ADAM SMITH AND THE CIRCLES OF SYMPATHY

WITHDRAWN

Collin College Library
SPRING CREEK CAMPUS
Plano, Texas 75074

Adam Smith and the Circles of Sympathy pursues Adam Smith's views on moral judgment, humanitarian care, commerce, justice and international law both in historical context and through a twenty-first-century cosmopolitan lens, making this a major and timely contribution not only to Smith studies but also to the history of cosmopolitan thought and to contemporary cosmopolitan discourse itself. Forman-Barzilai breaks new ground, demonstrating the spatial texture of Smith's moral psychology and the ways he believed that physical, affective and cultural distance constrain the identities, connections and ethical obligations of modern commercial people. Forman-Barzilai emphasizes Smith's resistance to the sort of relativism, moral insularity and cultural chauvinism that too often accompany localist critiques of cosmopolitan thought today. This is a timely, revisionist study that integrates the perspectives of intellectual history, moral philosophy, political theory, cultural theory, international relations theory and political economy, and will appeal widely across the humanities and social sciences.

FONNA FORMAN-BARZILAI is Associate Professor of Political Science at the University of California, San Diego, where she teaches political theory and the history of modern thought.

D1596350

IDEAS IN CONTEXT 96

Adam Smith and the Circles of Sympathy

Collin College Library
SPRING CREEK CAMPUS
Plano, Texas 75074

IDEAS IN CONTEXT

Edited by Quentin Skinner and James Tully

The books in this series will discuss the emergence of intellectual traditions and of related new disciplines. The procedures, aims and vocabularies that were generated will be set in the context of the alternatives available within the contemporary frameworks of ideas and institutions. Through detailed studies of the evolution of such traditions, and their modification by different audiences, it is hoped that a new picture will form of the development of ideas in their concrete contexts. By this means, artificial distinctions between the history of philosophy, of the various sciences, of society and politics, and of literature may be seen to dissolve.

The series is published with the support of the Exxon Foundation.

A list of books in the series will be found at the end of the volume.

ADAM SMITH AND THE CIRCLES OF SYMPATHY

Cosmopolitanism and Moral Theory

FONNA FORMAN-BARZILAI

University of California, San Diego

CAMBRIDGE
UNIVERSITY PRESS

CAMBRIDGE UNIVERSITY PRESS
Cambridge, New York, Melbourne, Madrid, Cape Town,
Singapore, São Paulo, Delhi, Tokyo, Mexico City

Cambridge University Press
The Edinburgh Building, Cambridge CB2 8RU, UK

Published in the United States of America by Cambridge University Press, New York

www.cambridge.org
Information on this title: www.cambridge.org/9781107402393

© Fonna Forman-Barzilai 2010

This publication is in copyright. Subject to statutory exception
and to the provisions of relevant collective licensing agreements,
no reproduction of any part may take place without the written
permission of Cambridge University Press.

First published 2010
First paperback edition 2011

A catalogue record for this publication is available from the British Library

Library of Congress Cataloguing in Publication data
Forman-Barzilai, Fonna, 1968–
Adam Smith and the circles of sympathy : cosmopolitanism and moral
theory / Fonna Forman-Barzilai.
p. cm. – (Ideas in context; 96)
Includes bibliographical references.
ISBN 978-0-521-76112-3
1. Smith, Adam, 1723–1790. 2. Ethics – History – 18th century.
3. Cosmopolitanism – History – 18th century. I. Title. II. Series.
HB103.A5.S43 2010
170.92–dc22
2010000022

ISBN 978-0-521-76112-3 Hardback
ISBN 978-1-107-40239-3 Paperback

Cambridge University Press has no responsibility for the persistence or
accuracy of URLs for external or third-party internet websites referred to in
this publication, and does not guarantee that any content on such websites is,
or will remain, accurate or appropriate.

To the memory of
Fay Forman
and
Rosalie Kaiman Nirenberg

Les lois de la conscience, que nous disons naître de nature, naissent de la coutume: chacun ayant en vénération interne les opinions et mœurs approuvées et reçues autour de lui …

Michel de Montaigne

Contents

Acknowledgments

As I sit to write these words at the end of a very long journey, I risk becoming precisely that person Smith described – the one "who skips and dances about with that intemperate and senseless joy which we cannot accompany him in." I hope the depth and sincerity of my gratitude will lessen the "contempt and indignation" Smith would heap upon me for the bursts of exuberance surely to follow. In good Smithian form I will try to remain temperate as my heart dances.

Best then to begin by acknowledging the various institutions that have provided material support for this project. My thanks go to the Charles E. Merriam Fellowship in Political Science at the University of Chicago; the Andrew W. Mellon Foundation whose generous funding enabled early travel and research; Balliol College, Oxford and then Master Colin Lucas for granting the visiting studentship that twice provided a home and research support; the Grodzins Prize Lectureship at the University of Chicago that enabled my first lectures on the Scottish Enlightenment; and the *Political Theory* editorial fellowship conceived by Stephen White that lured me to Virginia and provided full financial support during my last two years of writing. More recently, I am happy to acknowledge generous research support from the Division of Social Sciences and the Department of Political Science at the University of California, San Diego; the UCSD Committee on Research; the UCSD Faculty Career Development Program, and the Hellman Family Faculty Fellowship.

Variations on passages in chapters 1 and 6 were first published in *Critical Review*, vol. 14, no. 4 (2002). Variations on passages in chapters 3 and 5 were first published in *Political Theory*, vol. 28, no. 1 (2000); *Adam Smith Review*, vol. I (2004); *Political Theory*, vol. 33, no. 2 (2005); and in *New Voices on Adam Smith*, eds. Leonidas Montes and Eric Schliesser (Routledge, 2006). My thanks to Sage and Routledge for permission.

I was a law student in Madison when I first met Laurence Dickey; and it was he who reclaimed me from that dismal path and assured me through his own infectious example that the joys of studying European intellectual history were real and sustaining. He also introduced me to Adam Smith, my constant companion ever since. We have sparred continuously about method over the years, and always will; but we inevitably get to the same place on so many things, which I take as testimony to the underlying questions that drive us both and situate our sense of connection. Larry's support and confidence have sustained me through the years to a degree I am not sure he understands. These words of thanks could begin only with him, for he was my first and greatest teacher.

This project began as a dissertation in the Department of Political Science at the University of Chicago, and it is a great joy to thank the many people who inspired and supported me during those wonderful years in Hyde Park – Lloyd Rudolph especially, who from the very start encouraged my revisionist impulses regarding Smith and much else, engaged my ideas and read my work with the most exquisite sympathy. To this day, wherever he happens to be – Barnard, Kensington, Jaipur, Mussoorie, wherever – Lloyd forwards essays, news clippings and books, prods me with questions, requests my papers, and inquires about my well-being. I treasure his friendship and am humbled by the time, energy, and care he invested in me during his last years of university service, and over these now many years.

I thank Bernard Manin for encouraging me to integrate historical and theoretical rigor, demonstrating through his own work what it means to do history of ideas at its best. I thank Martha Nussbaum who first introduced me to cosmopolitan modes of thought and who took great interest in my work from the very start. Her continuing influence is evident on every page of this book. My emerging interests in cosmopolitan thought were encouraged by Larry Dickey and Bernie Yack who invited me at a fairly early stage to give a paper on Socratic cosmopolitanism at an annual CSPT conference on "Citizenship and Cosmopolitanism." That conference was a decisive experience and first set my work on its present course. Conversations with Joseph Cropsey, the late Leszek Kolakowski, Charles Larmore, Steve Pincus and Nathan Tarcov were formative; and the University of Chicago Political Theory Workshop provided a rigorous forum in which to present and discuss my work over the years. It is a great sadness that I never adequately thanked François Furet and Edward Shils for their guidance and encouragement during my early years in Chicago. I think they would have liked what became of my Adam Smith. My sincere thanks to Susan Stokes and the Center for Democracy at the University of Chicago for providing the sunlit office that became my sanctuary during my last two years in Hyde Park; and to Jack Cella at the Seminary Co-op Bookstore who indulged every request with joy and talked with me endlessly about books. Patchen Markell arrived just as I was leaving, and produced the most voluminous and perceptive comments I have ever received on this project – comments that resonated deeply over time and framed successive waves of revision. I am ever indebted to John McCormick and Jonathan Lear for their support and care, and to Stephen White who looked after me during my last years of writing while we worked together editing *Political Theory*, and ever since. My dissertation received the University of Chicago Social Sciences Dissertation Prize in 2002, an honor for which I am eternally grateful.

I cannot imagine a more stimulating environment in which to have written a dissertation on Adam Smith than the University of Chicago in the 1990s. For reasons that remain a mystery to those of us involved, Chicago was reverberating with Smithiana during those years. Jim Otteson had just finished up as Lauren Brubaker, Ryan Hanley, Eric Schliesser and I arrived to begin our projects on Smith. It was a perfect case of spontaneity: we arrived in different departments, worked in different traditions with predominantly different teachers who themselves had only marginal interests in Smith. Surely some of us wanted to pry Smith from the "Chicago school," though none of us came to Chicago for that purpose nor worked for a minute in the Economics Department. But we shared a profound fascination with the *Moral Sentiments* – and, though we would disagree quite vigorously at times and raise hell in whatever café we happened to be in, good book in hand, citing page and verse by heart, those engagements were formative for us all and cultivated a sense of community with roots that grew very deep over time, and deepen still. I thank my fellow "new voices" (the epithet is Schliesser's fault) for so many years of intellectual comradeship. Each will hear his own distinct voice in my book, no doubt.

For years of conversation, laughter and hijinks I am forever beholden to Michael Bloom, Venelin Ganev, Gretchen Helmke, John Kenny, Andrew Rehfeld, Eric Schliesser, and especially Robert Barros and Christina Tarnopolsky, who just get it, and to whom my debts are immeasurable. How I miss our days in Hyde Park.

Amidst the breezy palms of La Jolla, in a tangle of biotech labs, taquerias, strip malls and several major freeway systems, UCSD is another world; but it has proved a congenial academic home for the past seven years. The Department of Political Science has supported my research in every way. My thanks especially to Tracy Strong for his always careful and insightful reading of my work; to Sam Popkin who is a reservoir of optimism and perspective; to Phil Roeder from whom I learn more these days than from anyone; to Jee Baum, Amy Bridges, Scott Desposato, Karen Ferree, Clark Gibson, Harvey Goldman, Germaine Hoston, Alan Houston, and David Lake for their support and care along the way; to Robert Horwitz and Gershon Shafir additionally for invigorating collaborations; and to an exceptionally vibrant and convivial group of graduate students, among whom I am delighted to thank especially Christian Donath, Andrew Poe, and Wendy Wong, my indubitable first student-now-colleague. Above all I thank Gerry Mackie for his integrity, his genius, and his flawless advice at every turn.

I also acknowledge the support staff in the Department of Political Science, each and every one of them, for their efficiency and forbearance. Computer crashes have an uncanny sense of timing. Mine happened in the very last days of writing this book. Jeffrey Fritsch and Rafal Tamulsky dropped everything and saw me through those very tense days, salvaged every last file, and dragged me kicking and screaming into the twenty-first century by insisting I go Mac. I thank them every day for it.

I have been fortunate along the way to have encountered so many remarkable people who think about the world richly and variously. One of the joys of working on Smith in the revisionist way that I do is that he manages to captivate an astonishing range of audiences. I thank the following friends, colleagues, and teachers for particularly cogent and memorable comments, conversations, and interventions over the years on themes related to this book. My debt to them is immeasurable: Christopher Berry (who should be very pleased with the book's cover image), Richard Boyd, Lauren Brubaker, Roger Chartier, William Connolly, Joseph Cropsey, Avner de-Shalit, Douglas Den Uyl, Laurence Dickey, Michael Dubin, Peter Euben, Samuel Fleischacker, Christel Fricke, Jeffrey Friedman, the late François Furet, Harvey Goldman, Ruth Grant, Charles Griswold, Ryan Hanley, Russell Hardin, Maureen Harkin, Istvan Hont, Alan Houston, Fredrik Jonsson, Alexander Kaufman, Elias Khalil, Sharon Krause, Chris Laursen, David Levy, Jacob Levy, Jeff Lomonaco, Eric MacGilvray, Gerry Mackie, Bernard Manin, Kirstie McClure, Deirdre McCloskey, John McCormick, Iain McLean, Leonidas Montes, Martha Nussbaum, David Ohana, James Otteson, Sandra Peart, Jennifer Pitts, John Pocock, David Raphael, Jonathan Rick, Patrick Riley, John Robertson, Susanne Hoeber Rudolph, Amartya Sen, the late Edward Shils, Vernon Smith, Christina Tarnopolsky, Eduardo Velasquez, the late Iris Marion Young, and Michael Zöller. Additionally, I thank those who commented on all or parts of the manuscript at various stages: Charles Larmore, Patchen

Markell, Steve Pincus, Lloyd Rudolph, Eric Schliesser, Shannon Stimson, Tracy Strong, Lisa Wedeen, Stephen White, and Bernie Yack. Their advice has been priceless, and I have surely imperiled myself wherever I have not followed it. My gratitude as well to Richard Fisher and two anonymous referees at Cambridge University Press who offered rich and insightful comments, and to audiences at Chicago, Yale, Johns Hopkins, Michigan, William and Mary, the Hebrew University, Oxford, the London School of Economics, and UCSD, and at countless conferences, colloquia and workshops over the years, for their valuable contributions. In particular, I acknowledge the outstanding input I received at three recent conferences commemorating the 250th anniversary of Smith's *Moral Sentiments*: at Balliol College, Oxford, Smith's college, convened by Samuel Fleischacker and Vivienne Brown; at the University of Glasgow, convened by Christopher Berry; and in Berlin, convened by Michael Zöller. These interventions were exceptionally well timed: I deposited my final revisions just days after returning from the last.

In *Adam Smith and the Virtues of Enlightenment* (Cambridge, 1999) Charles Griswold illuminated Smith's salience for contemporary thought more richly than anyone ever has. The book was a brilliant demonstration of what one might *do* with Smith – a magnificently disruptive suggestion to me at a time when Donald Winch's *Adam Smith's Politics* (Cambridge, 1978) and Hont and Ignatieff's *Weath and Virtue* (Cambridge, 1986) set my agenda – when I firmly believed that the most effective way, perhaps the *only* way, to salvage Smith from what the economists had done to him, was to proceed historically. In a very fundamental way I still believe this. But Griswold's book, especially its emphasis on "ordinary morality," inspired something like a turning in my thought and approach: I began to think more critically about method – about what motivates the historian (this historian) to ask her questions, and about what history, done well, might bring to contemporary thought. Though it may seem that I sometimes distance myself from the book here, for I am not as optimistic as Griswold is about the adequacy of Smithian "therapy" for modernity, I hope the resonance of occasional academic quibbling doesn't overwhelm deeper harmonies and debts, and the extent that his book, more than any other, has situated my thoughts over the last decade.

My work has benefited enormously from my involvement with the International Adam Smith Society and its journal, *The Adam Smith Review*, of which I have recently become Editor. The Society and *Review* have done much in recent years to cultivate a sense of community among scholars across disciplines who are thinking innovatively about Smith and related themes. I am grateful to the members of the *Review's* Editorial Board for their confidence and support, and especially to Vivienne Brown, Doug Den Uyl, Sam Fleischacker, Charles Griswold, and Craig Smith, for making the transition such a happy one.

Working with Cambridge University Press ranks among the very finest experiences of my professional life. My thanks to Tom O'Reilly for stewarding my typescript expertly through production; to Martin Gleeson for superb copy-editing; to Teresa Lewis for many things, though perhaps mostly for working so hard to procure the image of my handsome young Smith from the Hunterian Museum; and to Jackie Taylor for transforming the image into a positively stunning cover. I am grateful to them all for their care and consummate professionalism. As for Richard Fisher, one can only marvel. As Executive Director of the Press, responsible essentially for its entire academic output, he continues to edit this iconic series with grace, attentiveness, remarkable efficiency and an open and enterprising spirit. What great good fortune that my first book landed in his hands. I am no less grateful to Quentin Skinner and Jim Tully for their encouragement in the last stages, and for their warmth and generosity since. Their support means a great deal to me.

My deepest gratitude goes to my family for seeing me through the joys and occasional traumas of this project, and for so much else: to Adam Forman, Neena and Richard Florsheim, and most inexpressibly to my parents, Sheldon and Narda Forman for the intensity of their devotion. For ten years David has been my most cherished interlocutor in life and thought. Too often he shouldered more than he should have, and I shall be eternally grateful for all that he enabled. My thanks to Noemi Canseco for her loving presence in our lives since Benjamin's birth; and to Allison Ciechanover for her wisdom and friendship at every turn: their reassurances helped nurture in me a sense of maternal wholeness that smoothed my return to campus and enabled the completion of this book. Benji is my treasure, and at four years old has managed to put everything into perspective. Choo choo, my little love ...

My grandmothers, Fay Forman and Rosalie Kaiman Nirenberg, passed away as this project was coming to a close. I will never again know compassion as pure as theirs, nor love as tender, and it brings great joy, though it is obviously no recompense at all, to dedicate this book to their memory.

Introduction: Smith's oikeiōsis

The idea of the *kosmou politēs* is very old, dating back at least to the ancient Stoics. But the idea that we might inhabit a realm beyond our own particular clans, nations, and states has re-emerged at various points throughout history, and with particular salience at the dawn of the twenty-first century. Cosmopolitanism has become a signifier of our times – the word is everywhere – though it has come to mean many things. The description "cosmopolitan" evokes a lifestyle that is enlightened, urban and worldly, one able to navigate the languages, tastes and cultures of the world's great cities with ease and panache. For many Americans the word conjures up images of Helen Gurley Brown's ideal of the independent, liberated "Cosmo" woman of the 1970s, an image reinvented for the 1990s in the wildly successful HBO television series "Sex in the City" and its celebration of "girl talk" over a pink martini-like libation known as a Cosmopolitan. The Cosmo woman's independence consisted in thinking for herself, experiencing her sexuality, and moving through the world loosened from the stifling conventions of domesticity and submissive femininity.

In modern ethical discourse, from Immanuel Kant to Martha Nussbaum and Kwame Anthony Appiah, the cosmopolitan ideal has embodied an imperative that we think for ourselves, that we become increasingly conscious of why we do what we do, that we resist giving ourselves over wholly to the conventions of time and place. *Sapere aude* – "dare to know" – Kant urged us, because one must cultivate independence of mind, or what Kant called "maturity," before one can recognize one's place in a larger, universal human community and begin the rational process of expanding the scope of one's moral concern beyond the confines and prejudices of place which are accidental, arbitrary and morally irrelevant from a cosmopolitan perspective.[1]

---

[1] On Kantian maturity see Immanuel Kant, "An Answer to the Question: What Is Enlightenment?," in *Political Writings*, ed. Hans Reiss, trans. H. B. Nisbet (Cambridge: Cambridge University Press, 1970), pp. 54–60.

Of course practitioners of identity politics and communitarians of diverse and colorful stripes promptly rejected the resurgence of ethical cosmopolitanism in the 1990s for this very reason – that in emphasizing our membership in a universal/cosmo polis, it seems to ask us to deny the earthy texture of our political, social and cultural selves; that it is thus too rationalist, too smug and imperialist, or perhaps just too optimistic for so flawed a species as we.[2] An entire "anti-cosmopolitan" – or perhaps "new cosmopolitan" – literature has cropped up in the last decade oriented around such challenges.[3]

Many who are troubled by the ethical cosmopolitan denial of particularity but who are nevertheless, in David Hollinger's words, "determined to max-imize species consciousness, to fashion tools for understanding and acting upon problems of a global scale, to diminish suffering regardless of colour, class, religion, sex and tribe," have attempted to reconceptualize a non-foundationalist or "postmetaphysical" cosmopolitanism, one with a weak or minimalist ontology, that seeks bridges while simultaneously affirming deep diversity and the integrity of cultural identity.[4] Others have sought to reframe the debate altogether, noting that identity *itself* has become complex and fragmented in our age of information, mobility and commodification. We are "mixed-up selves" living in a "mixed-up world," Jeremy Waldron writes (of himself), and conventional categories of culture and cosmopoli-tanism therefore no longer suit us very well.[5] Conceptualizing the intellectual landscape between reactionary localism and vapid universalism, between

---

[2] Martha Nussbaum emphasizes repeatedly that the cosmopolitan project does not entail that we surrender our "local identifications, which can be a source of great richness in life." She embraces a "concentric" model of Stoic cosmopolitanism for this reason. See notably Martha Nussbaum, "Patriotism and Cosmopolitanism," in *For Love of Country: Debating the Limits of Patriotism* (Boston: Beacon, 1996), pp. 3–17; and Martha Nussbaum, *Cultivating Humanity: A Classical Defense of Reform in Liberal Education* (Cambridge, MA: Harvard University Press, 1997).

[3] The first and perhaps defining debate was presented in Martha Nussbaum *et al.*, "Patriotism and Cosmopolitanism," *Boston Review*, October/November 1994; condensed Nussbaum, *Love of Country*.

[4] A defining collection in this movement was Pheng Chea and Bruce Robbins, eds., *Cosmopolitics: Thinking and Feeling beyond the Nation* (Minneapolis, MN: University of Minnesota Press, 1998). See also the special edition of *Public Culture* devoted to the new cosmopolitanism: Carol A. Breckenridge, Sheldon Pollock, Homi K. Bhabha and Dipesh Chakrabarty, eds., *Cosmopolitanism*. In *Public Culture*, vol. 12, no. 3 (2000). A very recent example, already much discussed, is Seyla Benhabib, *Another Cosmopolitanism* (Oxford: Oxford University Press, 2006). Bonnie Honig, in the same volume, doubts that Benhabib succeeds in her "postmetaphysical" mission, and posits an "agonistic cosmo-political" alternative. See Honig, "Another Cosmopolitanism?," pp. 102–127. David Hollinger's essay, "Not Universalists, Not Pluralists: The New Cosmopolitans Find Their Own Way," is an excellent example of how the "new cosmopolitanism" has arrayed itself against what it sees as the "polemically unmodified" cosmopolitanism of Martha Nussbaum and her "non-modified comrades": in Steven Vertovec and Robin Cohen, eds., *Conceiving Cosmopolitanism: Theory, Context, and Practice* (Oxford: Oxford University Press, 2002), pp. 227–239. The quoted text above comes from p. 230.

[5] Jeremy Waldron, "What Is Cosmopolitan?," *Journal of Political Philosophy*, vol. 8, no. 2 (2000), pp. 227–243, at p. 228. Note, however, that this complexity does not make the universalist ethical

"Jihad" and "McWorld" as Benjamin Barber put it, is where the debate in ethical cosmopolitanism has landed today, and it shows no real sign of resolving or slowing.[6]

But cosmopolitan debate is not limited to questions about ethics and culture. Cosmopolitanism has taken more explicitly political directions too, connected more or less overtly with the universalist ethical project associated with Kant. Political theorists influenced by Jürgen Habermas and his theory of communicative action are concerned less with identity or the scope and substance of our duties *per se*, and more with democratic procedures for talking about these things among others in a global setting. Cosmopolitan democrats like David Held, Daniele Archibugi, Andrew Linklater, Richard Falk and many others (the literature is flourishing) stress the superiority of democratic values to any particular ethnic conception of identity or nationality, and seek to expand democratic discourse ethics and institutions to the international realm – an agenda which a range of communitarian and identity-oriented critics have dismissed as presumptuous and imperialistic, and an implausible and potentially dangerous aspiration for world governance.[7]

Despite the vast and contentious ways that cosmopolitanism is articulated, re-articulated and challenged, however, one thing is very clear. Just as no early twentieth-century thinker would have neglected the impact of Marxism on the world, and no post-war thinker the impact of totalitarianism, we are all reflecting today on the directions that cosmopolitan currents are carrying individuals, groups, societies and states. We are dizzy with the pace of changes taking place around us, and are first beginning to make some sense of it. I have come to believe that Adam Smith's moral psychology has something to say to us today as we work to sort it out.

SMITH'S OIKEIŌSIS

Given the explosion of scholarship on Smith's thought in recent years, at the very moment that global and cosmopolitan issues have come to dominate public consciousness and academic discourse in the humanities and social sciences, it is surprising that we have no substantial interpretation of Smith's

---

project impossible for Waldron. Focusing on the reasons beneath cultural practices, and the accessibility of such reasons, Waldron ultimately aligns himself with the Kantian orientation and against the "practitioners of identity politics."

[6] Benjamin R. Barber, *Jihad vs. McWorld: How Globalism and Tribalism Are Reshaping the World* (New York: Ballantine Books, 1995).

[7] Several recent collections illustrate the range of positions in this discussion: Daniele Archibugi and David Held, eds., *Cosmopolitan Democracy: An Agenda for a New World Order* (Cambridge: Polity, 1995); David Held and Tony McGrew, eds., *Governing Globalization* (Cambridge: Polity, 2002); and Daniele Archibugi, ed., *Debating Cosmopolitics* (London: Verso, 2003).

moral philosophy for a global age.[8] What might it mean, for example, to extend his well-known ideas of "sympathy" and "spectatorship" to distant strangers?[9] Or to characterize his international political economy as "cosmopolitan"?[10] Or in a global context to say that Smith's jurisprudence has universal significance?[11] On reflection, it turns out that Adam Smith is an insightful participant in the ongoing debates about cosmopolitanism – what it is, what it assumes, what it can and cannot do.

In the vast and ever expanding sea of Smith scholarship, we have no interpretation of Smith that rigorously considers his thoughts about distance and proximity in the *Theory of Moral Sentiments* – that pays serious and central attention to the question of *spatial distance* in his moral philosophy.[12] This book is the first study to illuminate the spatial texture of Smith's

[8] For some very recent cosmopolitan interpretations and appropriations of Smith, across a variety of disciplines, see Luc Boltanski, *Distant Suffering: Morality, Media and Politics* (Cambridge: Cambridge University Press, 1999); Martha Nussbaum, *Poetic Justice: The Literary Imagination and Public Life* (Boston: Beacon, 1995); Amartya Sen, "Open and Closed Impartiality," *Journal of Philosophy*, vol. 99, no. 9 (2002), pp. 445–469; Margaret Chatterjee, "The Oceanic Circle," in Margaret Chatterjee, *Gandhi's Diagnostic Approach Rethought: Exploring a Perspective on His Life and Work* (New Delhi: Promilla and Co. and Bibliophile South Asia, 2007), esp. ch. 7; James Page, *Peace Education: Exploring Ethical and Philosophical Foundations* (New York: Information Age Publishing, 2008); David M. Levy and Sandra J. Peart, "Adam Smith and His Sources: The Evil of Independence," *Adam Smith Review*, vol. 4 (2008), pp. 57–87; and Martha C. Nussbaum, "'Mutilated and Deformed': Adam Smith on the Material Basis of Human Dignity," in Martha C. Nussbaum, *The Cosmopolitan Tradition* (Cambridge, MA: Harvard University Press, forthcoming). My thanks to Martha Nussbaum for sharing an early version of this chapter with me, since it expands on and qualifies some of her earlier assertions about Smith's "cosmopolitanism" of which I have been somewhat critical in other places.

[9] One frequently sees Smith's moral psychology invoked (and distorted) in literatures seeking to assert humanitarian and cosmopolitan duties toward distant strangers. For a particularly distorted example, which also happens to disfigure some of my own work, see Page, *Peace Education*, pp. 136–139. Two far worthier examples are Boltanski, *Distant Suffering*, which uses Smith's impartial spectator model to generate a humanitarian "politics of pity"; and Sen, "Impartiality," which emphasizes the global and cross-cultural significance of Smith's impartial spectator model. I will engage both at some length.

[10] See Fonna Forman-Barzilai, "Adam Smith as Globalization Theorist," *Critical Review* vol. 14, no. 4 (2002), pp. 391–419. For somewhat related formulations, that draw more general connections between free trade and the cultivation of humanitarian and cosmopolitan values in the eighteenth century, see Thomas J. Schlereth, *The Cosmopolitan Ideal in Enlightenment Thought* (Notre Dame, IN: University of Notre Dame Press, 1977), ch. 5; and Laurence W. Dickey, "*Doux-Commerce* and Humanitarian Values: Free Trade, Sociability and Universal Benevolence in Eighteenth-Century Thinking," in *Grotius and the Stoa*, ed. Hans W. Blom and Laurence C. Winkel (Assen: Van Gorcum, 2004), pp. 271–318.

[11] On the universalism of Smith's jurisprudence, one might begin with Knud Haakonssen's seminal chapter on "Smith's Critical Jurisprudence" in *The Science of a Legislator: The Natural Jurisprudence of David Hume and Adam Smith* (Cambridge: Cambridge University Press, 1981), pp. 134–153. See also Jennifer Pitts, *A Turn to Empire: The Rise of Imperial Liberalism in Britain and France* (Princeton, NJ: Princeton University Press, 2005), pp. 43–52, who has very interesting things to say about Smith's jurisprudence in a global context.

[12] Adam Smith, *The Theory of Moral Sentiments* (1759), ed. D. D. Raphael and A. L. Macfie, as vol. I of *The Glasgow Edition of the Works and Correspondence of Adam Smith* (Oxford: Oxford University Press; reprint Indianapolis, IN: Liberty Press, 1982).

thought, and to put him into direct conversation with global ethics discourse. I address Smith's place in the long-standing debates over cosmopolitanism, which were perhaps as vibrant in the eighteenth century as they are in our own. Specifically, I argue here that Smith's thoughts about *care* and *judgment* operate within remarkably narrow spatial limits. He argued (a) that our natural "beneficence" tends to fade as its object becomes further and further removed from the spectatorial center; and distinctly (b) that our judgments of others become less and less reliable as a justification for action or intervention. Understanding the spatial texture of Smith's thought will help clarify how both the moral psychology of care and the epistemology of moral judgment worked for him.[13] My book ultimately reflects on the localist implications that flow from Smith's orientation to space, demonstrates serious problems with enlisting the *Moral Sentiments* flatly for ethical cosmopolitan purposes, but ultimately points toward other resources in his thought, largely neglected in this context, for cultivating a twenty-first-century global ethics.

Those familiar with eighteenth-century European moral philosophy will detect a Humean sensibility in my assertion that Smith's thought operates within narrow spatial limits. David Hume famously observed that "sympathy ... is much fainter than our concern for ourselves, and sympathy with persons remote from us much fainter than that with persons near and contiguous."[14] Smith too believed that we tend naturally to connect affectively with those who are nearby or familiar to us, and that this connection tends to fade, become more tenuous, as an object becomes more "remote." Much will be said here about Hume's influence on Smith's way of thinking about distance, though I argue that Smith's account is richer and ultimately more provocative for us today. One of Smith's essential contributions beyond Hume, I argue, is that distance is a more complex and layered concept for him. It was not merely a physical concept. Smith approached distance in affective and cultural/historical terms as well – which means that I may be remote from someone sitting just before me, or close to someone across the globe. In this sense, Smith provides a framework for thinking in fresh ways about new sorts of human connection that emerge in a global age, for reflecting on what William Connolly has recently called "eccentric" connections that emerge in an age of speed and compressed distance – "crosscutting allegiances" that

---

[13] My thanks to Patchen Markell for first encouraging me to clarify the differences in Smith's thought between care and judgment.

[14] David Hume, *An Enquiry Concerning the Principles of Morals*, ed. J. B. Schneewind (Indianapolis, IN: Hackett, 1983), p. 49. In this passage, Hume used the word "sympathy" to mean other-concern, while Smith used the term "sympathy" very differently and distinctively to denote a general "fellow-feeling" with any passion whatsoever. I explore these differences later.

"exceed," "complicate" and often "compromise" the concentric connections of place that governed in ages when people lived slow, local lives.[15]

Moreover, Smith defined sympathy very differently than did Hume, so that distance and proximity played a different role in his thought. Sympathy for Smith was not about other-regarding affections which weaken or intensify depending on the physical proximity of another. Sympathy for Smith was primarily a principle of judgment and was impacted in very complex ways by the cultural, affective and physical proximity of the person or object being judged.

My case here rests on situating Smith's thoughts about distance in the *Moral Sentiments* in another much older context which very likely situated Hume's thoughts too. Here I emphasize ancient Stoic ethics, and specifically the Stoic idea of *oikeiōsis*, popularized by the second century CE Stoic, Hierocles, whose surviving fragments figure prominently in the writings of the fifth-century Macedonian anthologist Joannes Stobaeus – though the idea of *oikeiōsis* was most likely made known to Smith and the Scots generally through their familiarity with Cicero's *De Officiis*. The influence of Stoicism on Adam Smith's moral and political thought is widely appreciated, and has been given extensive treatment by the editors of the Glasgow edition of the *Moral Sentiments*, by Norbert Waszek, Vivienne Brown, Peter Clarke and most recently Gloria Vivenza, Leonidas Montes and Martha Nussbaum.[16] The Stoic dimension of Adam Smith's thought is apparent to

---

[15] William E. Connolly, "Eccentric Flows and Cosmopolitan Culture," in *Neuropolitics: Thinking, Culture, Speed* (Minneapolis, MN: University of Minnesota Press, 2002), pp. 177–201.

[16] See notably the editors' "Introduction" to Smith, *Moral Sentiments*, pp. 1–52, at pp. 5–10; Norbert Waszek, "Two Concepts of Morality: A Distinction of Adam Smith's Ethics and Its Stoic Origin," *Journal of the History of Ideas*, October 1984, pp. 591–604; and Norbert Waszek, *Man's Social Nature: A Topic of the Scottish Enlightenment in Its Historical Setting* (Frankfurt am Main: Peter Lang, 1986); Vivienne Brown, *Adam Smith's Discourse: Canonicity, Commerce and Conscience* (London: Routledge, 1994); P. A. Heise, "Stoicism in Adam Smith's Model of Human Behavior: The Philosophical Foundation of Self-Betterment and the Invisible Hand," *Ökonomie und Gesellschaft*, vol. 9 (1991), pp. 64–78; P. A. Heise, "Stoicism in the EPS: The Foundation of Adam Smith's Moral Philosophy," in *The Classical Tradition in Economic Thought: Perspectives on the History of Economic Thought*, vol. XI, ed. I. H. Rima (Aldershot: Edward Elgar, 1995); Peter H. Clarke, "Adam Smith and the Stoics: The Influence of Marcus Aurelius," University of the West of England, Faculty of Economics and Social Science, Working Papers in Economics No. 18, April 1996; and Peter H. Clarke, "Adam Smith, Stoicism and Religion in the 18th Century," *History of the Human Sciences*, vol. 13, no. 4 (2000), pp. 49–72; Jerry Z. Muller, *Adam Smith in His Time and Ours: Designing the Decent Society* (New York: Free Press, 1993; reprint Princeton, NJ: Princeton University Press, 1995); Fonna Forman-Barzilai, "Adam Smith as Globalization Theorist," *Critical Review*, vol. 14, no. 4 (2000), pp. 391–419; Charles L. Griswold, Jr., *Adam Smith and the Virtues of Enlightenment* (Cambridge: Cambridge University Press, 1999), pp. 217–227 and 317–324; Leonidas Montes, *Adam Smith in Context: A Critical Reassessment of Some Central Components of His Thought* (London: Palgrave Macmillan, 2004); Leonidas Montes, "Adam Smith as an Eclectic Stoic," *Adam Smith Review*, vol. 4 (2008),

even the most casual reader of the *Moral Sentiments*, for Smith spoke at great length about the Stoic project, about the elements of Stoicism that attracted him and those that he rejected. Throughout the *Moral Sentiments*, Smith regularly enlisted Stoic sources, mainly the *Discourses* of Epictetus, the *Meditations* of Marcus Aurelius, and less frequently, Cicero's *De Officiis* and *De Finibus* and Seneca's *Epistles*. He concerned himself very little with Stoic logic, physics and metaphysics, but concentrated on what he took often rather selectively to be Stoic "moral philosophy." Part VII of the *Moral Sentiments*, Smith's catalogue of the great schools within the history of moral philosophy, contains an entire chapter on Stoicism.[17] While he tended to think that the Stoic system was generally too rigorous in its demand for apathy toward life as lived by most people, he was nevertheless attracted to a moderated version of the Stoic idea of "self command," which became, arguably, the central virtue in his own moral philosophy.[18] In an extended discussion of self-command in Part VI Smith asserted that "Self-command is not only itself a great virtue, but from it all the other virtues seem to derive their principle lustre."[19] As such, it is not altogether surprising that most interpretations of Smith's Stoicism have focused on the prevalence of "self-command" and connected ideas in his thought. Many have also seized on the Stoic character of Smith's providentialism, which runs through (some would say governs entirely) both his ethical and economic ideas. But comparatively little attention has been given to Smith's cautious appropriation of the Stoic idea of *oikeiōsis*, which I have long found surprising given its direct relevance to contemporary debates about cosmopolitanism in moral philosophy, political theory and international ethics.[20]

---

pp. 30–56; Gloria Vivenza, *Adam Smith and the Classics: The Classical Heritage in Adam Smith's Thought* (Oxford: Oxford University Press, 2002), ch. 2 and pp. 191–212; and Nussbaum, "'Mutilated and Deformed.'" For the Stoic influence on the Scottish Enlightenment more generally, see Richard B. Sher, *Church and University in the Scottish Enlightenment: The Moderate Literati of Edinburgh* (Princeton, NJ: Princeton University Press, 1995), ch. 8; M. A. Stewart, "The Stoic Legacy in the Early Scottish Enlightenment," in *Atoms, Pneuma, and Tranquility: Epicurean and Stoic Themes in European Thought*, ed. Margaret J. Osler (Cambridge: Cambridge University Press, 1991), pp. 273–296; and J. C. Stewart-Robertson, "Cicero among the Shadows: Scottish Prelections of Virtue and Duty," *Rivista critica storia della filosofia* I (1983), pp. 25–49.

[17] *TMS* VII.ii.1 (pp. 267–314).　　[18] See notably *TMS* VI.iii (pp. 237–262).　　[19] *TMS* VI.iii.11 (p. 241).

[20] The notable exception here is Brown, *Discourse*, pp. 95–97. See also Montes, *Smith in Context*, p. 89, n. 62, who challenges Gloria Vivenza who (in *Smith and the Classics*) attributes Smith's thinking about the degrees of fellowship to Peripatetic influences, and doubts that it is Stoic in origin. See also Montes, "Adam Smith as an Eclectic Stoic." Just as I was completing this book, I discovered Levy and Peart, "The Evil of Independence." Though they never use the concept explicitly, Levy and Peart contribute to our understanding of Smith's *oikeiōsis* when they seek to "locate the foundations of Smith's egalitarianism in Stoic cosmopolitanism" (p. 2).

The word *oikeiōsis* derives from the Greek root *oikos*, which referred in ancient democratic life to the private realm of the household as distinct from the public realm of the *polis*, each of which entailed a different science of management, *oikonomeia* and *politika*. *Oikeiōsis* was a Stoic extrapolation from the familiarity that develops over time among those who inhabit the *oikos*, among those who very literally share physical space. Most fully developed by Cicero and Hierocles, *oikeiōsis* was the notion that human affection weakens as it radiates outward in degrees from the self. Thus, the Stoics mapped our affections concentrically, arguing that our affections are strongest at the center, closest and most familiar to the self, and that they weaken progressively as an object is removed further and further away. Imagine a dart board. According to Stoic *oikeiōsis*, the bullseye represents the self, the innermost ring represents one's family (those literally within the *oikos*), the next ring one's friends, the next one's neighbors, then one's tribe or community, then one's country, and so on; and ultimately the outermost and largest ring encompasses all of humanity. Surely, what determines the ordering of the circles, who will be regarded as "close," will vary with the kinship patterns in any particular culture.[21] But the process would seem to be a universal one for the ancient Stoics: human affection and care are ordered spatially around the self in a concentric pattern.

A central proposition in my interpretation here is that Smith's appropriation of Stoic *oikeiōsis* was conflicted and incomplete. He wholly embraced *oikeiōsis* as an empirical fact, as an accurate description of the concentric structure of human affection and care. Indeed, we will see that he organized his entire discussion of natural beneficence – of the natural "distribution of our good offices" – in *Moral Sentiments* VI.ii in concentric terms, mirroring the Stoic argument in remarkably precise detail. But while he embraced Stoic *oikeiōsis* as an empirical fact, as an accurate account of how human affection works, he decisively rejected Stoic cosmopolitan teleology which sought to overcome man's nature concentrically understood. Smith refused to follow the Stoic argument to its cosmopolitan conclusion that rational agents must cultivate "apathy" toward the near and dear, learn to resist *oikeiōsis* (the natural affection born of familiarity), to collapse the circles, and become "citizens of the world." In his engagement with Stoic teleology, then, Smith was distinctively *anti-cosmopolitan*.

---

[21] On this, see Margaret Chatterjee's fascinating discussion of Hierocles, Smith and Gandhi in "Oceanic Circle," p. 151. My thanks to Lloyd Rudolph for sending me Chatterjee's book just as I was finishing my own, prompting me, as he always does, to reflect on Smith's ideas outside of an Anglophone context.

THE ETHICS OF EXPANDING CIRCLES

The concentric model of ethical concern developed in Stoic thought has become something of a commonplace in ethics discourse today, and a centerpiece of the cosmopolitan agenda. In 1841, Ralph Waldo Emerson published his essay "Circles," which portrayed human life as a "self-evolving circle which, from a ring imperceptibly small, rushes on all sides outwards to new and larger circles, and that without end."[22] Not long after, historian W. E. H. Lecky drew on Emerson's metaphor of concentricity, and conceived of moral progress as an *expansion* of ethical responsibility, as an "expanding circle" with the individual and its intimates residing at the center, but which "soon ... includes first a class, then a nation, then a coalition of nations, then all humanity."[23] Lecky's formulation is so well known today that it is frequently invoked by intellectuals and practitioners as "Lecky's Circle."[24] Peter Singer's *Expanding the Circle* is a particularly well-known appropriation of Lecky's vision.[25] And this concentric way of thinking about our ethical duties is diffused throughout twentieth-century thought. Note for example Albert Einstein's "circle of compassion":

A human being is part of a whole, called by us the Universe, a part limited in time and space. He experiences himself, his thoughts and feelings, as something separated from the rest a kind of optical delusion of his consciousness. This delusion is a kind of prison for us, restricting us to our personal desires and to affection for a few persons nearest us. Our task must be to free ourselves from this prison by widening our circles of compassion to embrace all living creatures and the whole of nature in its beauty.[26]

Something very similar is at work in Gandhi's late political thought. Margaret Chatterjee recently explored affinities between Hierocles' circles and Gandhi's idea of the "oceanic circle," even noting important parallels with concentric themes in Emerson, Lecky and Adam Smith, all of whom Gandhi read with care.[27] In an editorial of April 1946 Gandhi wrote this:

Life will not be a pyramid with the apex sustained by the bottom. But it will be an oceanic circle whose centre will be the individual always ready to perish for the

[22] Ralph Waldo Emerson, "Circles," in *Emerson: Essays* (Cambridge, MA: Harvard University Press, 2005), pp. 320–345, at p. 323. My thanks to Eric MacGilvray for first bringing this essay to my attention.
[23] W. E. H. Lecky, *History of European Morals from Augustus to Charlemagne* (New York: George Braziller, 1955), vol. I, pp. 100–101.
[24] See, for example, James Bacchus, "Lecky's Circle: Thoughts from the Frontier of International Law," address to the Appellate Body of the World Trade Organization at the Institute of Advanced Legal Studies, University of London, April 10, 2003.
[25] Peter Singer, *The Expanding Circle: Ethics and Sociobiology* (New York: Farrar, Straus & Giroux, 1981).
[26] Albert Einstein, Letter of 1950, as quoted in the *New York Times*, March 29, 1972.
[27] Chatterjee, "Oceanic Circle."

village, the latter ready to perish for the circle of villages, til at last the whole becomes one life comprised of individuals, never aggressive in their arrogance, but ever humble, sharing the majesty of the oceanic circle of which they are integral units. Therefore, the outermost circle will not wield power to crush the inner circle, but will give strength to all within and will derive its own strength from it.[28]

A few things stand out in this passage. Note the profound difference between the "centre" of Gandhi's oceanic circle and the isolated, selfish individual who tends to reside at the center of Western appropriations of the Stoic model. Gandhi's center is an individual who is richly embedded in his village which, as Chatterjee points out, demonstrates how vastly different the concentric layout will look in cultures with different kinship patterns.[29] To a Western sensibility, an individual who is already ready to sacrifice himself to the village is a perplexing center, a foreign starting point. But for Gandhi the problem was not to overcome egoism in the Western sense, but to address tensions between tribe and nation, between local identity and a larger sense of unity organized around the idea of "India." Finally, Gandhi is not concerned in this particular passage with expanding concern to all of humanity (though of course this was essential to his overall vision). For him the "oceanic circle" confronted political problems internal to India. Gandhi rejected the conventional options of either state centralization, which is pyramid shaped and oppressive, or decentralized fragmentation, which is shapeless, and would undermine Indian unity. The oceanic circle was a device for navigating this tension between local self-determination and holistic unity. Gandhi inspires some very interesting thoughts about how we might use the circles to expand human connection, but in a way that respects the integrity of the inner-most circles – self, family, village.

Today the circles are perhaps most readily associated with Martha Nussbaum's extensive work on cosmopolitanism, which draws frequently on the Stoic model to tamp down parochial self-preference and expand our ethical concern. She argues that we "should work to make all human beings part of our community of dialogue and concern, base our political deliberations on that interlocking commonality; and give the circle that defines our humanity special attention and respect."[30]

---

[28] Gandhi, "Independence," cited in Chatterjee, "Oceanic Circle," p. 159.
[29] For an interesting discussion of the "moral circles" in Chinese thought, see *The Moral Circles and the Self: Chinese and Western Approaches*, ed. Kim-chong Chong, Sor-hoon Tan and C. L. Ten (Peru, IL: Open Court, 2003). Unfortunately, the book situates Adam Smith within a Western tradition that sees the individual as "isolated" and "egoistic" (p. xviii).
[30] Nussbaum, *Love of Country*, p. 9.

Although Smith in the *Moral Sentiments* ultimately rejected the cosmopolitan vision as it was articulated by the ancient Stoics, I am not suggesting here that cosmopolitans today should cast him aside. On the contrary! The arguments he mounted against the Stoic project add a fresh, distinctively Scottish sociological and moral psychological texture and depth to the steady onslaught of localist, communitarian and culturalist challenges leveled against the cosmopolitan project today. Like us, Smith struggled with surmounting spatial obstacles to human understanding and care, bringing his ethical thought front and center, and transforming Smith from a stodgy Scot long rebuffed by political theorists and moral philosophers for his vexing defense of free market capitalism in the *Wealth of Nations* and into a worthy interlocutor in the cosmopolitan debates who richly appreciated the local texture of human identity and can help us, in this sense, to grasp some of the limits of our own aspirations.

ADAM SMITH AND THE CIRCLES OF SYMPATHY

To demonstrate that Smith embraced *oikeiōsis* to turn Stoic cosmopolitanism on its head (or perhaps, as Marx claimed to have turned Hegel's system: "on its feet"[31]), I have found it most effective to proceed through my own argument concentrically. Following Smith's appropriation of the concentric pattern of Stoic *oikeiōsis* in *Moral Sentiments* VI.ii the book itself unfolds in circles, beginning in Part I with Smith's thoughts about the self; radiating outward in Part II to consider Smith's social thought; and concluding in Part III with his thoughts about broader spaces, what I call here the "circle of humanity." In other words, I replicate the concentric structure of Smith's discussion of beneficence in the *Moral Sentiments* VI.ii examining the gradations of affection and care in Smith's thought as they emerged passionately from the circle of the self, radiated outward further and further in the circles of various societies (family, neighborhoods, communities, nations), weakening all the while, until they ultimately faded away for Smith in the furthest domain of unknown strangers, the circle of humanity.

I begin in Stoic fashion with Smith's focus on the self. In Chapter 1, I revisit the "Adam Smith Problem" – the purported tension between Smith's ethics and economics, embodied in his two seminal texts, that has derailed many interpretations of Smith's thought over the last two

---

[31] See Karl Marx, "Preface" to *Capital: A Critique of Political Economy*, in *Marx and Engels: Basic Writings on Politics and Philosophy*, ed. Lewis S. Feuer (New York: Anchor, 1959), pp. 133–146, at p. 146.

centuries. Though I believe the tension is putatively artificial, as the majority of recent scholarship on Smith's thought has so effectively demonstrated,[32] I revisit the problem briefly here to challenge economic interpretations of the Smithian self as driven primarily by egoism and utility considerations, and the tendency among non-specialists and in public discourse generally to reduce the Smithian self to "economic man."[33] I argue that the self was complex for Smith, and often quite conflicted, struggling to negotiate tensions between its selfish and other-regarding tendencies. I demonstrate this complexity by (a) exploring Smith's rejection of the early-modern idea of "enlightened self-love," embraced by Thomas Hobbes, Samuel Pufendorf and Bernard Mandeville, and aligning him instead with what I describe as the more "complex" view taken by Bishop Joseph Butler and Jean-Jacques Rousseau; and (b) characterizing Smith's idea of "sympathy" as the very activity through which the conflicted self learns to cool passionate self-preference and resolve tensions between self and others.

I proceed in Chapter 2 to explore Smith's idea of sympathy as a sociological process through which the self in Smith's theory engages with other selves over time and evolves into a social being. Sympathy for Smith, thus, was not the spontaneous emotional connection with others that we tend to associate today with compassion or empathy, or what Hugo Grotius called *appetitus societatus*, Jean-Jacques Rousseau *pitié* and Francis Hutcheson benevolence. Sympathy was a social practice through which individuals who share physical space participate together in an ordinary exchange of approbation and shame, and through repetitive interactions over time learn

---

[32] References are provided in Ch. 1.

[33] Though I am critical of "economic man" interpretations of Smith's thought, I am significantly more perturbed by the adjective "economic" than the subject "man" in this formulation. I occasionally insert the female pronoun throughout the book to remind readers of Smith's contemporary appeal and that there is no reason why his account should have been confined to half the human race. However, I am only slightly ambivalent about the predominance of the male pronoun through this book, for anything otherwise would imply what a contextual orientation to Smith's thought should not. As one nineteenth-century English interpreter noted, "one-half of society has been almost entirely overlooked in his philosophy." T. E. Cliffe Leslie, "The Political Economy of Adam Smith," *Fortnightly Review*, November 1, 1870, p. 12. For further discussion of Smith's masculine morality, see Stuart Justman, *The Autonomous Male of Adam Smith* (Norman, OK: University of Oklahoma Press, 1993); and more recently Edith Kuiper, "The Construction of Masculine Identity in Adam Smith's *Theory of Moral Sentiments*," in Drucilla K. Barker and Edith Kuiper, eds., *Towards a Feminist Philosophy of Economics* (London: Routledge, 2003), pp. 145–160. For an excellent bibliography of work on the role of women in Smith's thought, and in early modern political economy generally, see the one accompanying Edith Kuiper, "Adam Smith and His Feminist Contemporaries," in *New Voices on Adam Smith*, ed. Leonidas Montes and Eric Schliesser (London: Routledge, 2006), pp. 3–60, at pp. 57–60.

to become "social" – learn to adjust their passions to a "pitch" commensurate with living in a society with others.[34] Man's natural desire for sympathetic concord inclines him to speculate how others will view him, to filter his desires and behavior through his society's particular expectations of him as a member of it, and to orient his sentiments around something external and social, what Smith called a "point of propriety."[35] Sympathy in this sense brings about a sort of affective coolness in the self and a "concord" of sentiments in society. Mediocrity (an Aristotelian might call it) and social order. In Chapter 2, I explore how sympathy functions as a social practice in Smith's thought, incorporating elements of Michel Foucault's accounts of "surveillance" and (in Chapter 3) "discipline" in *Discipline and Punish* to characterize the techniques and processes taught through which people are to "cool" their passions and channel them toward social ends.[36]

A guiding theme in my interpretation is that Smith was far less concerned in the *Moral Sentiments* with moral perfection than he was with the basic, minimal requirements of social coordination.[37] Indeed, social order was Smith's primary concern – just as it was "the peculiar and darling care of Nature."[38] He described the "welfare and preservation of society" as "the favorite ends of nature."[39] This is not to say that Smith didn't embrace the virtues of mutual respect and reciprocity inherent in the sympathy process, and central to modern practices of civility; clearly he did. Nor am I suggesting that Smith was unconcerned with individual self-perfection, or that the individual in his theory becomes a mere cog of society. Though he was modern and pluralist in his refusal to articulate a monistic *telos* for mankind, Smith believed in moral perfectibility and had much to say about moral development and maturity and the satisfactions of a properly human life, which were enabled only *within* society.[40] Nevertheless, I will argue here that Smith's perfectionism must be understood in the context of his

---

[34] *TMS* I.i.4.7 (p. 22); I.ii.intro.1 (p. 27); VI.iii.14 (pp. 242–243).

[35] *TMS* I.ii.intro.1 (p. 27); VI.iii.14 (pp. 242–243).

[36] Michel Foucault, *Discipline and Punish: The Birth of the Prison*, trans. Alan Sheridan (New York: Vintage, 1977–1995). On the theme of "coolness" in Smith, see for example *TMS* I.i.4.8 (p. 22).

[37] On Smith's preoccupation with social order, see Joseph Cropsey, *Polity and Economy: An Interpretation of the Principles of Adam Smith* (The Hague: Martinus Nijhoff, 1957), a thesis reinvigorated by Peter Minowitz, *Profits, Priests and Princes: Adam Smith's Emancipation of Economics from Politics and Religion* (Stanford, CA: Stanford University Press, 1993); and Douglas Den Uyl and Charles L. Griswold, "Adam Smith on Friendship and Love," *Review of Metaphysics*, vol. 49, March, pp. 609–637.

[38] *TMS* II.ii.3.4 (p. 86).   [39] *TMS* II.i.5.10 (p. 77).

[40] For further discussion, accompanied by a critique of Griswold and Den Uyl in "Friendship and Love" who note that Smith was ultimately concerned with "social cooperation" and not "the self-perfection of the individual (as in Aristotle)," see Samuel Fleischacker, *A Third Concept of Liberty: Judgement and Freedom in Kant and Adam Smith* (Princeton, NJ: Princeton University Press, 1999), pp. 143–149.

larger, distinctively modern concerns about social coordination. Indeed, an individual will not be free to unfold in a society plagued by disorder any more than he was free in a pre-modern society ordered by priests and princes. In a very rudimentary and foundational way, he observed that "no social intercourse can take place among men who do not generally abstain from injuring one another."[41] I argue here that Smith's central purpose in the *Moral Sentiments* was to identify an ordinary sociological process capable of ordering and unifying modern people without resting on strong, divisive theological foundations and without requiring archaic modes of coercion which would stifle modern (commercial) freedom and human progress. Smith challenged critics of progress and modernity who insisted that wealth and virtue were incompatible ends, and that properly functioning societies require that men be perpetually subjected to traditional moral prohibitions enforced by absolute rulers, a punitive clergy and a vengeful God. Instead Smith described a lighter, freer, self-regulating method of social coordination that worked endogenously – proof for critics of progress and modernity that free men could live sociably without consensus on the meaning of God's will, and without being coerced.[42] A key feature of Smith's moral system is that it functioned without transcendent truths supplied by religion or philosophy, which were always deeply contentious, and responsible for the intractable and bloody wars that moderns sought to bequeath to a barbarous history. Smith described the actual social practices through which modern people in their daily encounters and conversations with those nearest them learn to live together, to exchange their selfish passions for more sociable ones, to achieve consensus spontaneously and without ideological foundations on a wide range of issues, and ultimately to become members of a group. This is how I interpret the role of "sympathy" in the *Moral Sentiments*.

Knud Haakonssen characterizes Smith's moral philosophy as a "social theory of the self" – and I believe this comes through most clearly in Smith's sociological description of sympathetic exchange.[43] But sympathy is not merely a sociological account of emotional discipline for Smith, nor merely an account of how selves are socialized. Another guiding theme in my interpretation is that Smith's account of sympathy is also an important

Fleischacker asserts that "Society Shapes Us so That We Are Capable of Virtue" (p. 144). Indeed; though I tend to see this dimension as secondary to Smith's primary purpose of establishing social order in the *Moral Sentiments*.

[41] *TMS* II.ii.3.6 (p. 87).   [42] Freedom here as negatively and commercially understood.

[43] Knud Haakonssen, *Natural Law and Moral Philosophy: From Grotius to the Scottish Enlightenment* (Cambridge: Cambridge University Press, 1996), p. 131. There he writes that for Smith the self is "formed in our interactions with other people."

and highly original anthropological description of how *moral cultures* are cultivated and perpetuated over time.[44] Smith never used the language of "culture" to describe what he was doing in the *Moral Sentiments*. But he described the evolution of what *we* would call a moral culture, and so I am comfortable proceeding with this bit of anachronism. Describing Smith's project in cultural terms helps convey to a contemporary audience the salience of what he was doing for twenty-first-century cosmopolitan theory. Indeed, sympathy for Smith is the very process through which the self integrates the tastes and values of the people with whom it lives and interacts, becomes a member of that particular moral culture, and then passes that culture on to others. In this sense Smith's "social theory of the self" is also a highly original eighteenth-century cultural anthropology. Or, put differently, the individual is not the sole unit of analysis in Smith's account; he is not concerned only with the "sources of the self," to use Charles Taylor's formulation.[45] He was also talking about groups and their *mœurs*, though far less overtly for sure. My interpretation here resonates with what social scientists today call "constructivism," bringing Smith instantly into highly charged debates in the social sciences. Smith's alleged constructivism will become essential in later chapters when I consider the particularist implications of his anthropology for international ethics.

In Chapter 3, I turn from sympathy to explore Smith's idea of "conscience," or what he called, among other things, the "impartial spectator." Probing Smith's theory of conscience is essential in a book devoted to his relation to cosmopolitanism, for most interpreters who draw cosmopolitan inspiration from Smith's thought tend to focus on the purportedly transcendent character and capacities of the impartial spectator. My essential contention here is that conscience for Smith was in important ways continuous with his sociological account of sympathy and, as such, falls flat as a cosmopolitan device for getting us beyond ourselves. In other words,

---

[44] A note of gratitude to Bill Connolly for being first to suggest that I pursue the "cultural" implications of Smith's project. See Fonna Forman-Barzilai, "Smith on 'Connexion', Culture and Judgment," in *New Voices on Adam Smith*, ed. Leonidas Montes and Eric Schliesser (London: Routledge, 2006), pp. 89–114. For help in conceptualizing Smith's cultural anthropology I am indebted to Samuel Fleischacker, *On Adam Smith's Wealth of Nations* (Princeton, NJ: Princeton University Press, 2004), pp. 52–54; further elaborated in Samuel Fleischacker, "Smith and Cultural Relativism," trans. as "Smith und der Kulturrelativismus" in *Adam Smith als Moralphilosoph*, ed. Christel Fricke and Hans-Peter Schütt (Berlin: De Gruyter, 2005). My thanks to Sam Fleischacker for sharing the English version with me.

[45] Charles Taylor, *Sources of the Self: The Making of Modern Identity* (Cambridge, MA: Harvard University Press, 1989).

conscience too was a function of social experience, and inevitably constructed through that experience.[46]

I begin in Chapter 3 with the reasons Smith turned in his narrative from
sympathy to conscience, and demonstrate that conscience in the first
edition of the *Moral Sentiments* was not a transcendent source of knowledge
and truth for Smith but little more than a disciplinary function: the
psychological appropriation of the sympathy process over time, an internalization of social experience in a particular moral community that guides
individual judgment and action and secures social order. Smith maintained
that a sociological view of conscience was the perfect device for ordering
modern societies loosened from traditional forms of authority. In this light,
I characterize Smith's impartial spectator as a "socialized conscience,"
borrowed from Sheldon Wolin's classic account of liberal social conformity
in *Politics and Vision*.[47]

However, I argue that Smith became increasingly anxious about relying
on the socialized conscience to secure social order, revising his *Moral
Sentiments* five times between 1759 and 1790. He worried that it too easily
devolves into mere conventionalism, dependent on whatever norms happen
to prevail in a given place in time, affirming David Hume's well-known and,
to Smith, troubling assertion that we are nothing but habits, that "custom
[is] the foundation of all our judgments."[48] In private correspondence with
friends and colleagues, and in the revised text of the *Moral Sentiments* itself,
Smith gave voice to his growing concerns about conventionalism and
corruption: if conscience is understood merely as a disciplinary function,
as the psychological internalization of the sympathy process over time, it
may not have sufficient independence and maturity to resist cultural norms
and conventions when that might become necessary. Conscience might
simply reflect the norms and habits currently in vogue, whether altruistic or
greedy, peaceful or bellicose, hierarchical or democratic, and so on.

Smith's battle with conventionalism is at the center of my interpretation
here. When he described the genesis of and then struggled with the moral
insularity of culturally generated norms Smith tripped over questions that

---

[46] For interesting work on Smith's sociological view of conscience, see Edward G. Andrew, *Conscience
and Its Critics: Protestant Conscience, Enlightenment Reason, and Modern Subjectivity* (Toronto:
University of Toronto Press, 2001), esp. ch. 7; and Edward G. Andrew, "Anarchic Conscience and
Enlightenment Reason," in *Philosophical Designs for a Socio-Cultural Transformation*, ed. Tutsuju
Yamamoto (Ecole des Hautes Etudes en Sciences Culturelles and Rowman & Littlefield, 1998),
pp. 77–85.

[47] Sheldon Wolin, *Politics and Vision: Continuity and Innovation in Western Political Thought* (Boston:
Little, Brown, 1960), pp. 343–351.

[48] David Hume, *A Treatise of Human Nature* (London: Penguin Books, 1993), pp. 118 and 147.

would become central for later generations of moral and political theorists. Is morality a product of history, a cultural artifact? If so, does it condemn us to the shadows? To what extent is self-understanding and critique possible in ordinary moral life? To what extent can and should we judge others from within our own particularities, and act on those judgments? I believe that Smith identified what many today would refer to as the inescapable "thickness" of moral culture[49] – and that his attempt to transcend ordinary experience through the device of the impartial spectator was more problematic than he originally had supposed. Charles L. Griswold, Jr. in *Adam Smith and the Virtues of Enlightenment*, argues that Smith managed ultimately to steer a course between philosophy and ordinary morality through the "objectivity" of the impartial spectator. We are indebted to Griswold for illuminating this tension in Smith's thought better than anyone ever has. In doing so, he has opened entirely new vistas of interpretation, including mine. But I resist his reconciliation here – not because one might not somehow exist, but because I don't think Smith's thought gets us there.[50] I argue that the vivid tension between ordinary moral experience and reflective transcendence remains productively unresolved in Smith's thought – and that we stand to learn much about our own limitations by observing how Smith articulated the tension, struggled with it, and ultimately failed to resolve it.

Anxieties about conventionalism prompted Smith to rethink the sociological basis of conscience. Much like cosmopolitans today, he was uncomfortable with a thickly cultural view of morality, especially when particular moral cultures produced conventions that disturbed him – he frequently pointed to the examples of infant exposure, slavery and empire; and he linked the problems of "civil and ecclesiastical" faction and fanaticism to the same sort of cultural pathology. But he also seemed to include the lesser vices of modern profligacy and corruption in his list of disturbing cultural habits. Here we discover in Smith a mood of ambivalence and self-criticism that has received less attention than it merits. Over time he developed an argument that conscience needed to be more than the mere internalization of habit and social norm; it required a capacity to reflect on its own

---

[49] See, for example, Michael Walzer, *Thick and Thin: Moral Argument at Home and Abroad* (Notre Dame, IN: University of Notre Dame Press, 1994).

[50] For an earlier articulation of my argument, see Fonna Forman-Barzilai, "Book Review" of Charles Griswold, *Adam Smith and the Virtues of Enlightenment* in *Political Theory*, vol. 28, no. 1 (2000), pp. 122–130; and Fonna Forman-Barzilai, "Whose Justice? Which Impartiality?: Reflections on Griswold's Smith," *Perspectives on Political Science*, vol. 30, no. 3 (2001), pp. 146–150. For Griswold's reply, see Charles L. Griswold, Jr., "Reply to My Critics," *Perspectives on Political Science*, vol. 30, no. 3 (2001), pp. 163–167, at pp. 164–165.

WITHDRAWN

SPRING CREEK CAMPUS

experience, to reject and transcend itself when necessary. The theoretical quandary, of course, was how to characterize a conscience capable of doing this, how to endow conscience with what we might call "transcendent" qualities and capacities, given Smith's empirical methodological commitments, his sociological account of morality, and his explicit resistance to theism and moral casuistry of any sort. Where might such a thinker look for a transcendent epistemology?

Smith's growing concerns about conventionalism prompted a shift in later revisions of the *Moral Sentiments* from describing conscience in sociological terms to establishing the independence of conscience in what appear to be quasi-theological terms. In a move that has long perplexed Smith scholars, and has produced wildly divergent interpretations about Smith's orientation to God and religion, Smith began to integrate such exogenous, perfectionist elements as reason, God, moral rules, wisdom and maturity into his otherwise wholly empirical theory of conscience. According to Smith in the 1790 edition of the *Moral Sentiments*, for example, a mature individual learns to avert his eyes from the clamor of the world and heed the "demigod" that resides in his breast.[51] Looking inside ourselves to some *thing* we conceptualize as partly divine we learn to critique ourselves from a vantage point outside the world of social experience. I spend a good deal of time unpacking Smith's argument here, addressing the obvious problems with weaving religious language into an empirical theory of moral life. Did this perfectionist turn inward to what looks like the voice of God alter the essential empirical quality of Smith's project? Should we even take Smith seriously here? Surely he was more sober in his unbelief than his elder friend Hume whose avowed atheism frequently landed him in hot water; but there is also ample textual and biographical evidence to substantiate questions about Smith's personal faith. I don't speculate on Smith's biography in this book, but simply note that God in the *Moral Sentiments* appears as something of a deistic afterthought for him, issued most frequently in a Stoic key as a prime mover that sets Nature in motion, but also sometimes invoked to describe the ways that ordinary, God-fearing people are moved to decency. Either way, God for Smith was a philosophical addendum to an empirical model that tended without it to slide toward Humean relativity, undermining the local moral certainty and social stability Smith was always seeking. He understood his audience, and the ordinary moral sentiments about which he was writing.

In Chapter 4, I further explain and qualify Smith's perfectionism in the 1790 edition of the *Moral Sentiments* by emphasizing his engagement with the

---

[51] *TMS* III.2.32 (p. 131).

more strident variants of ethical perfectionism associated with Augustinian asceticism and Stoic cosmopolitanism, both of which Smith rejected outright for their rigoristic disdain for ordinary human tendencies and capacities, for human life as actually lived. Smith's anti-rigorism here is no mere caveat, but a key transition to my discussion in Section III of the "circle of humanity." Indeed, Smith insisted that Christian and Stoic imperatives to cultivate benevolence (the former by expanding brotherly love, the second by tamping down self-love) not only for one's fellows within "the circle of society" but for distant strangers in the "circle of humanity" – for "that great society of all sensible and intelligent beings," for "all the inhabitants of the universe"[52] – were too high-minded and unrealistic, suited perhaps to Christian saints and Stoic sages but inconsistent with the inclinations and capacities of ordinary people who were preoccupied with and best situated to engage local "humbler" concerns. For Smith, our obligations could not exceed our capacities; ought was limited by can. He acknowledged the beauty of great humanitarian exertion and magnanimity, but he insisted that we should not aspire to *live* that way.[53] Like his friend and intellectual companion Edmund Burke who famously directed our interests and energies to the "little platoons," Smith too was remarkably parochial, insisting that nature has attuned our sense of emotional connection to those realms over which we have some practical management – that we naturally care primarily for the near and dear, for "everything which Nature has prescribed to us as the proper business and occupation of our lives."[54] While mankind would focus on the "humbler departments," each tending to his own business, God and the great *œconomy* of Nature would tend to the business of universal happiness.

It was in this context of our limited obligations in Part VI of the *Moral Sentiments* that Smith appropriated the idea of *oikeiōsis*, the concentric pattern of human association advanced by the Stoics, but went on to reject the corollary Stoic imperative that proper reasoning helps us to overcome the concentric structure of our affections, collapse the circles and become

---

[52] *TMS* VI.ii.3.1–3 (p. 235). Throughout *TMS* VI.ii.3, Smith uses the designations "innocent," "sensible," "intelligent," and "rational" in various combinations to characterize "all the inhabitants of the universe."

[53] *TMS* VI.ii.3.6 (p. 237). See also *TMS* III.3.8–11 (pp. 139–141).

[54] *TMS* VII.ii.1.46 (pp. 292–293). One detects in this strand of Smith's thought important connections with Burke's naturalism, his anti-Stoicism and his formulation of the "little platoons" in *Reflections on the Revolution in France* in 1790: "To be attached to the subdivision, to love the little platoon we belong to in society, is the first principle (the germ as it were) of public affections. It is the first link in the series by which we proceed toward a love to our country and to mankind." Edmund Burke, *Reflections on the Revolution in France* (1790) in *The Writings and Speeches of Edmund Burke* (Oxford: Clarendon Press), vol. VIII. I will spend some time in ch. 4 examining these connections, though they are the subject of future work.

citizens of the world. Here Smith became what we might call today a "localist," asserting that our duties are limited to caring for the "humbler departments": for ourselves, our family, friends, groups, and so on, since caring in these circles is both more natural to us and likelier to be a more effective use of our knowledge and energies. An act of good-will, humanity and generosity that crosses this boundary was *supererogatory* for Smith – generally meritorious and deserving of praise, though not always, but certainly beyond what practical morality demands of us.

In Part III, entitled "The circle of humanity," I expand from Smith's social thought to his reflections on global and international themes. This is the most innovative dimension of my interpretation, I suspect, and of most immediate concern to contemporary political theory and international ethics. Few interpreters have appreciated the rich spatial texture of Smith's thought. In Chapter 5, I explore the extent to which notions of "proximity" and "distance" complicate Smith's moral psychology, making him highly relevant to contemporary cosmopolitan debates. Taking Smith's thoughts on proximity well beyond Hume's, I argue that Smith's description of our varied, layered and often conflictual affiliations, draws us into the spatial texture of sympathetic activity and stimulates further inquiry into three dimensions, or "spaces," in which sympathy takes place: (1) the physical; (2) the affective; and (3) the historical/cultural. I argue that Smith's orientation to space – physical space, affective space and cultural space – complicates his moral philosophy in ways not fully grasped by existing interpretations of his thought, and brings him into very current debates about the spatial texture of identity and connection in twenty-first-century life.

Distance means very different things in each of the three spaces I identify in Smith's thought, which means that attempting to transcend our natural biases toward the proximate in each space will entail different sorts of activity, require different sorts of aptitude, will be more or less difficult, and more or less likely to succeed. Put differently, Smith's particularism is not one of simple self-preference or bias, as is often alleged. My argument here is that Smith's understanding of bias was far more layered and inter- esting – that it works very differently in different spheres of human interaction. Ultimately, I argue that Smith's moral psychology in the *Moral Sentiments* was geared toward, and ultimately provided the resources necessary for, transcending physical and affective bias in the circle of society. In other words, his essential challenge was social coordination – how to overcome invidious passion and socialize the self in the "circle of society." With regard to cultural bias in broader circles, however, his thought about transcendence runs into problems, and for this reason becomes provocative for cosmopolitan thinking today. In my interpretation of Smith's moral psychology, I emphasize that sympathy is a process of social learning that explains how we become members and producers of particular moral cultures. Understood as such, Smith helps us to appreciate the profound difficulties of cultural self-reflection (knowing ourselves) and of cross-cultural understanding and judgment (knowing others) – essentially, the difficulties of transcending cultural bias. Smith's description of the moral life underscores the complex spatial barriers that the cosmopolitan agenda must inevitably confront in the realms of moral epistemology and judgment. These are not superficial and meaningless barriers to be sidelined as "post-modern academic perspectivism," but significant ones in the most profound sense. Ever since Socrates drank the hemlock, the difficulty of cultural self-reflection and the related tendency of groups violently to overreach have been deep and persistent problems, fraught with very real human dangers.

Moreover, ethical cosmopolitans will discover not only that Smith's moral psychology creates problems for cross-cultural judgment, but that the idea of "beneficence" itself, our duty to care, was remarkably localist and anti-cosmopolitan in Smith's outlook. Surely our benevolence and good-will know no boundaries. Though most of us are preoccupied with local interests and give very little thought to those out of sight, Smith acknowledged that it is relatively easy to *contemplate* good-will toward all sensible creatures from the comfort of our armchairs. But "beneficence," as Smith used it, which closely resembles what we would describe today as humanitarian action, operated within spatial boundaries that are woefully narrow from a cosmopolitan perspective. He referred to our "very limited powers of beneficence," and claimed that our only appropriate relation to all "innocent and sensible beings" – "all the inhabitants of the universe" – is "good-will."[55]

Given the "localist" and "particularist" implications of Smith's thought, did he ultimately believe that concern for the well-being of others is possible and ethically appropriate only within intimate spheres like family, friendship and citizenship? Should we take him at his word when he asked: "to what purpose should we trouble ourselves about the world in the moon?"[56] Taking him too seriously here would relieve us of considering his work further. Surely I wouldn't have traveled with Smith for so many years had I felt he abandoned us to the dark inertia of our particularities. What makes

---

[55] *TMS* VI.ii.intro.2 (p. 218); *TMS* VI.ii.3 (pp. 235–237). See also *TMS* III.3.8–11 (pp. 139–141).
[56] *TMS* III.3.9 (p. 140).

Smith's thought interesting and relevant for contemporary thought is that he aimed higher, aspired for more. He struggled with the implications of his sociological description of the moral life, both locally and beyond. We might think of Smith in this sense as a *troubled* particularist about morals, and a *troubled* realist about international order which resonates profoundly with the dilemmas faced today by those of us who are drawn to the virtues of a global humanity and repelled by the secrets and dangers of insular local-ism – and yet equally repelled by the ways that universalism can deny or marginalize local affiliations and identities. Cosmopolitanism today (and communitarianism alike, incidentally) has become far more "troubled" than the "unmodified cosmopolitanism" of the 1990s described by David Hollinger.[57] "New Cosmopolitans," as Hollinger refers to them, are devel-oping layered and sophisticated approaches to human identity and con-nection and are searching for new ways to conceptualize human interaction in a global age without succumbing to the binaries of thick localism and vapid universalism.[58] In the closing chapters of the book, I address tensions between Smith's rather bleak description of the world and his sincere desire to build bridges across spatial divides and to achieve international peace. My discussion about Smith's conciliatory impulses will prompt us to consider the cosmopolitan significance of the bridges Smith proposed in the realms of commerce and jurisprudence.

In Chapter 6, I address Smith's attempt to negotiate deep conflicts between his localism and his more noble aspirations for international peace. Indeed, localism was a central feature of Smith's moral psychology; and he resisted cosmopolitan aspirations for attempting to redirect us from the "humbler departments," from "everything which Nature has prescribed to us as the proper business and occupation of our lives."[59] Localism served for Smith as a sort of desirable middle terrain between the atomizing effects of selfishness and the ephemeral and ultimately meaningless unity of the "cosmopolis," as conceived by the ancient Stoics. His purpose in the *Moral*

---

[57] Hollinger, "New Cosmopolitans," p. 230.

[58] A recent book that has greatly influenced my thoughts on all this is James Tully, *Public Philosophy in a New Key* (Cambridge: Cambridge University Press, 2009), especially vol. 2.

[59] *TMS* VII.ii.1.46 (pp. 292–293). One detects in this strand of Smith's thought important connections with Burke's naturalism, his anti-Stoicism and his formulation of the "little platoons" in *Reflections on the Revolution in France* in 1790: "To be attached to the subdivision, to love the little platoon we belong to in society, is the first principle (the germ as it were) of public affections. It is the first link in the series by which we proceed toward a love to our country and to mankind." Edmund Burke, *Reflections on the Revolution in France* (1790) in *The Writings and Speeches of Edmund Burke* (Oxford: Clarendon Press), vol. VIII. I will spend some time in ch. 4 examining these connections, though they are the subject of future work.

Sentiments was to describe this middle terrain, to describe the ways that Nature had guaranteed her "favorite end": the "welfare and preservation of society."[60]

Nevertheless, Smith was deeply wary of group life, and its tendencies toward zeal and fanaticism. He reflected at length about the moral psychology of faction, both civil and ecclesiastical, and concluded that "of all the corrupters of moral sentiments ... faction and fanaticism have always been by far the greatest."[61] His discussion of civil faction and the psychology of "the man of system" is particularly poignant, published in 1790 just after the storming of the Bastille. Smith then expanded his reflections on group fanaticism in a discussion of the disturbing predominance of national self-interest and "public spirit" in international affairs, which "dispose[s] us to view, with the most malignant jealousy and envy, the prosperity and aggrandisement of any other neighboring nation."[62] To the extent that Smith was a localist, as I argue he was, he was nevertheless deeply troubled about group myopia and violence, and its implications for international stability and peace. I characterize this tension in Smith's thought as his *troubled realism.* And it is within this context of Smith's troubled realism that I situate his theory of commercial globalism – what I call the "commercial cosmopolis." Smith suggested that commercial intercourse among self-interested nations can emulate good-will on a global scale, balancing national interest and international peace without a coercive apparatus to enforce compliance with international law. We might say that "sympathy followed money" for Smith in the society of nations.[63]

I conclude in Chapter 7 with a discussion of Smith's *troubled particularism.* One of the cultural implications of Smith's moral psychology and the conventionalism it produces is that people tend to employ very partial, biased, criteria when judging the practices of others. The problem becomes especially acute when judging distant, unfamiliar strangers. How do we judge contexts and worlds of meaning that are unfamiliar to us without speculating about the other and forcing their practices into our own frames of reference? Smith's observations about the difficulties of assuming an impartial perspective when we judge illuminate how deeply entrenched our perspectives really are, how difficult it is to cultivate self-knowledge and critical distance from ourselves. In this sense, Smith is a perceptive

---

[60] *TMS* II.i.5.10 (p. 77). Cf. *TMS* II.ii.3.4 (p. 86).
[61] *TMS* III.3.42–43 (pp. 154–156); the quote is from *TMS* III.3.43 (p. 156).
[62] *TMS* VI.ii.2 (pp. 227–234), esp. at *TMS* II.ii.2.3–6 (pp. 228–230).
[63] My thanks to John Pocock for sharing this formulation with me.

and visionary cultural theorist, and a valuable ally for those who are committed today to preserving the category of "culture" and wary of the "thick" and "unreflective" universalisms so frequently brandished in political and academic discourse. But, in the end, what I find most compelling is that the *troubled particularist* in Smith refused to sit trapped in the proverbial box of moral relativity. The horrors around him – slavery, imperial conquest – demanded something firmer. Smith speaks most perceptively to political theory and international ethics today when he seeks to navigate his way jurisprudentially out of this box. I argue that despite the particularistic implications of Smith's anthropology his particularism didn't go "all the way down" so to speak. In the end, our cultural situatedness did not render self-critique or cross-cultural judgment impossible.

I characterize Smith's theory of "negative justice" as a strand of universalism in his thought – sometimes marginalized by interpreters since he said comparatively little about it, since what he did say was scattered, unsystematic and ultimately unfinished, and since it is overshadowed by other more prominent themes in his work. Nevertheless Smith's jurisprudence is arguably the most relevant dimension of his moral philosophy to contemporary discussions in international ethics. In Chapter 7, I gather Smith's reflections on the subject of justice scattered throughout the *Moral Sentiments*, the *Wealth of Nations* and his posthumously published *Lectures on Jurisprudence*, and weave them together into a coherent, universalist narrative. In short, Smith asserted that justice is a "negative virtue," grounded not in an abstract moral good, a *summum bonum*, which is inevitably arbitrary, particular and subject to great cultural variation and contestation, but in the human aversion to cruelty, a *summum malum* which struck Smith as "natural," "instinctive" and thus "universal" among people. I draw essential lines of connection between Smith and Judith Shklar in her work on cruelty in "Liberalism of Fear." I argue that Smith's idea of justice conceived "negatively" as the prohibition against inflicting cruelty was in fact *insulated from* and *prior to* the particularity of the moral sentiments, much the way Shklar asserted that the "liberalism of fear" was cosmopolitan for transcending cultural variation.[64] While Smith resisted slavery and imperial conquest, and Shklar Nazis in every guise, they shared an Archimedean impulse that cruelty was universally recognizable and

---

[64] See Judith N. Shklar, "Liberalism of Fear," in *Liberalism and the Moral Life*, ed. Nancy Rosenblum (Cambridge, MA, 1989), pp. 21–39; reprint *Political Thought and Political Thinkers*, ed. Stanley Hoffman, pp. 3–20 (Chicago: University of Chicago Press, 1998).

provided language for a genuinely global ethics – a natural jurisprudence, Smith called it, "independent of all positive institution."[65]

I conclude the book with some thoughts on Smith's relevance for contemporary political and moral theory, characterizing his theory of negative justice as a variant of ethical minimalism that resonates with discussions in political theory today about articulating moral goods in contexts of deep diversity.

INTERPRETATION

Given the very contemporary questions I ask of Smith, this project is situated at the conjunction of intellectual history and political theory, and integrates the demands of two sometimes proprietary disciplines. I should say a few words about this distinctive methodological imperative, and why I do not feel constrained by either approach.

I am committed to approaching the "historical Smith" as he emerged from his own unique cluster of influences and concerns. Clearly, much is missed when we "pillage" Smith's texts for evidence that confirms our suspicions or grounds our aspirations – the way economists long reified him as the Patron Saint of Capitalism without evaluating the full force of his thought in its own intellectual and political contexts.[66] At the same time, I remain wary of the claim that contextual method effectively insulates historical interpretation from the historian's critical impulses. More or less overtly we are driven to ask questions of history not merely because a text or a context demands it of us, as if questions are simply there like artifacts under the sand waiting for the asking, and not merely because certain questions may be professionally in vogue; but very often because we are stirred in our own lives by ethical and political questions that seem to find some bearing in earlier sets of questions. I don't think there is anything necessarily unhistorical about acknowledging what brings us to a particular period or a particular thinker. Indeed, if we wish to accept Collingwood's claim that the historian in history is a product of time and place – that since "St. Augustine looked at history from the

---

[65] *TMS* VII.iv.37 (p. 341).

[66] See Tuck, "The Contribution of History," p. 72. For an influential discussion on the "vulgar demand for relevance," see Quentin Skinner, "A Reply to My Critics," in *Meaning and Context: Quentin Skinner and His Critics*, ed. James Tully (Princeton: Princeton University Press, 1988), pp. 231–88, at 286–8. On the various methodological problems associated with forcing a thinker from the past into the scholar's own contemporary purposes, see Skinner, "Meaning and understanding in the history of ideas," *History and Theory* 8 (1969): 3–53; reprint ed. in *Meaning and Context*, pp. 29–67. In the case of Smith scholarship, see Donald Winch's introductory comments in *Adam Smith's Politics: An essay in historiographic revision* (Cambridge: Cambridge University Press, 1978).

point of view of the early Christian; Tillemont from that of a seventeenth-century Frenchman; Gibbon from that of an eighteenth-century Englishman; Mommsen, from that of a nineteenth-century German," then there is "no point in asking which was the right point of view" since "each was the *only one possible* for the man who adopted it"[67] – indeed, if we are to go along with this, how then can we with consistency exempt ourselves? We too are representatives of time and place, and the point of view that governs our work is more or less situated there. I am wary of conceiving the historian's perspective as a "view from nowhere" and am inclined to agree with Isaiah Berlin who ultimately doubted the possibility of historical "detachment": "What the historian says will, however careful he may be to use purely descriptive language, sooner or later convey his attitude."[68] Of course, this does not mean we should abandon history for critique, ferreting out the useful and dismissing all else as arcane. Clearly, the historian can be more or less conscious about preserving the historical integrity of her interpretation, more or less deliberate about precisely when her critical impulses are governing what she does. Some of course have no problem with conflating history and critique altogether. But I believe we are equally mistaken to insist on an impermeable demarcation line between them. I am committed to approaching Smith's thought with vigilant sensitivity to the particular motivations that he reveals to us through his texts. But I *come to* Smith very openly, with particular twenty-first century Anglophone cosmopolitan questions. And I *leave* Smith believing that his thought, once properly understood in context, is extraordinarily useful for illuminating various tensions in contemporary debate. In the end, my interpretation will stand among many – and my most valuable critics will be those who find it most productive to engage my interpretation at the level of insight.

---

[67] Cited in "Editor's Preface" to R. G. Collingwood, *The Idea of History* (Oxford: Oxford University Press, 1946–1980), p. xii.

[68] Isaiah Berlin, "Introduction" to *Five Essays on Liberty*, ed. Henry Hardy (Oxford: Oxford University Press, 2002), xxix.

PART I

The circle of the self

CHAPTER I

Conflicted self

We must soften into a credulity below the milkiness of infancy to think all men virtuous. We must be tainted with a malignity truly diabolical, to believe all the world to be equally wicked and corrupt.

Edmund Burke, *Thoughts on the Cause of the Present Discontents*

And what a malignant philosophy must it be that will not allow to humanity and friendship the same privileges which are undisputedly granted to the darker passions of enmity and resentment. Such a philosophy is more like a satyr than a true delineation or description of human nature, and may be a good foundation for paradoxical wit and raillery, but is a very bad one for any serious argument.

David Hume, *An Enquiry Concerning the Principles of Morals*

Until very recently, philosophers tended to ignore Adam Smith. They acknowledged his idea of sympathy in the *Theory of Moral Sentiments*, but generally regarded it as superficial and unsophisticated, and tended to dismiss Smith as a minor figure in the shadow of David Hume. Moreover, he was regularly cast aside as a crass materialist who reduced human motivation to selfishness and corrupted the world with a moral justification for capitalism. In this environment, Smith scholarship was left to the mercy of economists and historians of economics who because of their training and pressing worldly concerns tended to subordinate or ignore Smith's moral philosophy.

This tendency finds its earliest traces in a debate that began among late-nineteenth-century German capitalists and Marxists, on the extent to which Smith's two seminal books might be reconciled.[1] The so-called "Adam Smith problem" turned on how we might reconcile the *Theory of*

---

[1] For a useful history of the "Problem," see Richard Teichgraeber, "Rethinking *Das Adam Smith Problem*," *Journal of British Studies*, vol. 20, no. 2 (1981), pp. 106–123. On the German reception of Smith specifically, see Keith Tribe, "The German Reception of Adam Smith," in *A Critical Bibliography of Adam Smith* (London: Pickering and Chatto, 2002), pp. 120–152; and Montes, *Smith in Context*, pp. 20–39.

Moral Sentiments (1759) and its emphasis on sympathy with the *Wealth of Nations* (1776) and its emphasis on self-interest.[2] Are the books consistent or continuous? And if not, which in Smith's mind was prior? Was Smith primarily an ethical or an economic thinker? Were human beings driven primarily by sympathy or self-interest, virtue or vice? *Homo socius* or *homo oeconomicus*? Interpretation of Smith's thought throughout the last two centuries was dominated by "present-minded" people who wanted to say something or another about capitalism. In that environment the "Adam Smith Problem" was most often resolved in the direction of self-interest, with the *Wealth of Nations* and its purported "celebration of avarice"[3] rising triumphant as the motivating center of Smith's thought, and the *Moral Sentiments* set aside as puerile and academic. The most urgent of interpreters dismissed the "Adam Smith problem" altogether as an academic luxury.[4]

Saying something or another about capitalism is a worthy enterprise, no doubt. But as ideology goes, it tends to produce very bad history. And in Smith's case, it mattered very little where one stood on the political spectrum. Whether one extolled the virtues of capitalism or condemned its excesses and blindness; whether one advocated a small state or big one; there was general agreement about what Smith said and what he meant by it. Whether he was praised by liberals as a champion of individual freedom or maligned by Marxists as an "evil genius" responsible for inventing bourgeois ideology, interpretations generally "converged" around Smith as the founding father of liberal capitalism, leaving posterity with a ridiculously superficial, deeply flawed and selective interpretation of his thought.[5] The very idea of "Adam Smith," so frequently invoked in public debates today on the left and on the right, has not moved very far from this caricature – conveyed, for example, in such statements as those made by a recent US presidential candidate that China today acts like "Adam Smith on

---

[2] Adam Smith, *The Theory of Moral Sentiments* (1759), eds. D. D. Raphael and A. L. Macfie, as vol. I of *The Glasgow Edition of the Works and Correspondence of Adam Smith* (Oxford: Oxford University Press; reprint Indianapolis, IN: Liberty Press, 1982); Adam Smith, *An Inquiry into the Nature and Causes of the Wealth of Nations* (1776), eds. R. H. Campbell and A. S. Skinner, as vol. II of *The Glasgow Edition of the Works and Correspondence of Adam Smith* (Oxford: Oxford University Press; reprint Indianapolis, IN: Liberty Press, 1981), hereafter cited as *WN*.

[3] A formulation employed by Stephen Holmes to convey precisely what eighteenth-century liberalism was not. "The Secret History of Self-Interest," in *Beyond Self-Interest*, ed. Jane J. Mansbridge (Chicago: University of Chicago Press, 1990), pp. 267–286.

[4] For discussion, see Donald Winch's "Introduction" to *Adam Smith's Politics*, pp. 1–27; and Donald Winch, "Adam Smith and the Liberal Tradition," in *Traditions of Liberalism: Essays on John Locke, Adam Smith and John Stuart Mill*, ed. Knud Haakonssen (Sydney: Center for Independent Studies, 1988), pp. 82–104.

[5] Winch, *Adam Smith's Politics*, pp. 19 and 70.

steroids" when it buys oil from tyrants and sells its nuclear technology;[6] or by a well-known left-leaning journalist in the midst of the global economic crisis in early 2009 that Adam Smith's invisible hand has failed us.[7]

Among a majority of Smith scholars today in the humanities and social sciences, however, the unity of Smith's system is no longer in serious contention. Today we understand how thoroughly the nineteenth-century formulation of the "Adam Smith Problem" distorted what Smith meant by sympathy and self-interest, and missed the overall coherence of his moral philosophy and the place of political economy within it. From Smith's pupil John Millar, we know that Smith's lectures on moral philosophy at the University of Glasgow (1750–1764), delivered as Chair of Moral Philosophy, were divided into four tracks: natural religion, ethics, jurisprudence and political economy.[8] The second track later provided the basis for the *Theory of Moral Sentiments*, Smith's first book published in 1759; the third was published posthumously from student lecture notes as *Lectures on Jurisprudence*; and the fourth became the core of *The Wealth of Nations*. From a mere outline of Smith's lectures, one observes that political economy is one part of a far broader, comprehensive moral philosophical system, what Charles Griswold calls "a coherent whole."[9] Thus the nineteenth-century formulation of the "Adam Smith Problem" rests on a tension that was essentially foreign to Smith, but instead conveys the urgency of nineteenth-century debates about political economy. Knud Haakonssen and Donald Winch, in their recent discussion of Smith's legacy, speculated that Smith "could hardly have suspected that the

[6] Mitt Romney, speech at the Republican National Convention, September 3, 2008.

[7] Phil Donahue interview, Fox News, March 18, 2009.

[8] Dugald Stewart. *Biographical Memoirs of Adam Smith, of William Robertson, and of Thomas Reid* (Edinburgh: George Ramsay and Company, 1811), pp. 12–15.

[9] Griswold, *Virtues of Enlightenment*, pp. 29–39. This, despite the well-known historiographical problems with conjecturing about Smith's overall *corpus*. Accounts of Smith's coherence and continuity abound today. Some notable works in this tradition are Glenn R. Morrow, *The Ethical and Economic Theories of Adam Smith* (New York, 1923; reprint New York: Augustus M. Kelley, 1973); A. L. Macfie, *The Individual in Society* (London: Allen & Unwin, 1967); T. D. Campbell, *Adam Smith's Science of Morals* (London: Allen & Unwin, 1971); Robert Boyden Lamb, "Adam Smith's System: Sympathy Not Self-Interest," *Journal of the History of Ideas*, vol. 35 (1974), pp. 671–682; Andrew S. Skinner, *A System of Social Science: Papers Relating to Adam Smith* (Oxford: Clarendon Press, 1979); Athol Fitzgibbons, *Adam Smith's System of Liberty, Wealth and Virtue: The Moral and Political Foundations of the Wealth of Nations* (Oxford: Oxford University Press, 1995); Amartya Sen, *On Ethics and Economics* (Oxford: Basil Blackwell, 1987), pp. 1–28; Patricia Werhane, *Adam Smith and His Legacy for Modern Capitalism* (New York: Oxford University Press, 1991); Donald Winch, *Adam Smith's Politics*; and, more recently, James R. Otteson, *Adam Smith's Marketplace of Life* (Cambridge: Cambridge University Press, 2002); Fleischacker, *Wealth of Nations*.

question of systematic coherence and/or incompleteness in his intellectual endeavour would constitute an enduring part of his legacy."[10]

Economists began to lose their hold on Smith's legacy in the 1970s. An important moment in this story of Smith's twentieth-century recovery came in 1978 when Donald Winch confronted the "economist's Smith" head-on in his path-breaking book, *Adam Smith's Politics: An essay in historiographic revision.* Inspired by the "new" contextual approach to historical meaning (then) associated with Quentin Skinner and the so-called "Cambridge School" of intellectual history, Winch pursued various problems with interpreting Smith's thought through the anachronistic lens of nineteenth-century debates about liberal capitalism. Winch's particular focus was Adam Smith's politics. He wanted to unmask the "economist's Smith" in order to resuscitate the political elements of Smith's thought, which economists and economic historians had marginalized, or sublimated altogether, by claiming that politics, for better or for worse, was "epiphenomenal to the more profound economic forces at work in modern commercial society."[11] Properly contextualized, Winch demonstrated that Smith's thought drew explicitly upon a very old political language about virtue and corruption that his contemporaries would have identified with the Augustan humanism of Montesquieu and Hume.

One need not share Winch's historiographical orientation, his Cambridge proclivity for republican sentiments or his preoccupation with Smithian politics to recognize the value of approaching Smith's thought without ideologically charged nineteenth-century assumptions and with sensitivity to how Smith might have understood his own project. When permitted to speak in his own eighteenth-century voice, the "economist's Smith" begins to lose touch with himself. For one thing, the Chair of Moral Philosophy at the University of Glasgow never anchored human life on what George Stigler called the "granite" of self-interest.[12] Self-interest is a central dimension of human motivation, no doubt, but for Smith takes its place within a far richer motivational complex, marked as much by passion and imagination as by interest and reason. Why else would he have devoted a treatise to the subject of moral sentiment, demonstrating his life-long commitment to the project

---

[10] Knud Haakonssen and Donald Winch, "The Legacy of Adam Smith," in Knud Haakonssen, ed., *The Cambridge Companion to Adam Smith* (Cambridge: Cambridge University Press, 2006), pp. 366–394, at p. 369.

[11] Winch, *Adam Smith's Politics*, p. 27.

[12] George Stigler, "Smith's Travels on the Ship of State," *History of Political Economy*, vol. 3 (1971), pp. 265–277, at p. 265.

by revising it substantially five times over thirty-one years? Indeed, the enterprise of political economy was not itself at the center of Smith's thought, but takes its place in a larger project of moral philosophy.

What's more, Smith was ambivalent about commercial culture, and critical of the very economic totality he is accused of inventing and enshrining. Despite what history has made of him, he was never a flat-footed optimist about the effects of commercialism on the texture of human life, locally or globally. Modernity was never easy or uncomplicated for him. He did believe that a free market economy, supplemented by appropriate political and social institutions and policies, was modernity's best hope for general well-being. He was committed to reducing human poverty and misery and promoting human equality, and had great faith in the trajectory of history in this sense, leaving him justly susceptible to charges of woeful shortsightedness, well intentioned as it may have been.[13] But he also elaborated the dangers of commercial culture in detail and intensity matched only by Karl Marx himself. The "very meanest person" in eighteenth-century Europe might indeed be better off than "an African king," he once asserted.[14] But at the same time, he echoed Jean-Jacques Rousseau's counter-Enlightenment claims about the hypocrisies of modern happiness, charging that commercial life rested on a pervasive self-deception about our needs and our happiness, that it tended to corrupt our moral sentiments by encouraging vanity and conspicuous greed, and that it sapped our magnanimity and public-spiritedness. Smith encouraged commercial people to cultivate habits of personal thrift and to resist emulating the superfluities of the rich, which would lead to perpetual disappointment at best, failure and poverty at worst. Moreover, even at the very dawn of the industrial revolution, he observed that the division of labor dehumanized its participants through "mental mutilation," rendering them "as stupid and ignorant as it is possible for a human creature to become."[15] Smith was keenly aware of the "wonderful world" of early industrial capitalism so memorably conveyed in Robert Heilbronner's portrait of the tin mines of Cornwall and the textile

---

[13] For discussion of Smith's focus on ameliorating human poverty and misery, and his general preoccupation with the dignity of workers, see especially Samuel Fleischacker, *Wealth of Nations*; Emma Rothschild, *Economic Sentiments: Adam Smith, Condorcet, and the Enlightenment* (Cambridge, MA: Harvard University Press, 2001); and Nussbaum, "'Mutilated and Deformed.'"

[14] *WN* I.i.11 (pp. 23–24).

[15] *WN* V.i.f.50 (p. 782). For discussion of this theme in Smith, and its implications for a cosmopolitan interpretation of the *Wealth of Nations*, grounded in the material basis for human dignity, see Nussbaum, "'Mutilated and Deformed.'"

factories of Derby.[16] Indeed, Smith's orientation to modernity was one of genuine ambivalence – ultimately embracing the rise of commerce for its material benefits, its extension of human liberty, and its "ennobling byproducts," as Eric Schliesser puts it,[17] but also acknowledging and at times directly confronting the profound indignities and cruelties of modern commercial life, seeking to counter-balance some of them through the "expense" of public education.

The revisionist spirit Winch initiated in *Adam Smith's Politics* has reproduced itself in waves of scholarship committed to the project of wrestling Smith's thought from the economistic grip, unmasking the economists' hegemony over Smith's meaning, recovering new meanings that have a more solid claim to historical accuracy, and that are potentially useful for a generation no longer narrowly preoccupied with Marx and his legacy. And this momentum has not been confined to intellectual history. Smith revisionism is a truly multidisciplinary project within the humanities and social sciences. The last thirty years have witnessed a genuine renaissance of revisionist scholarship among moral philosophers, political and social theorists, anthropologists, psychologists, students of communication, of culture, of gender, of literature, among others.[18]

THE SMITHIAN SELF

Though their evaluations of the "Smithian legacy" radically diverged, Chicago-school types like Hayek, Friedman and Becker,[19] and Marxists like

---

[16] Robert L. Heilbronner, "The Wonderful World of Adam Smith," in *The Worldly Philosophers: The Lives, Times and Ideas of the Great Economic Thinkers* (New York: Simon & Schuster, 1953), pp. 40–72, at pp. 41–42. My thanks to Deirdre McCloskey for discussion on this, and for urging caution.

[17] Eric Schliesser, "Adam Smith's Benevolent and Self-Interested Conception of Philosophy," in Leonidas Montes and Eric Schliesser, eds., *New Voices on Adam Smith* (London: Routledge, 2006), pp. 328–357, at p. 351.

[18] This phenomenon is evident in the academic culture surrounding Smith scholarship today. The *Adam Smith Review*, published by Routledge and sponsored by the International Adam Smith Society, is situated at the heart of this, evident as well in several recent volumes of new scholarship: Christel Fricke and Hans-Peter Schütt, eds., *Adam Smith als Moralphilosoph* (Berlin: De Gruyter, 2005); Knud Haakonssen, *The Cambridge Companion to Adam Smith* (Cambridge: Cambridge University Press, 2006); and Leonidas Montes and Eric Schliesser, eds., *New Voices on Adam Smith* (London: Routledge, 2006). International conferences commemorating the 250th anniversary of the first edition of Smith's *Theory of Moral Sentiments* across the globe in 2009 (in Oxford, Glasgow, Oslo, Istanbul and Athens) are remarkably multidisciplinary.

[19] Friedrich A. von Hayek, *Individualism and the Economic Order* (Chicago: University of Chicago Press, 1948); Milton Friedman, *Essays in Positive Economics* (Chicago: University of Chicago Press, 1953); Gary S. Becker, *The Economic Approach to Human Behavior* (Chicago: University of Chicago Press, 1976). On Smith and the Chicago School, see the forthcoming essay by Steven G. Medema, "Adam Smith and the Chicago School," in *The Elgar Companion to Adam Smith*, ed. Jeffrey Young (Cheltenham: Edward Elgar, forthcoming 2009).

Macpherson and Dumont[20] generally agreed that the *Wealth of Nations* presented an essentially materialist, Hobbesian orientation to human motivation checked by a fundamental optimism that human egoism can be restrained autonomously, invisibly, through free competition in commerce. This is one thing interpreters mean when they refer to Smith as a "commercialized Hobbes"[21] – they mean his attempt to harness man's natural selfishness without sympathy, without moral philosophy, without the coercive political authority of a Leviathan or the skillful maneuvering of a wise mercantilist statesman,[22] but instead to socialize him through "enlightened self-love."[23] Enlightened self-love is the notion that self-love can be directed through reason to selfless ends.[24] On this account, sociable behavior is an instrument employed by rational egoists (i.e. Smith's "brewers, butchers and bakers"[25]) calculating future benefit, and little more. According to this instrumental view of society, sociability among men who were thoroughly egoistic and given easily to the suasion of their appetites could be attributed to no grander motive than its utility. Sympathy (usually interpreted wrongly by "Smith's economists," we shall see, as compassion, or benevolence, or some other related sort of ethical impulse) was nice to contemplate, but was unnecessary to sustain a viable social theory.

Smith scholarship in the past three decades has identified many problems with this general tendency to reduce Smith's thought to a materialist, utilitarian account of "enlightened egoism," or the "unintended consequences" of self-interest. In this chapter, I would like to emphasize two: one historiographical and methodological, the other theoretical. First, the conventional articulation of the "Adam Smith Problem," and the ultimate

---

[20] C. B. Macpherson, *The Political Theory of Possessive Individualism* (Oxford: Oxford University Press, 1962), the thesis of which was extended to Smith in his review of Winch's *Adam Smith's Politics*, *History of Political Economy*, vol. II (1979), pp. 450–454; Louis Dumont, *From Mandeville to Marx: The Genesis and Triumph of Economic Ideology* (Chicago: University of Chicago Press, 1977).

[21] See, for example, Cropsey, *Polity and Economy*, p. 72.

[22] For a good discussion of this tradition, as Smith in *WN* IV understood it, see Jacob Viner's classic "Power versus Plenty as Objectives of Foreign Policy in the Seventeenth and Eighteenth Centuries," *World Politics*, vol. I (October 1848), pp. 1–29; reprint in Jacob Viner, *Essays on the Intellectual History of Economics*, ed. Douglas A. Irwin (Princeton, NJ: Princeton University Press, 1991), pp. 128–153.

[23] See, for example, Milton Myers, *The Soul of Modern Economic Man: Ideas of Self-Interest, from Thomas Hobbes to Adam Smith* (Chicago: University of Chicago Press, 1983). A recent interpretation in this vein, from a critical perspective, is found in Michael J. Shapiro's extremely engaging *Reading "Adam Smith": Desire, History and Value* (Newbury Park, CA: Sage Publications, 1993), pp. 3–16. Shapiro claims that in Smith the "social" had become the primary alibi for the "political" (p. 11).

[24] The two classic accounts of "enlightened self-love" in early modern European thought are Arthur O. Lovejoy, *Reflections on Human Nature* (Baltimore, MD: Johns Hopkins University Press, 1961); and Albert O. Hirschman, *The Passions and the Interests: Political Arguments for Capitalism before Its Triumph* (Princeton, NJ: Princeton University Press, 1977).

[25] *WN* I.ii.2 (vol. I, pp. 26–27).

prioritization of Smith's materialism and his commercial egoism, fails to integrate the series of revisions Smith made to his *Moral Sentiments* over the course of his life.[26] Few scholars have given these revisions the careful attention they merit. Thought I don't intend to provide anything like a systematic account here, I shall signal in various places that Smith's thought becomes more intelligible when we recognize changes and adjustments that took place in his mind between 1759, when the first edition of the *Moral Sentiments* appeared, and the final sixth edition, published nearly thirty-one years later in 1790. When we acknowledge that the first edition was completed seventeen years before the 1776 publication of the *Wealth of Nations*, while the sixth edition surfaced fourteen years after, then the conventional articulation of the "Adam Smith Problem" is flawed, and in a distinctly historiographical way. One might even say that a new "Adam Smith Problem" emerges – that the question can no longer be simply the extent that the economic argument of the *Wealth of Nations* in 1776 flowed or departed from the ethical arguments of the *Moral Sentiments* of 1759, for the *Moral Sentiments* was not a static event. The question becomes: *why* did Smith revise his *Moral Sentiments* five times, and twice rather significantly? What so dissatisfied him? This issue of Smith's revisions will emerge again and again throughout my interpretation.

My second reason for rejecting an "egoistic" interpretation of Smith's thought is that Smith himself in many places flatly rejected it. As Donald Winch put it, he "did not make use of the construct known as 'economic man.'"[27] I would like to spend the balance of this chapter demonstrating that the Smithian self cannot be reduced to egoism, even though egoism played an undeniable and important role in his general description of human motivation. This will not come as earth-shattering news to anyone familiar with the recent debates. But what I do hope to illuminate here is the extent that the Smithian self was *conflicted,* ever struggling to negotiate tensions between its social and unsocial passions. First, I will introduce the notion of enlightened self-love which Smith in the *Moral Sentiments* took great pains to condemn, despite what neo-classical economists and public choice thinkers have wanted us to believe about him. Second, I will turn to Smith's conflicted self, and introduce the techniques through which people in his theory learn to negotiate their inner conflicts and become sociable.

---

[26] For insightful discussion, see Laurence Dickey, "Historicizing the 'Adam Smith Problem': Conceptual, Historiographical, and Textual Issues," *Journal of Modern History*, vol. 58, September (1986), pp. 579–609.
[27] Winch, *Adam Smith's Politics*, p. 167.

ENLIGHTENED SELF-LOVE

Adam Smith's understanding of self-love is not Hobbesian, but distinctively Stoic in origin. It arises, I believe, from the Stoic idea of *oikeiōsis*, the idea that human affection is spatially oriented concentrically around the self. We will see later in our discussion of the Stoic influence on Smith that Smith's discussion of beneficence in the *Moral Sentiments* (in a chapter titled "Of the Character of the Individual, so far as it can affect the Happiness of other People") is itself framed concentrically, considering first our self-love and our beneficence toward those closest to us; then toward various societies to which we belong; and finally toward the community of "all rational and sensible beings."[28] Smith adopted the fundamental assumption of the Stoic structure of human care, and began his own concentric journey with the Stoic observation that man's attention has been directed by nature to care for himself and for those who are "naturally the objects of his warmest affections" and "upon whose happiness or misery his conduct must have the greatest influence."[29] He argued:

Every man, as the Stoics used to say, is first and principally recommended to his own care; and every man is certainly, in every respect, fitter, and abler to take care of himself than of any other person.[30]

And yet, Smith condemned the practice of "deducing all our sentiments from certain refinements of self-love." Revealingly, he opened the *Moral Sentiments* with the following:

How selfish soever man may be supposed, there are evidently some principles in his nature, which interest him in the fortune of others, and render their happiness necessary to him, though he derives nothing from it except the pleasure of seeing it.[31]

Any educated eighteenth-century reader would have recognized that this assertion was directed at Thomas Hobbes and his followers, Samuel Pufendorf and Bernard Mandeville. In this well-known passage Smith rejected not only the claim that men were purely selfish beings without social impulses or needs, but also the corollary Mandevillean claim (embraced by many of his eighteenth-century contemporaries, and still attributed to Smith today) that any society or good-will to be found among them was little more than the by-product of enlightened selfishness.

"Enlightened self-love" is an old notion that egoism can be directed through reason to selfless ends. According to this instrumental view of

---

[28] *TMS* VI.ii (pp. 218–237).   [29] *TMS* VI.ii.1.2 (p. 219).
[30] *TMS* VI.ii.1.1 (p. 219).   [31] *TMS* I.i.1.1 (p. 9).

society, men are thoroughly selfish by nature, but are endowed with the faculty of foresight through which they are able to recognize future interests and to reason how most effectively to pursue them. The classical roots of this instrumental way of thinking about human motivation run deeper than I wish to go here. But in the generations just before Smith, the idea was often employed as a substitute for religious motivation in such diverse figures as the French Jansenist Pierre Nicole, the British natural theologian Bishop Joseph Butler, and the German natural lawyer Samuel Pufendorf, all of whom Smith was familiar with. Only later, when the eighteenth-century English physician-pamphleteer Bernard Mandeville popularized it, did the idea of "enlightened self-love" become commercialized, and an object of derision and ridicule among philosophers.

In his 1675 essay "De la charité et de l'amour-propre" ("Of Charity and Self-Love"), Pierre Nicole observed that man is naturally resistant to moral education because he

not only loves himself but loves himself beyond measure, loves only himself, and relates everything to himself. He wants every kind of property, honor pleasure, and he wants them only for himself. Placing himself at the center of everything, he would like to rule over everything and wishes that all creatures were occupied with nothing but pleasing him, praising him, and admiring him. This tyrannical disposition, being firmly implanted deep in the hearts of all men, makes them violent, unjust, cruel, ambitious, obsequious, envious, insolent, and quarrelsome.[32]

The tyrannical nature of self-love meant that men were highly immune to traditional moralism. More than a century later, Mandeville noted that even

---

[32] Pierre Nicole, "De la charité et de l'amour-propre," in *Oeuvres philosophiques et morales de Nicole, comprenant un choix de ses essais*, ed. Charles Jourdain (Paris: L. Hachette, 1845); trans. Elborg Forster, "Of Charity and Self-Love," in *Moral Philosophy from Montaigne to Kant, An Anthology*, 2 vols., ed. J. B. Schneewind (Cambridge: Cambridge University Press, 1990), vol. I, pp. 370–387, at p. 371. The date of the original French publication is not entirely clear, but scholars have placed it in *L'essais de morales*, vol. III, 1675. On the theme of *l'amour-propre éclairé* in Nicole, see Paul Bénichou, *Man and Ethics: Studies in French Classicism* (Paris: Editions Gallimard, 1948; trans. And ed. Elizabeth Hughes, New York: Anchor, 1971), chs. 3–4, esp. pp. 106–110; Lionel Rothkrug, *Opposition to Louis XIV: The Political and Social Origin of the French Enlightenment* (Princeton, NJ: Princeton University Press, 1965), pp. 47–51; Nannerl Keohane, *Philosophy and the State in France: The Renaissance to the Enlightenment* (Princeton, NJ: Princeton University Press, 1980), pp. 283–311; and especially Dale Van Kley, "Pierre Nicole, Jansenism and the Morality of Enlightened Self-Interest," in *Anticipations of the Enlightenment in England, France and Germany*, ed. Alan C. Kors and Paul Korshin (Philadelphia: University of Pennsylvania Press, 1987), pp. 69–85. Smith's familiarity with Nicole appears to be mostly secondary. We know that Nicole appears in one of Mandeville's later writings: *Free Thoughts on Religion, the Church, and National Happiness* (London,1729), pp. 68, 78 and 81, a book Smith was likely to have encountered. We also know that Smith possessed in his personal library a text on grammar that Nicole had co-authored with Arnauld and Lancelot, entitled "Grammaire générale et raisonée" (Amsterdam, 1703; reprint Paris, 1754). See James Bonar, ed., *A Catalogue of the Library of Adam Smith, Author of the "Moral Sentiments" and "The Wealth of Nations"* (1894; reprint New York: Augustus M. Kelley Publishers, 1966).

coercion was often insufficient to counter man's self-love: though "he may be subdued by superior Strength, it is impossible by Force alone to make him tractable."[33] For this reason, Mandeville observed, "Moralists and Philosophers of all Ages" attempted to *persuade* people "that it was more beneficial for every Body to conquer than indulge his Appetites, and much better to mind the Publick than what seemed his private Interest."[34] But the philosophers' attempts to persuade were always thwarted, Mandeville observed, because

whether Mankind would have ever believ'd it or not, it is not likely that any Body could have persuaded them to disapprove of their natural Inclinations, or prefer the good of others to their own, if at the same time he had not shew'd them an Equivalent to be enjoy'd as a Reward for the Violence, which by so doing they of necessity must commit upon themselves.[35]

This was where man's self-interest became a tool for the more persistent, inventive species of moralist: hence, Mandeville's claim that man is "an extraordinary selfish and headstrong, *as well as cunning* Animal."[36] Man's cunning enables him to recognize future interests, and to pursue them even at the cost of sacrificing certain immediate desires. In "Of Charity and Self-Love" Nicole advised that:

to banish all the vices, and all the gross Disorders therein, and to make Mankind happy even in this life, there needs only instead of Charity, to give everyone a harmless self-love, which may be able to discern its true Interests, and to incline thereto by the ways which true Reason shall discover to it.[37]

Likewise, in his *Sermons* of the 1720s, the English natural theologian Bishop Joseph Butler, grounded a practical morality in what he called "reasonable

[33] Bernard de Mandeville, "An Enquiry into the Origin of Moral Virtue," in *The Fable of the Bees, or Private Vices, Publick Benefits*, 2 vols., ed. F. B. Kaye (Oxford: Oxford University Press, 1924; reprint Indianapolis, IN: Liberty Press, 1988), vol. I, pp. 39–57, at pp. 41–42. On Mandeville's appropriation of the Jansenist position, see Arthur O. Lovejoy, *Reflections on Human Nature*, Lectures III–IV; Laurence Dickey, "Pride, Hypocrisy and Civility in Mandeville's Social and Historical Theory," *Critical Review*, Summer (1990), pp. 387–431; Thomas Horne, "Envy and Commercial Society: Mandeville and Smith on 'Private Vices, Public Benefits,'" *Political Theory*, vol. 9, no. 4 (1981), pp. 551–569; and E. J. Hundert, *The Enlightenment's Fable: Bernard Mandeville and the Discovery of Society* (Cambridge: Cambridge University Press, 1994), esp. pp. 30–36. See also the work of Jacob Viner: "Introduction," in Bernard Mandeville, *A Letter to Dion* (1732; Augustan Reprint Society, 1953), pp. 1–15; reprint in Irwin, ed., *Essays*, pp. 176–188; Jacob Viner, *The Role of Providence in the Social Order: An Essay in Intellectual History* (Princeton, NJ: Princeton University Press, 1972), ch. 3; and Jacob Viner, *Religious Thought and Economic Society* (Durham, NC: Duke University Press, 1978), pp. 130–139.
[34] Mandeville, "Moral Virtue," p. 42.   [35] *Ibid.*   [36] *Ibid.*   [37] Nicole, "Charity," p. 376.

self-love."[38] Employing categories and concepts strikingly similar to Nicole's, Butler argued that the presence of "virtue in the world depends on its appearing to have no contrariety to private interest and self-love":

Let it be allowed, though virtue or moral rectitude does indeed consist in affection to and pursuit of what is right and good, as such, yet, that when we sit down in a *cool hour*, we can neither justify to ourselves this or any other pursuit till we are convinced that it will be for our happiness or at least not contrary to it.[39]

For this reason Butler, like Nicole, insisted that religious leaders ought never "disown" the "principle of self-love."[40] He believed he was edifying rather than compromising his Christianity when he sought to "convince men that the course of life we would persuade them to is not contrary to their interest."[41] While "reasonable self-love" would never approximate the pure Pauline charity of the elect, it was a valuable substitute in a society of ordinary weak men because it so admirably contained the more extreme tendencies of self-love and imitated charity in a worldly way.

But *which* future interests were compelling enough to move man against himself, to quiet his passions? Mandeville asked: what could possibly inspire man to violate himself by "crossing his Appetites and subduing his dearest Inclinations"?[42] What "Equivalent" was "shew'd" to his self-love to justify the sacrifice? Nicole had fastened upon man's natural desire to be an object of love and esteem, an "inclination … so *cunning* and so subtle, and at the same time so pervasive, that there is no action into which it cannot creep."[43] Man's "violent temptations" are thus "weakened and counterbalanced" in Nicole's formulation by the "fear of men's judgments."[44]

Prompted by reason to seek the esteem and affection of men, self-love so perfectly imitates charity that if we consult it on how to conduct our outward actions, it will give us the same advice as charity will and launch us on the same course.[45]

Mandeville was doubtless drawing here on Nicole's argument about the civilizing effects of "esteem and affection" when he emphasized the "Power" that "Flattery" and "Contempt" had upon man's natural "Pride,"[46] and the extent to which man perceived his greater interest to lie in securing that

[38] Joseph Butler, *Five Sermons*, ed. Stephen L. Darwall (Indianapolis, IN: Hackett Publishing Co., 1983), pp. 57–67, at p. 65. "Sermon XII" is presented in the abridged Hackett edition as "Sermon V." Butler's complete works can be found in *The Works of Joseph Butler*, 2 vols., introduction and notes by J. H. Bernard (London: English Theological Library, 1900). Hundert reveals that Butler, in the course of his critique of Mandeville, became intimate with Jansenist moral psychology. Hundert, *Fable*, p. 134.
[39] Butler, *Sermon XI*, p. 56.   [40] *Ibid.*, p. 55.   [41] *Ibid.*, p. 56.
[42] Mandeville, "Moral Virtue," p. 51.   [43] Nicole, "Charity," p. 374.   [44] *Ibid.*, pp. 385–386.
[45] *Ibid.*, p. 377.   [46] Mandeville, "Moral Virtue," pp. 42–45 and 51–52.

"Flattery" and averting that "Contempt" by exercising "Self-denial"[47] – by harnessing, or at least "hiding or disguising,"[48] his natural appetites. To explain motives for virtuous action among intractably selfish creatures, Mandeville appropriated what Nicole and the Jansenists had called *l'amour-propre éclairé*, rendering into in rustic English as man's "Conquest of his own Passions out of a Rational Ambition of being good."[49] This is precisely what Mandeville meant when he claimed that "private vices" morally unchecked but enlightened through reason could yield "publick benefits." The practice of "Moral Virtue" among ordinary men could be attributed to no grander motive than this.

SMITH AND ENLIGHTENED SELF-LOVE

Little wonder so many interpreters have linked Mandeville and Smith with the idea that sociable behavior is little more than an instrument pursued by rational egoists calculating future benefit.[50] Famously, Smith argued in the *Wealth of Nations* that despite man's natural "passion for present enjoyment,"[51] human life wasn't fated to Hobbesian War, since the most urgent of man's passions were balanced by a foresight, by "a desire of bettering our condition, a desire which, though generally calm and dispassionate, comes with us from the womb, and never leaves us till we go into the grave."[52] In this particular passage, Smith was discussing incentives to "frugality" and against "profusion," but this instrumental way of thinking was by no means confined to his thoughts on personal spending habits. In fact, it is in this vein that interpreters regularly invoke Smith's famous reference to "the brewer the butcher and the baker," who act sociably toward their patrons not from benevolent intentions, not with a desire to cultivate society for its own sake, for its beauty or for its general utility, but in the interest of "bettering their condition."[53]

Smith maintained that "self-interest," or what he called the "selfish passions," held a sort of "middle" position between man's "social" and

---

[47] *Ibid.*, pp. 42, 43, 45, 51 and 56.   [48] *Ibid.*, pp. 44–45.   [49] *Ibid.*, pp. 48–49.
[50] See Hundert, *Enlightenment's Fable*, pp. 219–236; and Christopher J. Berry, *The Idea of Luxury: A Conceptual and Historical Investigation* (Cambridge: Cambridge University Press, 1994), pp. 152–173.
[51] *WN* II.iii.28 (vol. I, p. 341).
[52] *WN* II.iii.28 (vol. I, p. 341). See Albert Hirschman's discussion of calm passion and *doux-commerce* in *The Passions and the Interests*, pp. 9–66; sharpened in his "Rival Views of Market Society," *Journal of Economic Literature*, vol. 20, December (1982); reprinted in Albert O. Hirschman, *Rival Views of Market Society and Other Recent Essays* (Cambridge: Cambridge University Press, 1992), pp. 105–141. For an earlier, much neglected account, see Lovejoy, *Reflections*, esp. pp. 39–46.
[53] *WN* I.ii.2 (vol. I, pp. 26–27).

"unsocial" passions.[54] A "selfish" man employing his "reason" will recognize a certain "utility" in resisting his "unsocial" inclinations and, as best he can, feigning sociable ones. The butcher smiles to his customers as he envisions their next visit to buy meat. And with regard to his competitors, experience in the commercial world has taught him the norms of "fair play":

> In the race for wealth, and honours, and preferments, he may run as hard as he can, and strain every nerve and every muscle, in order to outstrip all his competitors. But if he should jostle, or throw down any of them, the indulgence of the spectators is entirely at an end. It is a violation of fair play, which they cannot admit of.[55]

I spend considerable time later exploring the ways that spectators constrain our behavior in commercial life as in most other spheres of life. But the point for now is to recognize Smith's claim that the world does not tolerate, does not sympathize with, open and flagrant violations of fair play. This knowledge makes the merchant gentle, *douceur*, in his interactions with customers and competitors – to invoke Albert Hirschman's famous description of the prudent actor in *The Passions and the Interests*. That "bettering our condition" can socialize in this negative way, Smith argued, requires that an individual through his reason is "capable" of "discerning the remote consequences" of his actions – "the advantage or detriment that is likely to result from them" in the future.[56] If the butcher takes advantage of his customers, willingly sells them a substandard product, they will likely turn elsewhere, and tell their neighbor to turn elsewhere – which will ruin his reputation, destroy his business, starve his family, and fuel the bourgeois cycle of fear that keeps him awake at night. The "prudence" of an action, therefore, represents an actor's rational choice that he would best be served by abstaining from various "immediate" impulses and interests in order to obtain a greater pleasure, or to avoid a worse pain, at a "future time."[57] It is worth noting now that Smith invoked this prudential, instrumental way of thinking when he reflected on the motivation of nations in international affairs – how to overcome the absence of good-will and cooperation among inescapably "selfish" national actors. This will be a subject for us later in Chapter 6.

Clearly, Smith's thoughts about prudence here were influenced by the Nicole–Butler orientation to "enlightened" or "reasonable" self-love. Butler

[54] *TMS* I.ii.4 (pp. 40–43); *TMS* III.6.6 (p. 172). See Knud Haakonssen, *The Science of a Legislator*, pp. 67–74 and 87–89; and D. D. Raphael, "Hume and Adam Smith on Justice and Utility," in *Proceedings of the Aristotelian Society* (London: Methuen & Co., 1972/73). New Series, vol. LXXIII, pp. 87–103.
[55] *TMS* II.ii.2.1 (p. 83).   [56] *TMS* IV.2.6 (p. 189).   [57] *TMS* IV.2.6–8 (pp. 189–190).

had defined "prudence" as the "reasonable endeavor to secure and promote" ones own "interest and happiness" in the future.[58] He contrasted this "cool" way of thinking with the heat of passion and impulse. "Imprudence" was "dissolutely to neglect" one's "greater good in the future" for the sake of a "present and lesser gratification."[59] Smith's description of the calculation was nearly identical.

Moreover, Smith agreed with Nicole and Butler that selfish rational choice emulated morality in a sociological way, permitting society to thrive in the absence of genuine affection, and without anachronistic forms of moral policing that too often rested on contentious assumptions about God and morals, and tended to stifle modern commercial aspirations. As Nicole observed,

However corrupt this society might be inwardly … outwardly nothing would be more orderly, courteous, just, peaceful, honorable, and generous; moreover, it would be an excellent thing that, everything being inspired and driven only by self-love, self-love would not show itself and that, society being entirely without charity, what one would see everywhere would be only the forms and outward marks of charity.

Indeed, one would live among self-lovers "as peacefully, safely and comfortably as if one were in a republic of saints."[60] Similarly, Smith argued that:

though among the different members of society there should be no mutual love or affection, the society, though less happy and agreeable, will not necessarily be dissolved. Society may subsist among different men, as among different merchants, from a sense of its utility, without any mutual love or affection.[61]

Istvan Hont suggests that Smith derived much of his optimism here from Pufendorf's notion of *socialitas*.[62] *Socialitas* was the idea that prior to any sort of social contract, prior to politics (*civitas*) and its institutional enforcement of positive law, man possessed a natural capacity to reason about how

[58] Butler, *Sermons*, p. 72. [59] *Ibid.* [60] Nicole, "Charity," p. 372. [61] *TMS* II.ii.3.2 (p. 86).
[62] Istvan Hont, "The Language of Sociability and Commerce: Samuel Pufendorf and the Theoretical Foundations of the 'Four-Stages Theory,'" in *The Languages of Political Theory in Early Modern Europe*, ed. Anthony Pagden (Cambridge: Cambridge University Press, 1987), pp. 253–276. On Pufendorf's idea of *socialitas*, see generally Leonard Krieger, *The Politics of Discretion: Pufendorf and the Acceptance of Natural Law* (Chicago: University of Chicago Press, 1965); Richard Tuck, *Natural Right Theories: Their Origin and Development* (Cambridge: Cambridge University Press, 1979), esp. pp. 176–177; Duncan Forbes, "Natural Law and the Scottish Enlightenment," in *The Origins and Nature of the Scottish Enlightenment*, eds. R. H. Campbell and A. S. Skinner (Edinburgh: John Donald Publishing Ltd, 1982), pp. 186–204; James Tully, "Introduction," in Samuel Pufendorf, *On the Duty of Man and Citizen*, ed. James Tully (Cambridge: Cambridge University Press, 1991), pp. xxi–xxix; and Robert Wokler, "Rousseau's Pufendorf: Natural Law and Foundations of Commercial Society," *History of Political Thought*, vol. 15, no. 3 (1994), pp. 373–402.

best to secure his own preservation. What gave this capacity ethical point for Pufendorf was that, unlike the beasts, man concluded that it was most useful to preserve himself by cooperating with other men. Hont suggested that the idea of *socialitas* finds its earliest expression in the Aristotelian idea that man's natural condition of need was implicitly a principle of *koinōnia*, of community.[63] Motivated by self-preservation, men came together without a contract, without a political apparatus, to deliberate about how to cooperate with one another.[64]

Similarly for Smith, the most rudimentary form of social existence is inspired not by a "natural love of society" or a "desire that the union of mankind should be preserved for its own sake," but through an enlightened form of "selfishness."[65] No one intends it, but society benefits nevertheless through the "unintended consequences" of prudence – what Martin Hollis has called a "cunning of reason."[66] Smith extended this way of thinking in his discussion of utility in Part IV of the *Moral Sentiments*. There he invoked his well-known formulation of the "invisible hand" to describe how the "rich" are led without knowledge or intention to benefit the "poor":

The rich only select from the heap what is most precious and agreeable. They consume little more than the poor, and in spite of their natural selfishness and

---

[63] Hont, "Pufendorf," p. 265. Similarly, Bernard Yack points out that man for Aristotle was not only *zoōn politikōn*, but first *zoōn koinōnikon*. Bernard Yack, *The Problems of a Political Animal: Community, Justice, and Conflict in Aristotelian Political Thought* (Berkeley, CA: University of California Press, 1993), pp. 25–33 and 64–65. Yack's treatment of Aristotelian *koinōnia* is sensitive to the role that reason and utility played in bridging individual motivations and communal ends.

[64] By conceiving natural cooperation through the medium of utilitarian reason, Pufendorf sought to bridge the monumental gap between Hugo Grotius and Thomas Hobbes. He could admit to a Hobbesian, individualist orientation to human nature, and avoid Grotius' natural sociality, but still achieve a non-political, non-Hobbesian conclusion about social life. See Hont, "Pufendorf," pp. 258 and 264. With Hont's interpretation, however, we almost forget about Pufendorf's absolutism. Obviously people don't *stay forever* for Pufendorf in *socialitas*. On how to understand Pufendorf's sociability in the *context of* his absolutism, see Daniel Gordon, *Citizens Without Sovereignty: Equality and Sociability in French Thought, 1670–1789* (Princeton, NJ: Princeton University Press, 1994), pp. 61–64; and especially Alfred Dufour's examination of Pufendorf's "two-fold" social contract in Alfred Dufour, "Pufendorf," in *The Cambridge History of Political Thought, 1450–1700*, ed. J. H. Burns and Mark Goldie (Cambridge: Cambridge University Press, 1991), pp. 561–588, at pp. 572–579. There, Dufour shows that Pufendorf's idea of sovereignty involved two distinct historical stages: First, *pactum associationis*, which corresponds to the utilitarian *socialitas* Hont described; and second, once men have united and contracted with one another in the first stage to cooperate for mutual preservation, they make a second contract, a "contract of subjection," which establishes the sovereign. This kind of thinking leads Richard Tuck to doubt Pufendorf's absolutism in *Natural Right Theories*, pp. 175–176.

[65] *TMS* II.ii.3.6–10 (pp. 88–90); *TMS* IV.2.3 (p. 188).

[66] Martin Hollis, *The Cunning of Reason* (Cambridge: Cambridge University Press, 1987). Similarly, Michael Ignatieff referred to this as a "cunning of Nature" in "Smith, Rousseau and the Republic of Needs," in *Scotland and Europe, 1200–1850*, ed. T. C. Smout (Edinburgh: John Donald Publishers, 1986), pp. 187–206, at p. 191.

rapacity, though they mean only their own conveniency, though the sole end which they propose from the labours of all the thousands whom they employ, be the gratification of their own vain and insatiable desires, they divide with the poor the produce of all their improvements. They are led by an invisible hand to make nearly the same distribution of the necessaries of life, which would have been made, had the earth been divided into equal portions among all its inhabitants, and thus without intending it, without knowing it, advance the interest of society, and afford means to the multiplication of the species.[67]

Nevertheless, we shouldn't inflate the "unintended consequences" dimension of Smith's thought beyond proper bounds. The *Moral Sentiments* was an extended and rich description of how "Nature" inclines man to *cultivate* his moral sentiments – not merely an account of how through selfishness he produces social ends without social intentions.[68] Even the most economistic of Smith's interpreters cannot deny this. But cold utility was in Smith's texts too, undeniably, perhaps for those turned callous by commercial life, perhaps as a supplement to moral sentiment when self-love spoke too loudly – a sort of insurance policy implanted in the world by Nature through what Smith often referred to as her benevolent "œconomy." Butler too seems to have conceived of enlightened self-love as an accommodation to an imperfect world. Instead of condemning utterly "the condition in this world,"[69] as a traditional moralist might do, Butler accommodated his ideals to the "present state of things, bad as it is" by seeking out resources for social coordination in the "familiar and daily intercourses among mankind."[70]

CONFLICTED SELF

Smith was preoccupied with social order and greatly influenced by Nicole, Butler and Pufendorf on the glue of modern society. The implications of this influence will emerge again and again throughout my interpretation of his thought. And yet, there are problems with reducing Smith to enlightened selfishness, as if he had nothing else to say on the subject of social cooperation. For one thing, it fails to account for Smith's suspicion of "prudence" as the sole motivation for action, and his outright condemnation of that Mandevillean species of "sophistry" that "deduce[s] all our

[67] *TMS* IV.1.10 (pp. 184–185).
[68] Hume, at *Enquiry* 5.2 (p. 50), argued that "utility ... is a foundation of the chief part of our morals." Smith challenged this idea, especially at *TMS* II.ii.3.6–12 (pp. 87–91) and IV (pp. 179–193).
[69] See Ignatieff, *Needs of Strangers*, p. 61.   [70] *Ibid.*, pp. 60–63.

sentiments from certain refinements of self-love."[71] From the first page of
the *Moral Sentiments*, the Patron Saint of neo-classical economics and
rational choice flatly rejected moral systems that conceived of man primarily
as a rational calculator of interests. In his discussion of ancient
Epicureanism in Chapter VII, for example, Smith distanced himself from
any practical morality that reduces human nature to selfishness and grounds
practical morality in prudential calculation.[72] There, he associated "prudence" with a spurious Epicurean "temperance." Since the "whole value of
this virtue arose from its utility, from its enabling us to postpone present
enjoyment for the sake of a greater to come," Smith regarded Epicurean
"temperance" as "nothing but prudence with regard to pleasure."[73] Since
"virtue," according to Smith's Epicurus, "did not deserve to be pursued for
its own sake," but "was eligible only upon account of its tendency to prevent
pain and to procure ease and pleasure" Smith decried Epicureanism as "no
doubt, altogether inconsistent with that which I have been endeavouring to
establish."[74]

More striking is the chapter Smith devoted to debunking the "ingenious
sophistry" of Mandeville's "licentious system."[75] In Smith's words:

Man, he observes, is naturally much more interested in his own happiness than in
that of others, and it is impossible that in his heart he can ever really prefer their
prosperity to his own. Whenever he appears to do so, we may be assured that he
imposes upon us, and that he is then acting from the same selfish motives as at all
other times ... All public spirit, therefore, all preference of public to private interest,

[71] *TMS* I.i.2.1 (pp. 13–14). See also *TMS* III.2.27 (p. 127); *TMS* VI.ii.4 (pp. 306–314); and *TMS* VII.iii.1
(pp. 315–317). On Smith's break with Mandeville, see for instance Lucio Colletti, "Mandeville,
Rousseau and Smith," in *From Rousseau to Lenin: Studies in Ideology and Society*, trans. John
Merrington and Judith White (New York: Monthly Review Press, 1972), pp. 195–216; Horne,
"Commercial Society," pp. 559–565. On the ambivalence of this break, however, see Donald
Winch, *Riches and Poverty: An Intellectual History of Political Economy in Britain, 1750–1834*
(Cambridge: Cambridge University Press, 1996), pp. 57–89; and the works of Dario Castiglione:
"Mandeville Moralized," *Annali della Fondazione Luigi Einaudi*, vol. 17 (1983), pp. 239–290;
"Considering Things Minutely: Reflections on Mandeville and the Eighteenth-Century Science of
Man," *History of Political Thought*, vol. 7 (1986), pp. 463–488; and "Excess, Frugality and the Spirit of
Capitalism: Readings of Mandeville on Commercial Society," in *Culture in History: Production,
Consumption and Values in Historical Perspective*, ed. Joseph Melling and Jonathan Barry (Exeter:
University of Exeter Press, 1992), pp. 155–179.
[72] *TMS* VII.ii.2 (pp. 294–300).   [73] *TMS* VII.ii.2.9 (p. 297).
[74] *TMS* VII.ii.2.17 (pp. 299–300); *TMS* VII.ii.2.13 (p. 298). We know, of course, by reading Seneca or
Cicero, that Epicurus himself was not regarded by his contemporaries as a theorist of sensual
indulgence, but that his thought is often confounded with what became of "Epicureanism." See
for example Seneca, *Letters From a Stoic*, trans. and ed. Robin Campbell (London: Penguin, 1969),
IX, p. 53; XVI, p. 65; XXVIII, p. 75. In 1790, Smith's attack on the Epicurean tendencies of prudence
will become far more systematic and severe as he begins to prioritize the Stoic idea of "propriety."
[75] *TMS* VI.ii.4 (pp. 306–314).

is, according to him [Mandeville], a mere cheat and imposition upon mankind; and that human virtue which is so much boasted of, and which is the occasion of so much emulation among men, is the mere offspring of flattery begot upon pride.[76]

In contrast, Smith asserted that man possesses a drive, a principle "in his nature" that conflicts with his baser, selfish passions, and inclines him toward the happiness of others "though he derives nothing from it except the pleasure of seeing it."[77]

It was a common strategy among early modern moral philosophers reflecting on human nature to craft a "middle way" to explain the foundations of society among men without succumbing to Hobbesian egoism or resorting to a sappy and implausible natural benevolence or moral sense. Joseph Butler, for example, attempted to wedge his view of human nature between the mutually obdurate categories of Hobbesian–Mandevillean self-love and Shaftesburian benevolence. He argued in 1726 in *Sermon XII* that the two extremes of "self-love" and "benevolence" actually exist in nature, by God's design, "in proportion" to one another in the minds and hearts of men – and that "virtue to be sure exists in the *due* proportion."[78] Jean-Jacques Rousseau's *Second Discourse* (1755) provides another useful example for us here,[79] since his attempt to "balance" human nature was so well known at the time, and because Smith read Rousseau's discourse with great care, and wrote a formal reply to Rousseau in the *Edinburgh Review* in 1756, just three years before the publication of his own *Moral Sentiments* in 1759.[80] Like Butler, Rousseau argued in the *Second Discourse* that the human soul operates in nature, before the cultivation of reason, according to two principles:

[76] *TMS* VII.ii.4.7 (pp. 308–309). That E. J. Hundert could conclude after reading *TMS* VII.ii.4 (pp. 306–315) that "Smith was never deeply concerned with the tangible licentiousness of Mandeville's conclusions" is puzzling (Hundert, *Fable*, p. 221).

[77] Once again, *TMS* I.i.1.1 (p. 9).

[78] Butler, *Sermons*, pp. 57–67, at p. 61. One of the few scholars to include Butler in a discussion of Adam Smith's anti-Hobbesism is Milton Myers in *The Soul of Modern Economic Man*. Despite the book's many shortcomings, which all seem to stem from it's narrow Anglo-centered approach to Smith's intellectual context, it is useful nevertheless for situating Smith's anti-Hobbesism in the context of British moral philosophy.

[79] Jean-Jacques Rousseau, *Discourse on the Origin of Inequality Among Men (Second Discourse)*, in *The Basic Political Writings*, trans. Donald A. Cress (Indianapolis, IN: Hackett, 1987), pp. 23–109.

[80] Adam Smith, "A Letter to the Authors of the Edinburgh Review," in *The Edinburgh Review, From July 1755 to January 1756* (Edinburgh, 1756), pp. 63–79. Citations from Adam Smith, *Essays on Philosophical Subjects*, ed. W. P. D. Wightman (Indianapolis, 1982). For discussion of the Letter and the influence of Rousseau's idea of human nature on Smith's thought in general, see Ryan Hanley, "Commerce and Corruption: Rousseau's Diagnosis, Adam Smith's Cure," *European Journal of Political Theory*, vol. 7, no. 2 (2008), pp. 137–158; Jeffrey Lomonaco, "Adam Smith's 'Letter to the Authors of the *Edinburgh Review*," *Journal of the History of Ideas*, vol. 64, no. 4 (2002), pp. 659–676; Dennis Rasmussen, "Rousseau's 'Philosophical Chemistry' and the Foundations of Adam Smith's Thought," *History of Political Thought*, vol. 27, no. 4 (2006), pp. 620–641.

of which one makes us ardently interested in our well-being and our self-preservation, and the other inspires in us a natural repugnance to seeing any sentient being, especially our fellow man, perish or suffer. It is from the conjunction and combination that our mind is in a position to make regarding these two principles, without the need for introducing that of sociability, that all the rules of natural right appear to me to flow."[81]

Smith agreed. Like Rousseau and Butler, he claimed that "the Deity" had implanted an "œconomy" in nature, endowing men with an "appetite" for both "self preservation and the propagation of the species."[82] At one point, he referred specifically to these appetites as our "social" and "unsocial" passions,[83] and repeated in several places that they coexist in a certain proportion to one another:

In every part of the universe we observe means adjusted with the nicest artifice to the ends which they are intended to produce; and in the mechanism of a plant, or animal body, admire how every thing is contrived for advancing the two great purposes of nature, the support of the individual and the propagation of the species.[84]

Sometimes, as in this passage, Smith attributed this "œconomy" and balance to the contrivance of "the Deity." In other places, confirming his affinity with natural theology, he referred to the "adjustments" of "Nature,"

And Nature, indeed, seems to have so happily adjusted our sentiments of approbation and disapprobation, to the conveniency both of the individual and of the society, that after the strictest examination it will be found, I believe, that this is universally the case.[85]

Characterizing human nature as a combination of selfish and social appetites – and referring to that combination as an "œconomy" implanted by the Deity, or as a "Natural" adjustment – it may seem as though Smith argued that our passions for self and society exist naturally in a harmonious relation with one another and require nothing additional from their mortal possessors. A reader attracted to the theme of spontaneous order in Smith's thought might be inclined to describe the adjustment here as such. But I believe we are mistaken to read Smith in this way. Like Butler, Rousseau and others, Smith placed an imperative on man to strike a practical balance between his "social" and "unsocial" passions. Indeed, the *Moral Sentiments* in its entirety might profitably be read as Smith's empirical description of

[81] Rousseau, *Second Discourse*, p. 35.   [82] *TMS* II.i.5.10 (p. 77).   [83] *TMS* I.ii.2 (pp. 31–43).
[84] *TMS* II.ii.3.5 (p. 87).   [85] *TMS* IV.2.3 (p. 188).

the very processes through which people learn actively to balance their social and unsocial passions, actively to put them into harmony.

The parallel here with Butler is again illuminating. Reflecting on the presence of both "self-love" and "benevolence" in the human heart, Butler argued that "virtue to be sure exists in the due proportion."[86] In other words, the burden was placed on man to put his divine gifts in order and to proper use. In the balance of this chapter, I explore what Smith meant when he said that our sentiments are "adjusted to the conveniency both of the individual and of the society," emphasizing that our "appetites" for each often come into conflict.

I argue that the self was conflicted for Smith, in three related ways – the first two I will address here; the third later in Chapter 4. First and foremost, people were ever struggling to negotiate conflicts that inevitably emerged in life between their selfish and social passions. Second, perhaps less frequently, they struggled to negotiate conflicts that emerged between the objects of their love – between filial obligation and patriotism, to take the classic Sophoclean example, or between patriotism and cosmopolitanism. Third, Smith observed that the self often conflicted with *itself* – that indeed human judgment and action did not always flow smoothly from steady rational decision in Smith's thought. What makes Smith's description of moral life so compelling, so much richer and more complex than the "rational man" reading that dominated for so long, is his psychological sensitivity to ways that the human mind often deludes and destabilizes itself. This is not an insignificant dimension of Smith's thought for he characterized it as the "source of half the disorders of human life."[87] For the moment, however, I would like to supplement the egoistic reading of Smith's thought with a more "complicated" and textured account of human motivation by discussing the first two sorts of struggle mentioned above: those between self and society; and those between conflicting loves. Later in Chapter 4, we will examine Smith's thoughts about why the self often deludes and disrupts itself, as well as the various solutions he offered to combat self-disruption.

SELF AND SOCIETY

While Smith fully acknowledged the selfish basis of human motivation, and frequently drew upon it to stabilize society in a very rudimentary way, he was also deeply concerned that our natural affections sometimes inspire

[86] Butler, *Sermons*, pp. 57–67, at p. 61.   [87] *TMS* III.4.6 (p. 158).

judgments and actions that neglect or overtly violate the well-being of those not particularly connected to us. It was therefore one of Smith's central objectives in the *Moral Sentiments* to *enlarge* the perspective of those whose judgments were easily led astray and often blinded by narrow affective entanglements. He illustrated the problem vividly in his famous discussion of the "Chinese earthquake," through which he attempted to provide some solution to Hume's troubling assertion that "it is not irrational for me to prefer the destruction of the entire world to the merest scratching of my little finger."[88] Without explicit reference to Hume's formulation (surely his readers would have needed no assistance) Smith compared the emotion one would experience over the news that a hundred million Chinese people (read: distant strangers) had been swallowed into the earth in a sudden massive earthquake, with the distress one would experience over the loss of one's own pinky finger – a great and tragic misfortune to distant strangers, in other words, versus a comparatively small misfortune to oneself. Smith speculated:

He would, I imagine, first of all, express very strongly his sorrow for the misfortune of that unhappy people, he would make many melancholy reflections upon the precariousness of human life, and the vanity of all the labours of man, which could thus be annihilated in a moment. He would too, perhaps, if he was a man of speculation, enter into many reasonings concerning the effects which this disaster might produce upon the commerce of Europe, and the trade and business of the world in general. And when all this fine philosophy was over, when all these humane sentiments had been once fairly expressed, he would pursue his business or his pleasure, take his repose or his diversion, with the same ease and tranquility, as if no such accident had happened. The most frivolous disaster which could befall himself would occasion a more real disturbance. If he was to lose his little finger tomorrow, he would not sleep to-night; but, provided he never saw them, he will snore with the most profound security over the ruin of a hundred millions of his brethren, and the destruction of that immense multitude seems plainly an object less interesting to him, than this paltry misfortune of his own.[89]

Smith likened the suasion of man's selfish passions to visual deception. Understanding why we often elevate our selfish needs shamelessly above the needs of others is much like understanding why an untrained eye will passively accept that a distant mountain it observes through a window is in reality smaller than the window through which it is observed. We are

---

[88] *TMS* III.3.4 (pp. 136–137). I write this in the aftermath of the massive Shandong earthquake of May 2008. Smith's example leaps from the page, especially as I reflect on the months that have passed since the media have thought it necessary to update us on the well-being of the earthquake victims. The reference to Hume is *Treatise on Human Nature*, II.ii.3 (p. 60).

[89] *TMS* III.3.4 (pp. 136–137).

sentimentally near-sighted. Our selfish passions tend to delude us into fantastic over-evaluations of ourselves, our own joys and pains, the importance of our place in the world relative to others.[90]

But given this natural propensity passively to elevate our own interests and concerns far above those of others, how can we possibly coexist in a world with others similarly inclined? The problem is sharp enough even in our own homes and communities, but Smith uses the case of distant strangers to illustrate the problem in its purest form. The distant Chinese stranger provided Smith with the most acute example of sufferers his audience would have had no physical, affective, cultural or economic connection with – no compelling reason, in other words, to stimulate concern. So, what is it for Smith that restrains us from sacrificing the well-being of others in order to save our little finger? He asked:

When our passive feelings are almost always so sordid and so selfish, how comes it that our active principles should often be so generous and so noble? When we are always so much more deeply affected by whatever concerns ourselves, than by whatever concerns other men; what is it that prompts the generous, upon all occasions, and the mean upon many, to sacrifice their own interests to the greater interests of others?[91]

For Smith the answer lies in man's conscience:

It is not the soft power of humanity, it is not that feeble spark of benevolence which Nature has lighted up in the human heart, that is thus capable of counteracting the strongest impulses of self-love. It is a stronger power, a more forcible motive, which exerts itself upon such occasions. *It is reason, principle, conscience, the inhabitant of the breast, the man within, the great judge and arbiter of our conduct.* It is he who, whenever we are about to act so as to affect the happiness of others, calls to us, with a voice capable of astonishing the most presumptuous of our passions, that we are but one of the multitude, in no respect better than any other in it; and that when we prefer ourselves so shamefully and so blindly to others, we become the proper objects of resentment, abhorrence, and execration. It is from him only that we learn the real littleness of ourselves, and of whatever relates to ourselves, and the natural misrepresentations of self-love can be corrected only by the eye of this impartial spectator.[92]

For Adam Smith there was something *inside* of us – "reason, principle, conscience, the inhabitant of the breast," etc. – that corrects our emotional near-sightedness by confronting us with the ugliness of our self-preference, and stabilizes our moral judgments by reminding us "that we are but one of

---

[90] *TMS* III.3.2–3 (pp. 134–136). [91] *TMS* III.3.4 (p. 137). [92] *TMS* III.3.4 (p. 137), emphasis added.

the multitude, in no respect better than any other in it."[93] I spend considerable time in this book exploring this internal faculty Smith identified and the ways it was used in his theory to socialize our judgments and actions and to stabilize modern society.

Interesting to note that Smith invoked this "internal tribunal" again when he reflected on how people adjudicate the second sorts of conflict I introduced above: those that emerge between *degrees* of social commitment. I turn next to this problem of "conflicting loves."

CONFLICTING LOVES

Smith observed that conflicts can arise when our affections are in tension or incompatible – when the claims they exert, or the actions they demand, draw in different directions or draw on finite or indivisible resources. John Rawls articulated the problem well when he observed that "benevolence is at sea as long as its many loves are in opposition in the persons of its many objects."[94] How does an individual in Smith's theory adjudicate such conflicts, when the claims of friendship collide with those of family, for example, or when family conflicts with country? In such cases, Smith insisted that the abstract priority rules advanced by ancient and modern casuists could provide no assistance: "When those different beneficent affections happen to draw different ways, to determine by any precise rules in what cases we ought to comply with the one, and in what with the other, is, perhaps, altogether impossible."[95] Priority rules in the case of conflicting duties, he claimed, are

impossible to accommodate to all the different shades and gradations of circumstance, character, and situation, to differences and distinctions which, though not imperceptible, are, by their nicety and delicacy, often altogether undefinable.[96]

Rules, for Smith, could not explain why in Voltaire's *Orphan of China* we admire both Zamti who is "willing to sacrifice the life of his own child, in order to preserve that of the only feeble remnant of his ancient sovereigns and masters" and Idame, his wife, "who reclaims her infant from the cruel hands of the Tartars, into which it had been delivered."[97]

If not by rules how then were conflicting affections and obligations to be negotiated? Charles Larmore observed that Smith's rejection of casuistic rule-following was accompanied by a claim that such conflicts could be

[93] *TMS* III.3.4 (p. 137).
[94] John Rawls, *A Theory of Justice* (Cambridge, MA: Belknap Press, 1971), p. 190.
[95] *TMS* VI.ii.1.22 (p. 226).   [96] *TMS* VI.ii.1.22 (p. 227).   [97] *TMS* VI.ii.1.22 (p. 227).

resolved through the "function of moral judgment."[98] I agree, for here Smith revived his idea of conscience, which figured so prominently earlier in the book (in Part III) in his discussion of self-preference in the Chinese earthquake example. There, we recall, Smith claimed that conscience was the moral faculty through which a person adjudicates conflicts that arise between his self-love and the claims of others, even distant, foreign others. Now, in Part VI, Smith extended this discussion of conscience to conflicts that emerged between *degrees* of social affection:

In what cases friendship ought to yield to gratitude, or gratitude to friendship; in what cases the strongest of all natural affections ought to yield to a regard for the safety of those superiors upon whose safety often depends that of the whole society; and in what cases natural affection may, without impropriety, prevail over that regard; must be left altogether to the decision of *the man within the breast, the supposed impartial spectator, the great judge and arbiter of our conduct.* If we place ourselves completely in his situation, if we really view ourselves with his eyes, and as he views us, and listen with diligent and reverential attention to what he suggests to us, his voice will never deceive us. We shall stand in need of no casuistic rules to direct our conduct.[99]

That Smith in this crucial passage appoints conscience the arbiter of conflicting duties, recalls Kant's discussion of conflicting imperfect duties in the *Metaphysical first principles of the doctrine of virtue*. I would venture to say that Smith came closer to Kant in this passage than in any other in any work. Though many have recognized the transcendental aim of Smithian conscience (even though, as we shall discover in the next chapter, it was formed empirically through the *a posteriori* processes of sociology and psychology,[100] even though it wasn't reason-ordained[101]), no one to my knowledge has explored the Kantian implications of Smith's resort to conscience for adjudicating conflicting duties.

To appreciate this, we recall Kant's idea of imperfect duties. For Kant, a perfect duty is strict, juridical and absolutely binding. The duty to respect others as ends in themselves is universal; it transcends the vicissitudes of context, the contingencies of time and place, categorically. Imperfect duties, on the other hand, such as the duty of active beneficence, are broad and flexible – not in the sense that they permit an agent to make random

[98] Charles E. Larmore, *Patterns of Moral Complexity* (Cambridge: Cambridge University Press, 1987), pp. 17–18 and p. 156, n. 26.
[99] *TMS* VI.ii.2.22 (pp. 226–227), emphasis added.
[100] Haakonssen, "Kantian Themes in Smith," pp. 151–152.
[101] Fleischacker, "Philosophy in Moral Practice: Kant and Adam Smith," *Kant-Studien* 82 (1991), pp. 249–269, at p. 266.

exceptions to the duty itself, but rather in the sense that context and
particular circumstances will bear on the manner in which the duty is to
be appropriately fulfilled. This is what is often referred to as the "latitudi-
narian" character of imperfect duty in Kant's moral philosophy. It refers
to an agent's permission to limit one maxim of duty by another (e.g. love
of one's neighbor in general by love of one's parents), by which the field
for the practice of virtue is widened.[102] In his discussion of the need for
latitude Kant pointed specifically to cases when duties of beneficence
collided. The resolution of such conflicts required a faculty he called
"judgment":

> ethics, because of the latitude it allows in its imperfect duties, unavoidably leads to
> questions that call upon judgment to decide how a maxim is to be applied in
> particular cases.[103]

But what exactly was this faculty for Kant? Kant had read Smith's *Moral
Sentiments* just before composing the *Metaphysics*.[104] Given this, it is stunning that he described this adjudicating faculty as "conscience"; and more
specifically, that he captured the dialogical quality of the Smithian impartial
spectator when he referred to conscience as "an internal court in the human
being," and "a business of a human being with himself."[105] The consonance
with Smith is remarkable indeed:

> Every human being has a conscience and finds himself observed, threatened, and,
> in general, kept in awe (respect coupled with fear) by an internal judge; and this
> authority watching over the law in him is not something that he himself (volun-
> tarily) makes, but something incorporated in his being.[106]

Of course, Kant's description of conscience as "incorporated" in a man's
being, as an "original and (since it is the thought of duty) moral predisposition,"[107] clashes importantly with what we shall discover about the
empirical basis of Smithian conscience. But its *functional* parity with
Smith's account of conscience as an internal adjudicator of conflicting duties
is significant, given what we know about Kant's interest in Smith's book.

   We turn in the next two chapters to Smith's idea of conscience – what it
was, where it came from, and how it operated. It is not obvious what

[102] Immanuel Kant, *The Metaphysics of Morals, Part II: Metaphysical First Principles of the Doctrine of Virtue*, in *Practical Philosophy*, trans. and ed. Mary J. Gregor, (Cambridge: Cambridge University Press, 1996), pp. 509–603, at Intro.VII, 6:390 (p. 521).
[103] Kant, *Doctrine of Virtue*, Intro.XVII, 6:411 (p. 538).
[104] See Fleischacker, "Kant and Adam Smith," pp. 249–255, for biographical details.
[105] Kant, *Doctrine of Virtue*, II.i.13, 6:438–440 (pp. 559–562).
[106] Kant, *Doctrine of Virtue*, II.i.13, 6:438 (p. 560).   [107] Kant, *Doctrine of Virtue*, II.1.13, 6:438 (p. 560).

conscience was for Smith for he referred to it throughout the treatise in a variety of ways: as "society within," "the man within," "the great inmate," "the great demigod in our breast," "reason" and "principle." These are very different ways of characterizing conscience, and we are left wondering which Smith *really* meant – or the extent to which they might be reconciled in his thought. What are we to make of Smithian conscience?

We know that Smith was certain about the *authority* of conscience in moral judgment and action:

Upon whatever we suppose that our moral faculties are founded, whether upon a certain modification of reason, upon an original instinct, called a moral sense, or upon some other principle of our nature, it cannot be doubted, that they were given us for the direction of our conduct in this life.[108]

But how did Smith *ground* man's moral faculties, certain as they apparently were to him? Recognizing the authority of conscience is one thing, and in eighteenth-century British moral philosophy, not a terribly controversial thing. But, identifying the source of moral knowledge was another question entirely. What, for Smith, was the source?

---

[108] *TMS* III.5.5 (pp. 164–165).

CHAPTER 2

Sympathetic self

'Tis with our judgments as our watches, none go just alike, yet each
believes his own.

Alexander Pope, Essay on Criticism

In Chapter 1, we examined Adam Smith's resistance in the *Moral Sentiments*
to deducing all moral sentiment from "certain refinements of self-love."[1]
From the opening lines of his treatise, Smith distinguished himself from
Mandeville and from other eighteenth-century attempts to "socialize" or
"commercialize" Hobbesian assumptions about human nature. Smith
rejected not only the claim that men were thoroughly selfish beings, but
he also rejected the corollary claim made by many of his contemporaries
that any "society" to be found among them was but a by-product of
enlightened selfishness. Men were not wholly selfish for Smith but in fact
deeply conflicted, ever struggling to negotiate conflicts that emerged in life
between their selfish and social appetites. We discovered that Smith identified a certain faculty inside of us that assists us as we adjudicate practical
conflicts between our selfish and social tendencies, helping us to resolve
them in the direction of sociality. In Chapter 1, I introduced Smith's
account of the conflicted self. Here I begin to explore the adjudicating
faculty Smith identified. He claimed that "to direct the judgments of this
inmate is the great purpose of all systems of morality."[2] But what was this
"inmate"? Where did it come from? How did it work?

One might begin by examining the language Smith used to describe it.
The problem, as I noted in the previous chapter, is that Smith referred to
conscience throughout the *Moral Sentiments* in a variety of ways: as
"society within," "the man within," "the great demigod in our breast,"
"reason" and "principle." These are very different ways of characterizing
conscience; and while there may be ways that an interpreter might go

---

[1] *TMS* I.i.2.1 (p. 13). See also *TMS* VII.iii.1 (pp. 315–317).   [2] *TMS* VII.iii.1.47 (p. 293).

about reconciling them, Smith did not do so explicitly. We are left to debate how he might have reconciled them, or which he really meant. Famously, Smith was something of a perfectionist regarding his written work, revising the *Moral Sentiments* five times over the course of thirty-one years, and consigning his unpublished work to the flames from his death-bed. It would be a stretch for us to suppose that these varieties of usage would have remained intact over so many years had the perfectionist in Smith found them the least bit incompatible.[3]

To get some grasp on Smith's idea of conscience, we might begin by isolating what Smith did *not* mean by it. For one thing, he did not attribute our moral faculties to God or any divine dispensation. He often said that God had arranged things in nature to maximize human happiness, and that it is reasonable for us to believe that we participate in His plan when we follow our natural tendencies. He claimed in several places that religious practice often helps "enforce" moral duty by giving it an added "sacredness" – and that a belief in God puts man "under an additional tie."[4] I will address Smith's deism later. But God did not ground or determine man's moral faculties for Smith. Nor did man's capacity to reason.[5] Smith's assault on "casuistry" is well known, and resonates powerfully with philosophical arguments today leveled against Kantian rationalism. "We shall stand in need of no

---

[3] I agree in principle with Emma Rothschild that Smith was not overly preoccupied with "foundational or metaethical questions" – "not tremendously interested in the foundations of his own or other people's systems." Emma Rothschild, "Dignity or Meanness," *Adam Smith Review*, vol. 45 (2004), pp. 150–165, at p. 152. Indeed, Smith was often vague about the origins of conscience – to what extent it emerges from the world, from reason, from God. I agree fully with this. However, I believe Rothschild overstates the case somewhat, particularly regarding Smith's later revisions to the *Moral Sentiments*, which seem to me largely inspired by foundational questions. But, even as such, a key assumption in my interpretation is that, regardless of Smith's vagueness or outright confusion, we ultimately learn much about our own foundational and metaethical commitments and tensions by considering his – for they were vivid, as we shall see.

[4] *TMS* III.5.12–13 (p. 170).

[5] I have learned a great deal about the debate in seventeenth- and eighteenth-century British moral philosophy between sensationalism and rationalism in the works of D. D. Raphael, especially *The Moral Sense* (Oxford: Oxford University Press, 1947); "The Impartial Spectator," in *Essays on Adam Smith*, ed. Andrew S. Skinner and Thomas Wilson (Oxford: Clarendon Press, 1975), pp. 83–99; *Moral Philosophy* (Oxford: Oxford University Press, 1981, 1984), chs. 2–3; and his edited collection, *British Moralists 1650–1800*, 2 vols. (Oxford: Clarendon Press, 1969; reprint Indianapolis, IN: Hackett, 1991). Also helpful has been Stephen Darwall, *The British Moralists and the Internal 'Ought': 1640–1740* (Cambridge: Cambridge University Press, 1995). On the debate between rationalism and theistic moralities, I have consulted John Gascoigne, *Cambridge in the Age of the Enlightenment: Science Religion and Politics from the Restoration to the French Revolution* (Cambridge: Cambridge University Press, 1988); the essays in Knud Haakonssen, ed., *Enlightenment and Religion: Rational Dissent in Eighteenth-Century Britain* (Cambridge: Cambridge University Press, 1996); and Frederick C. Beiser, *The Sovereignty of Reason: The Defense of Rationality in the Early English Enlightenment* (Princeton, NJ: Princeton University Press, 1996), esp. ch. 7, "Ethical Rationalism."

casuistic rules to direct our conduct," he declared.[6] In passages like this, Smith was targeting the "Cambridge Platonism" of Samuel Clarke and Richard Price who viewed the faculty of reason as the seat of moral knowledge, as the crucible of *a priori* duty.[7] Smith devoted an entire chapter in Part VII of the *Moral Sentiments* to analyzing this tradition and concluded that it was "altogether absurd and unintelligible to suppose that the first perceptions of right and wrong can be derived from reason."[8] He argued: "the original judgments of mankind with regard to right and wrong" are not like "decisions of a court of judicatory" reached "by considering first the general rule, and then, secondly, whether the particular action under consideration fell properly within its comprehension."[9] The fundamental problem with "casuistic rules" for Smith is that they are inherently incapable of "accommodating" the vicissitudes of human life:

> These [casuistic rules] it is often impossible to accommodate to all the different shades and gradations of circumstance, character, and situation, to differences and distinctions which, although not imperceptible, are, by their very nicety and delicacy, often altogether undefinable.[10]

Charles Griswold's discussion of Smith's skepticism in *Adam Smith and the Virtues of Enlightenment* is very helpful here. Smith rejected the "high-minded teleology" of traditional moral philosophy as well as the rationalism of his contemporaries for both tended to reduce human experience to "simple, systematic and univocal" patterns.[11] Griswold praises Smith for "saving the phenomena," for embracing our passions, our imperfections, our imagination, our finitude, and the ordinary, everyday understandings that make us who we are – in short, for recognizing that "prephilosophical ethical life" is the "main source of light" that moral philosophy possesses.[12] At the heart of the Smithian project, Griswold suggests, lies a humble respect for the lives of ordinary people, a willingness to take humanity as it is and to resist distorting the phenomena of ordinary life to fit our own partial views of how the world should be.[13]

Drawing on the physical sciences as a methodological model, eighteenth-century Scottish moral philosophers attempted through empirical inquiry to describe where actual moral judgments come from, given ordinary people

---

[6] *TMS* VI.ii.1.22 (p. 227).   [7] *TMS* VII.iii.2 (pp. 318–321).
[8] *TMS* VII.iii.2.7 (p. 320). An excellent discussion of Smith's skepticism and anti-rationalism is found in Charles L. Griswold, "Rhetoric and Ethics: Adam Smith on Theorizing about the Moral Sentiments," *Philosophy and Rhetoric*, vol. 24, no. 3 (1991), pp. 213–237, at pp. 224–229; and Charles L. Griswold, *Virtues of Enlightenment*, esp. ch. 4.
[9] *TMS* III.4.11 (p. 160).   [10] *TMS* VI.ii.1.22 (p. 227).
[11] Griswold, *Virtues of Enlightenment*, p. 52.   [12] *Ibid.*, p. 74.   [13] *Ibid.*, p. 52.

as they behave in the world as it appears.[14] Like Frances Hutcheson and David Hume, Smith presented a portrait of the actual sociological processes through which moral judgments are formed, and not a set of "abstruse" reflections upon man's moral aptitudes and tendencies. This is what it meant to produce an empirical *theory* of moral sentiments.

Others before me have detailed Smith's significant departures from British empiricism, and it is unnecessary to rehearse that again here. It is adequate to note that he generally took a great deal from it. Our "first perceptions of right and wrong," Smith agreed with Hutcheson, are grounded not in reason or in revelation, but in "immediate sense and feeling."[15] As Smith himself described it, Hutcheson's idea of a moral sense is

a particular power of perception exerted by the mind at the view of certain actions or affections; some of which affecting this faculty in an agreeable and others in a disagreeable manner, the former are stamped with the characters of right, laudable, and virtuous; the latter with those of wrong, blamable, and vicious.[16]

Smith agreed that the mind engaged in such "stamping," but he agreed with Hume that Hutcheson had overlooked the cognitive development of our moral faculties when he claimed that the mind can distinguish right from wrong prior to worldly experience. A. L. Macfie was right when he suggested that Smith sought to historicize Hutcheson's moral sense theory.[17] In a particularly well-known passage, Smith posited a fundamentally Humean claim that social intercourse precedes moral sensibility:

Were it possible that a human creature could grow up to manhood in some solitary place, without any communication with his own species, he could no more think of his own character, of the propriety or demerit of his own sentiments and conduct, of the beauty or deformity of his own mind, than of the beauty or deformity of his own face. All these are objects which he cannot easily see, which naturally he does not look at, and with regard to which he is provided with no mirror which can present them to his view. Bring him into society, and he is immediately provided with the mirror which he wanted before. It is placed in the countenance and

---

[14] On Smith's empirical critique of theism and rationalism, see Raphael, "Spectator," pp. 96–99. I have benefited from Bernard Williams' discussion of the comparable tendencies of religion and rationalism toward abstraction, in *Ethics and the Limits of Philosophy* (Cambridge, MA: Harvard University Press, 1985), pp. 195 and 197–198.

[15] *TMS* VII.iii.2.7 (p. 320).

[16] *TMS* VII.iii.3.2 (p. 321). For Smith's account of Hutchesonian "moral sense," see *TMS* VII.iii.3 (pp. 321–327). For helpful discussion, see Knud Haakonssen, "Natural Law and Moral Realism: The Scottish Synthesis," in *Studies in the Philosophy of the Scottish Enlightenment*, ed. M.A. Stewart (Oxford: Clarendon Press, 1990), pp. 61–85; and Knud Haakonssen, *Natural Law and Moral Philosophy*, pp. 65–85.

[17] Macfie, *The Individual in Society*, pp. 83–84.

behavior of those he lives with, which always mark when they enter into, and when they disapprove of his sentiments; and it is here that he first views the propriety and impropriety of his own passions, the beauty and deformity of his own mind.[18]

If we wish to grasp the epistemology of Smithian conscience this image of the "social mirror" may be the single most revealing passage in the *Moral Sentiments*. What this passage conveys is that Smith's orientation to our moral faculties began with a description of our immersion in society. This is how we come to know who we are, what the world is, and how to coordinate a balance between the two. Smith referred to this process as "sympathy." I argue here that sympathy is the foundation of conscience in Adam Smith's *Moral Sentiments* – that conscience emerges for him as sympathetic experience insinuates itself into the human soul, hardens over time, and ultimately becomes the inner tribunal that guides individual judgment and action. So, I begin below with Smith's account of sympathy as a prelude to his theory of conscience.

SYMPATHY

People often mistake the *Moral Sentiments* as a normative treatise about morality, but Smith rarely spoke in what we would refer to today as a "normative" voice. He tended to reject traditional moral philosophy for distorting the phenomena of ordinary life in its drive to promote abstract – Smith would say "abstruse"[19] – views of how the world should be.[20] In the tradition of Hutcheson and Hume, Smith was engaged in a far more *descriptive* activity. At one point he bluntly asserted "that the present inquiry is not concerning a matter of right ... but concerning a matter of fact."[21] Undoubtedly, there are moments in the text when he came rather close to offering a theory of moral justification, struggling with the erratic or unfortunate moral consequences of sympathy in certain contexts.[22] I shall say more about this later. But I argue here that Smith in the *Moral Sentiments* wanted primarily to convey as earnestly as possible the phenomena he observed in the social world around him. As such, he approached the subject of morality with the empirical eye of a moral psychologist, describing in rich detail the actual causal mechanisms through which sympathy generated moral sentiment, given people as they are in the world as it is.

[18] *TMS* III.1.3 (p. 110).   [19] See, for example, *TMS* III.3.21 (p. 145).
[20] A central theme in Griswold, *Virtues of Enlightenment*.   [21] *TMS* II.i.5.10 (p. 77).
[22] For an excellent discussion of the descriptive and normative dimensions of Smith's examination of morality, see Otteson, *Marketplace of Life*, pp. 199–257.

In the *Moral Sentiments*, Smith presented an empirical portrait of the way people go on, the way they relate to each other and produce morality together through ordinary daily interactions. Smith's empirical approach to morality demonstrates a commitment to taking humanity as it is and to resist distorting the phenomena of ordinary life to fit our own partial views of how the world should be. He rejected theology, the "high-minded teleology" of traditional moral philosophy, as well as the rationalism of his contemporaries for all tended to reduce human experience to simple patterns. As Griswold puts it, Smith wanted to "save the phenomena," to embrace the ordinary, "prephilosophical" understandings that make us who we are.[23] For Smith, moral life was not an abstract end that reason revealed to us in quiet contemplation, but a "social practice" conducted in shared spaces – or in Griswold's words, in a "context of mutual responsiveness."[24] No recourse to an independent order of moral facts was required for an adequate account of morality. Indeed, Smith suggested that we get over the fantasy that such an order outside ourselves even existed.[25] For an adequate account of morality, we needed simply to look at ourselves.

To contemporary social scientists nurtured on clear distinctions between facts and values, between what is and what ought to be, such an approach may seem a thoroughly empirical, scientific endeavor and not a philosophical one in the least.[26] But it is important to recognize that such a division of labor had not yet been conceived and professionalized in Smith's day. We must be wary of our own vocational specialization when interpreting a complex eighteenth-century thinker like Adam Smith, who was broadly educated and deeply insightful, perceptive and richly descriptive, obviously unconstrained by our twenty-first-century methodological biases and cautions, and guilty of countless border-crossings that transgressed the physical sciences, philosophy, history, politics, law, economics, psychology, anthropology, literary theory and social theory. Understanding Smith's project requires that we cultivate historical sensitivity to how Smith and his eighteenth-century audience would have understood the nature of his questions and methods. The positive/normative distinction that drives contemporary social science seems more than a slightly inappropriate heuristic for interpreting a "theory" that attempted to provide an empirical account of morals in the nebulous terms of "human nature," that moved quite freely between fact and value,

---

[23] Griswold, *Virtues of Enlightenment.*   [24] *Ibid.*, p. 49.   [25] *Ibid.*, p. 341.
[26] See, for example, T. D. Campbell, *Adam Smith's Science of Morals.* See especially pp. 19–21 on the question of whether Smith was doing philosophy or social science. It is not surprising given Campbell's answer that he characterizes Smith as a relativist.

between the actual and the ideal, and that – and this is true for any social observation, no matter how much objectivity it claims for itself – was inescapably guided by a variety of normative impulses, acknowledged or not.

So what was sympathy for Smith? On Smith's account, sympathy was not an innate human disposition that discharges mindlessly and spontaneously like Grotius' *appetitus societatus* or Rousseau's *pitie* or the *moral sense* of Shaftesbury[27] and Hutcheson; nor was it a rational telos toward which all healthy people strive, like Stoic *apatheia* or Lockean natural law. Though Smith rejected moral pessimism however it presented itself, and was keen to challenge the egoistic assumptions of Hobbes and his disciples (notably Pufendorf and Mandeville), as we have seen, he did not employ the idea of sympathy as a sappy signifier of human benevolence. Sympathy was not "automatic, passive, and mindless" for Adam Smith, as John Radner put it.[28] I demonstrate here that sympathy for Smith was a social practice through which ordinary people encountering one another in shared spaces, who are constrained by their selfishness, are nevertheless capable of coordinating with others and producing morality together without the artificial machinations of political coercion, philosophy, religion or formal education. As Smith described it, sympathy is a social process through which we learn to:

accommodate and to assimilate, as much as we can, our own sentiments, principles, and feelings, to those which we see fixed and rooted in the persons whom we are obliged to live and converse a great deal with.[29]

Milton Myers puts it very well when he claims that Smith's moral philosophy is "firmly based on the mundane and the visible, the common interpersonal pressures arising out of everyday life as these pressures act on people through the principle of sympathy."[30] John Durham Peters emphasizes its "publicity."[31] Henry Clark characterizes it helpfully as a "conversation."[32] Emma Rothschild too characterizes it as a "conversational

---

[27] Although, as Lawrence E. Klein emphasized in his excellent study, Shaftesbury in his *An Inquiry Concerning Virtue* never actually used the term. *Shaftesbury and the Culture of Politeness: Moral Discourse and Cultural Politics in Early Eighteenth-Century England* (Cambridge: Cambridge University Press, 1994), pp. 54–59.

[28] See Radner's discussion of the "mental effort" involved in both sympathy and selfishness in John Radner, "The Art of Sympathy in Eighteenth-Century British Moral Thought," *Studies in Eighteenth-Century Culture*, vol. 9 (1980), pp. 189–210.

[29] *TMS* VI.ii.1.17 (p. 224).

[30] Milton L. Myers, "Adam Smith as Critic of Ideas," *Journal of the History of Ideas*, vol. 32, no. 2 (1975), pp. 281–296.

[31] John Durham Peters, "Publicity and Pain: Self-Abstraction in Adam Smith's *Theory of Moral Sentiments*," *Public Culture*, vol. 7 (1995), pp. 657–684.

[32] Henry C. Clark, "Conversation and Moderate Virtue in Adam Smith's 'Theory of Moral Sentiments,'" *Review of Politics*, vol. 54, no. 2 (1992), pp. 185–210. However, I disagree with Clark's

morality."[33] Emphasizing the activities of "interaction" and "mutual exchange," James Otteson refers to it as a "market."[34] Knud Haakonssen describes a "mechanism for the selection of behavior that is adequate to ... the social situation" that "unintendedly creates common social standards."[35] Elsewhere he refers to this process as "education."[36] I agree fully with Radner above that sympathy is an activity of the mind; but I will emphasize along with those just cited, and others, that this activity of the mind takes place in a social context among other minds, mixing together in shared spaces, and that this situatedness has important implications for the role that sympathy plays in socialization, in the development of conscience, and in the creation and perpetuation of moral culture.

I shall present Smith's account of sympathy as a dramatic social practice that unfolds in two general "stages." The first, which I should like to call *surveillance*, is that in which a "spectator," any ordinary person, observes and judges the behavior of an "agent" and through some means communicates this judgment. The second stage, which I shall call *discipline*, will be discussed in Chapter 3. Discipline refers to the impact that the spectator's surveillance and judgment have upon the agent, the extent to which they motivate him to modify his conduct, and ultimately, through repetition, to become a member of a moral culture. I am deliberately drawing here upon Michel Foucault's account in *Discipline and Punish* of the turn in modern Western societies toward bloodless techniques of achieving social order of "governing conduct," as James Tully has put it.[37] I have appropriated Foucault's two well-known descriptions of modern life – "surveillance" and "discipline" – because they help to convey the relations of power that govern sympathetic activity in Smith's account and the moral culture that it produces. What gave sympathy ethical point for Smith was its power to

argument that for Smith such a conversation is possible only in "civilized societies." I will argue here that this process is a universal one for Smith, that it takes place wherever people live in physical proximity with one another.

[33] Emma Rothschild, *Economic Sentiments: Adam Smith, Condorcet, and the Enlightenment* (Cambridge, MA: Harvard University Press, 2001), p. 231.

[34] Otteson, *Marketplace of Life*. This claim is central to Otteson's reconciliation of Smith's seminal texts: "I think the concept of a market explains the development of all human social customs and institutions for Smith" (p. 7). See also Andreas Kalyvas and Ira Katznelson, "The Rhetoric of the Market: Adam Smith on Recognition, Speech and Exchange," *Review of Politics*, vol. 63, no. 3 (2001), pp. 549–579.

[35] Haakonssen, *Science of a Legislator*, p. 55.   [36] *Ibid.*, pp. 59–60.

[37] Foucault, *Discipline and Punish*. Smith himself used the word "discipline" over and again to describe the socializing work that sympathy performed in moral education: *TMS* III.3.20 (p. 145); *TMS* III.3.22 (p. 145); *TMS* III.3.24 (p. 146); *TMS* III.3.45 (p. 156); *TMS* III.5.1 (p. 163). He also often referred to our "undisciplined passions" and our "natural" and "untaught feelings": *TMS* I.iii.3.1 (p. 34); *TMS* III.3.28 (p. 148); *TMS* VI.iii.18 (p. 245). See James Tully, "Governing conduct," in *Conscience and Casuistry in Early Modern Europe*, ed. Edmund Leites (Cambridge: Cambridge University Press, 1988), pp. 12–71.

motivate people to modify their conduct to a pitch commensurable with social life. Surely, the Foucauldian or Benthamite architect is absent in Smith's account (indeed, we all seem to be accidental architects) but like Foucault's prisoner, who is subjected "to a field of visibility" and is thus transformed into a "principle of his own subjection," we become on Smith's account unwitting organs of panoptic coercion against ourselves and others.[38] What gave sympathy ethical point for Smith was its power through visibility to *discipline* modern individuals, to socialize them into the group, to marginalize or sublimate their differences and perpetuate cultural norms without traditional (bloody) forms of coercion.

One prefatory comment before pursuing the "stages" of surveillance and discipline further. It is potentially misleading to refer to the engagements in Smith's description as "stages" or moments since they often fire quite rapidly, often simultaneously, and tend to live on in the mind and world long after they take place. Mindful not to lock the sympathy dynamic into a mechanical sequence I use the temporal signifier "stage" since it conveys distinct social experiences within Smith's description. I use "stage" to emphasize the inter-subjectivity of Smith's account – that sympathy for him was not a moral disposition or a telos but a dynamic that stimulated agents (and the future agents of agents) to accommodate themselves to the demands of social life.

A second prefatory comment about my use of Foucault, a twentieth-century continental postmodern, to interpret an eighteenth-century Scot. I have not engaged Foucault here to be stylish or provocative, and I would encourage readers inclined to bristle at my use of Foucault in this context to pause and reflect on the reasons one might wish to juxtapose his views on surveillance and discipline with Smith's. I find Foucault's language for speaking about socially disciplined norms deeply perceptive and resonant with Smith's description of how norms are passed along through sympa-thetic exchange. I wish to emphasize Smith's salience for contemporary political, moral and social theory by mapping Foucauldian language onto his description of sympathy as a social practice through which our moral criteria are disciplined as we move through the watching world. Putting their accounts against one another is a fruitful exercise because Foucault's categories help convey to a contemporary audience the power relations that govern sympathetic activity and the sort of morality that it produces. I am not imputing menacing intentions to Smith, though I do intend to suggest ultimately that the autonomy and independence he valued might be under-cut ultimately by the disciplinary mechanism he so richly described.

[38] Foucault, *Discipline and Punish*, pp. 202–203.

"SURVEILLANCE" AND FELLOW-FEELING

The first "stage" of sympathy is that in which a spectator – any ordinary, richly constituted, inescapably partial individual – observes the behavior of an agent, arrives at a judgment, and somehow (verbally or otherwise) communicates her judgment to the agent. In this act of judging, Smith noted, the spectator is unable to experience the agent's joys and griefs in a primary and immediate way since she is quite literally a different being, incapable of going "beyond" her own flesh and mind, "beyond" her own "person."[39] The only way a spectator can generate fellow-feeling for the agent, according to Smith, is imaginatively to project herself into the agent's world and to ask herself whether she would be motivated by his circumstances to feel and act as he does. Since "we have no immediate experience of what other men feel," Smith argued, "we can form no idea of the manner in which they are affected, but by conceiving what we ourselves should feel in the like situation."[40]

Though our brother is upon the rack, as long as we ourselves are at our ease, our senses will never inform us of what he suffers. They never did, and never can, carry us beyond our own person, and it is by the imagination only that we can form any conception of what are his sensations. Neither can that faculty help us to this any other way, than by representing to us what would be our own, if we were in his case. It is the impressions of our own senses only, not those of his, which our imaginations copy. By the imagination we place ourselves in his situation, we conceive ourselves enduring all the same torments, we enter as it were into his body, and become in some measure the same person with him, and thence form some idea of his sensations, and feel something which, though weaker in degree, is not altogether unlike them.[41]

Smith's account of imagination in this passage takes place within a spatial forum, a shared space, upon a sort of dramatic stage.[42] The spectator as audience, or "by-stander,"[43] *sees* the spectacle of suffering before him, in all its colorful and compelling detail, and imagines what the sufferer endures.

Smith often referred to spectators as "fair," "impartial" and "indifferent"[44] and he differentiated his project from a "selfish" morality that is based entirely

[39] *TMS* I.i.1.2 (p. 9).   [40] *TMS* I.i.1.2 (p. 9).   [41] *TMS* I.i.1.2 (p. 9).
[42] On the "drama" and "theatricality" of Smithian sympathy, see David Marshall, "Adam Smith and the Theatricality of Moral Sentiments," *Critical Inquiry*, vol. 10, June (1984), pp. 592–613, esp. p. 612, n. 14; and David Marshall, *The Figure of Theatre: Shaftesbury, Defoe, Adam Smith, and George Eliot* (New York: Columbia University Press, 1986).
[43] *TMS* I.i.1.4 (p. 10); *TMS* II.i.2.2 (p. 69).
[44] That Smith characterized actual spectators (and not merely the supposed "impartial spectator") as fair, impartial and indifferent, see *TMS* I.i.5.8 (p. 26); *TMS* I.ii.4.1 (p. 39); *TMS* II.i.2.2 (p. 69); *TMS* II.ii.1.3 (p. 78); *TMS* II.ii.2 (pp. 82–85); *TMS* II.ii.2.4 (p. 85); and *TMS* III.3.42 (p. 154).

on self projection. Contemporary scholars have often debated the implications of the spectator's change of position in Smith's theory, and the extent to which we might call such a theory of sympathetic imagination "egoistic" since judgment entails that a spectator bring the case of another "home to himself" – in a sense to make the case his own, imagining that *he* was the person principally concerned. Smith himself insisted that this "selfish" reading of the sympathetic imagination was misguided. A spectator's commiseration is given *entirely* upon the account of the sufferer, and cannot, in this sense, be considered "selfish." He insisted that the spectator does not place himself, *as himself,* into the position of the agent. Rather he tries actually to *take on* the person of the agent, to become *him* as far as possible, to imagine what *he* feels in *his* circumstances. For Stephen Darwall, this sort of projection in Smith's account of sympathy entails "identification with, and thus respect for, the other as having a different point of view."[45] It assumes a framework of "moral community among independent equal persons."[46] A spectator sympathizes with an agent not because he believes *he* would be motivated in those circumstances to do the same thing, but because he finds that the agent did the proper thing, *as him*. Therefore, Smith argued that the spectator's commiseration (or lack thereof) is given (or withheld) *entirely on the account* of the agent, and can in no way be considered "selfish":

> yet this imaginary change is not supposed to happen to me in my own person and character, but in that of the person with whom I sympathize. When I condole with you for the loss of your only son, in order to enter into your grief I do not consider what I, as a person of such a character and profession, should suffer, if I had a son, and if that son was unfortunately to die: but I consider what I should suffer *if I was really you*, and I not only change circumstances with you, but I change persons and characters. My grief, therefore, is *entirely upon your account*, and not in the least upon my own. It is not, therefore, in the least selfish.[47]

Only through the imagination, through his attempt "in fancy" to get as close to the agent as possible, to "enter as it were into his body and become in some

---

[45] Stephen Darwall, "Equal Dignity in Adam Smith," *Adam Smith Review*, vol. 1 (2004), pp. 129–134, at p. 132.

[46] *Ibid.* Smith's egalitarian impulses have been treated at length by Emma Rothschild, *Economic Sentiments: Adam Smith, Condorcet, and the Enlightenment* (Cambridge, MA: Harvard University Press, 2001) – but also note her caution regarding Darwall's reading of the "grounding" of Smith's egalitarianism in "Dignity or Meanness," pp. 150–154. Rothschild notes there how little Smith was "concerned with what we would call either foundational or metaethical questions" (p. 152). On Smith's egalitarianism, see also Samuel Fleischacker, *A Third Concept of Liberty*; and Samuel Fleischacker, *Wealth of Nations* (Princeton, NJ: Princeton University Press, 2004), pp. 72–80, and Iain McLean, *Adam Smith: Radical and Egalitarian: An Interpretation for the 21st Century* (Edinburgh: Edinburgh University Press, 2006).

[47] *TMS* VII.iii.1.4 (p. 317), emphasis added.

measure the same person with him,"[48] to "bring home to himself every little circumstance of distress which can possibly occur to the sufferer,"[49] can the spectator come to understand why the agent acts and feels as he does. In other words, only imaginary closeness can produce understanding. But it is key to note that the sympathy model is effective for Smith for producing impartial moral judgments because the spectator is *at once* both involved *and* detached. Once "changing places in fancy" the spectator is said to understand the agent and his conditions *well enough* to "form some idea of his sensations," to feel *with* him and achieve a sufficient "correspondence" or "concord." And yet, she is coolly removed from his distress or pleasure; her change of position is only "imaginary" and "momentary." Since she remains safe while the agent suffers, since she remains poor while he prospers, lonely while he loves, the sentiment she generates is necessarily "lower" in degree and it "varies in kind" from the agent's primary sentiments.[50] Smith wrote:

Our imagination not having run in the same channel with that of the lover, we cannot enter into the eagerness of his emotions.[51]

A spectator's understanding can never be perfect for Smith since spectators never *really* become one with those they observe since they never for a moment lose sight of the very separateness that their spectatorship entails. As John Durham Peters put it: "Sympathy ... is not a matching of emotions, a heart-to-heart transfer from one person to another, but a judgment made by an observer, an interpretation."[52] Surely Smith did not make Rousseau's more radical claim about the man whose reason "isolates him and moves him to say in secret, at the sight of a suffering man, 'Perish if you will; I am safe and sound'," the man who needs only to "place his hands over his ears and argue with himself a little in order to prevent nature, which rebels within him, from identifying him with the man being assassinated."[53] But he did assert that even the most refined imagination must fall short of primary experience, that a complete "unison" of sentiment between different people differently situated is impossible.[54] It is central to understanding Smith's thought, however, that this unbridgeable gap between spectator and agent was not terribly problematic for him.[55] Smith's acknowledgment

---

[48] *TMS* I.i.1.2 (p. 9).   [49] *TMS* I.i.1.2 (p. 9).   [50] *TMS* I.i.4.7 (pp. 21–22).
[51] *TMS* I.ii.2.1 (p. 31).   [52] Peters, "Publicity and Pain," p. 660.
[53] Rousseau, *Second Discourse*, pp. 54–55.   [54] *TMS* I.i.4.7 (p. 22).
[55] To the extent that understanding is possible among physically discrete individuals, we shall see later that Smith believed it is likelier when a spectator is "closer" physically to the other, able to ascertain the minute and total circumstances of other's case. See *TMS* I.i.4.6 (p. 21). It also helps to be as familiar as possible with the world of meanings that situate those circumstances for the other. See *TMS* I.ii.1.7 (p. 220).

of the fundamental unbridgeability of perspectives and positions, and his resistance to erecting unstable bridges, may be one of his most important lessons for moderns struggling with deep diversity and cross-cultural intelligibility. We can get only so close, understand only so much. Smith was not seeking a complete "unison" among different people differently situated and constituted – he understood the fundamental impossibility of this – but rather, was affirming the possibility of what he observed as a less fulfilling but nevertheless sufficient "concord" of sentiment, supported by the nature of human sociality. Indeed, he believed this concord, achieved through the sympathy dynamic, was sufficient for social order: "These two sentiments … [that of the spectator and that of the agent] … have such a correspondence with one another, as is sufficient for the harmony of society. Though they will never be unisons, they may be concords, and this is all that is warranted or required."[56]

Moreover, and perhaps equally important for the integrity of Smith's project, this inherent and unbridgeable distance between spectator and agent was the *very thing* that enabled a spectator to judge *impartially* – to be sufficiently "fair" and "indifferent" and ultimately positioned to judge whether or not an agent's behavior is "proper."[57] A spectator cannot literally experience an agent's sensations but he sees his blood and his tears, hears his laughter, and he finds himself drawn into the "cause which excites them."[58] Nearness will improve, and distance will diminish, the preciseness with which he can understand "the case of his companion with all its minutest incidents."[59] In other words, proximity will help the spectator better understand *why* the agent responded to particular causes the way he did, and to evaluate more accurately whether or not the agent's response was appropriate, or what Smith called "proper."

Now, think of propriety as a kind of "suitability" to circumstance. Here Smith followed David Hume who rejected a tendency among moral philosophers in his day to reduce moral judgment to a consideration of consequences alone, or to what Smith called the "tendency of affections."

Philosophers have, of late years, considered chiefly the tendency of affections, and have given little attention to the relation which they stand in to the cause which excites them. In common life, however, when we judge of any person's conduct, and of the sentiments which directed it, we constantly consider them under both these aspects. When we blame in another man the excesses of love, of grief, of resentment, we not only consider the ruinous effects which they tend to produce,

[56] *TMS* I.i.4.7 (p. 22).   [57] *TMS* I.i.1.2–3 (pp. 9–10).
[58] *TMS* I.i.1.8 (p. 18).   [59] *TMS* I.i.4.6 (p. 21).

but the little occasion which was given for them. The merit of his favourite, we say, is not so great, his misfortune is not so dreadful, his provocation is not so extraordinary, as to justify so violent a passion. We should have indulged, we say; perhaps have approved of the violence of his emotion, had the cause been in any respect proportioned to it.[60]

Here, Smith was following Hume who resisted the unjust potential of consequentialism, claiming that a "moral decision" must rest upon a refined knowledge of "all the circumstances and relations" that bear upon a case:

While we are ignorant whether a man were aggressor or not, how can we determine whether the person who killed him be a criminal or innocent?[61]

I may think I see an act of aggression before me, but a more refined understanding of the circumstances might reveal that the "bully" was merely fending off an attack. Distance distorts what we see, obscures the "whole case." We become "fair" and "impartial," Smith argued, only after we "bring home to ourselves every little circumstance of distress which can possibly occur to the sufferer."[62] We need to understand the "whole case"[63] in order to determine whether or not the agent's behavior was "proper," "suitable to its object," "proportioned," appropriate to the particular cause which excited it.[64] A judgment is not "fair" if it merely considers whether the consequences of the behavior merit praise, though clearly they might.

But how does a spectator decide whether an action or feeling is suitable to its cause and therefore proper? On what criteria – or, to use Smith's language, on what "standards and measures"[65] – does she *base* her judgment? What, in other words, is propriety? A Smithian spectator does not judge others with an abstract measure, as if he has come upon the scene a disembedded and stripped down self, behind a Rawlsian veil of ignorance. Rawls himself noted that a crucial "contrast" between impartial spectator theory and his own theory of the original position was that in the former, parties "possess all the requisite information" and "relevant knowledge" of their "natural assets or social situation," while in the latter, parties are

---

[60] *TMS* I.i.3.7 (p. 18), emphasis added.   [61] Hume, *Enquiry*, Appendix I, p. 85.

[62] *TMS* I.i.4.6 (p. 21). It must also be noted here that Smith acknowledged that a spectator might be moved by a vivid narrative of distant joy or suffering. Departing slightly from Hume, who claimed that an event described in "an old history or remote gazette … is so infinitely removed as to affect the senses, neither with light nor with heat" (*Enquiry* V.2 (p. 221)), Smith argued that we can in fact sympathize upon reading a story. The vividness of the description replicates proximity: "We can sympathize with the distress which excessive hunger occasions when we read the description of it in the journal of a siege, or of a sea voyage. We imagine ourselves in the situation of the sufferers, and thence readily conceive the grief, the fear and consternation, which must necessarily distract them" (*TMS* I.ii.1.1 (p. 28)).

[63] *TMS* I.i.4.6 (p. 21).   [64] *TMS* I.i.3.1 (p. 16).   [65] *TMS* I.i.3.1 (p. 17). See also *TMS* I.i.3.10 (p. 19).

"subject to a veil of ignorance."[66] As John Durham Peters puts it, "There is, for Smith, no transcendence of subjective experience."[67] Smith never expected an impartial spectator to strip himself of his own prior experiences, to take up a "view from nowhere," to import and to exaggerate (but only a little) Thomas Nagel's provocative formulation.[68] Since the spectator never forgets that his change of position is "imaginary" and "momentary" – that he remains safe while the agent suffers, that he remains poor while the agent prospers – his sentiment is necessarily "lower" in degree and it "varies in kind" from the agent's primary sentiments.[69]

On the contrary, Smith maintained that spectators employ what we would call today a *subjective*, or *self-referential* standpoint, which means that we judge the actions and opinions of others "as right, as accurate, as agreeable to truth and reality ... *for no other reason* but because we find that it agrees with our own."[70] In short, a Smithian spectator has no resource but her own lights – another dimension of his thought that resonates profoundly for contemporary debates on impartiality and perspective: Something of the spectator will always remain behind the lens for Smith, safe on dry land.

I judge of your sight by my sight, of your ear by my ear, of your reason by my reason, of your resentment by my resentment, of your love by my love. I neither have, *nor can have*, any other way of judging about them.[71]

And again:

when we judge ... of any affection ... it is scarce possible that we should make use of any other rule or canon but the correspondent affection in ourselves.[72]

Two points of clarification will help us better understand the self-reference of the spectator's perspective in Smith's thought. First, it is interesting to note the extent to which spectators can become invested in their perspectives when observing and judging others. Smith observed that spectators typically experience pleasure when they discover that the passions and affections of others "coincide" and "tally" with their own. Like the astronomical order in the heavens which so fascinated Smith, concordance, harmony and equilibrium among people are always experienced as pleasant

---

[66] Rawls, *Theory of Justice*, pp. 183–187. See also Campbell, *Science of Morals*, pp. 127–141; Raphael, "Impartial Spectator," pp. 96–97; Fleischacker, "Kant and Adam Smith," p. 258; and Haakonssen, "Kantian Themes in Smith," pp. 151–152.

[67] Peters, "Publicity and Pain," p. 660.

[68] Thomas Nagel, *The View from Nowhere* (Oxford: Oxford University Press, 1986), esp. pp. 67–71.

[69] *TMS* I.i.4.7 (pp. 21–22).   [70] *TMS* I.i.4.4 (p. 20), emphasis added.

[71] *TMS* I.i.3.10 (p. 19), emphasis added.   [72] *TMS* I.i.3.9 (p. 18).

phenomena in Smith's thought; cacophony, disharmony and disequilibrium always jarring and deeply disturbing.

A second point of clarification: characterizing the perspective of spectators as self-referential is not incompatible with a claim that the spectator's perspective is a product of social experience, the fruits of social discipline. A spectator's perspective will reflect her experiences living in a particular time and place, absorbing its moral culture. Smith described the spectators' standpoint as self-referential since the spectator makes judgments with his own faculties and without absolute algorithms to guide him. But the spectator comes to know who he is and what he believes through a lifetime of gazing into the "mirror of society," participating in sympathetic exchange. To recall a well-known passage addressed earlier in my discussion of the social origins of self-knowledge, Smith speculated that a self in solitude "could no more think of his own character, of the propriety or demerit of his own sentiments and conduct, of the beauty or deformity of his own mind than of the beauty or deformity of his own face."[73] Society provides a mirror, situates the self in a "field of visibility" to invoke Foucault once again, and engenders the criteria by which the self will come to mirror and judge others.

I shall leave aside until later the question of whether Smith's account of sympathy can produce the "impartiality" that he was seeking, particularly in contexts that are unfamiliar and foreign to the spectator. But I sound the warning bell now, loudly, and encourage the reader patiently to journey along as we work toward a fuller understanding of Smith's project – and particularly his attempt to innoculate his theory against bias and other irregularities in judgment by exploring a conscience-like faculty he called the "impartial spectator." In due course, we will see that Smith struggled intensely with the problems of bias and partiality in his *Moral Sentiments*, and worked and re-worked his theory over thirty-one years to identify new and productive ways of stabilizing moral judgment.

---

[73] *TMS* III.1.3 (p. 110).

PART II

The circle of society

CHAPTER 3

Discipline and the socialized conscience

The Other is the indispensable mediator between myself and me ...
I see myself because somebody sees me.
                    Jean-Paul Sartre, *Being and Nothingness*

For in truth habit is a violent and treacherous schoolmistress. She
establishes in us, little by little, stealthfully, the foothold of her authority; but having by this mild and humble beginning settled and planted
it with the help of time, she soon uncovers to us a furious and
tyrannical face against which we no longer have the liberty even of
raising our eyes. We see her at every turn forcing the rules of nature.
                    Michel de Montaigne, *Of Custom, and not easily
                    changing an accepted law*

In our attempt to understand what Smith meant by "conscience" we have, so
far, examined his thoughts on sympathetic judgment, and have noted the self-
referential nature of the criteria spectators use when they judge. But we need
to move beyond this conventional understanding of Smith's idea of sympathy
"as judgment" to consider the socializing function of sympathy in Smith's
larger argument. Moral life is not only about judgment, but about action
and the reasons for action. No account of ordinary morality in Smith's
thought is adequate if it overlooks the *disciplinary* effects the spectator's
surveillance and judgment have upon the agent, the extent to which the
spectator motivates her to modify her conduct, to act in a "proper" way, in a
way the spectator can indulge, in what Smith often referred to as a "moral"
way. Sympathy in Smith's theory works like an act of *surveillance* in a
relatively closed physical space which exerts a certain kind of disciplinary
power over those being watched. When compounded over time these disciplinary experiences progressively constrain the agent's understanding of
herself, of others, and of the world, and serve to condition the moral criteria
("my ear," "my reason," "my resentment," and so on) that she will deploy
when she inevitably finds herself in the position of spectator. Moral culture
is thus passed from each generation to the next, through the infinite

repetition of sympathetic contacts – what Christopher J. Berry very nicely refers to in his account of eighteenth-century Scottish socialization theory as the "stickiness" of "social institutions."[1]

I begin this chapter by elaborating the disciplinary effects of sympathy in Smith's thought. I then argue that his theory of conscience in the first edition of the *Moral Sentiments* is developmentally continuous with his sociological description of sympathetic discipline. This means that the device of the impartial spectator ultimately has little independence from the judgments of actual spectators in the world – at least as it functions most often in most people. As such, I refer to Smithian conscience in this chapter somewhat provocatively as a "socialized conscience," borrowed from Sheldon Wolin's classic critique of liberal social conformity in *Politics and Vision*.[2] However, we will discover that Smith became increasingly anxious about his sociological theory of conscience once critics leveled charges of moral conventionalism against the first edition of his book. These critiques prompted Smith to revise his *Moral Sentiments* five times between 1759 and 1790. I argue that Smith's central purpose in these revisions was to assert the independence of conscience. By the final edition in 1790, we shall see, his narrative had shifted profoundly from describing conscience in sociological terms to establishing the independence of conscience in quasi-theological perfectionist terms.

DISCIPLINE

In his discussion of moral judgment, Smith always emphasized the activity of spectators, what it means for a spectator to become fair and impartial when he imaginatively "enters into" and judges the circumstances of those potentially very differently situated and constituted. When a spectator does that, Smith said, he is participating in the virtues of "indulgent humanity," a code throughout the *Moral Sentiments* for "the great law of Christianity" which, he said, consists in loving our neighbor as we love ourselves.[3] Here now we move to the flip side of the sympathy dynamic, what I am calling the "disciplinary" stage, in which an agent is motivated by a spectator's gaze and judgment to respond. In other words, in the disciplinary stage, Smith's focus shifts from spectators to agents being observed – from Foucault's

---

[1] Christopher J. Berry, "Sociality and Socialisation," in *The Cambridge Companion to the Scottish Enlightenment*, ed. Alexander Broadie (Cambridge: Cambridge University Press, 2003), pp. 243–257.

[2] Sheldon Wolin, "Liberalism and Conformity: The Socialized Conscience," in *Politics and Vision*, pp. 343–351.

[3] *TMS* I.i.45.1 (p. 23); *TMS* I.i.5.5 (p. 25). See also *TMS* III.3.8 (p. 139).

"inspector's lodge" to the prisoner in his cell. Insofar as an agent is motivated by observation and judgment to adjust himself, his actions, we are told, arise from a different set of virtues than those of indulgent Christianity. Smith explained the difference:

Upon these two different efforts, upon that of the spectator to enter into the sentiments of the person principally concerned, and upon that of the person principally concerned, to bring down his emotions to what the spectator can go along with, are founded two different sets of virtues. The soft, the gentle, the amiable virtues of candid condescension and indulgent humanity, are founded upon the one: the great, the awful and respectable, the virtues of self-denial, of self-government, of that command of the passions which subjects all the movements of our nature to what our own dignity and honour, and the propriety of our own conduct require, take their origin from the other.[4]

Whenever Smith invoked the "awful and respectable virtues," he was referring to Stoic self-command, which was discussed in the greatest detail in those portions of the *Moral Sentiments* that Smith added to his text in its sixth edition in 1790 (in Part VI and a good deal of Part III). While Christian "humanity" in the surveillance stage implored a spectator to love his neighbor as he loves himself, Stoic self-command in the discipline stage implored an agent to love himself *only as* he loves his neighbor, or inversely, as his neighbor is capable of loving him.[5] Both activities, in other words, begin with the assumption that people tend to love themselves more than they love others – a theme that runs through the *Moral Sentiments*, and is common to both the Christian view of original sin and Stoic views on human nature – but the first entails that a spectator share that love with others by endeavoring to "put himself in the situation of the other, and to bring home to himself every little circumstance of the distress which can possibly occur to the sufferer,"[6] while the second entails that agents restrain their self-love to a degree commensurable with their diminished love for others. Ernst Tugendhat emphasizes that both kinds of "intersubjective attitude" – that of sensitivity and that of self-control – are necessary before any reciprocal adjustment of sentiments can take place: "Both the person participating and the one primarily affected must have developed an *enabling general disposition* that makes an appropriate affective attunement possible."[7]

---

[4] *TMS* I.i.5.1 (p. 23). [5] *TMS* I.i.5.5 (p. 25). See also *TMS* III.3.8 (p. 139). [6] *TMS* I.i.4.6 (p. 21).
[7] Ernst Tugendhat, "Universalistically Approved Intersubjective Attitudes: Adam Smith," trans. Bernard Schreibl, *Adam Smith Review*, vol. 1 (2004), pp. 88–104, at p. 91.

Now, how is an agent disciplined on Smith's account? What motivates him to adjust his conduct, to violate "his natural, his untaught and undisciplined feelings"?[8] For Smith, the answer lies in man's natural "approbativeness." He observed that the very "presence" of others "composes" us because we desire to be loved and approved of.[9]

> Nature, when she formed man for society, endowed him with an original desire to please, and an original aversion to offend his brethren. She taught him to feel pleasure in their favorable, and pain in their unfavorable regard. She rendered their approbation most flattering and most agreeable to him for its own sake; and their disapprobation most mortifying and most offensive.[10]

Smith always contrasted the heated intensity of emotion and passion with the "cool" rationality of "proper" behaviour,[11] indulgence in present gratification with the pursuit of a duller but nevertheless agreeable and more mature enjoyment of love, approval and congenial relations with peers.[12]

> Though every man may, according to the proverb, be the whole world to himself, to the rest of mankind he is a most insignificant part of it. Though his own happiness may be of more importance to him than that of all the world besides, to every other person it is of no more consequence than that of any other man. Though it may be true, therefore, that every individual, in his own breast, naturally prefers himself to all mankind, yet he dares not look mankind in the face, and avow that he acts according to this principle. He feels that in this preference they can never go along with him, and that how natural soever it may be to him, it must always appear excessive and extravagant to them. When he views himself in the light in which he is conscious that others will view him ... he must, upon this, as upon all other occasions, humble the arrogance of his self-love, and bring it down to something which other men can go along with.[13]

Once an agent brings his emotions into "harmony and concord with the emotions of those who are about him," he is said to have struck the "point of propriety."[14] Most often, as the passage above indicates, striking that point will require that an agent silence himself, "lower" his passion, "bring it down," since spectators, as spectators, are able only to *imagine* the condition

---

[8] *TMS* III.3.28 (p. 148).   [9] *TMS* I.i.4.7–10 (pp. 22–23).   [10] *TMS* III.2.6 (p. 116).
[11] Smith's frequent use of the term "coolness" might have been borrowed from Bishop Joseph Butler. See his discussion in *Sermons* xi, 20–1, of "coolness" and "reasonable self-love." Joseph Butler, *Fifteen Sermons Preached at the Rolls Chapel*, vol. I, in *The Works of Bishop Butler*, 2 vols., ed. J. H. Bernard (1726; London: Macmillan, 1900). Smith's references throughout the *Moral Sentiments* indicate that he was familiar with this (*TMS* I.iii.1.1 (p. 43); *TMS* III.5.5 (pp. 164–165)).
[12] *TMS* I.i.4.7 (p. 22). On the importance of desire and pleasure in Smith's account of sympathy, from a French "intersubjectivist" perspective that draws on the work of René Girard, see Jean-Pierre Dupuy, "Invidious Sympathy in the *Theory of Moral Sentiments*," *Adam Smith Review*, vol. 2 (2006), pp. 98–123.
[13] *TMS* II.ii.2.1 (p. 83).   [14] *TMS* I.i.4.7 (p. 22).

of agents and therefore cannot possibly enter into the intensity of what the agent experiences. Smith emphasized over and again that spectators have only a "dull sensibility to the afflictions of others."[15] Observe the following:

> when we condole with our friends in their afflictions, how little do we feel, in comparison of what they feel? We sit down by them, we look at them, and while they relate to us the circumstances of their misfortune, we listen to them with gravity and attention. But while their narration is every moment interrupted by those natural bursts of passion which often seem almost to choak [*sic*] them in the midst of it; how far are the languid emotions of our hearts from keeping time to the transports of theirs?[16]

This "dull insensibility" augments disciplinary power, for agents are keenly aware of it – that spectators "though naturally sympathetic, never conceive, for what has befallen another, that degree of passion which naturally animates the person principally concerned."[17] "Sensible" of this limitation on the spectator (for he himself has been a spectator), the agent understands that he will achieve the "complete sympathy" he "passionately desires" only by restraining himself in the presence of his judge.[18] His anger and his resentment, his jealousy and his pain, all that shocks the norm, must be lowered "to that pitch in which the spectators are capable of going along with him. He must flatten … the sharpness of its natural tone."[19] He must become "master" of himself.[20]

A note here about the Stoic quality of propriety in these passages, for it will become important to my arguments later in Chapter 4 about why Smith rejected Stoic perfectionism. Lowering or flattening passion to a "point of propriety" incorporates notions of balance, of moderation, of equilibrium – different goals entirely than the severe Stoic idea of "extirpating" all passion and irrational attachment. Smith's idea of propriety aims at far less when it seeks harmony with the emotions of others rather than harmony with the abstractions of reason or nature. Indeed, for Smith man is always the measure; and coordination among them always the goal.

Moreover, diverging from the Stoic position even further, Smith recognized that harmony is not always achieved by "lowering" or "flattening" passion. Sometimes, propriety requires an agent to "raise" his passion, to augment and "bring it up," a dimension of his thought that departs significantly from the Stoic theme of self-command and aligns instead with Aristotelian "mediocrity" which, as Smith acknowledged in Part VII,

---

[15] *TMS* I.iii.1.13 (p. 47).   [16] *TMS* I.iii.1.12 (p. 47).   [17] *TMS* I.i.4.7 (p. 21).
[18] *TMS* I.i.4.7 (p. 22).   [19] *TMS* I.i.4.7 (p. 22).   [20] *TMS* III.3.22 (p. 145).

"lies in a kind of middle between two opposite vices."[21] In the following two passages, in unmistakably Aristotelian terms, Smith argued that an agent sometimes elevates passion to achieve the point of propriety:

The propriety of every passion excited by objects peculiarly related to ourselves, the pitch which the spectator can go along with, must lie, it is evident, in a certain mediocrity. If the passion is too high, or if it is too low, he cannot enter into it … This mediocrity, however, in which the point of propriety consists, is different in different passions. It is high in some and low in others. There are some passions which it is indecent to express very strongly … And there are others of which the strongest expressions are upon many occasions extremely graceful.[22]

And again, in Part VI, added in 1790. Note here the Aristotelian language of "excess" and "defect":

the point of propriety, the degree of passion which the impartial spectator approves of, is differently situated in different passions. In some passions the excess is less disagreeable than the defect; and in such passions the point of propriety seems to stand high, or nearer to the excess than to the defect. In other passions, the defect is less disagreeable than the excess; and in such passions the point of propriety seems to stand low, or nearer to the defect than to the excess.[23]

Smith thereafter presented a typology of passion, illustrating which passions required raising and which required lowering, contrasting those passions "which tend to unite men in society, to humanity, kindness, natural affection, friendship, esteem," with those "which drive men from one another, and which tend, as it were, to break the bands of human society; the disposition to anger, hatred, envy, malice, revenge."[24] Smith referred to these two types of passion as the "social passions" in which the point of propriety is generally quite high[25] and the "unsocial passions" in which the point of propriety is comparatively low.[26]

An *excess* in social passion, in other words, is "never regarded with aversion":

[21] *TMS* VII.ii.1.12 (pp. 270–271). In Part VII, Smith claimed that Aristotelian virtue "corresponds … pretty exactly with what has been said above concerning the propriety and impropriety of conduct" (*TMS* VII.ii.1.12 (p. 271)). It is important to note, however, that, while Smith embraces Aristotelianism here, he does not characterize mediocrity *as virtue*, but *as propriety*. Smith, in other words, is not adopting Aristotle's account of virtue as his own, but is, rather, appropriating Aristotelian virtue as his own notion of propriety.

[22] *TMS* I.ii.intro (p. 27).   [23] *TMS* VI.iii.14 (p. 242).

[24] The typology runs though *TMS* I.ii (pp. 27–43), repeated in Aristotelian terms at VI.iii.14–22 (pp. 242–246). The passage quoted comes from *TMS* VI.iii.15–16 (p. 243). My thanks to Martha Nussbaum for helping me to conceptualize the discussion that follows.

[25] *TMS* I.ii.4 (pp. 38–40).   [26] *TMS* I.ii.3 (pp. 34–38).

The too tender mother, the too indulgent father, the too generous and affectionate friend, may sometimes, perhaps, on account of the softness of their natures, be looked upon with a species of pity ... but can never be regarded with hatred and aversion, nor even with contempt, unless by the most brutal and worthless of mankind ... There is nothing in itself which renders it either ungraceful or disagreeable.[27]

Excessive humanity, then, is "agreeable" and often "delicious," but a *defect* is universally condemned as "hardness of heart."[28] He insisted that "stoical apathy" is appropriate with regard to our own pains and sicknesses, but that it "appears always peculiarly odious" when one's child, for example, is sick or in pain.[29] With regard to personal, and especially bodily, pain:

We esteem the man who supports pain and even torture with manhood and firmness; and we have little regard for him who sinks under them, and abandons himself to useless outcries and womanish lamentations.[30]

But with regard to the pain and torture of one's child:

The man who appears to feel nothing for his own children, but who treats them upon all occasions with unmerited severity and harshness, seems of all brutes the most detestable.[31]

Smith likened this sort of insensibility to "stoical apathy," which "is, in such cases, never agreeable, and all the metaphysical sophisms by which it is supported can seldom serve any other purpose than to blow up the hard insensibility of a coxcomb to ten times its native impertinence."[32] As such:

A parent without parental tenderness, a child devoid of all filial reverence, appear monsters, the objects, not of hatred only, but of horror.[33]

When we shift focus from the "social passions" to the "unsocial passions" – those passions and affections "which drive men from one another" – the point of propriety is comparatively low.[34] As Smith put it:

It was, it seems, the intention of Nature, that those rougher and more unamiable emotions, which drive men from one another, should be less easily and more rarely communicated.[35]

As such, an *excess* of unsocial passion will always render a man "the object of hatred, and sometimes even of horror, to other people."[36] Smith charged:

[27] *TMS* I.ii.4.3 (p. 40).　[28] *TMS* VI.iii.15 (p. 243).　[29] *TMS* III.3.14 (p. 143).
[30] *TMS* VI.iii.17 (p. 244).　[31] *TMS* III.3.14 (p. 143).　[32] *TMS* III.3.16 (p. 143).
[33] *TMS* VI.ii.1.7 (p. 220).　[34] *TMS* I.ii.3 (pp. 34–38).
[35] *TMS* I.ii.3.5 (p. 37).　[36] *TMS* VI.iii.16 (p. 243).

Too violent a propensity to those detestable passions, renders a person the object of universal dread and abhorrence, who, like a wild beast, ought, we think, to be hunted out of all civil society.[37]

A *defect* in "unsocial Passions," however, "is seldom ever complained of."[38] Smith offered the example of "resentment":

How many things are requisite to render the gratification of resentment completely agreeable, and to make the spectator thoroughly sympathize with our revenge? ... We should resent more from a sense of the propriety of resentment, from a sense that mankind expect and require it of us, than because we feel in ourselves the furies of that disagreeable passion. There is no passion, of which the human mind is capable, concerning whose justness we ought to be so doubtful, concerning whose indulgence we ought so carefully to consult our natural sense of propriety, or so diligently to consider what will be the sentiments of the cool and impartial spectator. Magnanimity, or a regard to maintain our own rank and dignity in society, is the only motive which can ennoble the expressions of this disagreeable passion.[39]

Nevertheless, Smith insisted that *some defects* in "unsocial Passions" were disagreeable and begged for arousal. He offered several examples: the "young man who has no relish for the diversions and amusements that are natural and suitable to his age, who talks of nothing but his book or his business,"[40] the person with a poor "self-estimation," who thinks "meanly" of himself;[41] and Smith's favorite example, the man who submits passively to insult and injury.[42]

We sometimes complain that a particular person shows too little spirit, and has too little sense of the injuries that have been done to him; and we are ready to despise him for the defect, as to hate him for the excess of this passion.[43]

Indeed, sometimes a defect in "unsocial Passion" will arise to "a most essential defect in the manly character."[44] "A want of proper indignation ... renders a man incapable of protecting either himself or his friends from insult and injustice."[45] Indeed, some unsocial passions, like proper indignation

are regarded as necessary parts of the character of human nature. A person becomes contemptible who tamely sits still, and submits to insults, without attempting either to repel or to revenge them. We cannot enter into his indifference and insensibility: we call his behaviour mean-spiritedness, and are as really provoked by

---

[37] *TMS* I.ii.4.3 (p. 40).   [38] *TMS* VI.iii.16 (p. 243).   [39] *TMS* I.ii.3.8 (p. 38).
[40] *TMS* VI.iii.21 (p. 246).   [41] *TMS* VI.iii.22 (p. 246).
[42] *TMS* I.ii.3.3 (pp. 34–35); *TMS* VI.iii.16 (p. 243).   [43] *TMS* II.i.5.8 (p. 77).
[44] *TMS* VI.iii.16 (p. 243).   [45] *TMS* VI.iii.16 (p. 243).

it as by the insolence of his adversary. Even the mob are enraged to see any man submit patiently to affronts and ill usage. They desire to see this insolence resented, and resented by the person who suffers from it. They cry to him with fury, to defend, or to revenge himself. If his indignation rouses at last, they heartily applaud, and sympathize with it ... provided it is not immoderate.[46]

And so, propriety in some circumstances requires that an agent "raise" his passions rather than "lower" them. An Aristotelian qualification of his Stoicism indeed. Not feeling indignant and resentful when one sustains injustice and injury is a "stupid insensibility to the events of human life," Smith insisted, echoing his rejection in Part VII of severe Stoic "apathy," which

by endeavouring, not merely to moderate, but to eradicate all our private, partial, and selfish affections ... endeavours to render us altogether indifferent and uncon- cerned in the success or miscarriage of everything which Nature has prescribed to us as the proper business and occupation of our lives.[47]

So while self-command in pursuit of propriety had undeniable Stoic resonances, Smith did not endorse Stoic "insensibility" or "apathy." He rejected the ancient Stoic aim of "extirpating" the passions. He articulated the distinction between moderation and extirpation, between self- command and insensibility, in terms that will become central later to his rejection of Stoic cosmopolitanism:

Insensibility and that noble firmness, that exalted self-command, which is founded in the sense of dignity and propriety, are so far from being altogether the same, that in proportion as the former takes place, the merit of the latter is, in many cases, entirely taken away.[48]

But Smith's qualification of Stoicism went further yet. Corollary to his discussion about proper indignation was Smith's novel claim that a keen sensibility "to our own injuries and to our own misfortunes" was in fact

---

[46] *TMS* I.ii.3.3 (pp. 34–35).

[47] "Stupid insensibility" comes from *TMS* VI.iii.18 (p. 244). The longer passage is from *TMS* VII.ii.1.46 (pp. 292–293).

[48] *TMS* VI.iii.18 (p. 245). Like Griswold (in *Virtues of Enlightenment*, p. 320) and Rothschild (*Economic Sentiments*, p. 132), Nussbaum acknowledges Smith's general break from Stoic apathy and indiffer- ence, but she also notes a troubling "asymmetry" regarding Smith's Stoicism in his additions to the 1790 edition, in which he continues to reject Stoic insensitivity to the suffering of loved ones, but augments his reverence for the man of self-command who is able to maintain a noble indifference toward his own misfortunes. Nussbaum, "Mutilated and Deformed." In such cases, Smith argues: "there are but very few cases in which we can approach too near to the stoical apathy and indifference" (*TMS* III.3.16 (p. 143)).

necessary before one could become sensible to the injuries and misfortunes of others.[49]

The man who feels little for his own misfortunes must always feel less for those of other people, and be less disposed to relieve them. The man who has little resentment for the injuries which are done to himself, must always have less for those which are done to other people, and be less disposed either to protect or to avenge them. A stupid insensibility to the events of human life necessarily extinguishes all that keen and earnest attention to the propriety of our own conduct, which constitutes the real essence of virtue.[50]

Curiously, Smith didn't articulate the obvious conclusion, but he had demonstrated by logical turns that Stoic apathy and insensibility to self, in the end, served to undermine the very selflessness that it sought to cultivate. The argument would have served him well had he pursued it further and developed it.

The *Moral Sentiments* is a treasure box filled with colorful and perceptive illustrations of the "proper" exercise of passion, those which required raising and those which required lowering – from cold parents to bratty children, from scholars too bookish to enjoy the diversions of youth to cowards without proper indignation, from the womanish man who cries out in pain to the "savage" who endures pain for the sake of honor. In a private letter to Smith acknowledging the publication of the *Moral Sentiments* in 1759, Edmund Burke complimented the liveliness of Smith's illustrations:

I own I am particularly pleased with those easy and happy illustrations from common Life and manners in which your work abounds more than any other that I know by far.[51]

The point in all of his (incidentally, rather masculine[52]) vignettes throughout the book, is that the person who adjusts his behavior does so coolly under surveillance, under the watchful and critical eye of spectators. The anticipation of judgment disciplines the agent, motivates him to soften his temper, to restrain his resentment, more Stoically to endure physical discomfort, to elevate other-concern, to augment proper indignation, and so on. In all of these examples, discipline takes place under surveillance.

[49] *TMS* VI.iii.18 (p. 244).   [50] *TMS* VI.iii.18 (p. 244).
[51] "Letter to Smith from Edmund Burke, 10 September 1759" as "Letter #38" in *Correspondence of Adam Smith*, ed. Ernest Campbell Mossner and Ian Simpson Ross as vol. VI of *The Glasgow Edition of the Works and Correspondence of Adam Smith* (Oxford: Oxford University Press 1977; reprint Indianapolis, IN: Liberty Press, 1987), pp. 46–47, at p. 46.
[52] See Nussbaum, "Mutilated and Deformed," on Smith's "macho Stoicism."

CONSCIENCE AND THE "EYES OF OTHER PEOPLE"

In Foucault's description of Bentham's panoptic prison, the prisoner is perpetually subject to a "field of visibility." He becomes a "principle in his own subjection" because he is never quite sure whether an inspector sits in the central lodge, looming large before him with its shrouded windows. The prisoner's permanent "visibility," combined with the "invisibility" of the inspector, becomes a powerful "guarantor of order." What this means is that the prisoner's mind has become disciplined; he will conform even when no one is verifiably present watching and judging him. Power here functions automatically.

Hence the major effect of the Panopticon: to induce in the inmate a state of conscious and permanent visibility that assures the automatic functioning of power. So to arrange things that the surveillance is permanent in its effects, even if it is discontinuous in its action; that the perfection of power should tend to render its actual exercise unnecessary.[53]

We recall that the Smithian self only becomes aware of his "character," and "the beauty and deformity of his own mind" when he encounters the "mirror" of society. A creature "who from his birth was a stranger to society" would be occupied solely with the "objects of his passions, the external bodies which either pleased or hurt him."[54] But "bring him into society"

and all his own passions will immediately become the causes of new passions. He will observe that mankind approve of some of them, and are disgusted by others. He will be elevated in the one case, and cast down in the other; his desires and aversions, his joys and sorrows, will now often become the causes of new desires and aversions, new joys and sorrows.[55]

Smith's account of sympathy emphasized the power that social surveillance has on the desiring self. What happens, then, when the Smithian self is alone and out of sight, liberated from the constraints of surveillance and judgment? How does an agent in Smith's theory go on beyond the gaze of his neighbors? With the proverbial ring of Gyges turned inward, does he rush headlong to satisfy his most base and unsocial passions? When no one watches him, does he kill and steal and rape and plunder? As Glaucon asked in *Republic* Book II, does he:

stay on the path of justice or stay away from other people's property, when he could take whatever he wanted from the marketplace with impunity, go into people's houses and have sex with anyone he wished, kill or release from prison

---

[53] Foucault, *Discipline and Punish*, p. 201.   [54] *TMS* III.i.3 (p. 110).   [55] *TMS* III.i.3 (p. 111).

anyone he wished, and do all the other things that would make him like a god among humans?[56]

Later in the *Republic* Socrates described the "shameless" dreams of tyrannical men, what they desire as "the rest of the soul – the rational, gentle, and ruling part – slumbers":

> Then the beastly and savage part, full of food and drink, casts off sleep and seeks to find a way to gratify itself. You know that there is nothing it won't dare to do at such a time, *free of all control by shame or reason*. It doesn't shrink from trying to have sex with a mother, as it supposes, or with anyone else at all, whether man, god, or beast. It will commit any foul murder, and there is no food it refuses to eat. In a word, it omits no act of folly or shamelessness.[57]

How does a person in Smith's theory manage temptation, navigate conflicts between his "unsocial" and "social" passions, when there are no actual spectators to motivate him with approbation or shame? Is it merely the fear of getting caught? If a magic ring could ensure invisibility, does the Smithian self too become a tyrannical monster, a "god among humans"?

It is precisely on this question of self-judgment in solitude that Smith introduced the subject of conscience. Smith's account of conscience comprises the entirety of Part III of the *Moral Sentiments*, entitled "Of the Foundation of *our* Judgments concerning *our own* Sentiments and Conduct, and of the Sense of Duty."[58] I emphasize Smith's reference here to "our" judgments, concerning "our own" sentiments and conduct, for this is the first time in the treatise that he discussed moral judgment in a subjective (rather than in an intersubjective) way, and the first time he addressed the standards people use to judge themselves outside of actual social scrutiny. As Smith described it, the impartial spectator enables us to maintain our equilibrium when society is not present to guide us, or at those moments when our partial sentiments speak too loudly and threaten to distort our moral judgments and produce unsocial behavior. Like the Panoptic prisoner who becomes the "principle of his own subjection," the Smithian self learns to discipline himself outside of social surveillance. For this reason, Christopher J. Berry accurately refers to conscience in Smith's thought as a "learnt resource."[59] The "eyes of other people" become embedded in his soul, capable of guiding him without their actual, physical presence. The practice of sympathy is driven inside and we become capable of self-judgment.

---

[56] Plato, *Republic*, trans. G. M. A. Grube, ed. C. D. C. Reeve (Indianapolis, IN: Hackett, 1992), 360b–c (p. 36).
[57] Plato, *Republic*, 572b.   [58] *TMS* III (pp. 109–178).   [59] Berry, "Sociality and Socialisation," p. 253.

Smith was far less concerned with moral perfection than with the basic, minimal requirements of social coordination. Eager to confront preachy critics of progress and modernity who insisted that social order required traditional moral prohibitions enforced by kings, lords and priests, Smith described a freer, self-regulating method of social coordination that worked without archaic hierarchies. This is how I have interpreted "sympathy" in the *Moral Sentiments*.

I argue here that Smith's theory of conscience in the early editions of the *Moral Sentiments* was largely an extension of his sociological description of sympathy and fundamentally consistent with Hume's emphasis on custom and habit. The order in which these ideas appear in the *Moral Sentiments* – sympathy in Parts I and II; conscience in Part III – is no accident for the ideas are sociologically continuous for Smith. Recall, sympathy centers on how spectators judge us, how we respond in turn, and how we ultimately become disciplined social creatures through repetitive contacts. Conscience now is primarily an account of how we come to judge *ourselves*.[60] On the first page of Part III, in Smith's introduction to the subject of conscience, he emphasized that these two activities – judging others and judging ourselves – greatly resemble one another. He wrote:

The principle by which we naturally either approve or disapprove of our own conduct, seems to be altogether the same with that by which we exercise the like judgments concerning the conduct of other people. We either approve or disapprove of the conduct of another man according as we feel that, when we bring his case home to ourselves, we either can or cannot entirely sympathize with the sentiments and motives which directed it. And in the same manner, we either approve or disapprove of our own conduct, according as we feel that, when we place ourselves in the situation of another man, and view it, as it were, with his eyes and from his station, we either can or cannot entirely enter into and sympathize with the sentiments and motives which influenced it.[61]

The process of judging oneself looks very much like the process by which we judge others, with the obvious difference that we cannot literally observe our own actions without also experiencing them – we cannot but be "judges in our own cases," to recall John Locke's formulation.[62] The only way we might view our own actions with some impartiality, Smith argued, is by attempting to view ourselves "with the eyes of other people":

---

[60] D. D. Raphael has always emphasized that Smith developed the impartial spectator as a theory of judgment about one's own actions. See most recently *The Impartial Spectator*.

[61] *TMS* III.1.2 (pp. 109–110).

[62] John Locke, *The Second Treatise of Government*, in *Two Treatises of Government*, ed. Peter Laslett (Cambridge: Cambridge University Press, 1960–1992), pp. 265–428, 14.17 (p. 276).

We examine our persons limb by limb, and by placing ourselves before a looking-glass, or by some such expedient, endeavour, as much as possible, to view ourselves at the distance and *with the eyes of other people.*[63]

And again:

We suppose ourselves the spectators of our own behaviour, and endeavour to imagine what effect it would, in this light, produce on us. This is the only looking-glass by which we can, in some measure, *with the eyes of other people*, scrutinize the propriety of our own conduct.[64]

Ultimately, Smith argued that the impartial spectator is the "only" way we have of "correcting the natural misrepresentations of self-love," of learning "the real littleness of ourselves, and of whatever relates to ourselves."[65]

David Marshall and Vivienne Brown have drawn on the work of Mikhail Bakhtin to characterize Smith's description of conscience as a "dialogical" process[66] that echoes the theatricality of Shaftesburian soliloquy:

When I endeavor to examine my own conduct, when I endeavor to pass sentence upon it, and either to approve or condemn it, it is evident that, in all such cases, I divide myself, as it were, into two persons; and that I, the examiner and judge, represent a different character from that other I, the person whose conduct is examined into and judged of. The first is the spectator, whose sentiments with regard to my own conduct I endeavor to enter into, by placing myself in his situation, and by considering how it would appear to me, when seen from that particular point of view. The second is the agent, the person whom I properly call myself, and of whose conduct, under the character of a spectator, I was endeavouring to form some opinion. The first is the judge; the second the person judged of. But that the judge should, in every respect, be the same with the person judged of, is as impossible, as that the cause should, in every respect, be the same with the effect.[67]

This account of conscience as an internal "conversation" or "dialogue" that one conducts with oneself replicates Smith's account of actual sympathy in

[63] *TMS* III.i.4 (p. 111–112), emphasis added.
[64] *TMS* III.i.5 (p. 112), emphasis added.   [65] *TMS* III.3.4 (p. 137).
[66] See David Marshall, "Theatricality," p. 612, n. 14; and David Marshall, *The Figure of Theatre.* Also Vivienne Brown, *Adam Smith's Discourse*, pp. 9–75, for an interpretation committed to the dialogical approach of Mikhail Bakhtin.
[67] *TMS* III.1.6 (p. 113). See especially Shaftesbury's, "Soliloquy or Advice to an Author," in *Characteristics of Men, Manner, Opinions, Times, etc.*, 2 vols., ed. John M. Robertson (Gloucester, MA, 1963), vol. I, p. 121; excerpted recently in *Moral Philosophy from Montaigne to Kant, An Anthology*, 2 vols., ed. J. B. Schneewind (Cambridge: Cambridge University Press, 1990), vol. I, pp. 486–488. I have learned much about Shaftesburian "soliloquy" in David Marshall's work, cited in n. 66 above. See also Thomas Fries, "Dialog und Soliloquium," in *Dialog der Aufklärung, Shaftesbury, Rousseau, Solger* (Tübingen: Francke Verlag, 1993), pp. 49–97. Thanks to Mila Ganev for her assistance in translation.

the world. When an agent deliberates with this imagined spectator in his breast, and adjusts his conduct to a pitch that this imagined spectator can "enter into," he is exercising self-command with an eye to propriety, just as he would in his intersubjective relations with actual spectators.

I believe Smith asserted a congruity between judging others and judging ourselves in order to demonstrate that it was possible for us to cultivate some measure of impartiality regarding ourselves, just as we are able to do regarding others. This is what the procedure of using "the eyes of other people" as we judge ourselves is meant to *do*. But I would like to raise a question about what exactly Smith meant when he referred to the "eyes of other people." Was he claiming very simply that the basic *procedure* for judging is congruous – that, as Emma Rothschild puts it:

> by sympathizing with other people – with "you", as it were – and by observing your responses to her conduct, the individual can get a sense of what it would be like to be the impartial spectator of her own conduct.[68]

Or, was he saying something more profound and potentially problematic, that when we judge ourselves we employ the *very same criteria* used by "the eyes of other people" when they judge us in the social world? I believe that the resemblance of *procedure* between judging others and judging ourselves is obvious but far less important for understanding and evaluating Smith's idea of conscience than the more substantive and culturally far-reaching question of whether the criteria are the same. Does my social experience engaging real spectators ultimately condition my understanding of the "eyes of other people" when I come to judge myself? Is Smith, in other words, describing a developmental process through which sympathy *generates* conscience over time, driving social values deep into the soul? Much will hang on the answers to these questions. Indeed, if the impartial spectator merely absorbs the norms of social propriety; if within the logic of Smith's account of ordinary morality conscience does nothing more than recapitulate and protect conventional wisdom, then Smith's idea of conscience will look far more like a Humean habit or perhaps a Freudian super-ego than a mature, independent foundation for moral judgment.

My central claim here is that Smithian conscience emerges developmentally from the sympathy process itself, and is therefore, at its root, deeply continuous with it both procedurally *and* substantively. Note in the following passage the way Smith conflated the procedural meaning of the "eyes of

---

[68] Emma Rothschild, "Dignity or Meanness," p. 153.

other people" with the very criteria we use when judging our *own* sentiments and motives:

> We can never survey our own sentiments and motives, we can never form any judgment concerning them; unless we remove ourselves, as it were, from our own natural station, and endeavour to view them as at a certain distance from us. But we can do this in no other way than by endeavouring to view them *with the eyes of other people, or as other people are likely to view them.* Whatever judgments we can form concerning them, accordingly, must always bear some *secret reference,* either to what are, or to what, upon a certain condition, would be, or to what, we imagine, ought to be the *judgment of others.*[69]

We don't merely use the "eyes of other people" as a way of gaining distance, of stepping outside ourselves and cooling ourselves off, but we align ourselves with the very *way* other people are likely to view our sentiments and motives. We adopt their criteria; and as Smith put it, the judgments we make about ourselves "must always bear some secret reference" to these criteria. This confirms my earlier claim that Smith offers not merely a "social theory of the self" but also a "cultural anthropology," for how do we come to know how other people are likely to view our sentiments and motives? Through the sympathy process, through a lifetime gazing into the mirror of society. To state my claim more provocatively, conscience is the psychological effect of sympathetic discipline. Or as Jean-Pierre Dupuy put it, the "Smithian self is fundamentally mimetic, always ready to lose itself in the many mirrors held forth by others."[70] This will have important implications later in the book when we evaluate whether the Smithian conscience is capable of reflecting on the moral culture that produces it, and able when necessary to stand up against it.

Some have claimed that Smith's account of conscience as a social censor constructed in the mind over time has strong affinities with the Freudian super-ego.[71] This argument about internalized society implies that there are two "persons" or "parts" inside of the Smithian self – one passionate (which Fleischacker calls "an incipient version of the id"[72]), the other a representation of actual repression (the super-ego) – engaged in a sort of deliberation with one another. Freud emphasized the negative, strangling effects of disapproval and fear produced by a repressive upbringing while Smith was describing ordinary moral psychology and the internalization of both

---

[69] *TMS* III.i.2 (p. 110), emphasis added.   [70] Dupuy, "Invidious Sympathy," p. 109.
[71] Campbell, *Science of Morals*, pp. 149 and 165; Raphael, "Impartial Spectator," pp. 97–98; D. D. Raphael, *Adam Smith* (Oxford: Oxford University Press, 1985), pp. 41–44; and D. D. Raphael, *The Impartial Spectator*, pp. 48–49; and Fleischacker, "Kant and Adam Smith," p. 259.
[72] Fleischacker, "Kant and Adam Smith," p. 259, n. 41.

"favorable and unfavorable attitudes," as Raphael put it.[73] For Raphael this difference makes comparisons between Freud and Smith largely unhelpful. But I would suggest that despite important differences the comparison is compelling and quite interesting. Freud and Smith obviously came from different traditions with very different purposes and audiences. But the phenomena they described were remarkably similar: no less than the very psychological processes by which an individual internalizes and then reproduces her world. While Freud sought to free a patient from a suffocating super-ego, Smith found her self-command useful, put her discipline to work in the world, in the service of social order. I believe this is what drove Sheldon Wolin's claim that Smith's *Moral Sentiments*, more systematically and overtly than perhaps any other modern liberal text, emphasized the "necessity" and "desirability" of social conformity at the level of *internal* conscience:

the external quality [of social norms] must be overcome so that they can be appropriated into the inner life of the individual. In short, social norms should be internalized and, as such, operate as the individual's conscience. Conscience thus becomes social rather than individual.[74]

What makes conscience so effective in perpetuating social norms, Smith observed, is that "habit and experience have taught us to do this [appeal to conscience] so easily and so readily, that we are scarce sensible that we do it."[75]

Of course, there has been much debate among interpreters of Smith's thought in recent years about the extent to which conscience "reflects actual social attitudes," as Raphael puts it; or becomes what Christopher Berry calls a "mere reflex of prevalent social norms."[76] Vincent Hope, Samuel Fleischacker and others insist on Smith's underlying conventionalism.[77] Fleischacker characterizes the impartial spectator as "an extension or

---

[73] Raphael, *Impartial Spectator*, p. 49.
[74] Wolin, *Politics and Vision*, p. 344.   [75] *TMS* III.3.3 (pp. 135–136).
[76] Berry, "Sociality and Socialisation," p. 253. Berry's formulation is useful here, though I should note that he believed Smith's account of conscience was ultimately capable of "an evaluative assessment of the complexity of social life" – and that he uses Smith's thoughts on infanticide as his evidence (p. 254). I will have much to say later about this in ch. 6, and so I resist engaging for now.
[77] See Vincent Hope's work, "Smith's Demigod," in *Philosophers of the Scottish Enlightenment*, ed. Vincent Hope (Edinburgh: Edinburgh University Press, 1984), pp. 157–167; and Vincent Hope, *Virtue by Consensus: The Moral Philosophy of Hutcheson, Hume and Adam Smith* (Oxford: Clarendon Press, 1989), pp. 1–11 and 83–117. See also Samuel Fleischacker, *On Adam Smith's Wealth of Nations* (Princeton, NJ: Princeton University Press, 2004, *passim*; and "Smith and Cultural Relativism," trans. as "Smith und der Kulturrelativismus" in *Adam Smith als Moralphilosoph*, ed. Christel Fricke and Hans-Peter Schütt (Berlin: De Gruyter, 2005).

idealization of our society's mode of moral judgment,"[78] and an "idealized version of our friends and neighbors."[79] Edward Andrew calls it an "internalized radar of social expectations."[80] Others have strongly disagreed, perhaps Martha Nussbaum most so, who has drawn parallels between the impartial spectator and John Rawls' device of the "original position."[81] Similarly Luc Boltanski suggests that Smith's impartial spectator is "aperspectival."[82] Amartya Sen too emphasizes that Smith's impartial spectator is able to remove itself "objectively" from accepted conventions and biases.[83] Knud Haakonssen, Charles Griswold and most recently Jennifer Pitts find themselves somewhere mid-way – recognizing that conscience is sociologically embedded, but emphasizing its distinct ability to "detach" itself from "social morality"[84] – that it employs a "standard of right ... over and above the judgements of the moment."[85] Pitts argues that our judgments for Smith are "formed in social contexts, but they are also independent of such contexts."[86]

What are we to make of such divergent interpretations? I agree in principle with Emma Rothschild that Smith "provides only a very nonchalant explanation of the origin of the ... tribunal within us," that he was "not tremendously interested in the foundations of his own or other people's systems."[87] Indeed, he was relatively unconcerned with "grounds and groundworks."[88] Clearly, part of the explanation for this is that Smith's system was designed to work without a "fundamental principle of judgment." As Rothschild put it:

The principle of moral judgment, that is to say, is that there is no fundamental principle of moral judgment. There is no foundation; all there is, is the correction and convergence of sentiments.[89]

Nevertheless, Smith was often very vague about the origin of conscience – to what extent it emerges from the world, from reason, from God – which surely leaves room for creative interpolation. Ultimately I think the debate over Smith's epistemology rests to some extent on historiographical

---

[78] Fleischacker, *Wealth of Nations*, p. 52.   [79] Fleischacker, "Smith and Cultural Relativism," p. 8.
[80] Andrew, "Anarchic Conscience," p. 82.   [81] Nussbaum, *Poetic Justice*, p. 134, n. 23.
[82] Boltanski, *Distant Suffering*, p. 49.   [83] Sen, "Impartiality."
[84] Haakonssen, *The Science of a Legislator*, p. 56.
[85] Griswold, *Adam Smith and the Virtues of Enlightenment*, p. 281.
[86] Pitts, *A Turn to Empire*, pp. 43–52, at p. 43.
[87] Rothschild, "Dignity or Meanness," pp. 152 and 154. I do believe Rothschild overstates the case somewhat, particularly regarding Smith's later revisions of the *Moral Sentiments*, which seem to me largely motivated by epistemic questions.
[88] Rothschild, "Dignity or Meanness," p. 154.   [89] Rothschild, *Economic Sentiments*, p. 231.

confusion.[90] Again, Smith revised his *Moral Sentiments* five times over thirty-one years. He became increasingly anxious about the inherent conventionalism of a sociological view of conscience between the first and sixth editions of the book. As a result, I believe his interest in foundational questions deepened and became more explicit. The historiographical point I am making here is that there is ample textual evidence in remnants of the early editions to sustain arguments that Smith was a Humean conventionalist, committed to what Rothschild calls a "conversationalist morality";[91] and there is ample evidence in the revisions to sustain arguments that he strove for something firmer, more stable, less contingent.

We will discover that Smith's understanding of conscience and of mature moral judgment began to shift in later editions of the book.[92] Very soon after he formulated his idea of conscience, he observed that the question of moral epistemology was crucially different than the question of how man *employs* what he knows in practical moral judgments.[93] Smith became increasingly anxious and dissatisfied with his idea of conscience between the first and sixth editions of the *Moral Sentiments*, which spanned nearly thirty-one years. He decided that his articulation of conscience needed clearer *independence* from the relativity of social attitudes.[94]

DIGRESSION ON SECULARIZATION

Smith's evolving view of conscience was often articulated in religious language and was steeped in a distinctive religious sensibility. I will argue that Smith deliberately fused the traditions of Protestant theology and eighteenth-century sociability – let's call them "God within" and "society without" – to advance a theory of conscience useful to free men in modern societies. This move, I shall suggest, distanced Smith further from his Scottish friend David Hume and established him as a deistic eighteenth-century translator of the Protestant tradition of Luther, Knox and Milton. Before pursuing Smith's evolving view of conscience, a word should be said

---

[90] See Dickey, "Historicizing the 'Adam Smith Problem.'"

[91] Rothschild, *Economic Sentiments*, p. 231.

[92] See Raphael's discussion of Smith's various revisions of the *Moral Sentiments* and his evolving view of conscience, in *The Impartial Spectator*, pp. 32–42.

[93] Samuel Fleischacker recognizes the difference and claims that Smith was concerned far more with the question of moral action than with moral epistemology. "Philosophy in Moral Practice: Kant and Adam Smith," *Kant-Studien* 82 (1991), pp. 249–269, at pp. 255–256. I agree, although I shall argue that gnawing concerns about moral action forced him ultimately to reconsider his earlier epistemological commitments.

[94] *TMS* I.iii.3 (pp. 61–66); *TMS* III.2 (pp. 113–134).

about the historiographical significance of such a fusion for our under-standing of modern secularization.

Conventional interpretations of Enlightenment secularization tend to stress anticlericalism and the separation of church and state, obscuring the presence of Christian "plot structures" in modern thought.[95] There is an acute problem of anachronism, however, in the assumption that eighteenth-century thought had moved beyond religion, that secularization was accomplished in one fatal blow. Too often historians dismiss the gradualism in intellectual transition; and this is particularly true in the case of secularization. They cancel the "old" and emphasize only what they wish for various reasons to characterize as "new." The problem with this, of course, is that there is no future yet when a thinker in history is thinking. Novelty is a concept that must be contextualized to have any meaning whatsoever.

I suggest that we consider the significance of "hybrid" concepts in transitional thought. I borrow the idea from Lewis F. Green who defined a "hybrid" as the "recharging of a traditional concept with quite new overtones."[96] A hybrid is created when a tradition of discourse is carried into a new setting, converging with the ideas and purposes of later thinkers. My interpretation here of Smith's idea of conscience as a deliberate fusion of Protestant theology with the eighteenth-century discourse of sociability is a hybrid in this very sense. Too often, however, historians fail to recognize the hybridity of eighteenth-century ideas. Consider Reinhard Koselleck's claim that the eighteenth century, in its linear drive toward the future, had "detached" itself "from everything that all previous experiences had to offer."[97] There are many possible explanations for such anachronism. The most obvious, of course, is that some historians "pillage" history for their

[95] On the importance of understanding secularization as a gradual shifting of "index symbols," see Ernst Cassirer, *The Philosophy of the Enlightenment*, trans. Fritz C. A. Koelln and James P. Pettegrove (Princeton, NJ: Princeton University Press, 1951), pp. 134–196. The revisionist literature on secularization is vast. Four influential works that address the importance of plot and symbol are: Erich Auerbach, *Mimesis: The Representation of Reality in Western Literature* (Berne: A. Francke Ltd, 1946; trans. And ed. Willard R. Trask, Princeton, NJ: Princeton University Press, 1968), esp. pp. 160–173, 246–250 and 258–261; Karl Löwith, *Meaning in History* (Chicago: University of Chicago Press, 1949), esp. pp. 1–19, 60–61 and 182–203; Anders Nygren, *Eros and Agape* (London: SPCK, 1954), esp. pp. 160–166, 179–181, 205–207 and 272–277; and M. H. Abrams, *Natural Supernaturalism: Tradition and Revolution in Romantic Literature* (New York: W. W. Norton and Company, 1971), esp. pp. 65–70.
[96] Lewis F. Green, *Chronicle into History: An Essay on the Interpretation of History in Florentine Fourteenth-Century Chronicles* (Cambridge: Cambridge University Press, 1972), p. 59. For a similar formulation, see J. G. A. Pocock, "Time Institutions and Action: An Essay on Traditions and Their Understanding," in *Politics, Language and Time: Essays on Political Thought and History* (Chicago: University of Chicago Press, 1989), pp. 233–272, at p. 234.
[97] Reinhart Koselleck, *Futures Past: On the Semantics of Historical Time* (Frankfurt: Suhrkamp Verlag, 1979; trans. And ed. Keith Tribe, Cambridge, MA: MIT Press, 1985), p. 220. For an excellent recent account of

own purposes.[98] Sometimes the language of a tradition will "change" as the tradition is adapted, obscuring its lineage.[99] Other times, the archaic traditions that comprise a hybrid concept are so deeply embedded in the cultural and intellectual milieu that a thinker seeks overtly to upset, that it seems paradoxical for the historian to situate the thinker within them. This is particularly true in the case of eighteenth-century secular thought, where the dispute with Christianity was frequently so venomous.

As for Smith, he was notoriously anticlerical in his writings, deeply suspicious of religious fanaticism and manipulation. He spoke frequently of the "factious and party zeal" of "worthless" cabals who teach men "that by sacrifices, and ceremonies, and vain supplications, they can bargain with the Deity for fraud, and perfidy, and violence."[100] God, he observed, is frequently invoked by "zealots" – both "civil" and "ecclesiastical" – to whom "they impute all their own prejudices, and often view that Divine Being as animated by all their own vindictive and implacable passions."[101] In a discussion of the "unhappy delusions" of false religion, Smith declared Voltaire's *Mahomet* "one of the most interesting, and perhaps the most instructive spectacles that was ever introduced upon any theatre" for he understood that Voltaire's true target was not Islam or even Mahomet himself, but "false notions of religious duty" that were perhaps as real a problem in eighteenth-century Europe as they were in seventh-century Arabia: "Such as are our sentiments for the unhappy Seid and Palmira, such ought we feel for every person who is in this manner misled by religion."[102] Nevertheless, despite Smith's unwavering assault on the hypocrisies, corruptions and abuses of religion, my general point here is that we cannot possibly make historical sense of his moral thought, and particularly his articulation of an independent conscience, without acknowledging the Protestant context from which it sprang, and the impact he knew his representation would have on an eighteenth-century audience that would have included many believers. Without historiographical sensitivity to the hybridity of Smith's thought, we miss his place in the long and often

---

Smith's stadial theory of development that is sensitive to his distance from the chauvinistic and "triumphalist" view of European progress, see Jennifer Pitts, *A Turn to Empire: The Rise of Imperial Liberalism in Britain and France* (Princeton, NJ: Princeton University Press, 2005), pp. 25–58.

[98] The word belongs to Tuck, "The Contribution of History," p. 72.

[99] See the essays in Terence Ball, James Farr and Russell L. Hanson, eds., *Political Innovation and Conceptual Change* (Cambridge: Cambridge University Press, 1989), esp. Quentin Skinner, "Language and Political Change," pp. 6–23.

[100] *TMS* III.5.13 (p. 170).   [101] *TMS* III.3.43 (pp. 155–156).

[102] The discussion runs through *TMS* III.6.12 (pp. 176–177).

circuitous intellectual history of secularization. His theory of conscience to which we now turn is a case in point.

THE INDEPENDENT CONSCIENCE: FROM SOCIOLOGY TO THEOLOGY

Asserting the independence of conscience became a central objective for Smith in the revisions to his *Moral Sentiments* after critics leveled charges of moral conventionalism against him. Smith's old friend, Sir Gilbert Elliot, recognized the problem soon after the first edition appeared in 1759, and pressed Smith in a private letter on how his idea of conscience would transcend social opinion and become a moral check on corruption when necessary.[103] If conscience is merely a representation of society internalized in the agent, it "consists in doing what is conventionally expected, whether the convention is right or not," as Vincent Hope observed.[104] What, then, is the point of conscience? Gilbert seems to have touched a nerve in Smith. For the next thirty-one years, from the second edition of the *Moral Sentiments* through the last in 1790, Smith was preoccupied with establishing the *independence* of conscience, moving him further from Humean sociology I believe and as close as he would ever come to a Protestant theory of conscience.

I often wonder if conventionalism would have troubled Smith in a society that esteemed what he believed was properly estimable. What we know is that Smith was revolted by the vulgar displays of wealth and power parading themselves as virtue and greatness in eighteenth-century British life. Michael Ignatieff argues that Smith came close here to Rousseau in reviving a Stoic argument that moral corruption is a product of conventional belief, and in so doing, had advanced the first "specifically modern theory of false consciousness."[105] Although the sober Scot rarely acknowledged his intellectual debt to the contentious Genevan, whom he once referred to in a letter to David Hume as a "hypocritical Pedant,"[106] Smith agreed with Rousseau that social

---

[103] On the circumstances surrounding Sir Gilbert Elliot's letter to Smith, see D. D. Raphael and A. L. Macfie's editorial "Introduction" to *Moral Sentiments*, pp. 16–17; and Raphael, "Spectator," pp. 90–93. For biographical information, see Ian Simpson Ross, *The Life of Adam Smith* (Oxford: Clarendon Press, 1995), pp. 113, 153, 157 and 183.

[104] Hope, "Smith's Demigod," p. 167.

[105] See Ignatieff, "Republic of Needs," pp. 201–202. See also ch. 4 of his related book, *The Needs of Strangers* (London: Chatto & Windus, 1984; reprint London: Hogarth Press, 1990), pp. 105–131.

[106] "Adam Smith to David Hume," July 6, 1766, *Corres.*, No. 93 (pp. 112–113). On the circumstances surrounding this famous letter, and the incident between Hume and Rousseau that inspired it, see

experience transmutes conventional *"points d'honneur"* or *"objets ... de estime"* into truths.[107] In his evolving views on conscience, however, Smith was probably influenced less by Rousseau and more by various Stoic theories of moral education, particularly their "radical critique of convention and ordinary belief" and their emphasis on rational self-reflection.[108]

From the earliest editions of the *Moral Sentiments* Smith worried about the effects of upper-class profligacy on the aspirations of the middling classes and warned:

Never enter the place from whence so few have been able to return; never come within the circle of ambition; nor ever bring yourself into comparison with those masters of the earth who have already engrossed the attention of half mankind before you.

In the 1790 revisions Smith's tone intensified and turned from warning to scolding in a new chapter devoted to the very "corruption of our moral sentiments."[109] Now he described the middling classes as a "mob" imitating the "vices and follies" of "the rich and great."[110] This "corruption of our moral sentiments" became a central preoccupation for Smith in the 1790 edition, prompting him to rethink the very sufficiency of a sociological theory of moral life. A purely sociological view abandons conscience to the winds of opinion and slips into a precarious moral relativity dictated by the

---

David Hume's letter to Adam Smith, October 8, 1767, *Corres.*, No. 111 (pp. 133–137), and various letters of 1775–1776 from Hume to others collected in *Rousseau's Political Writings*, ed. Alan Ritter and Julia Conaway Bondanella (New York: W. W. Norton, 1988), pp. 195–199.

[107] See *Lettre à M. D'Alembert sur son Article Genève*, ed. Michel Launay (Paris: Garnier-Flammarion, 1967), pp. 141–156; and *Du Contrat Social; ou, principes de droit politique*, in *Jean-Jacques Rousseau: Œuvres complètes*, 4 vols., ed. Bernard Gagnebin and Marcel Raymond (Paris: Gallimard, Bibliothèque de la Pléiade, 1959–66), vol. III, pp. 347–470, at IV.vii (p. 458). This way of thinking is central to several of Rousseau's *Fragments politiques* written in the early- and mid-1750s, especially "De l'Honneur et de la Vertu," in *ibid.*, vol. III, pp. 501–508, and "Le Luxe, le Commerce et les Arts," in *ibid.*, vol. III, pp. 516–524. Finally, this theme pervaded Rousseau's political works later in life: *Considérations sur le gouvernement de Pologne et sur sa réformation projettée*, in *ibid.*, vol. III, pp. 951–1041, and *Projet de constitution pour la Corse*, in *ibid.*, vol. III, pp. 899–950.

[108] On the Stoics' "radical critique of convention and ordinary belief," see Martha C. Nussbaum, *The Therapy of Desire: Theory and Practice in Hellenistic Ethics* (Princeton, NJ: Princeton University Press, 1994), pp. 13–47, 318–329, 333 and 488–490. I have learned a great deal about Stoic "self-reflexion" from Troels Engberg-Pedersen, "Discovering the Good: Oikeiōsis and Kathēkonta in Stoic Ethics," in *The Norms of Nature: Studies in Hellenistic Ethics*, ed. Malcolm Schofield and Gisela Striker (Cambridge: Cambridge University Press, 1986; and Paris: Editions de la Maison des Sciences de l'Homme, 1986), pp. 145–183, esp. pp. 158–171.

[109] *TMS* I.iii.3. For a useful interpretation, see D. D. Raphael, "Adam Smith 1790." See also Dickey, "Historicizing the 'Adam Smith Problem,'" esp. pp. 595–599; and Dwyer, "Theory and Discourse."

[110] See *TMS* I.iii.3.7 (p. 64).

whimsy of the "rich and great." I resist making too functionalist a claim here, but one must be struck by Smith's change in tone thirty years later.[111]

By relativity I do not mean the relativism we associate today with problems of articulating universal moral standards, though I do argue later that Smith's cultural anthropology is ultimately very relevant to this problem. For the moment I mean very simply that disturbing norms were emerging spontaneously from within his own society, disrupting social order, and Smith's empirical commitments afforded no obvious stable ground from which to challenge them. Social man had become "unreliable" since he had succumbed to the "lure of luxury."[112] This is precisely why I say that Smith was anxious about "relativity."

Conscience, he decided, needed genuine *independence* from convention.[113] It needed the capacity to *reflect* on its own experience. The burden for Smith, of course, was to find a way to establish the independence of conscience without abstracting morals entirely from their sociological roots.[114] He needed a way to stabilize judgment without grandly leaping into the easy metaphysical salve of rationalism or theism or intuitionism, which he had always rejected for being "abstruse." Smith needed to steer a course between the empirical and the transcendental, between what Jonathan Lear has called the "contentful" and the "vacuous."[115] He needed, in Charles Griswold's words, "to carve out logical space for reasoning that is neither free from historicity nor reducible to it."[116] How could Smith transcend the relativity of the socialized conscience in a way that was still consistent with the phenomenology of moral life?

After the first edition of the *Moral Sentiments* and through to the sixth, Smith worked at this. His most settled response came in elaborate portions of text added to Part III in 1790, in which he attempted to craft a distinction between immature and mature moral judgments – characterizing the former as mere social assimilation driven by a childish desire for praise, and the latter as the ability to reflect on and abstract oneself from what is

---

[111] Thanks to Istvan Hont who warned me against this many years ago.

[112] Dickey, "Historicizing the 'Adam Smith Problem,'" p. 598.

[113] See esp. *TMS* I.iii.3 (pp. 61–66).

[114] Raphael, "Impartial Spectator," pp. 90–99, is illuminating on how Smith's empiricism can accommodate conscience's independence from social attitudes. See also his editorial "Introduction" (with Macfie) to *Moral Sentiments*, pp. 15–19.

[115] Jonathan Lear is illuminating in "Transcendental Anthropology," in *Subject, Thought, and Context*, ed. Philip Pettit and John McDowell (Oxford: Clarendon Press, 1986), pp. 267–298, esp. pp. 270–272 and 293.

[116] Charles L. Griswold, Jr., "On the Incompleteness of Adam Smith's System," *Adam Smith Review*, vol. 2 (2006), pp. 181–186.

conventionally praised in the world.[117] He demonstrated this distinction to his readers through a developmental, perfectionist account of conscience which described a gradual transformation in the nature of rational activity itself – a weaning away from a purely instrumental, childish sort of rationality, through which a person regulates his passions only to obtain actual praise and to avoid censure, what Smith once described as "the frivolous desire of praise at any rate," and towards a mature capacity for reflective reason, which aspires to "praise-*worthiness*."[118] Smith suggested that conscience matures as a person's rational capacity evolves from an archaic, self-preserving tool into a higher sort of self-reflection. As the conscience matures, the nature of reason itself transforms so that it can call its own experience into question.

Smith's developmental account of conscience in the 1790 revisions unfolded as follows: He began his argument in Stoic fashion with the cultivation of self-command in children. A child, we are told, learns to exercise self-command only when he enters school and discovers that his peers will not accept the behavior once tolerated by his parents and nurses.[119] Because the child naturally desires to gain the favor and avoid the contempt of his new play-fellows, he soon learns to become "master" of himself. He becomes "disciplined."[120] People of the weakest constitution, Smith continued, are much like school children. They are young in moral strength, immature, for they never have learned to command their passions for any reason but to obtain favor and to avoid censure.[121] Such people are motivated solely by the prospects of praise and blame, so that they know only how to mask their base appetites instrumentally, and in the presence of others.[122] Immature men long for the ring of Gyges, long for the license that invisibility enables. As Smith put it, such a person "naturally prefers himself to all mankind, yet he dares not look mankind in the face, and avow that he

---

[117] Most of *TMS* III.2–3 (pp. 113–156) was added in 1790. There is evidence that Smith began turning to this view as early as the second edition. See *TMS* III.1.7 (p. 113). For further discussion of Smith's distinction here, see Griswold, *Virtues of Enlightenment*, pp. 210–212; and Ryan Hanley, "Adam Smith, Aristotle and Virtue Ethics," in *New Voices on Adam Smith*, ed. Leonidas Montes and Eric Schliesser (London: Routledge, 2006), pp. 17–39.

[118] *TMS* VII.ii.4.9 (p. 310). For Smith's developmental account of conscience, see *TMS* III.3.21–25 (pp. 145–147). For his distinction between praise and praise-worthiness, see specifically *TMS* III.1.7 (p. 113); *TMS* III.2 (pp. 113–134). Even in the 1759 edition, Smith averred that one who acts "solely from a regard to what is right and fit to be done ... acts from the most sublime and godlike motive which human nature is even capable of conceiving." VII.ii.4.8–10 (pp. 309–11). This theme was greatly augmented in the revisions.

[119] *TMS* III.3.22 (p. 145).   [120] *TMS* III.3.22 (p. 145).

[121] See especially *TMS* III.3.21–25 (pp. 145–147).   [122] *TMS* III.3.23–24 (pp. 145–146).

acts according to this principle."[123] Whenever no one is watching, his
passions "rush headlong" to their own "gratification," much like "a child
that has not yet gone to school," much like Glaucon's description of the
unjust man in Book II of Plato's *Republic*.[124] Understood as an act of
masking or sublimation, sociable behavior requires great concentration
and exertion. Even with the incentive of praise, it is difficult for an agent
to sustain for too long. Since he has not "been well inured to the hard
discipline of self-command," Smith argued, "he soon grows weary of this
restraint":[125]

Upon some occasions ... passions are restrained ... by prudential considerations of
the bad consequences which might follow from their indulgence. In such cases, the
passions, though restrained, are not always subdued, but often remain lurking in
the breast with all their original fury.[126]

Indeed, passions are "frequently inflamed by the restraint, and sometimes
(long after the provocation given, and when nobody is thinking about it)
burst out absurdly and unexpectedly, and with tenfold fury and violence."[127] In this 1790 passage we have a striking eighteenth-century account
of psychological repression, and why a life devoted to seeking praise and
"making friends" was bound to fail miserably as a key to both individual
happiness and social order.[128]

   Smith's favorite person, the "man of real constancy and firmness," we are
told, is so "thoroughly bred in the great school of self-command" that he
"whether in solitude or in society, wears nearly the same countenance."[129]
He doesn't tire of self-restraint. He doesn't merely sublimate his passions,
but actually "moderates and subdues" them.[130] The virtue of the "man of
real constancy and firmness" consists in his thorough identification with his
conscience. Smith praised the great exertions of this "wise and just man":

He has never dared to forget for one moment the judgment which the impartial
spectator would pass upon his sentiments and conduct. He has never dared to
suffer the man within the breast to be absent one moment from his attention. With
the eyes of this great inmate he has always been accustomed to regard whatever

[123] *TMS* II.ii.2.1 (p. 83).   [124] *TMS* VI.concl.2 (p. 263); *TMS* III.3.23 (p. 145).
[125] *TMS* III.3.24 (p. 146).   [126] *TMS* VI.concl.3 (p. 263).   [127] *TMS* VI.concl.4 (p. 263).
[128] See Jean Starobinski's Freudian discussion of "dissimulated violence" in the eighteenth-century idea
of *civilization* in *Blessings in Disguise; or, The Morality of Evil*, trans. Arthur Goldhammer (1989;
Cambridge, MA: Harvard University Press, 1993), pp. 1–35 (esp. pp. 7 and 10–11) and pp. 194–212
(esp. pp. 203–206). Also see Pierre Saint-Amand's provocative thesis about the violence lurking
beneath eighteenth-century optimism in *The Laws of Hostility: Politics, Violence, and the
Enlightenment*, trans. Jennifer Curtiss Gage (Paris, 1992; Minneapolis, MN: University of
Minnesota Press, 1996).
[129] *TMS* III.3.25 (p. 146).   [130] *TMS* VI.concl.3–4 (p. 263).

relates to himself. This habit has become perfectly familiar to him. He has been in the constant practice, and, indeed, under the constant necessity, of modelling, or of endeavouring to model, not only his outward conduct and behaviour, but, as much as he can, even his inward sentiments and feelings, according to those of this awful and respectable judge. He does not merely affect the sentiments of the impartial spectator. He really adopts them. He almost identifies himself with, he almost becomes himself that impartial spectator, and scarce even feels but as that great arbiter of his conduct directs him to feel.[131]

Obvious here is Smith's affinity with Kant, who had defined "immaturity" in "What is Enlightenment?" as "the inability to use one's own understanding without the guidance of another."[132] This may help us understand why Smith, in the second edition of the *Moral Sentiments* and onward to the sixth, began to string "reason" together with "conscience, the inhabitant of the breast, the man within, the great judge and arbiter of our conduct."[133] He didn't capitulate to the rationalism of Price and Clark, but rather attempted to differentiate the two "tribunals" we consult when making moral judgments, each of which entailed different *sorts* of rational activity: The tribunal of the "man without" was comprised of our fellows and operated according to the dynamics of actual praise; the second tribunal, the "man within," enabled rational reflection about what was genuinely praise-worthy, independent of society's "groundless acclamations."[134]

The "two tribunals" argument represents Smith's best attempt to innoculate his sociological account of conscience against charges of conventionalism. Note, however, that the argument, as I have presented it to this point, does not yet explain how conscience *gains* its independence from prevailing norms. Surely Smith enjoined us to appeal to the higher tribunal. In fact this was always his argument, though he expanded and refined it in the 1790 revision. Where Smith went further now was that he attempted to say more about what the higher tribunal *knows*, and how it knows what it knows. In other words, what makes something *praise-worthy*? Who decides? Very literally, what determines worth?

At precisely this moment, a deistic God emerges in Smith's narrative. Smith attempted to fortify his account of conscience by personifying the impartial spectator as a "demigod within the breast" – "partly of immortal,

---

[131] *TMS* III.3.25 (pp. 146–147).
[132] Immanuel Kant, "An Answer to the Question: What Is Enlightenment?," trans. H. B. Nisbet, in *Political Writings*, ed. Hans Reiss (Cambridge: Cambridge University Press, 1970–1991), pp. 54–60, at p. 54.
[133] *TMS* III.3.4 (p. 137).   [134] *TMS* III.2.32 (p. 131).

yet partly too of mortal extraction."[135] A perfect illustration of my contention above that Smith sought to combat conventionalism by forging a third way between the empirical and the transcendental. The "demigod within the breast" is very literally a third way since it is comprised of both human and divine elements. Smith says very little about this composite tribunal beyond its function. We know that it served for Smith as a "standard," as an "idea of exact propriety and perfection."[136] We also know that "every man" possessed this "idea" to some degree. Indeed, Smith conceived of mature moral judgment in perfectionist terms as a "slow, gradual, and progressive" unfolding of wisdom and virtue that takes place, to some extent, in us all:

> The wise and virtuous man directs his principal attention to the first standard; the idea of exact propriety and perfection. There exists in the mind of every man, an idea of this kind, gradually formed from his observations upon the character and conduct both of himself and of other people. It is the slow, gradual, and progressive work of the great demigod in the breast, the great judge and arbiter of our conduct. This idea is in every man more or less accurately drawn, its colouring is more or less just, its outlines are more or less exactly designed, according to the delicacy and acuteness of that sensibility, with which those observations were made, and according to the care and attention employed in making them.[137]

Beyond this, we know little more about the demigod – whose God it is, how the human and divine get on together in such close quarters! But the key for us is to recognize its function in Smith's argument; and on this Smith was clear. He used the "demigod in the breast" as a standard of "perfection," to combat the force of public opinion, the "vehemence and clamour," the "false judgment" and "groundless acclamations" of "ignorant and weak man."[138]

I read Smith's characterization of conscience as a demigod voicing "the idea of exact propriety and perfection" as a deistic formulation of the independent and irrefutable authority of the Protestant conscience. Smith comes closer in these passages to the Protestant tradition than anywhere else in his work. He recognized the power in Luther's assertion that conscience is "like a ball kicked about the earth" when it is "separated from the Word of God" but he gives the "Word of God" an unmistakably deistic spin:

---

[135] *TMS* III.2.32 (p. 131). See also *TMS* VI.iii.25 (p. 247), also added in 1790, in which Smith elaborated on the two very different "standards" that we can employ when we judge. The higher standard, employed by men of conscience, is "the idea of exact propriety and perfection" established by the "demigod within the breast"; the lower standard, employed by "the greater part of our friends and companions … our rivals and competitors" is "an approximation to that idea which is commonly attained in the world" (*TMS* VI.iii.25 (p. 247)).

[136] *TMS* VI.iii.25 (p. 247).   [137] *TMS* VI.iii.25 (p. 247).   [138] *TMS* III.2.32 (p. 131).

When his judgments are steadily and firmly directed by the sense of praise-worthiness and blame-worthiness, he *seems* to act suitably to his divine extraction: But when he suffers himself to be astonished and confounded by the judgments of ignorant and weak man, he discovers his connexion with mortality, and *appears* to act suitably, rather to the human, than to the divine, part of his origin.[139]

That Smith uses the language of "seeming" and "appearing" in this passage – that our judgments look to us *as if* they conform to the "divine" when we aspire to perfection and to the "human" when we capitulate to the mob – not that they actually *do* – confirms that Smith was making a deistic argument that it is natural and reasonable for us to believe that our mature moral judgments conform to God's will. This deistic way of thinking about conscience, and about man's relation to God and religion in general, is infused throughout the *Moral Sentiments* in all its various editions.

One particularly fine example – which I will explore at length in the next chapter – is found in a 1759 portion of Part III in which Smith invokes divine law to describe how ordinary folk are motivated to curb their self-love when confronted with particularly challenging circumstances, and ultimately to behave on most occasions with "tolerable decency."[140] In the 1759 text, he insisted that even ordinary people – people driven primarily by the external tribunal of approbation and shame – are led nevertheless to establish moral rules for themselves through a sort of rational extrapolation from ordinary experience, and to attribute those rules to the will of God who will punish their transgression in the next world. I spend considerable time in the next chapter exploring this argument in light of Smith's preoccupation with modern social order and his resistance to Christian and Stoic perfectionism. But it is fascinating to pause here to compare Smith's theology there with the "two tribunals" argument I have explored in this chapter. Clearly both arguments are offered in a deistic key – that it is natural and reasonable for us to believe that our moral judgments reflect God's will and subject us to his rewards and punishments in a life to come. But there is a crucial difference between them that illuminates the profound evolution in Smith's thinking about the socialized conscience in later revisions of the *Moral Sentiments*. In the 1759 passages, we shall see, Smith invoked divine law to maintain social order, to encourage decency and conformity, to prevent society from "crumbling into nothing." In the later 1790 passages discussed here, however, Smith invoked the demigod for precisely the opposite reason: to challenge the social order for its falsehood and corruption, to provide refuge for man *from* society when it violates his

[139] *TMS* III.2.32 (p. 131).   [140] *TMS* III.4–5 (pp. 156–170).

inner sense of what is right. Indeed, resisting social opinion often requires that the "man within" put himself into direct *conflict* with the "man without." This is what it means for a person to exercise moral maturity and independence of conscience. I find it profoundly interesting to note in this context that Smith referred us to "a still higher tribunal" – "to that of the all-seeing Judge of the world, whose eye can never be deceived, and whose judgments can never be perverted."[141] To me, this passage resonates with Locke's "appeal to heaven" – though Locke of course was establishing the right of a people to revolt collectively against political tyranny, and Smith was providing "effectual consolation" for the lonely individual conscience confronting the mob that "in due time" truth will win out.[142] Despite the obvious differences, however, one is struck by the functional equivalence of these appeals that reach beyond the realm of human judgment, and the moments at which they appear in both Locke's and Smith's arguments. When there is no umpire on earth the highest tribunal is God.

TOWARDS A MIDDLING MORALITY

Interpreters have long debated the extent that Smith's perfectionist moves in the 1790 revisions transformed his project from a properly empirical one to a normative and philosophical, or even a theistic, one. I argued in Chapter 2 that Smith did not perceive his own options in this way; he was not constrained by our orientation to facts and values and would have seen no obvious tension between a description of ordinary moral life and an observation that some people attune their minds and aspirations to problematic models. So, I do not wish to suggest that Smith abandoned the empiricism for which he is best known.

In fact, these shifts in Smith's thought might be interpreted through a distinctively empirical lens. When Smith observed the world about him, what he saw was the "great mob of mankind" becoming "the admirers and worshipers of wealth and greatness" – that the standards of "praiseworthiness" were being set by what he called "fashionable profligacy." Such a phenomenal irregularity was bound to shock his Newtonian soul and make him uneasy. Smith was a systematic thinker, and it makes sense that his restlessness would have compelled him to find an explanation for it, and to adjust his system by looking for resources *in the world* with which to relieve the disequilibrium. Smith was more than slightly obsessed with

---

[141] *TMS* III.2.33 (p. 132).   [142] Locke, *Second Treatise*, ch. 14; and *TMS* III.2.33 (pp. 131–132).

connecting and harmonizing disjointed phenomena, both in the natural and social sciences. A reading of his *History of Astronomy* surely confirms this.[143]

And yet, just as Smith didn't abandon his empiricism, neither did he soothe himself with metaphysical comfort. Despite Smith's perfectionist moves, he conceded that most people were narrowly self-concerned, attached to familiar people and things, externally driven in their behavior rather than internally driven, and were incapable of cultivating the more reflective sort of moral judgment he had described and advocated in his 1790 revisions to Part III of *Moral Sentiments*. Very much a realist about the practical limits of moral philosophy, Smith never expected more of people than the middling propriety of which he thought they, in various "shades and gradations," were capable. It is to this very "middling morality" of the *Moral Sentiments* that I turn next.

---

[143] Adam Smith, "The History of Astronomy," in *Essays on Philosophical Subjects*, ed. W. L. D. Wightman, as vol. III of *The Glasgow Edition of the Works and Correspondence of Adam Smith* (Oxford: Oxford University Press; reprint Indianapolis, IN: Liberty Press, 1982), pp. 33–105.

CHAPTER 4

Perfectionism and social order

> [A]lmost all worthwhile human life lies between the extremes that
> morality puts before us.
>
> Bernard Williams, *Ethics and the Limits of Philosophy*

Smith's portraits in the last chapter of the "weak man" and the "wise and
virtuous man" are ideal types. Most people fall somewhere in the middle. Like
Cicero's *De Officiis*, which Smith characterized as a doctrine of "imperfect,
but attainable virtues," the *Moral Sentiments* seeks to describe the morality
of ordinary people, to whom Smith variously referred as "tolerably good
soldiers," "commonly honest men," the "mean," the "many," the "greater
part," the "crude," the "mass," the "vulgar," the "coarse clay of mankind."[1]
Cicero described the nature of his project in the following way:

> The duties that I discuss in these books are, then, those that the Stoics call
> "middle". They are shared and widely accessible.[2]

In this chapter, I do four things. First, I argue that Smith was primarily
concerned in the *Moral Sentiments* with describing and legitimating the
morality of ordinary people for its stabilizing effects on modern society.
This will mean, ultimately, that much of the perfectionist rhetoric in his
thought should be bracketed from, or at least interpreted within, the central
thrust of his practical morality, which was oriented around social order.
Here I fundamentally agree with Joseph Cropsey, Charles Griswold and
Douglas Den Uyl, among others, that Smith was primarily concerned in
the *Moral Sentiments* with social coordination.[3] I believe that Smith's

---

[1] See, for example, *TMS* I.i.5.9 (p. 26); *TMS* I.iii.3.5 (p. 63); *TMS* III.3.4 (p. 137); *TMS* III.3.6 (p. 138);
TMS III.5.1 (p. 162); and *TMS* VI.ii.23–27 (pp. 247–249). See also Smith's discussion of the
"imperfect, but attainable virtues" of Roman Stoicism at *TMS* VII.ii.1.42 (pp. 291–292).

[2] Cicero, *On Duties*, trans. M. T. Griffin and E. M. Atkins (Cambridge: Cambridge University Press, 1991).

[3] Cropsey, *Polity and Economy*; Minowitz, *Profits Priests and Princes*; and Griswold and Den Uyl,
"Friendship and Love." Here I depart from Fleischacker, who suggested in *Third Concept*, pp. 143–144,
that social coordination was secondary to self-perfection for Smith in the *Moral Sentiments*.

perfectionism is best understood in the context of this larger, distinctively modern agenda. Indeed, an individual will be no freer to become what he might be in a society rent by violence and disorder than he was in pre-modern societies ordered monistically from above. Social order is the bedrock of modern selfhood for Adam Smith. It is not insignificant here that he referred to "the welfare and preservation of society" as "the favorite ends of nature," and elsewhere, likewise, as "the great, the immense fabric of human society," the "association of mankind," and the "peculiar and darling care of Nature."[4] The *Moral Sentiments* should be read as a description of how Nature exercises this care. Second, I demonstrate that Smith's emphases on ordinary morality and social order share much in common with several older moral systems that similarly rejected the most severe and rigoristic sorts of moral perfectionism by carving out a middle space for "decent" or "tolerable" behavior between the binary extremes of moral success and failure. Third, I argue that Smith's anti-rigorism, and his assertion that ordinary morality grounds modern social order, comes through most clearly in his discussion of moral rules, which guide ordinary people who, for various reasons that emerge from both mind and world, become deluded and derailed, surely less attuned to the voice of the "impartial spectator" than a wise and virtuous man would be.[5] I argue that Smith's incorporation of reason and God into his description of moral rules should not be interpreted as perfectionist slippage from his sociological account of morality, but rather as an empirical observation about how ordinary people, who tend to fear God and gravitate naturally toward rule-following, maintain a basic moral equilibrium when the world tempts and challenges them. Finally, I will explore Smith's anti-rigorism in greater detail through his rejection of the severe perfectionism embodied in Christian and Stoic variants of cosmopolitanism.[6]

ORDINARY PEOPLE, ORDINARY MORALITY

When Smith spoke in the binary language of maturity and immaturity, internal and external, wisdom and folly, he was constructing a theoretical continuum of the "shades and gradations of weakness and self-command, as we meet them in common life."[7] For Smith "virtue" was a polar symbol, an

---

[4] *TMS* II.i.5.10 (p. 77) and *TMS* II.ii.3.4 (p. 86), respectively.   [5] *TMS* III.4–5 (pp. 156–170).
[6] See notably *TMS* III.3.8–21 (pp. 139–145); *TMS* III.6 (pp. 171–178); *TMS* VI.iii (pp. 237–262); *TMS* VII.ii.1.15–47 (pp. 272–293).
[7] *TMS* III.3.21 (p. 145).

"idea of exact propriety and perfection" – and while some people are better than others at "assimilating" themselves to this ideal, Smith conceded that the "greater part" of mankind, who are weak and imperfect, easily deluded, driven by self-love and generally preoccupied with their own particular endeavors, would never come very close. Among the various things Smith called virtue throughout the *Moral Sentiments* were "an idea of perfection,"[8] a "model" or a "picture,"[9] an "archetype of perfection,"[10] the "standard of ideal … perfection,"[11] "the most sublime and godlike motive which human nature is even capable of conceiving,"[12] and so forth. Virtue was an imaginary of perfection that stood somehow beyond sociology for Smith, outside of history, serving as a transcendent model against which people might compare their own mortal and imperfect characters.[13] For Smith, "perfection" was an ideal "which no human conduct ever did, or ever can come up to."[14] Yet, the model fostered humility by demonstrating "in how many features the mortal copy falls short of the immortal original."[15]

From the first page of the *Moral Sentiments* Smith insisted that even "middling" or "ordinary" men, whom Cicero had called *vulgus*, or those whose *sapientia perfecta non est*,[16] had the capacity to "approximate" wisdom and virtue, to move toward *honestum*.[17] The same sort of optimism is reflected in Smith's perfectionist discussion in 1790 of the "shades and gradations of weakness and self-command, as we meet them in common life."[18] In these passages, Smith described how a person's conscience can mature over time. The most important point, however, is that a failure to *attain* perfect wisdom and virtue in this process of self-perfection did not condemn a person to complete moral failure, according to Smith. Indeed, men were not gods, but needy and imperfect:

It is not easy to conceive what other motive an independent and all-perfect Being, who stands in need of nothing external, and whose happiness is complete in himself, can act from. But whatever the case with the Deity, so imperfect a creature as man, the support of whose existence requires so many things external to him, must often act from many other motives. The conditions of human nature were peculiarly hard, if those affections, which, by the very nature of our being, ought frequently to influence our conduct, could upon no occasion appear virtuous, or deserve esteem and commendation from anybody.[19]

---

[8] *TMS* I.i.5.9–10 (p. 26).   [9] *TMS* VI iii.25 (p. 248).   [10] *TMS* VI.ii.25 (p. 247).
[11] *TMS* VI.iii.25–26 (p. 248).   [12] *TMS* VII.ii.4.10 (p. 311).
[13] See esp. *TMS* I.i.5.8–10 (pp. 25–26); *TMS* I.iii.3 (pp. 61–66); *TMS* VI.iii.23–27 (pp. 247–250).
[14] *TMS* I.i.5.9 (p. 26).   [15] *TMS* VI.iii.25 (p. 247).   [16] "[W]isdom is not perfect."
[17] Cicero, *De Officiis*, III.13–17, p. 105.   [18] *TMS* III.3.20–25 (pp. 145–147), at III.3.21 (p. 145).
[19] *TMS* VII.ii.3.18 (p. 305).

Elsewhere, in a Ciceronian key, Smith argued that there "may frequently be a considerable degree of virtue in those actions which fall short of the most perfect propriety."[20] I interpret Smith's thoughts about ordinary morality here as highly egalitarian. For Smith even the most childish, externally driven sort of self-restraint, with all of its psychological pitfalls, was valued nevertheless for mitigating the most pernicious and anti-social manifestations of self-love.

THE EGALITARIAN MIDDLE

This way of thinking about the social value of ordinary morality has a long history. In a series of passages in Plato's *Phaedo*, Socrates differentiated *sophrosyne* (self-restraint) that is recommended by philosophy and driven by reason, and the sort of restraint that is inspired only by considerations of self-interest – what we might think of in Smith's terms as a differentiation between the morality of a wise man and ordinary morality. Socrates insisted that those who practice *sophrosyne* "by nature and habit without philosophy or reason" are ethically "worthy" nevertheless.[21] Their mere "social and civil virtue" is not the true *sophrosyne* of the philosopher. Indeed, "most men" (*oi polloi*) are "self-restrained" only through "a kind of self-indulgence."[22] Because they "fear that they may be deprived of certain pleasures which they desire ... they refrain from some because they are under the sway of others."[23] Specifically, "most men" resist "bodily desires" because they fear the "loss of property" or "the dishonor or disgrace of wickedness."[24] In their "seemly" conduct,[25] they simply "substitute" base, "bodily desires" for other more sociable ones, "exchanging" them "as if they were coins."[26] But, while there was something "slavish" and "impure" about this *skiagraphia*,[27] this "painted imitation of virtue" that had "nothing healthy or true in it,"[28] there was, astonishingly, something ethically "worthy" about it for Socrates. While it wouldn't make philosophers of ordinary men, it served admirably to restrain the more vicious tendencies of *akolasia* (self-indulgence) from "conquering" them, ultimately rendering the "human race" more "social and gentle."[29]

---

[20] *TMS* I.i.5.8 (p. 25).
[21] Plato, *Phaedo*, trans. Harold North Fowler (Cambridge, MA: Harvard University Press, 1914), 82(A)–(B). My thanks to Joseph Cropsey for extended conversations about this dimension of the *Phaedo* and its relation to various themes in modern economic thought.
[22] *Phaedo*, 68(E)–69(B).   [23] *Phaedo*.   [24] *Phaedo*, 82(B)–(C).   [25] *Phaedo*, 68(C).
[26] *Phaedo*, 69(A)–(B).   [27] *Phaedo*, 69(B).   [28] *Phaedo*, 69(C).
[29] *Phaedo*, 69(A) and 82(A)–(B). My thanks to Joseph Cropsey for endless conversation on this.

Aristotle, in his more celebrated discussion of the "mean" in *Nicomachean Ethics*, more systematically differentiated the ethical triad we find in the *Phaedo*.[30] His "poles," like Plato's, are true *sophrosyne* at one end, and *akolasia* at the other.[31] The *sophron* (self-controlled man) follows *sophia* (theoretical wisdom) always, practices *sophrosyne* perfectly and is never tempted to turn from it.[32] At the other end sits the man infected with *akolasia*, who is entirely, "wickedly" self-indulgent and feels no regret about it.[33] Between these two extremes, however, lies the sphere of practical ethics. In Book VII, Aristotle differentiates two distinct personality types that constitute this middle sphere, according to their moral resolve.[34] On the one hand, there is the *enkrates*, the man who has sufficient *dynamis* (capacity) to follow the voice of *phronesis* (practical wisdom), to resist temptation and to control his passions by striving for the mean in every situation. On the other hand, there is the *akrates*, the man who is morally weak, given to temptation, able to recognize *phronesis* (which differentiates him from the man infected with *akolasia*[35]) but rarely to follow it. The point is that both the *enkrates* and the *akrates* reside in the realm of practical ethics. Though one is morally strong and the other is morally weak, both recognize *phronesis*, and they both in varying degrees have the *dynamis* to avoid *akolasia* even if they will never achieve the true *sophrosyne* of the *sophron*.[36]

Jacob Viner demonstrated the predominance in early modernity of this triadic way of thinking about morality, and its relation to the evolution of economic ideas. He focused on the Jansenists Pierre Nicole (discussed here in Chapter 1, and with whom Smith was most likely familiar) and Jean Domat, who articulated an ethical scheme comprised of three "levels": the Christian "elect" representing pure virtue at one pole; vicious "rogues" at the other; and an "intermediate level" comprised of *honnêtes hommes* – "ordinary men" who had learned to temper their *amour-propre* through

---

[30] Martin Ostwald, in his notes on the *Nicomachean Ethics*, recognized that *Phaedo* (69(A)–(B)) is a unique moment in the Platonic corpus, and that it "comes very close to Aristotle's own position." Aristotle, *Nicomachean Ethics*, trans. and ed. Martin Oswald (Indianapolis, IN: Bobbs-Merrill, 1962), p. 171, n. 60. A helpful discussion of Aristotle's "taxonomic analysis" can be found in Amélie O. Rorty, "Akrasia and Pleasure," in *Essays on Aristotle's Ethics*, ed. Amélie O. Rorty (Berkeley, CA: University of California Press, 1980), pp. 267–284.

[31] Rowe, *Phaedo*, p. 148, recognizes that *akolasia* functions as the opposite of *sophrosyne* in the *Phaedo*.

[32] Aristotle, *Nicomachean Ethics*, III.10–11 (pp. 77–81).

[33] *Nicomachean Ethics*, III.12 (pp. 81–82); *Nicomachean Ethics*, VII.8 (pp. 197–199).

[34] *Nicomachean Ethics*, VII (pp. 174–213).

[35] On the idea that there is a difference between the *akrates* and the man who is dominated entirely by *akolasia*, see *Nicomachean Ethics*, VII.8 (pp. 197–199).

[36] See Oswald's comments, *Nicomachean Ethics*, pp. 313–314. See Smith's assertion that the "character" of Aristotelian "virtue" turns on the "practical habits" of "reasonable moderation" in *TMS* VII.ii.1.13–14 (pp. 271–272).

a code of Christian *civilité*.[37] In "Of Charity and Self-Love," as we saw in Chapter 1, Nicole observed that *honnêtes hommes* are not "animated" by the "spirit of God" like the Christian elect. But while their *civilité* is "not animated and stirred *but* by self-love," they nevertheless should not be "intermixed together with the wicked," with the "rogues," since their "exterior behavior," their *l'amour-propre éclairé*, so admirably "imitated" the virtues of "Christian charity" – it "so much resembled supernatural and divine actions."[38]

Like Socrates and Aristotle, like Nicole and Domat, Smith believed there was something far greater and more noble and beautiful than that which the bulk of mankind would ever attain, that which "no human conduct ever did, or ever can come up to."[39] But it was the bulk of mankind and their "middling" capacity for decency and social order with which Smith was primarily concerned in the *Theory of Moral Sentiments*. Nearly every chapter of this manifesto of middle-class mores refers in one way or another to the capacities of the "tolerably good soldier," the "commonly honest man" and the social utility of his decency.[40]

Smith's modern faith in the morality of ordinary people compelled him to draw a demarcation line between "virtue" and "mere propriety." He wrote:

As in the common degree of the intellectual qualities, there is no abilities; so in the common degree of the moral there is no virtue. Virtue is excellence, something uncommonly great and beautiful, which rises far above what is vulgar and ordinary ... There is, in this respect, a considerable difference between *virtue* and *mere propriety*; between those qualities and actions which deserve to be admired and celebrated, and those which simply deserve to be approved of.[41]

To a contemporary reader, this all rings uncomfortably elitist; and among some Smith's thought has helped to edify such elitism. If one is inclined to find a basis for elitism and inegalitarianism in Smith's work, here and elsewhere, it would not be difficult to find one. Smith, as D. D. Raphael put it, was "always a stratifier, never a leveler."[42] Sometimes the "wise and virtuous man" appears to be a class of people who have special access to a

---

[37] Viner, "Introduction," pp. 180–182 and 186–188; and Viner, *Religious Thought*, pp. 130–139. Viner argued that the ethical potential that seventeenth-century Jansenist social theory discovered in enlightened self-love was essential conceptually to the eventual secular creation of a self-regulating commercial space.

[38] Nicole, "Charity," *passim*.   [39] *TMS* I.i.5.9 (p. 26).

[40] These formulations from *TMS* III.3.5–6 (p. 138) are typical of Smith's general attitude toward ordinary morality.

[41] *TMS* I.i.5.6–7 (p. 25).   [42] Raphael, "Hume and Adam Smith," p. 101.

truth that eludes the rest of us – like Aristotelian *phronimoi*.[43] At other times, however, the man of "birth and fortune" seems to emerge as Smith's preferred elite in modern society: "Nature has wisely judged that distinction of ranks, the peace and order of society, would rest more securely upon the plain and palpable difference of birth and fortune, than upon the invisible and uncertain difference of wisdom and virtue."[44] Interpreters have long debated the implications of Smith's often obsessive attachment to the "distinction of ranks" and the "stability" it produced.

Nevertheless, if we read Smith's distinction between virtue and propriety in the current discussion in light of his modern rejection of ethical rigorism – in particular the rigoristic "perfection-or-failure"[45] ethical systems of neo-Augustinianism and Stoicism – his thought appears less elitist than a very deliberate egalitarian leveling of modern ethical life. Distinguishing virtue and propriety in a book written explicitly to legitimate the latter, Smith opened an ethical space for the majority *between* the poles of perfection and failure, grounded in a realistic orientation to the practical limits of moral philosophy, and suited to the needs of modern, free people.

In the balance of this chapter I will explore how Smith carved out such a space. First, I will explore his discussion of moral rules, in which this space is very clearly presented. Second, I will explore Smith's rejection of Christian and Stoic rigorism, against which his own middling alternative is asserted.

"SELF-DELUSION" AND RULE-FOLLOWING

A recurring theme in the *Moral Sentiments* is the intransigence of self-love. Despite our best intentions, we often find ourselves whipped off-course by sudden emotional upheavals, unhealthy desires, self-delusion, paranoia, a distorted reliance on the opinion of others, and so on. Smith's description of our psychological instability is crackling with insight. And yet this all made

---

[43] On Aristotelian themes of "moral nobility" in Smith's thought, see Ryan Hanley, "Adam Smith, Aristotle and Virtue Ethics," in *New Voices on Adam Smith*, ed. Leonidas Montes and Eric Schliesser (London: Routledge, 2006), pp. 17–39. The Aristotle reference comes from p. 21. Although themes of moral nobility, excellence and genuine superiority weave through Smith's narrative, I see them as far less central to Smith's ultimate egalitarian purposes than does Hanley.

[44] See notably *TMS* VI.ii.1.20 (p. 226). See also *TMS* I.iii.2.3 (p. 52); *TMS* VI.iii.30 (p. 252). The editors of *TMS* commented on Smith's "complacency" in this regard at *TMS*, "Introduction," pp. 17–18. For more discussion on the intentions behind Smith's "élitism," see Norbert Waszek, "Two Concepts of Morality," pp. 592–597.

[45] I borrow this useful term from Waszek, "Two Concepts," p. 599.

him deeply anxious. Note the connection between psychological instability and social disorder in the following passage:

This self-deceit, this fatal weakness of mankind, is the source of half the disorders of human life ... Nature, however, has not left this weakness, which is of so much importance, altogether without a remedy; nor has she abandoned us entirely to the delusions of self-love. Our continual observations upon the conduct of others, insensibly lead us to form to ourselves certain general rules concerning what is fit and proper either to be done or to be avoided.[46]

A pervasive theme in my interpretation is Smith's preoccupation with social order. This seems to be precisely why he first introduced the idea of "general Rules of Morality." They guide us when self-love overpowers the voice of conscience and subjects society to the dangers of our instability.[47] It is not coincidental that Smith's discussion of general rules follows directly on the heels of his description of the "wise and just man who has been thoroughly bred in the great school of self-command" and "identifies himself" completely with his conscience.[48] Surely most of us will never achieve such perfection. For the rest of us Smith turned to the subject of general rules. Note in the following two passages how he introduced the subject, linking moral rules explicitly with the "tolerable decency" of ordinary people:

The regard to those general rules of conduct, is what is properly called a sense of duty, a principle of the greatest consequence in human life, and the only principle by which the bulk of mankind are capable of directing their actions. Many men behave very decently, and through the whole of their lives avoid any considerable degree of blame, who yet, perhaps, never felt the sentiment upon the propriety of which we found our approbation of their conduct, but acted merely from a regard to what they saw were the established rules of behaviour.

And again:

The coarse clay of which the bulk of mankind are formed, can not be wrought up to such perfection. There is scare any man, however, who by discipline, education, and example, may not be so impressed with a regard to general rules, as to act upon almost every occasion with tolerable decency, and through the whole of his life to avoid any considerable degree of blame.[49]

Moral rules are the "only way" ordinary people learn to act with "tolerable decency," according to Smith. Without them, he suggested, "there is no man whose conduct can be much depended upon."[50] This is a sharp claim

---

[46] *TMS* III.4.6–7 (pp. 158–159).
[47] *TMS* III.4 (pp. 156–161). See Samuel Fleischacker's penetrating discussion of Kant's parallel use of moral rules against self-delusion in "Kant and Adam Smith," pp. 260–265.
[48] *TMS* III.3.25 (pp. 146–147).   [49] *TMS* III.5.1 (pp. 162–163).   [50] *TMS* III.5.2 (p. 163).

in a book written to demonstrate the role of sentiment in social coordination. Smith's tone intensified as he reflected further on ordinary people and the social consequences of their limited moral resolve. He insisted that "the very existence of human society ... would crumble into nothing" if "mankind were not generally impressed with a reverence for those important rules of conduct."[51] Smith's anxiety about this was sufficiently acute that he added yet another chapter in which he "further enhanced" the observance of moral rules by linking them with "the commands and laws of the Deity," who will "finally reward the obedient, and punish the transgressors of their duty."[52] At this point in Smith's argument, Panoptic surveillance has become truly all-seeing, swarming around us in every possible dimension of our lives. As we have seen, the ordinary person in Smith's theory is under the continual eye of his neighbor (sympathy); he hears the voice of his neighbors resonating in his soul, disciplining him from within (the impartial spectator, understood as a socialized conscience). And now too, "the eye ... of God" – the "great avenger of injustice."[53] A vengeful God "enhances" rule-following and protects society from disintegration:

When the general rules which determine the merit and demerit of actions, come thus to be regarded as the laws of an All-powerful Being, who watches over our conduct, and who, in a life to come, will reward the observance, and punish the breach of them; they necessarily acquire a new sacredness from this consideration ... The idea that, however we may escape the observation of man, or be placed above the reach of human punishment, yet we are always acting under the eye, and exposed to the punishment of God, the great avenger of injustice, is a motive capable of restraining the most headstrong passions.[54]

When moral rules are shrouded as divine transgression is demonized. "The very thought of disobedience appears to involve in it the most shocking impropriety."[55]

Passages like these have inspired much reflection on Smith's relation to religion and God. At moments Smith sounds rather sincere, as if the general rules originate in a theistic sense from belief in God. Indeed, in his chapter title Smith asserted that the general rules of morality are "*justly* regarded as the Laws of the Deity," insisting later that this "can be doubted of by nobody who believes his existence."[56] He frequently claimed that we "co-operate with the Deity" and "advance ... the plan of Providence" when we act according to the "dictates of our moral faculties."[57] He often characterized man as God's

---

[51] *TMS* III.5.2 (p. 163).   [52] *TMS* III.5 (pp. 161–170); and *TMS* III.5.3 (p. 163).
[53] *TMS* III.5.12 (p. 170).   [54] *TMS* III.5.12 (p. 170).   [55] *TMS* III.5.12 (p. 170).
[56] *TMS* III.5.12 (p. 170).   [57] *TMS* III.5.7 (p. 166).

"vicegerent" on earth "to superintend the behaviour of his brethren."[58] Smith's affinity with natural religion comes through clearly in such passages. That God has so ordered things in nature with an intention to promote human happiness, that things "divine" and "natural" are interchangeable in this sense, is a theme that runs like a red thread through the book, sustaining Smith's most famous idea about spontaneous order.[59] But none of this overrides Smith's basic assertion in the *Moral Sentiments* that man's moral sentiments are sociologically rooted. All Smith was really saying here is that philosophy can "recommend" the "opinion" that God's will is compatible with our moral sentiments and the general rules that flow from them.[60] He was not starting theistically from God's will to establish our moral sentiments and general rules; rather, he started by positing the sentiments and rules and then made a philosophical argument that it is natural and reasonable for us to believe that God intended them and will punish their violation:

This reverence is still further enhanced by an opinion which is first impressed by nature, and afterwards confirmed by reasoning and philosophy, that those important rules of morality are the commands and laws of the Deity, who will finally reward the obedient, and punish the transgressors of their duty.[61]

Moreover, recall that this entire discussion about divine law follows on a lengthy meditation on the general lack of moral stability among ordinary folk. Read in this light, Smith was actually making (what today might seem like) a rather cynical sociological observation about the utility of belief, about the social benefits of encouraging simple, God-fearing people to *regard* the general rules of morality as the laws of a vengeful God. Why else would he emphasize man's "natural fear" of "mysterious beings" and "unknown intelligences."[62]

---

[58] *TMS* III.2.31 (p. 130).
[59] The classic statement: Jacob Viner, *The Role of Providence in the Social Order*. See also Otteson, *Marketplace of Life*; Richard A. Kleer, "Final Causes in Adam Smith's *Theory of Moral Sentiments*," *Journal of the History of Philosophy*, vol. 33, no. 2 (1995), pp. 275–300; "The Role of Teleology in Adam Smith's *Wealth of Nations*," *History of Economics Review*, vol. 31 (2000), pp. 14–29; and Lisa Hill, "The Hidden Theology of Adam Smith," *European Journal of the History of Economic Thought*, vol. 8, no. 1 (2001), pp. 1–29. Peter Minowitz, in *Profits, Priests and Princes*, characterizes this move of replacing the revelationary or biblical "form" of the "moral mechanism" with a "natural form" (pp. 47 and 208) as an "emancipation from religion," giving far too little validity I think not only to the influence of natural theology in the *Moral Sentiments*, but also to the religious character of modern secularization itself. Minowitz relies far too heavily on the absence of "biblicism" and Augustinianism in Smith's texts (esp. pp. 141–157). He dismisses any "religiosity" in the *TMS* as "insincere," reflecting most likely Smith's "concern" in old age "with avoiding notoriety for religious unorthodoxy" (p. 188).
[60] *TMS* III.5.3 (p. 163).   [61] *TMS* III.5.3 (p. 163).   [62] *TMS* III.5.3–4 (pp. 163–164).

How vain, how absurd would it be for man, either to oppose or to neglect the commands that were laid upon him by Infinite Wisdom, and Infinite Power![63]

One senses a profound restlessness in Smith's successive presentation of chapters in Part III, which began with a description of conscience with which only wise and just men are able fully to identify (III.3); proceeded by fortifying conscience with a rationalistic discussion of moral rules intended to combat intransigent self-love and self-deceit among ordinary people (III.4); and ended up resorting to the "Infinite Wisdom and Infinite Power!" of God's will to terrify ordinary, God-fearing people into submission (III.5).

I turn next to Smith's thoughts about Augustinian and Stoic perfectionism, for it was in the course of describing and then ultimately rejecting them that Smith most clearly articulated his own practical morality.

NEO-AUGUSTINIANISM PERFECTIONISM

Smith rejected the "ascetic doctrine" of Christian moralists like à Kempis and Pascal who "placed virtue in the entire extirpation and annihilation of all our passions,"[64] who praised "the solitary monk in his cell, obliged to mortify the flesh and to subject it to the spirit ... supported by the hope of an assured recompense, and by the secret unction of that grace which softens the yoke."[65] As à Kempis put it in 1413 in a chapter of *The Imitation of Christ* entitled "On the Love of Solitude and Silence":

No one is worthy of heavenly comfort, unless they have diligently exercised themselves in holy contrition. If you desire heartfelt contrition, enter your room, and shut out the clamor of the world, as it is written, "commune with your own heart, and in your chamber, and be still" (Ps. iv, 4; Isa. xxvi, 20). Within your cell you will discover what you will only too often lose abroad.[66]

More influential among Smith's intellectual milieu was Blaise Pascal who insisted that any endeavor to endow worldly human activity with religious or moral significance was hypocrisy, merely a disguise for *amour-propre*, a futile attempt to escape original sin through *divertissement* in society rather than to confront it with self-knowledge in solitude. In his *Pensées* in 1660, Pascal wrote:

---

[63] *TMS* III.5.12 (p. 170).   [64] *TMS* VII.ii.4.12 (p. 313).   [65] *TMS* III.2.34 (p. 133).

[66] Thomas à Kempis, *The Imitation of Christ*, trans. Leo Sherley-Price (London: Penguin, 1952), I.xxi (p. 51).

If a man were happy, he would be the more so, the less he was diverted, like the Saints and God. – Yes; but is it not to be happy to have a faculty of being amused by diversion? – No; for that comes from elsewhere and from without, and is thus dependent, and therefore subject to be disturbed by a thousand accidents, which bring inevitable griefs.[67]

Augustinians maintained that all goodness is grounded in the love of God – and that any act of generosity or public-spiritedness motivated by something less pure was a vain attempt to purchase salvation.[68] As Smith described the ascetic position:

All affections for particular objects, ought to be extinguished in our breast, and one great affection take the place of all others, the love of the Deity, the desire of rendering ourselves agreeable to him, and of directing our conduct, in every respect according to his will. We ought not to be grateful from gratitude, we ought not to be charitable from humanity, we ought not to be public-spirited from the love of our country, nor generous and just from the love of mankind. The sole principle and motive of our conduct in the performance of all those different duties, ought to be a sense that god has commanded us to perform them.[69]

Smith further described the severity of the ascetic position:

It is this spirit, however, which, while it has reserved the celestial regions for monks and friars, or for those whose conduct and conversation resembled those of monks and friars, has condemned to the infernal all the heroes, all the states-men and lawgivers, all the poets and philosophers of former ages; all those who have invented, improved, or excelled in the arts which contribute to the sub-sistence, to the conveniency, or to the ornament of human life; all the great protectors, instructors, and benefactors of mankind; all those to whom our natural sense of praise-worthiness forces us to ascribe the highest merit and most exalted virtue.[70]

An interesting oddity in the history of philosophy is the extent that nihilistic doctrines so often resemble ascetic perfectionism in their practical effects. Smith observed that Bernard Mandeville's "licentious" system seemed to be founded on this very ascetic tradition of neo-Augustinianism. Smith recog-nized a profound irony in Mandeville's logic that eludes many interpreters still: that Mandeville's thought arose conceptually from a rigoristic

---

[67] Blaise Pascal, *Penseés*, trans. W. F. Trotter (New York: E. P. Dutton, 1958), #170 (p. 49).
[68] For an excellent discussion of this rigoristic tradition, see Anthony Levi, *French Moralists: The Theory of the Passions, 1585–1659* (Oxford: Oxford University Press, 1964), pp. 202–233.
[69] *TMS* III.6.1 (p. 171).   [70] *TMS* III.2.35 (p. 134).

position.[71] He recognized that Pascallian rigorism had given rise to a new kind of secular pessimism in modern thought that became "licentious" when it was put into practice.

Some popular ascetic doctrines which had been current before his time, and which placed virtue in the entire extirpation and annihilation of all our passions, were the real foundation of this licentious system.[72]

Indeed, Smith often drew parallels between the "whining and melancholy moralism" of Pascal and the Hobbesists of his own century, Bernard Mandeville in particular.[73] He devoted an entire section in the *Moral Sentiments* (VII.ii.4) to the task of differentiating his project from Mandevillean "licentiousness," and the Pascallian "asceticism" on which it rested.[74] Like Pascal, Mandeville took "away altogether the distinction between vice and virtue" and held all of human conduct to a moral standard of "complete self-denial": "Wherever our reserve with regard to pleasure falls short of the most ascetic abstinence, he treats it as gross luxury and sensuality."[75] The only real difference between Pascal and Mandeville is that while both saw all behavior short of perfection as an illusion of virtue, "a concealed indulgence of our passions,"[76] a "mere cheat and imposition upon mankind,"[77] Pascal condemned it as *hypocrisie* and *divertissement*, while the crafty Mandeville put that very hypocrisy to work to contain base egoism in the commercial world. Indeed, Mandeville argued that the hypocrisy of social posturing was the only real alternative in a thriving modern state for its ability to emulate the effects of genuine ethical motivation without stifling human industriousness.[78] If "Jove" would enter the Mandevillean bee-hive to "fling down" the "mask" of

---

[71] See, for example, *TMS* VII.ii.4.12 (pp. 312–313). For an excellent introduction to how eighteenth-century secular literature had co-opted a religious orientation to man's "inner corruption," see Lovejoy, *Reflections*, esp. pp. 14–21. On Mandeville's "rigorism" and "Augustinianism," see Viner, "Mandeville," pp. 179–182; Lovejoy, *Reflections*, Lectures III–V, *passim*; Dickey, "Mandeville"; Shelley Burtt, *Virtue Transformed: Political Argument in England, 1688–1740* (Cambridge: Cambridge University Press, 1992), esp. pp. 133–135; and Thomas Horne, "Envy and Commercial Society." Horne's essay has the virtue of distinguishing Mandeville's rigorous "two-fold" ethical system from the "three-fold" systems of Shaftesbury, Hutcheson and Smith. Mandeville's system, in other words, fails to concede a "morally neutral" space (pp. 561–562). For a similar formulation, see Lawrence E. Klein's discussion of how Shaftesbury had aligned Hobbes' "Epicureanism" and LaRochefoucauld's "Augustinian Jansenism," in *Shaftesbury*, pp. 63–64. Most recently, see Pierre Force, *Self-Interest before Adam Smith: A Genealogy of Economic Science* (Cambridge: Cambridge University Press, 2003), pp. 48–57, who argues that Augustinianism and Epicureanism cohere around the idea that "each is led by his own pleasure" (p. 57).

[72] *TMS* VII.ii.4 (p. 313, and more generally pp. 306–317). See also *TMS* III.2.27 (p. 127).

[73] *TMS* III.3.9 (p. 139); *TMS* VII.ii.4.12 (pp. 312–313).

[74] *TMS* VII.ii.4 (pp. 306–317); See also *TMS* III.2.27 (p. 127).

[75] *TMS* VII.ii.4.11 (p. 312).   [76] *TMS* VII.ii.4.11 (p. 312).   [77] *TMS* VII.ii.4.12 (p. 313).

[78] *T MS* VII.ii.4.11–13 (pp. 311–313).

"hypocrisy," industry would collapse, and the honest bees "would be forced to take up a more humble residence in a hollow tree trunk."[79] For Smith, this was the "ingenious sophistry of his reasoning."[80]

It was easy for Dr. Mandeville to prove, first, that this entire conquest [of passion] never actually took place among men; and secondly, that, if it was to take place universally, it would be pernicious to society, by putting an end to all industry and commerce, and in a manner to the whole business of human life. By the first of these propositions he seemed to prove that there was no real virtue ... and by the second, that private vices were public benefits, since without them no society could prosper or flourish.[81]

Now, given Francis Hutcheson's acerbic condemnation of Mandeville,[82] there is again more than a little irony that Smith discovered great similarities between the two. Smith's reference to "whining and melancholy moralists ... who regard as impious the natural joy of prosperity"[83] echoes his rejection of Hutchesonian benevolence, in which the "mixture of any selfish motive, like that of a baser alloy, diminished or took away altogether the merit which would otherwise have belonged to any action."[84] Certainly Hutcheson didn't take the Mandevillean leap into "licentiousness," but he agreed that "virtue must consist in pure and disinterested benevolence alone."[85] Smith explained:

Dr. Hutcheson was so far from allowing self-love to be in any case a motive of virtuous actions, that even a regard to the pleasure of self-approbation, to the comfortable applause of our own consciences, according to him, diminished the merit of a benevolent action.[86]

Smith proceeded to reject his teacher's otherwise "amiable system" for its unacceptable dualism. I cited this passage earlier to demonstrate Smith's emphasis on middling morality. Here we have it now it in its fuller context as a refutation of Hutcheson:

so this system seems to have the ... defect, of not sufficiently explaining from whence arises our approbation of the inferior virtues of prudence, vigilance, circumspection, temperance, constancy, firmness ... Benevolence may, perhaps, be the sole principle of action in the Deity, and there are several, not improbable,

[79] Mandeville, *Fable*, vol. I, pp. 33 and 35. See *TMS* IV.1.10–11 (pp. 183–187).
[80] *TMS* VII.ii.4.11 (p. 312).
[81] *TMS* VII.ii.4.12 (p. 313). Of course, Smith also resisted moral rigorism for this reason, since it would repress the "little affairs of this world" – the "business of society" (see *TMS* III.2.31–32 (pp. 128–131)). For a similar formulation, see Hume, *Enquiry*, Conclusion, pp. 73–74.
[82] Francis Hutcheson, *Reflections upon Laughter and Remarks upon the 'Fable of the Bees'*, in *Collected Works of Francis Hutcheson*, 7 vols. (Hildesheim: G. Olds, 1971), vol. 7: *Opera Minora*, pp. 144–156.
[83] *TMS* III.3.9 (p. 139). [84] *TMS* VII.ii.3.6 (p. 302). [85] *TMS* VII.ii.3.6 (p. 302).
[86] *TMS* VII.ii.3.13 (p. 303).

arguments which tend to persuade us that it is so. It is not easy to conceive what other motive an independent and all-perfect Being, who stands in need of nothing external, and whose happiness is complete in himself, can act from. But whatever may be the case with the Deity, so imperfect a creature as man, the support of whose existence requires so many things external to him, must often act from many other motives. The conditions of human nature were peculiarly hard, if those affections, which, by the very nature of our being, ought frequently to influence our conduct, could upon no occasion appear virtuous, or deserve esteem and commendation from any body.[87]

If Smith's rejection of Augustinian Christianity – Pascallian, Mandevillian (by derivation) or Hutchesonian – constituted one wave of his assault on rigorism, his rejection of Stoicism surely constituted the other.[88] "Both," he insisted, "have carried their doctrines a good deal beyond the just standard of nature and propriety."[89]

SMITH AND STOIC COSMOPOLITANISM

The influence of Stoicism on Smith's thought is well acknowledged.[90] Here I am particularly interested in Smith's conflicted orientation to Stoic *oikeiōsis*. The Stoics argued that human affection is oriented spatially around the self, and that it naturally weakens progressively as its object radiates outward, further and further from the self. However, the center-piece of Stoic perfectionism was an imperative to collapse the natural concentric structure of our affections. This was what the Stoic cosmo-politan project was ultimately about. While Christian ethics sought "to increase our sensibility to the interests of others" and "have us feel for others as we naturally feel for ourselves," Stoicism on the other hand sought to "diminish" our self-interest, and to "have us feel for ourselves as we naturally feel for others."[91] The end result was perhaps not easily distinguishable – the circles collapse in both cases – but according to Smith Christianity sought to accomplish this end by augmenting

[87] *TMS* VII.ii.3.15 (p. 304); *TMS* VII.ii.3.18 (p. 305).

[88] Indeed, he often linked the rigorist strains of Christianity and Stoicism in just this way. See notably *TMS* III.3.8–21 (pp. 139–145). See also the Stoical quality of his description of ascetic Christianity at *TMS* III.6.1 (p. 171), and, inversely, the ascetic Christian cadence of his description of Stoic cosmopolitanism ("universal benevolence") at *TMS* VI.ii.3 (pp. 235–237).

[89] *TMS* III.3.8 (p. 139). That Smith's arguments against Christianity and Stoicism are cut from the same cloth, see Rothschild, *Economic Sentiments*, p. 133.

[90] See "Introduction" chapter, n. 16, above, for a list of those who have addressed the Stoic connection in some depth.

[91] *TMS* III.3.8 (p. 139). Compare *TMS* I.i.5.5 (p. 25): "As to love our neighbor as we love ourselves is the great law of Christianity, so it is the great precept of nature [read: Stoicism] to love ourselves only as we love our neighbor, or what comes to the same thing, as our neighbor is capable of loving us."

beneficence; Stoicism by extirpating self-preference. The Stoics believed that mature, rational individuals should cultivate apathy toward the familiar and all that was most natural to them, and ultimately become "citizens of the world." I demonstrate here that Smith very deliberately appropriated the concentric structure of Stoic *oikeiōsis* in his extended discussion of human beneficence in Part VI.ii of the *Moral Sentiments* – but only to turn the theory decisively *on its head* for its unrealistic perfectionism.

Because Hierocles' account of *oikeiōsis* in the second century AD is magnificently clear, but largely unfamiliar to non-specialists who, like Smith, tend to be more familiar with Cicero's well-known account of the "degrees of fellowship" in *De Officiis*,[92] I begin my discussion by citing at length several portions of the Papyrus fragment in which Hierocles' account is found:

Each of us is as it were entirely encompassed by many circles, some smaller, others larger, the latter enclosing the former on the basis of their different and unequal dispositions relative to each other. The first and closest circle is the one which a person has drawn as though around a centre, his own mind. This circle encloses the body and anything taken for the sake of the body. For it is virtually the smallest circle, and almost touches the centre itself. Next, the second one further removed from the centre but enclosing the first circle; this contains parents, siblings, wife and children. The third one has in it uncles and aunts, grandparents, nephews, nieces, and cousins. The next circle includes the other relatives, and this is followed by the circle of local residents, then the circle of fellow-tribesmen, next that of fellow-citizens, and then in the same way the circle of people from neighboring towns, and the circle of fellow-countrymen. The outermost and largest circle, which encompasses all the rest, is that of the whole human race.[93]

The Stoics posited this concentric structure both for descriptive purposes and for normative cosmopolitan purposes. On the one hand they offered an empirical portrait of human affection, describing the natural ties of ordinary people as a function of proximity and familiarity. But they also argued that

[92] Cicero, *Of Duties*, ed. M. T. Griffin and E. M. Atkins (Cambridge: Cambridge University Press, 1991), Book I, 46–59 (pp. 20–25).

[93] For Hierocles' fragment, see A. A. Long and D. N. Sedley, *The Hellenistic philosophers*, 2 vols. (Cambridge: Cambridge University Press, 1987), 57.G (vol. I, pp. 349–350; vol. II, pp. 347–348). For discussion of Hierocles and *oikeiōsis*, see Brad Inwood, "Hierocles: Theory and Argument in the Second Century AD," *Oxford Studies in Ancient Philosophy* (Oxford: Oxford University Press, 1984), vol. 2, pp. 151–183; Engberg-Pedersen, "Discovering the Good," esp. pp. 175–177; Julia Annas, *The Morality of Happiness* (Oxford: Oxford University Press, 1993), pp. 262–276; Martha Nussbaum, *The Therapy of Desire*, pp. 341–344; Martha Nussbaum, "Kant and Stoic Cosmopolitanism," *Journal of Political Philosophy* (1995); and Gisela Striker, "The Role of *Oikeiōsis* in Stoic Ethics," in *Essays on Hellenistic Epistemology and Ethics* (Cambridge: Cambridge University Press, 1996), pp. 281–297.

mature moral agents will cultivate apathy: they will overcome the natural pull of human affection which develops through familiarity, and collapse the circles inward, concentrically toward the center, so that humanity *writ large* ultimately makes the same ethical claims as those with more immediate connections. Hierocles counseled:

Once these [circles] have all been surveyed, it is the task of a well tempered man, in his proper treatment of each group, to draw the circles together somehow towards the centre, and to keep zealously transferring those from the enclosing circles into the enclosed ones ... It is incumbent on us to respect people from the third circle as if they were those from the second, and again to respect our other relatives as if they were those from the third circle. For although the greater distance in blood will remove some affection, we must try hard to assimilate them. The right point will be reached if, through our own initiative, we reduce the distance of the relationship with each person.[94]

The Stoic activity of cultivating apathy and contracting the circles is like collapsing a telescope. One familiarizes oneself with people in the outermost circle by conceptualizing them as people in the smaller circle contained within it, and so forth; and repeats the process over and over until all of humanity rests inside the inner circle accompanying the agent himself. Once a moral agent completes this process the Stoics considered him a "citizen of the world," a cosmopolitan.[95]

Smith's appropriation of Stoic *oikeiōsis* in the *Moral Sentiments* is particularly clear in Section IV.ii. There, in a sequence of three chapters, Smith demonstrated "our very limited powers of beneficence" by deliberately reproducing the concentric pattern of human affection.[96] Chapter 1 examines the order in which "*Individuals* are recommended by Nature to our care and attention";[97] Chapter 2 radiates outward to consider the "order in which *Societies* are by nature recommended to our Beneficence";[98] and Chapter 3 radiates further yet to consider "*Universal* benevolence" which, we shall see, Smith applauds for its beauty, but ultimately brackets from his discussion of practical morality.[99] The same concentric structure holds true for the internal organization of the chapters. As we might expect, the first chapter on "Individuals" begins, and thus Smith's Stoic argument about the circles of familiarity and affection begins, with a discussion of a man's relation *to himself*. Smith claimed:

---

[94] Long and Sedley, *Hellenistic Philosophers* 57.G (vol. I, pp. 349–350; vol. II, pp. 347–348).
[95] See *TMS* III.3.11 (p. 140).   [96] *TMS* VI.ii (pp. 218–237).   [97] *TMS* VII.ii.1 (pp. 219–227).
[98] *TMS* VII.ii.2 (pp. 227–234).   [99] *TMS* VII.ii.3 (pp. 235–237). See also *TMS* I.ii.4.1 (pp. 38–39).

Every man, as the Stoics used to say, is first and principally recommended to his own care; and every man is certainly, in every respect, fitter and abler to take care of himself than of any other person. Every man feels his own pleasures and his own pains more sensibly than those of other people.[100]

This of course is a Smith all too familiar to economists who have reduced his thought to selfishness and egoism. Earlier in the book, I addressed the economistic distortion of Smith's thought that prevailed in the nineteenth century and throughout much of the twentieth. These passages on beneficence reveal just how distorted the "economic man" reading of Smith really is. Surely Smith appropriated the Stoic assumption that caring for oneself is natural and appropriate for human beings. But this is hardly the whole of human motivation for Smith, or the essence of our social constitution. We recall the famous opening paragraph of the *Moral Sentiments* in which Smith denied the supposition of man's utter selfishness and asserted that there are "principles in man's nature which interest him in the fortune of others."[101] I argue here that Smith's Stoic discussion of beneficence at Section VI.ii of the *Moral Sentiments* should be read as a spatial exploration of his well-known opening statement about man's social nature, which he directed to Hobbes and his followers. Indeed all of Section VI.ii is devoted to describing the natural gradation or "distribution" of our natural interests in the fortune of others. Smith clearly defined his task: "In the present section I shall only endeavour to explain the foundation of that order which nature seems to have traced out for the distribution of our good offices."[102]

Following his Stoic discussion of the self that is situated at the concentric center of this "order," Smith proceeded in Section VI.ii.1 to radiate his circles outward, justifying his arrangement not according to the force of blood (which "I am afraid, exists no-where but in tragedies and romances"[103]) but with the centripetal pull of "habitual sympathy."[104] The parallel here with the Stoic idea of familiarity is striking, especially since both characterize human affection as derivative, as emerging from physical closeness and intimacy. Smith wrote: "Relations being usually placed in situations which naturally create this habitual sympathy, it is expected that a suitable degree of affection should take place among them."[105] Recalling the ancient *oikos* and the familiarity generated within it, the circles situated closest in proximity to the self and therefore most affectively compelling for Smith encompassed family members of varying degrees of intimacy – those who are "naturally the objects of his warmest affections" and "upon whose happiness or misery his

---

[100] *TMS* VI.ii.1.1 (p. 219).   [101] *TMS* I.i.1 (p. 9).   [102] *TMS* VI.ii.intro.2 (p. 218).
[103] *TMS* VI.ii.1.11 (p. 222).   [104] *TMS* I.ii.1.7 (p. 220).   [105] *TMS* I.ii.1.7 (p. 220).

conduct must have the greatest influence"[106] – and eventually radiated outward, with weakening intensity, to business colleagues and neighbors, and eventually in Chapter 2, to the various and sometimes competing "orders and societies" and "states," "sovereignties," "governments," "nations," "countries" to which we belong.[107] For Smith the affective pull of these collectivities rests contingently on the connection they have to those we love and care about in a primary, more "natural" way, and who are best situated to benefit from our interest and care:

The state or sovereignty in which we have been born and educated, and under the protection of which we continue to live, is, in ordinary cases, the greatest society upon whose happiness or misery, our good or bad conduct can have much influence. It is, accordingly by nature, most strongly recommended to us. Not only we ourselves, but all the objects of our kindest affections, our children, our parents, our relations, our friends, our benefactors, all those whom we naturally love and revere the most, are commonly comprehended within it; and their prosperity and safety depend in some measure upon its prosperity and safety. It is by nature, therefore, endeared to us, not only by all our selfish, but by all our private benevolent affections.[108]

The outermost circle, which makes the very weakest claims on our "limited power of beneficence" encompass humanity as a whole – the "care ... of all rational and sensible beings."[109] Our "good-will is circumscribed by no boundary" for Smith "but may embrace the immensity of the universe."[110] Our ability to act on that good-will, however, is naturally quite limited. As such, Smith leaves the "administration" of universal benevolence to God.

Thus, in Section VI.ii of the *Moral Sentiments* Smith seems to have embraced Stoic *oikeiōsis* as an empirical fact. As Jacob Viner once observed, "spatial distance operates to intensify psychological distance" for Smith:

---

[106] *TMS* VI ii.1.2 (p. 219).
[107] A note on Smith's language in *TMS* VI.ii.2 (pp. 227–234). In the chapter title, Smith refers in general to "Societies." Within the chapter itself, he often invokes the phrase "orders and societies" to refer to (what we think of today as) sub-national affiliations. When he speaks of civil faction and fanaticism in "times of public discontent" he tends to refer to such divisions as "parties." Also included in Smith's discussion of "Societies" are the "states," "sovereignties," "governments," "nations," and "countries" to which we belong. He uses all these concepts in the chapter to refer to what we would characterize today as the modern nation-state – though it is very interesting to note that he tends to invoke the more affectively charged concepts of "nation" and "country" when reflecting on the problems of prejudice, jealousy and hatred toward other nation-states, while preferring "state," "sovereignty" or "government" when discussing more sober obligations. I will have more to say about Smith's thoughts on the pathologies of nationalism in Chapter 6.
[108] *TMS* VI.ii.2.2 (p. 227).   [109] *TMS* VI.ii.3 (pp. 235–237), at VI.ii.3.1 (p. 235).
[110] *TMS* VI.ii.3.1 (p. 235).

the sentiments weaken progressively as one moves from one's immediate family to one's intimate friends, to one's neighbors in a small community, to fellow-citizens in a great city, to members in general of one's own country, to foreigners, to mankind taken in the large, to the inhabitants, if any, of distant planets.[111]

But beyond this point of empirical congruity with the Stoics, however, Smith diverged sharply. For Smith Stoic *oikeiōsis* seems to have captured so precisely the way human affection operates in the world that as a practical moralist he refused to make the Stoic leap into cosmopolitan deconstruction. *Oikeiōsis* was a compelling representation of the human condition that should be accommodated by moral philosophy – and not a mere accident of birth to be dismissed as morally irrelevant. Smith argued that human experience was staunchly resistant to the artificial manipulations of reason, that affection could not be shifted about willy-nilly from object to object at will. In this, Smith agreed with Cicero that fellowships based on "familiarity" (*familiaritate*) were stronger and more resilient than any other.[112] Most people were incapable of cultivating "apathy" or "insensibility" toward the familiar. Nor, as we shall discover, was it possible for them to experience anything *but* a heightened apathy and insensibility for those who were far away and unfamiliar to them.

I continue my exploration of Smith's conflicted orientation to Stoic *oikeiōsis* by considering his elaborate discussion of apathy in his lengthy account of Stoic moral philosophy in Book VII of the *Moral Sentiments*:

By the perfect apathy which it prescribes to us, by endeavoring, not merely to moderate, but to eradicate all our private, partial, and selfish affections, by suffering us to feel for whatever can befall ourselves, our friends, our country, not even the sympathetic and reduced passions of the impartial spectator, it endeavors to render us altogether indifferent and unconcerned in the success or miscarriage of every thing which Nature has prescribed to us as the proper business and occupation of our lives.[113]

What stands out in this passage is Smith's assertion that our "private, partial and selfish affections" are natural, and that by "prescribing" us to "eradicate" them, Stoicism asks us to become "indifferent and unconcerned" toward everything that is most natural to us. We have two conflicting imperatives here; two voices; two "prescriptions" – that of "Nature" and that of (Stoic) philosophy, each asserting very different claims about what man should be. The first demands that we live according to our affections and the local concerns that they stimulate; the second that we live according

[111] Viner, *Providence*, pp. 80–81.   [112] Cicero, *On Duties* I (p. 23).   [113] *TMS* VII.ii.1.46 (pp. 292–293).

to a sort of rational indifference that turns its back on natural affection. The first tends toward localism; the second finds time and place a mere accident of birth and morally irrelevant. Whether or not interpreters today would find these binaries in Smith's narrative to be rigid and artificial, Smith's orientation in this debate, as he understood and articulated it, was clear. While he accepted *oikeiōsis* as an empirical fact about human affection, he turned sharply from Stoic cosmopolitan teleology which advocated a revolt against nature. The attempt to overcome the natural structure of human affection and collapse the circles toward the center was not only psychologically improbable for most moral agents, but ultimately, for this reason, morally objectionable.

Smith argued that "affection" is neither a product of accident or reason, but rather the result of "habitual sympathy," which is a prephilosophical, sociological phenomenon that takes place in a context of human relation. Smith's view of affection in the following passage is entirely consistent with his anthropological description of how moral communities emerge and perpetuate in shared spaces over time, which I explored at length in Chapters 2 and 3. Indeed it is not surprising that he attributes affection here to a kind of sympathy that has become "habitual" through repetition:

> *What is called affection, is in reality nothing but habitual sympathy.* Our concern in the happiness or misery of those who are the objects of what we call our affections; our desire to promote the one, and to prevent the other; *are either the actual feeling of that habitual sympathy, or the necessary consequences of that feeling.* Relations being usually placed in situations which naturally create this habitual sympathy, it is expected that a suitable degree of affection should take place among them. We generally find that it actually does take place; we therefore naturally expect that it should.[114]

Though he focused on habitual sympathy in passages like this, Smith didn't entirely neglect other bases for affection. He recognized for example that we *naturally* feel attachments to those whose character is virtuous,[115] to those from whom we have previously experienced beneficence,[116] and to those whose personal condition is either extraordinarily great or impoverished.[117] Surely these criteria share something in common with what we might describe as the "rationalized" bases of loyalty in Cicero's *De Officiis*.[118] But Smith's overriding assertion was that our affections were driven most powerfully by our habits sympathizing with those nearest us in the *oikos*.

[114] *TMS* I.ii.1.7 (p. 220), emphasis added.   [115] *TMS* VI.ii.1.18 (pp. 224–225).
[116] *TMS* VI.ii.1.19 (p. 225).   [117] *TMS* VI.ii.1.20–21 (pp. 225–226).
[118] Cicero, *De Officiis*, I.45–59. Thanks to Martha Nussbaum for this point.

One recalls Rousseau's account of familial love in the *Second Discourse* – that "the habit of living together gave rise to the sweetest sentiments known to men: conjugal love" and "paternal love."[119] Similarly, Smith illustrated the affective pull of habitual sympathy by offering the example of a father and son, or a brother and sister, who have been estranged by some accident during what would have been the formative years of their relationship. Despite their most fervent hopes and efforts they will never recover what has been lost to them. Never will they replicate "that cordial satisfaction, that delicious sympathy, that confidential openness and ease, which naturally take place in the conversation of those who have lived long and familiarly with one another."[120]

But the Stoics maintained that with proper effort, with the proper cultivation and use of our reason, we could overcome the affective partiality generated by living with others in close proximity, and that we could cultivate something resembling familiarity with those far removed from our daily intercourses. Again, Hierocles' fragment is instructive, for he described how the "well tempered man" goes about "contracting" the circles, drawing them together, and thus in the same moment expanding his "respect" and "affection" for those who are spatially removed. He emphasized our "initiative" in contracting the circles – that it requires effort, that we must "try hard" to overcome our partiality toward those who are near and to extend our "affection" to those who are further removed from us. The Stoics recognized the work involved, and that the hurdles were very high.

In this Smith wholly agreed – which is precisely why he maintained that cosmopolitanism was possible for and therefore appropriate only to the Stoic sage, he who lives his life in perfect *apatheia*, in perfect tranquility, transparency and happiness, consistently sacrificing his own "private, partial and selfish affections" for the greater good of the universe. Smith described the apathy of the Stoic sage:

He is at all times willing that his own private interest should be sacrificed to the public interest of his own particular order or society. He is at all times willing, too, that the interest of this order or society should be sacrificed to the greater interest of the state or sovereignty, of which it is only a subordinate part. He should, therefore, be equally willing that all those inferior interests should be sacrificed to the greater interest of the universe, to the interest of that great society of all sensible and

[119] Rousseau, *Second Discourse*, p. 63.

[120] *TMS* VI.ii.1.8 (p. 221). This surely explains Smith's case against sending children to boarding schools in England and on the continent, a practice that had become fashionable among urbane eighteenth-century Scots (*TMS* VI.ii.1.10 (p. 222)). I will address this issue further in ch. 5.

intelligent beings, of which God himself is the immediate administrator and director. If he is deeply impressed with the habitual and thorough conviction that this benevolent and all-wise Being can admit into the system of his government, no partial evil which is not necessary for the universal good, he must consider all the misfortunes which may befall himself, his friends, his society, or his country, as necessary for the prosperity of the universe, and therefore as what he ought, not only to submit to with resignation, but as what he himself, if he had known all the connexions and dependencies of things, ought sincerely and devoutly to have wished for.[121]

In his resignation, this "wise and virtuous man" is a "citizen of the world." He regards himself

not as something separated and detached, but as a citizen of the world, a member of the vast commonwealth of nature. To the interest of this great community, he ought at all times be willing that his own little interest should be sacrificed. Whatever concerns himself, ought to affect him no more than whatever concerns any other equally important part of this immense system.[122]

As we saw earlier in Chapter 3, Smith admired those who exhibited great acts of beneficence, especially toward strangers.[123] And he routinely expressed disgust with the "hard-hearted," those who "shut their breasts against compassion, and refuse to relieve the misery of their fellow creatures, when they can with the greatest ease."[124] Indeed, such "hardness of heart ... excludes [a man] from the friendship of all the world."[125] But he found the severity of Stoic cosmopolitanism morally objectionable, because most of us are entirely incapable of achieving the unnatural distance toward familiarity upon which Smith believed Stoic ends ultimately rested. "The Stoical philosophy," Smith wrote,

teaches us to interest ourselves earnestly and anxiously in no events, external to the good order of our own minds, to the propriety of our own choosing and rejecting, except in those which concern a department where we neither have nor ought to have any sort of management or direction, the department of the great Superintendent of the universe. By the perfect apathy which it prescribes to us, by endeavouring, not merely to moderate, but to eradicate all our private, partial, and selfish affections, by suffering us to feel for whatever can befall ourselves, our friends, our country, not even the sympathetic and reduced passions of the impartial spectator, it endeavours to render us altogether indifferent and unconcerned in the success or miscarriage of every thing which Nature has prescribed to us as the proper business and occupation of our lives.[126]

---

[121] *TMS* VI.ii.3.3 (pp. 235–236).   [122] *TMS* III.3.11 (p. 140).   [123] *TMS* I.ii.4.1 (pp. 38–39).
[124] *TMS* II.ii.1.7 (p. 81); see also *TMS* VI.iii.15 (p. 243).   [125] *TMS* VI.iii.15 (p. 243).
[126] *TMS* VII.ii.1.46 (pp. 292–293).

The "perfect apathy" of Stoic sages requires a sensibility that eludes ordinary people affectively pulled toward the local, given over to what their own "private, partial, and selfish affections" demand. Smith agreed with Hume who observed that:

A parent flies to the relief of his child, transported by that natural sympathy which actuates him, and which affords no leisure to reflect on the sentiments or conduct of the rest of mankind in like circumstances.[127]

Smith was a "practical moralist" who embraced human limitations and imperfections, who insisted that the way we go on must serve as the basis of any plausible theory about our duties. For a practical moralist like Smith, moral philosophy needed to accommodate human passions and imperfections rather than attempt to extirpate, "eradicate," them through reason. And so, in language that echoed his rejection of ascetic Christian perfectionism, Smith lodged his complaint with the rigorism of the severe Stoic position:

As all those who had arrived at this state of perfection [perfect apathy], were equally happy; so all those who fell in the smallest degree short of it, how nearly soever they might approach to it, were equally miserable. As the man, they said, who was but an inch below the surface of the water, could no more breathe than he who was a hundred yards below it; so the man who had not completely subdued all his private, partial, and selfish passions, who had any other earnest desire but that for the universal happiness, who had not completely emerged from that abyss of misery and disorder into which his anxiety for the gratification of those private, partial, and selfish passions had involved him, could no more breathe the free air of liberty and independency, could no more enjoy the security and happiness of the wise man, than he who was most remote from that situation. As all the actions of the wise man were perfect, and equally perfect; so all those of the man who had not arrived at this supreme wisdom were faulty, and, as some Stoics pretended, equally faulty.[128]

Smith attributed this sort of "metaphysical sophism"[129] to Chrysippus, for he refused to believe that men of such "sublime eloquence" as Zeno and Cleanthes would subscribe to an imperative so "dialectical" and "scholastic" that it would equate the killing of a "cock" with the killing of one's "father," the "bursting of a bubble" with the "bursting of a world."[130] Indeed, Smith acknowledged correctly that "the Stoics in general seem to have admitted

---

[127] Hume, *Enquiry*, Appendix III, p. 93.   [128] *TMS* VII.ii.1.40 (pp. 290–291).
[129] *TMS* III.3.14 (p. 143).
[130] *TMS* VII.ii.1.39–41 (pp. 289–291). For discussion of Chrysippus and his break with the ethical thought of Zeno and Cleanthes, see generally A. A. Long, *Hellenistic Philosophy*, pp. 184–187 and 219–220; and F. H. Sandbach, *The Stoics* (Indianapolis, IN: Hackett, 1994), pp. 42–48.

that there *might* be a degree of proficiency in those who had not advanced to perfect virtue and happiness."[131] He continued:

They distributed those proficients into different classes, according to the degree of their advancement; and they called the imperfect virtues which they supposed them capable of exercising, not rectitudes, but proprieties, fitnesses, decent and becoming actions, for which a plausible or probable reason could be assigned, what Cicero expresses by the Latin word *officia*, and Seneca, I think more exactly, by that of *convenientia*. The doctrine of those perfect, but attainable virtues, seems to have constituted what we may call the practical morality of the Stoics. It is the subject of Cicero's Offices; and is said to have been that of another book written by Marcus Brutus, but which is now lost.[132]

Smith pointed specifically to the practical moralism of Cicero and Seneca, who conceded that the majority of men could coexist peaceably and cooperatively with one another somewhere between the extremes of perfect apathy and utter depravity if they lived by a code of appropriateness and performed appropriate acts, what the Greek Stoa called *kathēkonta*, and the Roman Stoa, either *officia* (Cicero) or *convenientia* (Seneca).[133] Indeed, Smith fully embraced the "middle-Stoic" distinction, as we would call it today, between virtuous acts and acts that were appropriate – in Greek Stoicism, the distinction between the *katorthōmata* and *kathōkonta*, and in Cicero's Latin appropriation of the Greek in *De Finibus*, between *recte facta* and *officia*.[134] For Smith, opening up this egalitarian middle space had become the key to social order in modern European life. Indeed, one might say that his entire project in the *Moral Sentiments* was directed toward conceptualizing this middle space. It certainly inspired his key distinction in the *Moral Sentiments* between "virtue" and "propriety" – or, to be more exact, between "the excellence of virtue" which "deserves to be admired and celebrated" and the "mere propriety" of the many which "simply deserve[s] to be approved of"

---

[131] *TMS* VII.ii.1.42 (p. 291).

[132] *TMS* VII.ii.1.42 (pp. 291–292). Incidentally, we know that Marcus Brutus' book was entitled *Peri Kathōkontos*, which, Cicero tells us in *De Finibus* III, is the Greek Stoic equivalent of his own Latin rendering of *officiis*. Cicero, *De Finibus Bonorum et Malorum*, trans. H. Rackham (Cambridge, MA: Harvard University Press), III:20 (p. 238).

[133] Waszek, "Two Concepts," *passim*; Brown, *Adam Smith's Discourse*, pp. 76–99. At least two other scholars have recognized Smith's "threefold" approach to moral philosophy, though they have not identified the opening of this space as a neo-Stoic move: Jacob Viner links it with the "tripartite" ethical character of the seventeenth-century Jansenist social theories of Pierre Nicole and Jean Domat, in "Introduction," pp. 180–182 and 186–188; while Thomas Horne in "Envy in Commercial Society," pp. 560–562, links it (mistakenly I think) with Hutcheson and (mistakenly again) with Shaftesbury's "distinction between natural affections, self-affections, and unnatural affections."

[134] Cicero, *De Finibus*, III:20 and III:24.

for its social utility.[135] For Smith, the imperfect but attainable and useful proprieties that "simply deserve to be approved of" consisted in fulfilling what our ordinary experiences recommended to us. Henry Clark put the matter as such:

> The perfect moral agent, then, is not the saint; self-denial belongs to that "ascetic" morality by which Christianity has corrupted moral philosophy in modern Europe. It is rather the one who has achieved a proper perspective on the relationship between respect for self and others.[136]

THE "HUMBLER DEPARTMENTS"

One should not conclude from the foregoing that benevolence is problematic in itself for Smith. In fact, the opposite is true: "We have always ... the strongest disposition to sympathize with the benevolent affections."

> Generosity, humanity, kindness, compassion, mutual friendship and esteem, all the social and benevolent affections, when expressed in the countenance or behaviour, even toward those who are not peculiarly connected with ourselves, please the indifferent spectator upon almost every occasion.[137]

Note that in this passage the spectator approves of benevolent affections expressed even toward strangers, toward those "not peculiarly connected with ourselves." Nevertheless, for Smith, our active duties could not exceed our "very limited powers of beneficence" – our *natural capacity to act* effectively on our benevolent affections. Smith conceived of our active duties as imperfect rather than perfect, ordinary rather than supererogatory,[138] consisting not in something as grand as caring for the happiness of the universe, but for the more modest aim of striving for the happiness of those toward whom we are naturally "partial":

---

[135] *TMS* I.i.5.6–7 (p. 25).   [136] Clark, "Conversation and Moderate Virtue," pp. 199–200.
[137] *TMS* I.ii.4.1 (pp. 38–39).
[138] On the doctrine of supererogation generally, see J. O. Urmson's seminal essay, "Saints and Heroes," in *Essays in Moral Philosophy*, ed. A. I. Melden (Seattle: University of Washington Press, 1958), pp. 198–216. See also Joel Feinberg, "Supererogation and Rules," in *Doing and Deserving: Essays in the Theory of Responsibility* (Princeton, NJ: Princeton University Press, 1970), pp. 3–24; David Heyd, *Supererogation: Its Status in Ethical Theory* (Cambridge: Cambridge University Press, 1982); and Susan Wolf, "Moral Saints," *Journal of Philosophy*, vol. 79, no. 8 (1982), pp. 419–439. Little has been written on Stoic supererogation. On the supererogatory character of Seneca's *beneficium* in the *Moral Essays*, see Heyd, *Supererogation*, pp. 40–42. That Cicero's idea of *officium perfectum* in the *De Officiis* is supererogatory, see Gregory des Jardins, "Terms of *de Officiis* in Hume and Kant," *Journal of the History of Ideas*, vol. 28 (1967), pp. 237–242, at p. 239. Vincent Hope in "Smith's Demigod," p. 162, has recognized the supererogatory elements of Smith's moral philosophy.

To man is allotted a much humbler department, but one much more suitable to the weakness of his powers, and to the narrowness of his comprehension; the care of his own happiness, of that of his family, his friends, his country.[139]

As such, Smith leaves the "administration" of universal benevolence to:

the immediate care and protection of that great, benevolent, and all-wise Being, who directs all the movements of nature; and who is determined, by his own unalterable perfections, to maintain in it, at all times, the greatest possible quantity of happiness.[140]

I have not focused in this chapter on Smith's affinities with Stoic providentialism, but his explicit appropriation here, situated at the heart of his discussion of universal benevolence in Section VI.ii, is unmistakable and noteworthy. Observe parallels with the following passage in which Smith elsewhere in the *Moral Sentiments* described the Stoic view of God's role in maintaining universal happiness:

The ancient Stoics were of opinion, that as the world was governed by the all-ruling providence of a wise, powerful, and good God, every single event ought to be regarded, as making a necessary part of the plan of the universe, and as tending to promote the general order and happiness of the whole.[141]

Smith's orientation to Stoicism, in Section VI.ii of the *Moral Sentiments*, is complex indeed! Note what he has done here: He managed to combine Stoic ideas of providential order with an explicit *rejection* of the Stoic cosmopolitan agenda, grounding this rejection in a full embrace of Stoic *oikeiōsis* as an empirical fact. In other words, because people were naturally inclined and best suited to care for their own, and were essentially incapable of extending that concern fruitfully toward grander departments, Smith rejected the Stoic cosmopolitan agenda, yet embraced the Stoic "conviction" that while each cares for his part, God minds the happiness of the whole. After essentially surrendering the fate of "all the unknown regions of infinite and incomprehensible space" to a benevolent Stoic God which would be "filled with nothing but endless misery and wretchedness" without his protection, it is not terribly surprising that Smith characterized "the very suspicion of a fatherless world ... the most melancholy of all reflections."[142]

Smith's rejection of Stoic cosmopolitanism, and his less heady, practical commitment to man's "humbler department" has an immediate Burkean quality to it. The resonance here is not surprising: it is well known that

---

[139] *TMS* VI.ii.3.6 (p. 237).   [140] *TMS* VI.ii.3.2 (p. 235).   [141] *TMS* I.ii.3.4 (p. 36).
[142] *TMS* VI.ii.3.2 (p. 235).

Burke and Smith were friends, participated in the same intellectual society in the 1770s and 1780s ("The Club"), and avidly consumed each other's work. In a private letter to Smith dated 10 September 1759, just months after the first edition of the *Moral Sentiments* had been delivered to him by Smith's publishers, Burke praised Smith for his

fine Picture of the Stoic Philosophy towards the end of your first part which is dressed out in all the grandeur and Pomp that becomes that magnificent delusion.[143]

We get some insight into what Burke meant by "delusion" in other parts of his letter. He seems to have meant that the Stoic system was precarious, unstable, not "sensible," similar to the products of "those Gothic architects who were fond of turning great Vaults upon a single slender Pillar."[144] Given Smith's and Burke's affinity on the Stoic failure, it makes good sense that they resisted Stoicism on much the same grounds, essentially that it denied the natural structure of human affection. As one interpretation of Smith recently put it: "Stoical disdain for this central fact of place denied the innate sociability of humans with those close to them. Smith is contemptuous of the stoic doctrine of the irrelevance of experience in which the murder of one's father is said to be no more important than the death of a chicken."[145] Burke and Smith, each in their own way, asserted that human beings are affectively drawn to the local, are better able to care for the local – and that Stoic imperatives, in attempting to overcome all this, had lost touch with ordinary human life as it is lived. In this sense, Smith's formulation of the "humble department" has a clear affiliation with Burke's formulation of the "little platoons" in *Reflections on the Revolution in France* in 1790.[146] Interesting too, from an historical perspective, is that Smith first used this formulation of the "humbler department" in his new Chapter VI in the 1790 edition of *Moral Sentiments* – in other words, at the same precise moment as Burke did. In the following passage, also penned by Smith in the 1790 edition, we see again references to the "little department":

By Nature the events which immediately affect that little department in which we ourselves have some little management and direction, which immediately affect

[143] "Letter to Smith from Edmund Burke, 10 September 1759" as "Letter #38" in *Corres.*, pp. 46–47, at p. 47. For discussion of the events surrounding this letter, see Ross, *Life of Adam Smith*, pp. 157–158 and 181.

[144] *Corres.*, p. 46.   [145] Levy and Peart. "Adam Smith and His Sources," p. 62.

[146] "To be attached to the subdivision, to love the little platoon we belong to in society, is the first principle (the germ as it were) of public affections. It is the first link in the series by which we proceed toward a love to our country and to mankind." Edmund Burke, *Reflections on the Revolution in France* (1790) in *The Writings and Speeches of Edmund Burke* (Oxford: Clarendon Press), vol. VIII.

ourselves, our friends, our country, are the events which interest us the most, and which chiefly excite our desires and aversions, our hopes and fears, our joys and sorrows.[147]

So a cluster of factors – our natural affection for our own, our interests in promoting what we love, and our superior ability to assist in that realm all together explain Smith's Burkean conclusion that "the plan and system which Nature has sketched out for our conduct, seems to be altogether different from that of the Stoical philosophy."[148] Note too that Smith resisted Stoic apathy here not only because it was unnatural, but also because he believed it was ultimately unnecessary for combating parochial "vehemence." Drawing somewhat ironically on Stoic providence, Smith assuaged his more rigoristic critics:

Should those [humbler] passions be, what they are apt to be, too vehement, Nature has provided a proper remedy and correction. The real or even the imaginary presence of the impartial spectator, the authority of the man within the breast, is always at hand to overawe them into the proper tone and temper of moderation.[149]

This chapter, and thus our discussion of the "Circle of Society," ends on a rather parochial note. And yet Smith never seemed to surrender completely his loftier aspirations for humankind, the perfectionism that always dwelled just beneath the surface of his cool descriptions of the world. At times Smith is even melancholy: "We only regret that it is unfit for the world, because the world is unworthy of it."[150]

---

[147] *TMS* VII.ii.1.44 (p. 292).   [148] *TMS* VII.ii.1.43 (p. 292).   [149] *TMS* VII.ii.1.44 (p. 292).
[150] *TMS* I.i.4.3 (p. 40).

PART III

The circle of humanity

CHAPTER 5

Sympathy in space

Sympathy, we shall allow, is much fainter than our concern for ourselves, and sympathy with persons remote from us, much fainter than that with persons near and contiguous.

David Hume, *An Enquiry Concerning the Principle of Morals*

In this book I have provided an interpretation of sympathy in Adam Smith's thought that opens itself quite naturally to questions about ethics in a global age, in an age marked by dramatic changes in the spatial arrangement of human life. In brief, I have argued that Smithian sympathy is best understood as a *social practice* through which morality is intersubjectively produced in shared physical spaces. Challenging a frequent assumption that sympathy is an emotion for Smith, or a virtue, I have emphasized the dramatic activities of surveillance and discipline, concluding that Smith's description of sympathetic activity is also a rich anthropology of culture formation. Understanding sympathy as such will help us now, in the present chapter, as we inquire into the spatial texture and the cosmopolitan significance of sympathetic activity as Smith presented it.

Smith's account of sympathy in the *Moral Sentiments* surely ranks among the subtlest accounts we have of the nature of sympathetic activity and of its prominence in human life. It is certainly the best known dimension of his moral thought among both students and casual consumers of Smith. And yet, in a time when so many of us are thinking about globalization and various cosmopolitical conundrums, there has been little exploration of Smith's thoughts on sympathy and proximity.[1] David Hume is regularly cited for his thoughts about the impact of proximity on our sentiments and judgments in the *Enquiry Concerning the Principles of Morals*; but little has

---

[1] A couple of notable exceptions: Russell Neili, "Spheres of Intimacy and the Adam Smith Problem," *Journal of the History of Ideas*, vol. 47, no. 4 (1986), pp. 611–624; and Boltanski, *Distant Suffering*. However, Smith is somewhat incidental to Boltanski's larger project, and his thoughts on distance are not fully investigated.

been said about similar ideas in Smith, which I believe are considerably richer and more interesting than were Hume's. Hume observed that our sentiments are constrained by proximity, and that we therefore needed a firmer, more impartial foundation than sentiment to ground our moral judgments. He famously located this foundation in the general standards that are drawn from "social intercourse" and "general usefulness."[2]

In this chapter I demonstrate that Smith absorbed much of Hume's basic orientation to proximity, and that he too sought to discover an *enlarged* method of judging others, untainted by the natural partiality of our passive feelings. As we saw in Chapter 3, this attempt was embodied in Smith's well-known account of the "Impartial Spectator." Much ink has been spilled on the relation between Hume's and Smith's general accounts of sympathy – notably their divergence over Hume's association of sympathy with considerations of utility. I do not intend to rehearse all that here.[3] I invoke Hume for the simple reason that he guided Smith's general orientation to the effects of proximity on sentiment – that our sympathy tends to fade as an object becomes further and further removed.

Drawing on my discussion of *oikeiōsis* in Chapter 4, I argue here that Smith's Humean orientation to proximity is rooted in a genealogical observation drawn substantially from Stoic moral psychology that physical proximity begets familiarity, which in turn makes affection and interest stronger, understanding more accurate, care a more efficient use of our very limited resources, and beneficent action therefore more natural and appropriate. The spatial texture of Smith's thought has not been widely appreciated or discussed. Indeed, people continue to cite Hume, never Smith, on the relation between sympathy and distance. But I shall demonstrate here

---

[2] Hume, *Enquiry*, pp. 48–50.
[3] For a classic statement, see the Editors' "Introduction" to *TMS*, pp. 10–15. Useful accounts can be found in: Stephen Darwall, "Empathy, Sympathy, Care," *Philosophical Studies*, vol. 89 (1998), pp. 261–282; Haakonssen, *Science of a Legislator*; Hope, *Virtue by Consensus*; Glenn R. Morrow, "The Significance of the Doctrine of Sympathy in Hume and Adam Smith," *Philosophical Review*, vol. 32, no. 1 (1923), pp. 60–78; David Raynor, "Hume's Abstract of Adam Smith's *Theory of Moral Sentiments*," *Journal of the History of Philosophy*, vol. 22 (1984), pp. 52–79; and F. L. von Holthoon, "Adam Smith and David Hume: with Sympathy," *Utilitas*, vol. 5, no. 1 (1993), pp. 36–48. One might summarize the relation as follows: that, while Smith adopted and integrated Hume's description of sympathy in *A Treatise of Human Nature* as the "communication" of sentiments along with Hume's subsequent shift in the *Enquiry*, in which sympathy was associated more conventionally with benevolence, Smith ultimately rejected Hume's claim in the *Enquiry* that sympathy was grounded in utility. At *TMS* IV.2.5 (p. 188), Smith considered Hume: "The same ingenious and agreeable author who first explained why utility pleases, has been so struck with this view of things, as to resolve our whole approbation of virtue into a perception of this species of beauty which results from the appearance of utility ... But I still affirm that it is not the view of this utility or hurtfulness which is either the first principle or source of our approbation or disapprobation."

that Smith's description of sympathy was not only more extensive and explicit than was Hume's, but also more subtle and textured, more complex and psychological, and ultimately more compelling for contemporary moral and political theory. In this, I agree fully with Stephen Darwall's assessment that "Smith's theory of sympathy and its role in our emotional lives is richer, more sophisticated, and, arguably, more suggestive for a wider range of issues."[4] One central reason from my perspective is that Smith's colorful and perceptive descriptions of our various attachments and affections (and the inevitable conflicts among them) draws us into the rich spatial texture of sympathetic response.[5] Specifically, Smith stimulates further inquiry into a variety of *spaces* in which sympathetic activity takes place. Familiarity for Smith and the Stoics seems initially to be a function of physical proximity. But reflecting further, familiarity is considerably more layered than mere physical presence, for familiarity need not entail physical proximity. There are other ways than physically that people might be "proximate" and thus familiar to one another, ways that may have little or nothing to do with where one is situated physically. Moreover, physical proximity need not produce familiarity. An important dimension of my argument is that Smith helps us to explore the spatial complexities of Stoic *oikeiōsis* – and particularly in the modern setting where encounters with others have become more frequent, more serendipitous, more *eccentric*,[6] moving us into new sorts of space that the Stoics could not have considered.

SPATIAL COMPLEXITY

In this chapter I productively complicate the notion of proximity in Adam Smith's thought by differentiating three dimensions, or spaces, in which sympathy operates: the physical, the affective, and the historical/cultural. Ultimately, I wish to demonstrate that a rich and complicated understanding of proximity exposes the difficulties (though not necessarily the impossibility) of maneuvering sympathy beyond the narrow spaces it naturally inhabits. Can sympathy transcend its particular genealogy and be shifted about? To what extent does Smith's "impartial spectator" model succeed in correcting the sentimental nearsightedness of sympathy, in detaching us

---

[4] Stephen Darwall, "Sympathetic Liberalism: Recent Work on Adam Smith," *Philosophy and Public Affairs*, vol. 28, no. 2 (1999), pp. 139–164, at p. 140.
[5] I suspect Darwall would agree here, given the contextual implications of his characterization of Humean sympathy as "emotional contagion" and Smithian sympathy as "projective empathy." See Darwall, "Empathy," p. 267.
[6] See Connolly, "Eccentric Flows."

from and getting us *beyond* the particularity generated by our physical, affective and cultural entanglements?

In a well-known passage in *An Enquiry Concerning the Principles of Morals*, David Hume observed that proximity tends to stimulate sympathy, and that distance tends to diminish it:

Sympathy, we shall allow, is much fainter than our concern for ourselves, and sympathy with persons remote from us, much fainter than that with persons near and contiguous.[7]

Hume's spatial concepts in this passage – "remoteness," "nearness" and "contiguity" – all seem to have a *physical* implication: that we sympathize more vibrantly with people who are literally close by and less so with those who are not. And yet, these concepts seem to signify something other or more than shared physical space. For example, Hume noted that our *relationships and associations* will affect the scope of our sentiments. To cite another famous passage, he observed that an account of a generous action reported in an "old history or remote gazette" is "so infinitely removed, as to affect the senses with light nor heat" – but, that if the virtue is brought "nearer, by our acquaintance or connexion with the persons" involved, then "our hearts are immediately caught" and "our sympathy [is] enlivened."[8] Related to this, Hume also noted that our *interests* tend to influence the scope of our sentiments. He maintained that since our real and present interests are always "in view," it is unlikely that an "imaginary interest" in "distant ages and countries" will incite "real sentiments," particularly if these interests happen to draw in different directions.[9]

What all this suggests is that there are other ways than *physically* that a person can be "near" or "remote." Hume points us in the right direction: we need to complicate the notion of proximity to signify other sorts of space than physical space. I may be revolted by my neighbor, familiarity breeding proverbial contempt, yet feel *affectively* connected with an old schoolmate or lover who lives in another country. As William Connolly observes in his study of "eccentric connection" which he posited as a challenge to conventional "concentric" understandings of our relations with others:

you may well have a sense of belonging to the family that nourishes you or wish to participate in the state that governs you ... [but] during a time when speed compresses distance – concentric circles of political culture are complicated and compromised by numerous crosscutting allegiances, connections, and modes of collaboration.[10]

---

[7] Hume, *Enquiry*, p. 49.   [8] *Ibid.*, p. 50.   [9] *Ibid.*, p. 41.
[10] See Connolly, "Eccentric Flows," p. 186.

I might sympathize with a person thousands of miles away upon hearing a narrative that she, like me, has a special fondness for doing *tai chi* or for the paintings of Mark Rothko; or that, unlike me, lives next to a radioactive waste dump. What's more, I may be sitting just across a table from someone but find myself entirely incapable of understanding or sympathizing with her world of meanings. I might be more familiar in a *cultural* sense with the religious or dietary practices of a person living in Yemen than with the practices of my dinner companion, yielding in such a case a more refined sympathetic judgment of the physically remote, and a relative insensibility toward the near.[11] Imaginatively obtuse grown-ups simply could not recognize that Saint Exupéry's little prince had drawn not a hat but an elephant inside a boa-constrictor. Indeed, the issue of physical proximity seems to rouse more questions than it resolves, for it seems to be neither a necessary nor a sufficient condition for sympathetic response. The question of proximity seems to demand affective and cultural considerations as well.

Adam Smith's rich moral psychology in the *Moral Sentiments* helps us to appreciate the spatial complexities of sympathetic activity, perhaps better so than any other eighteenth-century work on the sentiments. In this chapter I will consider three spaces in which sympathy seems to operate on Smith's account: physical space, affective space and historical/cultural space.[12] I identify and differentiate these three spaces, while stressing interesting occasional overlaps and glaring tensions among them. We might conceptualize each of these dimensions as continua along which any act of sympathy can be situated (i.e. physically proximate or remote, affectively connected or not, historically familiar or unfamiliar). In other words, any given act of sympathy can be situated somewhere along each of these three continua, with the result that any act of sympathy will be a particular *confluence* of the three. I shall now examine each of these spaces in further detail.

A. PHYSICAL IMMEDIACY

Everybody knows that when it is noon in the United States the sun is setting over France. If you could fly to France in just one minute, you could go straight into the

---

[11] See Jeremy Waldron's colorful description of the Guatemalan who "shares a faith and a church with the Irish, and also with the Italians, Poles, Brazilians, Japanese Catholics and Filipinas" and thus identifies more readily with them than with the "distinctiveness" of Guatemalan culture. Waldron, "What Is Cosmopolitan?," p. 233.

[12] There may be others. Henry Clark, for example, suggests that "the scale of our sympathy may be said to follow the range of our conversation." Clark, "Conversation and Moderate Virtue," p. 202. One might argue that this is conceptually distinct from my spaces, though it might in fact be a hybrid of two, or perhaps of all three.

sunset, right from noon. Unfortunately France is too far away for that. But on your tiny planet, my little prince, all you need do is move your chair a few steps. You can see the day end and the twilight falling whenever you like. (Antoine de Saint Exupéry, *The Little Prince*)

We will discover in the following three sections that Adam Smith was less concerned in the *Moral Sentiments* with examining how physical proximity and distance impact our sympathetic responses and judgments than he was with describing the ways that affective "connections" and shared experiences and interests do.[13] Nevertheless, it would be inaccurate to say that physical space was unimportant in Smith's moral psychology given the emphasis he placed on the faculty of sight. Throughout the entire first section of the treatise, Smith spoke regularly about the ways that we "view" and "look at" others, of the "very appearances" that their emotions convey to us, that we rejoice in "observing" fellow-feeling in them, that people tend to "parade" certain parts of themselves, "conceal" others, and so on. His account of the mechanics of sympathy assumed that the spectator is positioned near enough to "see," to "gaze at," to "look upon" another person, in order to appreciate the particular circumstances that motivate the other to feel and act as he does.[14] Smith's language revolved around the faculty of sight, and the way that seeing something mediates the imagination. Indeed, he described sympathy as an activity that takes place in physical space, upon a sort of dramatic stage.[15] As Knud Haakonssen notes, he:

always takes as a matter of course that man is social, that he is bound to be together with his fellows. This means that he will always literally have to look upon them; he is forced to watch them and see what they are like.[16]

The spectator thus is an audience to his fellows, or in Smith's words a "bystander"[17] who *watches* and is *affected* by the spectacle of suffering or joy before him, in all its colorful and compelling detail. And the agents who perform before him will respond to being seen, like Sartre's man in the park whose physical space is violently penetrated the moment he is seen by another.[18] To take a couple of Smith's illustrations of the influence of physical

---

[13] At one point, Smith said explicitly that "moral" connection is more important to understanding natural affection than is "physical connection." *TMS* VI.ii.1.14 (p. 223). In this passage, Smith was discussing relations between parent and child, which would seem to be an extreme case, thus making the general point readily applicable to far less intimate relations.

[14] *TMS* I.i.1–2 (pp. 9–16).

[15] On the "drama" of Smithian sympathy, see Marshall: "Theatricality" and *Figure of Theatre*.

[16] Haakonssen, *Science of a Legislator*, p. 52.   [17] *TMS* I.i.1.3 (p. 10).

[18] Jean-Paul Sartre, *Being and Nothingness*, trans. Hazel E. Barnes (New York: Philosophical Library, 1956), pp. 254–259.

space on sympathetic discipline: small children learn by observing the responses of those physically closest to them, notably their "play-fellows," what it means to act appropriately.[19] Watching my three-year-old son evolve into a social being in his Montessori pre-school, has confirmed for me just how right Smith was about this. That I feel "offense" when a spectator "seems not to be affected by my misery" or when she refuses to "wear a serious countenance" is a function of the physical proximity between me and her.[20] I see her insensibility and the effects are "instantaneous."[21] As Luc Boltanski describes it, we "regulate our reciprocal expectations by interpreting external signs accessible to sight."[22] In short, Smith assumes a basic physical proximity, a face-to-face transaction, between spectator and agent in his description of both "stages" of sympathetic interaction – surveillance and discipline – although we will see that physical proximity is neither a necessary nor a sufficient condition for sympathetic response.

For the moment, the relevant insight is that physical proximity will improve the preciseness with which the spectator/by-stander can under-stand the circumstances of the agent when he "enters into" his reality, and that distance will diminish it. He cannot physically experience the agent's sensations or feel his emotions, but he sees his blood and tears, hears his cries and laughter, and he finds himself drawn into the circumstances that gave rise to them. Physical proximity will help the spectator better understand *why* the agent responded to particular causes the way he did, and to evaluate more accurately whether or not the agent's response was "proper" or "suitable." For example, a spectator might believe he sees an act of harm when from afar he observes an agent strike another with force, but a more refined understanding of the circumstances, *seeing more*, can reveal that the "bully" was merely fending off an attack, or perhaps helping his friend by crushing a mosquito on its bite, or helping to dislodge a piece of meat from his throat. Distance (physical, temporal) distorts what the spectator can see, obscures the whole story, and leads him to evaluate the agent's behavior as "improper." Bring the scene nearer to the eye, and the spectator will likely adjust his judgment to accommodate the incidents that motivated the agent's behavior – the prior attack, the mosquito biting, the choking.

In this Smith was closely following David Hume, who argued that a "moral decision" that lacks previous knowledge of "all the circumstances and relations" of a case are only "speculative propositions":

---

[19] *TMS* III.3.22 (p. 145). [20] *TMS* I.i.2.4 (p. 15). [21] For example, at *TMS* I.i.4.9 (p. 23).
[22] Boltanski, *Distant Suffering*, p. 39.

in moral deliberations we must be acquainted beforehand with all the objects, and all their relations to each other ... If any material circumstance be yet unknown or doubtful, we must first employ our inquiry or intellectual faculties to assure us of it; and must suspend for a time all moral decision or sentiment. While we are ignorant whether a man were aggressor or not, how can we determine whether the person who killed him be a criminal or innocent? But after every circumstance, every relation is known, the understanding has no further room to operate, nor any object on which it could employ itself.[23]

For Hume and for Smith, precise detail is most *im*-mediately acquired through the faculty of sight. And sight is more precise when we are proximate, physically nearer, to something.

Nevertheless, while physical proximity assists the spectator in acquiring a more precise and accurate understanding of an event, we should not assume that it is either necessary or sufficient for sympathetic response on Smith's account. Regarding necessity, I might hear about or read in graphic detail (as Smith surely might have) an account of the public execution of Damiens the regicide, and without *seeing* the events – the "red-hot pincers," the "boiling potion," the "tugging horses," the prisoner's cries for his Lord's pardon – experience some dimension of sympathy for him and the pain he endures.[24] Although Smith's primary description of sympathetic activity rested on the faculty of sight, he acknowledged that a spectator might be moved by literature (he frequently drew on tragedy for his examples), or a vivid narrative of distant joy or suffering. The vividness of the description *replicates* physical proximity, imagination carries the distant back to us, and ultimately elicits the very sentiments that physical proximity would have produced – confirming that proximity served as a sort of baseline in Smith's account of how we come to sympathize. Departing slightly from Hume, who claimed, as we saw above, that an event described in "an old history or remote gazette ... is so infinitely removed as to affect the senses, neither with light nor with heat,"[25] Smith argued that we can in fact sympathize upon reading a vivid story:

We can sympathize with the distress which excessive hunger occasions when we read the description of it in the journal of a siege, or of a sea voyage. We imagine ourselves in the situation of the sufferers, and thence readily conceive the grief, the fear and consternation, which must necessarily distract them. We feel, ourselves, some degree of those passions, and therefore sympathize with them: but as we do

---

[23] Hume, *Enquiry*, Appendix I, p. 85.
[24] I am referring here to Foucault's memorable overture in *Discipline and Punish*, pp. 3–6.
[25] Hume, *Enquiry*, p. 50.

not grow hungry by reading the description, we cannot properly, even in this case, be said to sympathize with their hunger.[26]

These insights seem particularly relevant today, when the idea of physical proximity is complicated by information, mobility and speed, when travel is easy and encounter frequent, and when images and narratives of distant suffering are transported digitally into the living rooms and computer screens of remote spectators.[27] Smith would have had much to say were he reflecting today on the impact of the media on our moral sentiments, with its vivid narratives about ethnic cleansing, graphic depictions of starving infants, of young girls being genitally mutilated, of grinning soldiers torturing naked prisoners, and so on.

As physical proximity appears not to be necessary for sympathy, it also does not seem to be sufficient. Smith offered a fine illustration in his *Lectures on Jurisprudence* of the insufficiency of physical proximity to explain sympathy. He observed that a nobleman "who is far removed from the conditions of his servant" has a less refined ability to "feel with" him than do ordinary farmers who work side-by-side in the fields and eat with their servants. Despite the nobleman's physical proximity to the servant who may be shaving his face in the morning or clipping his toenails, only the farmer "considers his servant as almost an equal with himself, and is therefore more capable of *feeling with* him."[28] In this example, the nobleman's sense of superiority (we might call it "distance in status") dulls the sympathetic imagination, regardless of his physical proximity to his servant. A sense of helplessness might produce a similar numbing effect: as when one visits an impoverished city and comes upon throngs of homeless children begging for money, or when one is besieged by television images of starving infants.

In the end, however, despite the callousness of the nobleman in the example above, the dominant strain in Smith's thought regarding physical

---

[26] *TMS* I.ii.1.1 (p. 28). Note also: "Our joy for the deliverance of those heroes of tragedy or romance who interest us, is as sincere as our grief for their distress" (*TMS* I.i.1.4 (p. 10)). However, elsewhere, Smith seems to return somewhat to Hume when he argues against the Stoic imperative to cultivate sympathy for distant tragedy: "No speculation of this kind, however, how deeply soever it might be rooted in the mind, could diminish our natural abhorrence for vice, whose immediate effects are so destructive, and whose remote ones are too distant to be traced by the imagination" (*TMS* VII.ii.1.45 (p. 292)).

[27] Luc Boltanski has offered a very thoughtful discussion of Smithian sympathy and media representations of "distant suffering" in *Distant Suffering*. For discussion, see Fonna Forman-Barzilai, "And Thus Spoke the Spectator: Adam Smith for Humanitarians," *Adam Smith Review*, vol. 1, September (2004), pp. 167–174.

[28] Adam Smith, *Lectures on Jurisprudence (1762–1766)*, ed. R. L. Meek, D. D. Raphael and P. G. Stein, as vol. V of *The Glasgow Edition of the Works and Correspondence of Adam Smith* (Oxford: Oxford University Press; reprint Indianapolis, IN: Liberty Press, 1982), A iii.109, emphasis added.

space is that physical proximity makes contact likelier and sympathy therefore more precise. These two elements of contact and knowledge combined
for Smith to ground an affirmative duty to assist. As we discovered in
Chapter 4 Smith was very much a localist in this sense, and resisted the
Stoic cosmopolitan urge to expand this duty to distant strangers. Recall the
following passages:

To man is allotted a much humbler department, but one much more suitable to the
weakness of his powers, and to the narrowness of his comprehension; the care of his
own happiness, of that of his family, his friends, his country.[29]

And again:

By Nature the events which immediately affect that little department in which we
ourselves have some little management and direction, which immediately affect
ourselves, our friends, our country, are the events which interest us the most, and
which chiefly excite our desires and aversions, our hopes and fears, our joys and
sorrows.[30]

Surely these passages incorporate affective considerations (interest, desire,
aversion, joy, sorrow) which we will address in the next section on affective
space; but note for now Smith's emphasis here on comprehension (what we
know) and the relative weakness and effectiveness of our power to care,
which seems to be a function of where we are situated physically with regard
to the object of our intended care.[31]

Luc Boltanski suggests that Smith never really considered the impact of
physical distance on his theory of spectatorship – that he overlooked

the tension between a necessarily local face to face encounter, as in the figure of
compassion, and the conveyance over distance of a representation of suffering that
is required by a general politics of pity, as if the second figure could be directly
derived, smoothly and uninterruptedly, by extension of the first.[32]

But this cannot be right. Smith was quite explicit about the barriers that
distance creates for sympathetic imagination. I should like to close my
discussion of physical space with the following passage from the 1759 edition
of the *Moral Sentiments*, in which Smith challenged the "whiny and

---

[29] *TMS* VI.ii.3.6 (p. 237).   [30] *TMS* VII.ii.1.44 (p. 292).

[31] For an interesting discussion of the significance of geography in discussions about partiality and
benevolence, see David Smith, "How Far Should We Care? On the Spatial Scope of Beneficence,"
Progress in Human Geography, vol. 22, no. 1 (1998), pp. 15–38.

[32] Boltanski, *Distant Suffering*, p. 37. Boltanski does acknowledge that Smith incorporated a "kind of
distance" into his theory by positing a spectator that was uninvolved, impartial, without ties or pre-
commitments to the sufferer. And he praises Smith for invoking imagination as a way of traversing
that distance (pp. 37–38).

melancholy" moralism of Christian cosmopolitanism explicitly on physical grounds.[33] I will cite the passage in its entirely since I believe it best demonstrates Smith's vivid and somewhat troubling account of distance, as well as the reasons that distance circumscribed his understanding of our duties.

extreme sympathy with misfortunes which we know nothing about, seems altogether absurd and unreasonable. Take the whole earth at an average, for one man who suffers pain or misery, you will find twenty in prosperity and joy, or at least in tolerable circumstances. No reason, surely, can be assigned why we should rather weep with the one than rejoice with the twenty. This artificial commiseration, besides, is not only absurd, but seems altogether unattainable; and those who affect this character have commonly nothing but a certain affected and sentimental sadness, which, without reaching the heart, serves only to render the countenance and conversation impertinently dismal and disagreeable. And last of all, this disposition of mind, though it could be attained, would be perfectly useless, and could serve no other purpose than to render miserable the person who possessed it. Whatever interest we take in the fortune of those with whom we have no acquaintance or connexion, and who are placed altogether out of the sphere of our activity, can produce only anxiety to ourselves, without any manner of advantage to them. To what purpose should we trouble ourselves about the world in the moon? All men, even those at the greatest distance, are no doubt entitled to our good wishes, and our good wishes we naturally give them. But if, notwithstanding, they should be unfortunate, to give ourselves any anxiety upon that account, seems to be no part of our duty. That we should be but little interested, therefore, in the fortune of those whom we can neither serve nor hurt, and who are in every respect so very remote from us, seems wisely ordered by Nature; and if it were possible to alter in this respect the original constitution of our frame, we could yet gain nothing by the change.[34]

What do we make of this striking passage? Smith argued here that preoccupying oneself with distant suffering is (1) absurd; (2) pathological; and in the end (3) perfectly useless. It is "absurd" because, even though he conceded that he didn't really "know" much about it, he decided that most men were living "in prosperity and joy, or at least in tolerable circumstances." Smith seems more than a little out of touch with the difficulties of life for so many people even in proximate eighteenth-century England and Scotland.[35] Earlier he castigated Christian moralists for

reproaching us with our happiness, while so many of our brethren are in misery, who regard as impious the natural joy of prosperity, which does not think of the

[33] *TMS* III.3.8 (p. 139).   [34] *TMS* III.3.9 (p. 140).
[35] See Robert Heilbronner's classic account of eighteenth-century English tin miners, agricultural harvesters and factory workers in "The Wonderful World of Adam Smith," pp. 41–43.

many wretches that are at every instant labouring under all sorts of calamities, in the languor of poverty, in the agony of disease, in the horrors of death, under the insult and oppression of their enemies.[36]

Smith's flippant attitude toward human suffering here is stunning; and I find it remarkable that he retained these callous passages from the original 1759 text after having so forcefully articulated his concerns about the suffering of modern working people in the *Wealth of Nations* of 1776.[37] But the argument goes even further: those who preoccupy themselves with imagined misfortunes and "unattainable" compassion are described by Smith as emotionally unhealthy, unpleasant and dour in demeanor – "whining and melancholy moralists, who are perpetually reproaching us with our happiness, while so many of our brethren are in misery."[38] Elsewhere he observed:

Commiseration for those miseries which we never saw, which we never heard of, but which we may be assured are at all times infesting such numbers of our fellow-creatures, ought, they think, to damp the pleasures of the fortunate, and to render a certain melancholy dejection habitual to all men.[39]

In these passages, we detect distinct resonances of Hume's discussion of "distant ages and remote countries" in the *Enquiry Concerning the Principles of Morals*, where he claimed that it is unlikely that "a *real* sentiment or passion can ever arise from an *imaginary* interest; especially when our *real* interest is still kept in view."[40] Hume's emphasis on known, local interests captures precisely Smith's views on the relation between knowledge and care. And yet Smith goes further yet. Even if people were actually suffering far off, and we somehow learned of it and brought it home to ourselves – in other words, somehow made it "real" – such commiseration would be "perfectly useless" since the sufferers are "placed altogether out of the sphere of our activity." Simply put, there was nothing we could do about it. Smith was ever preoccupied with useful, purposive, "effectual" action, and had little patience for indolence and waste. And so he asks, "To what purpose should we trouble ourselves about the world in the moon?"[41] For Smith, benevolence without the possibility of action was wasted emotion, and deserved little real merit. He referred to it as "indolent benevolence":

---

[36] *TMS* III.3.9 (p. 139).
[37] For discussion, see Fleischacker, *Wealth of Nations*; Rothschild, *Economic Sentiments*, and especially Nussbaum, "Mutilated and Deformed."
[38] *TMS* III.3.9 (p. 139).   [39] *TMS* III.3.9 (pp. 139–140).   [40] Hume, *Enquiry*, p. 41.
[41] *TMS* III.3.9 (p. 140).

Man ... must not be satisfied with indolent benevolence, nor fancy himself the friend of mankind, because in his heart he wishes well to the prosperity of the world ... The man who has performed no single act of importance, but whose whole conversation and deportment expresses the justest, the noblest, and most generous sentiments, can be entitled to demand no very high reward, *even though his inutility should be owing to nothing but the want of an opportunity to serve.*[42]

A guiding theme in Smith's thought, we have seen, is that Nature has attuned our sentiments and interests toward the sphere over which we have some management; and it was within this sphere – the "humble department" – that our duties were always directed for Smith. For this reason, Smith came down rather hard on the *vita contemplativa*. Even the "sublime speculation of the contemplative philosopher can scarce compensate the neglect of the smallest active duty." His example was Marcus Antoninus:

that he is occupied in contemplating the more sublime, can never be an excuse for his neglecting the more humble department; and he must not expose himself to the charge which Avidius Cassius is said to have brought, perhaps unjustly, against Marcus Antoninus; that while he employed himself in philosophical speculations, and contemplated the prosperity of the universe, he neglected that of the Roman empire.[43]

These passages are surely the most overtly anti-cosmopolitan in all of Smith's published work; and to my mind they sit rather uncomfortably alongside so many other moments of genuine humanity and open-heartedness in his thought. But what ultimately strikes the reader in the foregoing discussion is not merely Smith's cool attitude toward the suffering of others (even Clifford Geertz, this century's most influential proponent of localism, would likely have characterized the sort of localism defended in these passages as "parochialism without tears."[44]) but perhaps moreso, how vastly different Smith's world was from our own – the slowness, the difficulty of travel and communication, the dearth of information about the condition of distant peoples, the comparative insularity of state and corporate activity, the impotence of international law, the absence of international and transnational dialogue, as well as international and non-governmental agencies that might assist distant spectators in their desire to act, and so on. How might Smith have adjusted his orientation in different circumstances? John Durham Peters has suggested that we consider the

---

[42] *TMS* II.iii.3.3 (p. 106), emphasis added.   [43] *TMS* VI.ii.3.6 (p. 237).

[44] Clifford Geertz, "The Uses of Diversity," *Michigan Quarterly Review*, vol. 25 (1986), pp. 105–123, at p. 122; discussed in David Hollinger, "How Wide Is the Circle of the 'We'?," *American Historical Review*, vol. 98, no. 2 (1993), pp. 317–337, at p. 328.

"circumference of authentic sympathy" in Smith's thought with historical sensitivity:

> Smith's historical universe is able to contain the pathos of suffering at a distance in a way that ours is not. His social theory does not imagine that the inhabitants of China could ever be anything but an abstraction for Scotsmen. Sympathy is adjusted to human finitude in Smith in a way that it cannot be for us two centuries later. Social relations for him take place in a face-to-face setting on a circumscribed portion of the earth's surface ... Smith is secure in the limited range of his humanity in a way that dwellers within the fractured global flows of people, images, words, money, technology, and actions can be only at the peril of a guilty conscience.[45]

Clearly, Smith's localism was grounded in what he believed were mankind's very practical constraints in the realms of knowing and assisting. He never argued that we ought to wish harm to those beyond our "sphere of activity," or that "all innocent and sensible beings" didn't merit our good wishes. Indeed, in his discussion of "universal Benevolence" in Section VI.ii.3, he insisted:

> Though our effectual good offices can very seldom be extended to any wider society than that of our own country; our good-will is circumscribed by no boundary; but may embrace the entirety of the universe. We can not form the idea of any innocent and sensible being, whose happiness we should not desire, or whose misery, when distinctly brought home to the imagination, we should not have some degree of aversion.[46]

For those of us interested in Smith's salience for today, we must pause to consider how our global condition – and its vast networks of knowing and assisting – might have changed Smith's mind about the proper scope of our duties. Surely our tiny planet is not the world described in the passages discussed above, where "knowing" about distant suffering was unlikely or where assisting was beyond our capacity. Of course there are also barriers and complications today that Smith could not have considered: media bias, over-saturation and mind-numbing complexity which tend to deaden the effects of knowledge, the staggering number of actors involved in any forum of distress which can bewilder our desire to act, to name just a few.[47]

It is fitting to conclude that physical proximity in Smith's *Moral Sentiments* was something of litmus test, most frequently characterized as a *necessary condition* for knowledge, ethical concern and action. But it would be a mistake to move forward without reflecting briefly on the *sufficiency* of physical proximity for ethical concern, an issue Smith didn't address

---

[45] Peters, "Publicity and Pain," pp. 564–565.   [46] *TMS* VI.ii.3.1 (p. 235).
[47] My thanks to Eric Schliesser here for reminding me how complex our world is!

explicitly but which seems to be entailed by his conclusions, and by many of his illustrations. In *Becoming Evil*, a fascinating study of the social psychology of genocide, James Waller examined a series of clinical experiments that all tended to support the conclusion that physical proximity tends to render violence among humans less likely, and that "killing is made easier as the distance between perpetrators and their victims increases."[48] Stanley Milgram's well-known obedience experiments demonstrated, for example, that we are less likely to obey orders to commit harm the closer we are to our victim physically. How do we then make sense of the unimaginable brutality that takes place during a genocide among people who share physical space? Genocide seems to provide a profound limiting case for claims about the inverse relation of distance and killing. Surely there are cases far less extreme.

It turns out that a lack of affective connection, or a carefully crafted break-down of affective connection, can powerfully diminish our sense of ethical concern, even toward people with whom we live in close physical contact. To achieve their ends, genocidal regimes are extraordinarily successful at dehumanizing their victims, subjecting them to what Waller calls a "social death" before ever inflicting physical harm.[49] Well before the Nazi genocide began, Goebbels' propaganda regime tapped into long-standing anti-Semitic sensibilities in the German psyche and presented the Jew as vermin, as a plague, as a microbe infecting the purity and hygiene of the Aryan race. Tutsis became "cockroaches" at the mercy of Hutu machetes. Nanking became a city of "hogs" to their Japanese assailants. Once a victim is dehumanized through language, once the affective connection between perpetrator and victim is severed, once the victim is presented as the cause of death and not a subject of it, once children are transformed from a natural object of care into "nits that make lice,"[50] exterminating one's neighbors is normalized – not an immoral act of burning hatred which ordinary people are always loathe to commit, but an act of decency, of patriotism and love, a natural extension of the perpetrator's noble affection to his own group.[51]

We turn next to Smith's thoughts about affective "connexion" to one's own, and how he dealt with its potential for excess and even ferocity.

[48] James Waller. *Becoming Evil: How Ordinary People Commit Genocide and Mass Killing*, 2nd edn (New York: Oxford University Press, 2007), pp. 196–197.
[49] Waller, *Becoming Evil*, pp. 196–220. [50] *Ibid.*, pp. 25–31.
[51] See Saul Friedländer, *Reflections of Nazism: An Essay on Kitsch and Death* (New York: Harper & Row, 1981), esp. pp. 102–105.

B. AFFECTIVE "CONNEXION": ON "FEELING
TOO STRONGLY"

The greatest crimes do not arise from a want of feeling for others but from an over-sensibility for ourselves and an over-indulgence to our own desires. (Edmund Burke to the Chevalier de Rivarol (1791))

We come now to the second space in which Smith considered the phenom-enon of sympathy. Here I explore Smith's thoughts on affective "connexion" and its effects on moral judgment, and his description of how we surmount affective bias and enlarge our judgments through the mechanisms of sym-pathy and the impartial spectator. The presentation that follows rests on my contention throughout this book that Smith was primarily concerned in the *Moral Sentiments* with social order, with maintaining the "fabric of society," the "association of mankind," "human society," etc.[52] Not insignificantly, as we have seen, he also described the aim of preserving and maintaining social order as the "peculiar and darling care of Nature."[53] For Smith, affective bias was the most significant impediment to social order, and a subject that every moral philosophy needed to confront. In the *Moral Sentiments* he considered the problem in both its individualistic and collective manifestations. Just as individual self-preference unchecked can destabilize man's relations with his immediate fellows, the collective self-preference of societies, parties, "civil" and "ecclesiastical" factions and nations can become fanatical under certain conditions and produce instability and war on a much vaster scale. Indeed, for Smith, "of all the corrupters of moral sentiments ... faction and fanaticism have always been by far the greatest."[54] Smith's remarks on the dangers of collective sentiment in the 1790 edition of the *Moral Sentiments* are pro-foundly interesting when considered in light of the localist texture of his moral psychology in general. Indeed, by leaving man to the "humbler depart-ments" and legitimating a relatively narrow concern with local events, he abandoned mankind to the very prejudices and hatreds of group life that so alarmed him. In 1790 he spent a good deal of time reflecting on group psychology and its effects on national and international stability and prosper-ity. In this section of Chapter 5, I will focus primarily on the problem of affective bias among individuals. In Chapter 6, I will address Smith's concerns with collective bias.

---

[52] These formulations are drawn from *TMS* II.ii.3.4 (p. 86) and *TMS* II.5.2 (p. 163), both of which are concerned explicitly with how Nature prevents society from "crumbling into atoms," from "crum-bling into nothing."

[53] *TMS* II.ii.3.4 (p. 86).   [54] *TMS* III.3.43 (p. 156).

Smith's concern with affective bias as a defining element of human nature is presented most clearly in the following passage. Note too his reference to the mitigating effects of "particular connexion" with specific others, which will become essential later in our discussion of collective bias.

Men, though naturally sympathetic, feel so little for another, with whom they have no particular connexion, in comparison with what they feel for themselves; the misery of one, who is merely their fellow-creature, is of so little importance to them in comparison even of a small conveniency of their own; they have it so much in their power to hurt him, and may have so many temptations to do so.[55]

Because he believed with the Stoics that affective bias was man's natural disposition, but that it was also deeply problematic from the perspective of society, the *Moral Sentiments* was devoted to thickly describing the ordinary sociological methods through which a person in concert with his neighbors spontaneously coordinates a balance between his self-regarding and other-regarding tendencies. Without the intervention of Nature and society men would be like "wild beasts" and would "enter an assembly of men as he enters a den of lions."[56]

Affection for Smith was the emotional product of "association" and "connexion" with others over time, which commonly evolve through physical proximity and shared experiences with them.[57] As we have seen, Smith's orientation to human affection is decisively Stoic in origin. He embraced Stoic *oikeiōsis* as an empirical fact about human "affection." He agreed that we tend to feel affection for those with whom we share physical space and are most familiar, and likewise that "spatial distance operates to intensify psychological distance," as Jacob Viner put it.[58] This Stoic way of understanding human connectedness is captured nicely in Smith's observation that "affection" is in reality nothing but habitual sympathy":

Our concern in the happiness or misery of those who are the objects of what we call our affections; our desire to promote the one, and to prevent the other; are either the actual feeling of that habitual sympathy, or the necessary consequences of that feeling. Relations being usually placed in situations which naturally create this habitual sympathy, it is expected that a suitable degree of affection should take

---

[55] *TMS* II.ii.3.4 (p. 86).   [56] *TMS* II.ii.3.4 (p. 86).
[57] Although Smith did acknowledge that we can feel affection, regardless of such "connexion," for a person who has demonstrated exceptional "personal qualities," for someone exceptionally needy, or for someone from whom we have experienced "past services." *TMS* VI.ii.1.14–20 (pp. 223–236).
[58] Viner, *Providence*, pp. 80–81.

place among them. We generally find that it actually does take place; we therefore naturally expect that it should.[59]

For Smith, affection does not originate in blood, a fallacy which holds force for him "no-where but in tragedies and romances."[60] Nor is it an abstract entity like benevolence or compassion, which moralists traditionally attempted to teach and to shift about from object to object. For Smith, the relation between physical and affective proximity meant that the Stoic circles were firmly grounded in human experience and were therefore resistant to philosophical or religious manipulation. As such, while he was greatly impressed with and indebted to Stoic moral psychology, Smith rejected the Stoic's "absurd and unreasonable" cosmopolitan assertion that we should aspire to collapse the natural concentric structure of human relationships through the exercise of our reason.[61] He simply could not accept that our highest human aspiration is to rebuke nature, nourish apathy toward those who are near, and become "citizens of the world."[62] As we have seen before, he refused to take the leap "from primary impulse to virtue," to borrow A. A. Long's description of the Stoic cosmopolitan imperative.[63] Smith wrote:

By the perfect apathy which [the "stoical philosophy"] prescribes to us, by endeavoring, not merely to moderate, but to eradicate all our private, partial, and selfish affections, by suffering us to feel for whatever can befall ourselves, our friends, our country ... it endeavors to render us altogether indifferent and unconcerned in the success or miscarriage of every thing which Nature has prescribed to us as the proper business and occupation of our lives.[64]

With regard to our duties, therefore, Smith concluded:

All men, even those at the greatest distance, are no doubt entitled to our good wishes, and our good wishes we naturally give them. But if, notwithstanding, they should be unfortunate, to give ourselves any anxiety upon that account, seems to be no part of our duty.[65]

This apparently callous disregard for the condition of distant strangers may seem odd coming from a moral philosopher so often championed as a prophet of human sympathy. But I believe our judgment should be tempered somewhat by remembering that "can" for Smith always limited

[59] *TMS* I.ii.1.7 (p. 220). For discussion of the "familiarity principle" in Smith (in both *WN* and *TMS*), see Otteson, *Marketplace*, pp. 183–189. An interesting discussion of Smith's "spheres of intimacy" and the way it helps resolve the Adam Smith Problem, can be found in Neili, "Spheres of Intimacy."
[60] *TMS* VI.ii.1.11 (p. 222).   [61] *TMS* III.3.9 (p. 140).   [62] *TMS* III.3.11 (p. 140).
[63] Long, *Hellenistic Philosophy*, pp. 184–189.   [64] *TMS* VII.ii.1.46 (pp. 292–293).
[65] *TMS* III.3.9 (p. 140).

"ought," and that he found it absurd and cynical to extend duty to actions that were beyond the capacities of the ordinary eighteenth-century people he observed around him, who were not only limited in their knowledge and capacity to assist, but were driven primarily by their personal interests and affective attachments. Smith may have underestimated the humanitarian interests and capacities of his own century, let alone those of centuries to come, but he insisted that we are best positioned to assist those for whom we have affection, understanding and direct contact[66] – and he believed deeply that humanity profited, borough by borough, through a sort of divine œconomy, through this natural arrangement. He believed this arrangement was "wisely ordered by Nature," and that "if it were possible to alter in this respect the original distribution of our frame, we could yet gain nothing from the change."[67] Indeed, Smith unlike the Stoics believed that affective concentricity was not only natural but *good* for he believed that "the great society of mankind would be best promoted by directing the principal attention of each individual to that particular portion of it, which was most within the sphere both of his abilities and of his understanding."[68]

And yet, Smith recognized that this natural structure threatened to bias the sympathy process, to distort our perceptions and judgments, ultimately to divide and factionalize humankind. In the remainder of this section I explore why affection was morally problematic for Smith. As he put it, "feeling too strongly" tends to delude us into fantastic over-evaluations of ourselves and our loved ones, of our own pains and joys, the importance of our place in the world relative to others.[69] Calm and settled judgment is easily blown off course by what he described as a "paroxysm of emotion," an "eagerness of passion" which can "discolour our view of things" and lead us to elevate our own immediate ends above all else. He observed:

In the same manner, to the selfish and original passions of human nature, the loss or gain of a very small interest of our own, appears to be of vastly more importance, excites a much more passionate joy or sorrow, a much more ardent desire or aversion, than the greatest concern of another with whom we have no particular connexion. His interests, as long as they are surveyed from this station, can never be put into the balance with our own.[70]

---

[66] Recall *TMS* VII.ii.1.44 (p. 292): "By nature the events which immediately affect that little department in which we ourselves have some management and direction, which immediately affect ourselves, our friends, our country, are the events which interest us the most, and which chiefly excite our desires and aversions, our hopes and fears, our joys and sorrows."

[67] *TMS* III.3.9 (p. 140).   [68] *TMS* VI.ii.2.4 (p. 229).   [69] *TMS* III.3.38 (pp. 153–154).

[70] *TMS* III.3.2–3 (pp. 134–135), emphasis added.

In a well-known passage that I considered earlier, Smith speculated that most of us would be considerably more distressed by the loss of our pinky finger than by the sudden death of millions of distant strangers swallowed up in a massive earthquake.[71]

He seems to have fastened onto Locke's observation in the *Second Treatise* that self-love makes men "partial to themselves and their Friends" – that we are "biased" when we are "judges in our own case."[72] David Hume too was instructive when he observed in the *Enquiry* that we passively tend to prefer ourselves and those "contiguous" and "intimately connected" with us.[73] Like Locke and Hume, Smith suggested that we take a cool, *affective distance* from the heat of our self-love. While Locke turned to the umpire of civil government "to restrain the partiality and Violence of men,"[74] and Hume counseled common sense and "calm judgment," encouraging us to "render our sentiments more public and social" by employing "general and unalterable standards" drawn from "the intercourse of sentiments ... in society and conversation,"[75] Smith introduced us to the "Impartial Spectator," a conscience-like faculty inside each of us that ensures that our passive sentiments will not give way to radically partial judgments and actions.[76] This "inhabitant of the breast, the man within, the great judge and arbiter of our conduct" succeeds in cooling us off, "astonishing the most presumptuous of our passions"[77] and protecting the weak and innocent, Smith maintained, because it forces us to imagine how we would appear to an impartial observer, a "third person who has no particular connexion" with us – an impartial person – if we were to lose control and surrender to our passive sentiments.[78] The impartial spectator imposes a sort of affective distance on us and prompts us to reflect, to be less partial, more objective, judges:

> Should those passions be, what they are very apt to be, too vehement, Nature has provided a proper remedy and correction. The real or even the imaginary presence of the impartial spectator, the authority of the man within the breast, is always at hand to overawe them into the proper tone and temper of moderation.[79]

---

[71] *TMS* II.3.4 (pp. 136–137).   [72] Locke, *Second Treatise*, pp. 275–276.   [73] Hume, *Enquiry*, p. 49.
[74] Locke, *Second Treatise*, pp. 275–276.   [75] Hume, *Enquiry*, p. 49.
[76] *TMS* III.3 (pp. 134–156). Of course, when Smith turned from the issue of biased judgment to deal in other parts of his treatise with more serious instances of willful acts of injustice, so often animated by delusive partiality, he did not neglect the importance of courts of justice in "well-governed states." He wrote: "To prevent the confusion which would attend upon every man's doing justice to himself, the magistrate, in all governments that have acquired any considerable authority, undertakes to do justice to all, and promises to hear and to redress every complaint of injury." *TMS* VII.iv.36 (p. 340). He continued on in Lockean terms: "without this precaution, civil society would become a scene of bloodshed and disorder, every man revenging himself at his own hand whenever he fancied he was injured."
[77] *TMS* III.3.4 (p. 137).   [78] *TMS* III.3.3 (p. 135).   [79] *TMS* VII.ii.1.44 (p. 292).

The impartial spectator brings order to a troubled mind, brings certainty into moral judgment, "calls to us, with a voice capable of astonishing the most presumptuous of our passions, that we are but one of the multitude, in no respect better than any other in it."[80] And yet, even after we "enter more coolly into the sentiments of the indifferent spectator," we can easily fall victim to "self-deceit" and "delusion" which prevent us from seeing ourselves in too humiliating a light, and ultimately reproduce "like errors in time to come."[81] We frequently sublimate what is most obviously wrong with us, and press confidently forward convincing ourselves that we have done no wrong.

It is so disagreeable to think ill of ourselves, that we often purposely turn away our view from those circumstances which might render that judgment unfavorable. He is a bold surgeon, they say, whose hand does not tremble when he performs an operation upon his own person; and he is often equally bold who does not hesitate to pull off the mysterious veil of self-delusion, which covers from his view the deformities of his own conduct. Rather than see our own behaviour under so disagreeable an aspect, we too often, foolishly and weakly, endeavour to exasperate anew those unjust passions which had formerly misled us; we endeavour by artifice to awaken old hatreds, and irritate afresh our almost forgotten resentments: we even exert ourselves for this miserable purpose, and thus persevere in injustice, merely because we once were unjust, and because we are ashamed and afraid to see that we were so.[82]

As Robert Shaver puts it, "Since the relevant spectator is my creation, it is tempting for me to create one who will let me approve of myself."[83] According to Smith, this phenomenon of "feeling too strongly," of delusion, and committing "like errors in time to come" is particularly acute when we live too solitary a life, isolated from the reality check of society.

In solitude, we are apt to feel too strongly whatever relates to ourselves: we are apt to over-rate the good offices we may have done, and the injuries we may have suffered: we are apt to be too much elated by our own good, and too much dejected by our own bad fortune.[84]

---

[80] *TMS* III.3.4 (p. 137).

[81] *TMS* III.4.4 (p. 158). For discussion, see Harvey Mitchell, "The Mysterious Veil of Self-Delusion in Adam Smith's *Theory of Moral Sentiments*," *Eighteenth-Century Studies*, vol. 20 (1987), pp. 405–421.

[82] *TMS* III.4.4 (p. 158). See also *TMS* III.4.3 (p. 157): "His own natural feeling of his own distress, his own natural view of his own situation, presses hard upon him, and he cannot, without very great effort, fix his attention upon that of the impartial spectator. Both views present themselves to him at the same time. His sense of honour, his regard to his own dignity, directs him to fix his whole attention upon the one view. His natural, his untaught and undisciplined feelings, are continually calling it off to the other."

[83] Robert Shaver, "Virtues, Utility, and Rules," in *The Cambridge Companion to Adam Smith*, ed. Knud Haakonssen (Cambridge: Cambridge University Press, 2006), pp. 189–213, at p. 204.

[84] *TMS* III.3.38 (p. 153).

158 *The circle of humanity*

Smith encouraged the deluded to look outside themselves, to surround themselves with umpires who have "no particular connexion," no affective tie, and who are therefore unlikely to be caught up in the same web of self-inflation and delusion. This meant avoiding solitude and seeking the company of friends, and better yet, strangers. Indeed, strangers who care little for us are better spectators, more "impartial" than our friends or neighbors. For,

If we saw ourselves in the light in which others see us, or in which they would see us of they knew all, a reformation would generally be unavoidable. We could not otherwise endure the sight.[85]

Only an impartial observer can "awaken" a deluded conscience from its slumber:

The conversation of a friend brings us to a better, that of a stranger to a still better temper. The man within the breast, the abstract and ideal spectator of our sentiments and conduct, requires often to be awakened and put in mind of his duty, by the presence of the real spectator: and it is always from that spectator, from which we can expect the least sympathy and indulgence, that we are likely to learn the most complete lesson of self-command.[86]

As such he concluded that "brooding" alone over one's gripes and misfortunes was far less preferable to airing them openly and moderately in the presence of others: "Society and conversation, therefore, are the most powerful remedies for restoring the mind to its tranquility":

Men of retirement and speculation, who are apt to sit brooding at home over either grief or resentment, though they may often have more humanity, more generosity, and a nicer sense of honour, yet seldom possess that equality of temper which is so common among men of the world.[87]

We will see in Chapter 6 that Smith extended this insight about solitary self-preference and distortion to the fanatical tendencies of civil factions and entire nations as well, which is why he was wary of isolationism in international affairs where the "partial spectator is at hand: the impartial one at a great distance."[88] Smith was notoriously critical of factionalism and nationalism – affection *writ large*: "Of all the corrupters of moral sentiments, therefore, faction and fanaticism have always been by far the greatest."[89] The "contagion" of group sentiment was a serious problem for Smith, and we will see

[85] *TMS* III.4.6 (pp. 158–159).
[86] *TMS* III.3.38 (pp. 153–154). For further discussion of the role of strangers in Smith's system, see Clark, "Conversation and Moderate Virtue," pp. 195–198.
[87] *TMS* I.i.4.10 (p. 23). [88] *TMS* III.3.41 (p. 154). [89] *TMS* III.3.43 (p. 156).

in Chapter 6 that he struggled with ways to replicate impartial spectatorship in broader spaces of human relation.[90]

This discussion of affective partiality brings out an apparent tension in Smith's thought about the relation between physical space and affective space. On the one hand, as I discussed above, Smith speaks regularly about the importance of physical proximity for accurate and well-informed judgments – that a spectator be near enough to a situation to know the details, to "enter into" its "minutest incidents." And yet, we learn now that spectators must be affectively removed from a situation to evaluate it impartially. Apparently, understanding requires proximity, and impartiality requires a sort of cool distance.

If an agent is my friend, and I care for her well-being, my partiality toward her makes me likelier to accommodate her self-indulgence, to brush it aside. I already want to understand her, I want her to thrive, I have memories of her behaving better, of her similarly indulging me, and so on, so I forgive her lapse and judge her gently – in a way that a stranger or mere acquaintance would not. In Smith's words, "we expect less sympathy from a common acquaintance than a friend … [and] still less sympathy from an assembly of strangers."[91] And yet, despite the affective partiality which softens my judgment, I am nearer to my friend in a physical sense than a stranger is, and am therefore far likelier to "see" and understand the "minutest incidents," the "little circumstances" surrounding my friend's behavior.[92] In other words, though my judgment is partial, my understanding is rich.

An impartial stranger, on the other hand, does not have the same affective pull. His distance becomes a remedy for partiality – but of course not without adverse implications. Distant strangers, though impartial, will have a less refined and precise understanding of the circumstances they evaluate. Strangers, unlike friends, will not have an intimate or complex appreciation of why an agent behaves as she does. She "cannot open to the former all those little circumstances which [she] can unfold to the latter."[93] But in extreme situations, as we have seen, strangers are an effective disciplinary force, Smith decided, in shaking extreme prejudice out of partiality, in "restoring the mind to its tranquility."[94] In the end, it seems that the ideal Smithian perspective will be that of a spectator who is essentially Janus-faced: near enough to access the meanings and vicissitudes of a particular situation, but distant enough not to be entangled within them – both hot

[90] *TMS* III.3.41–43 (pp. 154–156); *TMS* VI.ii.2 (pp. 227–234).   [91] *TMS* I.i.4.10 (p. 23).
[92] *TMS* I.i.4.6, 10 (pp. 21 and 23).   [93] *TMS* I.i.4.9 (p. 23).   [94] *TMS* I.i.4.10 (p. 23).

and cool.[95] This tension is not entirely resolvable but Smith seemed to think that reflective moral agents could navigate it more or less successfully.

C. HISTORICAL FAMILIARITY

Custom reconciles us to everything. (Edmund Burke, *A Philosophical Inquiry into the Origin of Our Ideas of the Sublime and Beautiful*)

The tenuous balance between physical and affective space is profoundly unsettled by a third space, likely the most relevant and complicated space in which sympathetic judgment moves in Smith's thought: that of history, or culture. We saw in the previous two sections that Smith's spectator was able, with varying degrees of success, to *transcend* both physical and affective concentricity and *enlarge* his moral perspective. In both cases, judgment was naturally biased toward the near, but was ultimately enlarged in various ways. In the case of physical space, for example, we saw that a vivid narrative or image could serve to bring the distant near and thus arouse our sympathy. In the case of affective space, we saw that Smith's turn toward the impartial spectator helped us to transcend our affective biases. Overall, I think Smith's description of sympathy and the impartial spectator are together a plausible account of how people learn to surmount affective bias. We might say that Smith succeeds in his project of affective *enlargement*.

But surely there are other sorts of bias than affective bias that a successful moral philosophy must address. I am thinking specifically of *cultural* bias, a subject of considerable importance and academic attention today. In this section, I argue that Smith's account of sympathy and the impartial spectator, on its own, does not explain sufficiently how people might surmount cultural bias. My argument rests on the assertion, which I have explored already at length, that Smith's account of the moral life should be interpreted as a highly original anthropology of culture formation – thicker, more textured and complex than perhaps any other in the eighteenth century. In the *Moral Sentiments* Smith described in rich detail how moral culture is shaped, sustained and perpetuated by its own participants, without a value-giver, without formal education, without traditional forms of authority. Smith's description of the moral life, understood anthropologically, confirms that the

---

[95] Luc Boltanski in *Distant Suffering* has a relevant discussion about the necessity of both hot and cool judgment for humanitarian thought and speech. He argues that Smith's theory successfully integrates them. In Boltanski's language, Smith's system permits "reflexivity" which "makes it possible to introduce a symmetry which reduces the tension between an aperspectival objectivism and moral involvement" (p. 43).

standards people use when they judge themselves and others derive from their own social experiences and are thus largely particular to those experiences. I am not arguing here that moral cultures cannot overlap and coincide with one another and therefore become in varying degrees intelligible to one another on Smith's model, but there is nothing in his anthropology to suggest that they must or will. Coincidence is left to chance.

Since Smith employed his spectator model to bridge affective distance between people – the fact that I as spectator cannot literally experience what you are experiencing but can use my imagination to get some "sense" of it – some interpreters have claimed that his theory has cosmopolitan significance, that it can help spectators transcend *cultural* bias and come to understand and generate fellow-feeling for those who are physically, affectively and *culturally* remote. In what follows I will argue that this kind of appropriation forces an alien agenda on Smith – and more important, that it neglects one of his most original insights: that sympathy is a social practice oriented around criteria that vary from one forum of ordinary experience to another. This has important anthropological implications for interaction across moral contexts. I argue here that Smith's moral psychology has difficulties enlarging the perspective of spectators entangled within historical space. While it does generate a transitory, affective sort of coolness, moderating our selfishness and enlarging us by reminding us that "we are but one of the multitude, in no respect better than any other in it,"[96] I argue that it is ultimately incapable of generating the sort of impartiality necessary for calling our own cultural experience into question, a critical space in which we might come to know ourselves better and to evaluate those who are culturally remote without assimilating them to ourselves. Because Smith's moral psychology was ultimately an anthropological description of how moral culture develops and sustains itself over time, and not a theory of how we become conscious about that process or how we might transcend it when necessary, this enlargement is substantially more complex and difficult to realize in the case of cultural bias. Smith's moral psychology thickly describes how deeply entrenched our perspectives really are, how difficult it is to cultivate a critical distance from ourselves, and to approach others without historical bias. It is for this reason, I submit, and not for his alleged cosmopolitanism, that Smith speaks most perceptively to moral and political theory today.[97]

---

[96] *TMS* III.3.4 (p. 137).
[97] For an excellent discussion of the tensions between anthropological relativism and philosophical universalism in Smith's thought, see Fleischacker, "Smith and Cultural Relativism."

CULTURE AND JUDGMENT

By designating this last space "historical" I am referring to the constructed, historical nature of the criteria spectators deploy when they judge – or, to use Smith's language, the "standards and measures" against which they discern "propriety" in other people.[98] Smith did not use the language of "culture" or "moral culture" to describe his project; but in contemporary terms this is precisely what he was doing. The "point of propriety" that Smith so often spoke of, which served to orient and constrain sentiment and action, is not a universally normative measure that can be grafted onto any moral context. What is proper in one moral culture might be rude and insensitive in another. You belch at my table and I am put off; I wear shoes at yours and you are. Smith's anthropology reveals that the *content* of propriety – that which designates a given sentiment or action as "praise-worthy" and "proper" – is particular to those who articulate it, part of a moral culture and as such deeply consensual. We might say that the formal category of propriety is universal for Smith (all moral cultures have some understanding of it), but that the content is necessarily plural. It must not be confused with what some might wish to characterize as universally normative or transcultural. In Part V of the *Moral Sentiments*, Smith explored what we would call "cultural pluralism," and there he concluded:

> The different situations of different ages and countries are apt … to give different characters to the generality of those who live in them, and their sentiments concerning the particular degree of each quality, that is either blamable or praise-worthy, vary, according to that degree which is usual in their own country, and in their own times.[99]

I will have much to say later about Smith's view of cultural pluralism in Part V and its relation to cosmopolitan theory today. In due course we will encounter thinkers who have attempted to draw cosmopolitan and universalist conclusions from Smith's account of the moral life – but we will discover, with Knud Haakonssen, that Smith "does not have access to a universal morality nor is an underlying logos any part of his system."[100]

To better understand Smith's orientation to historical space, let's revisit his account of the criteria we use when we judge others, which I discussed at some length in Chapter 2. Our moral criteria are self-referential for Smith. He described them as such:

---

[98] *TMS* I.i.3 (pp. 16–19).   [99] *TMS* V.2.7 (p. 204).
[100] Knud Haakonssen, "Introduction," in Adam Smith, *Theory of Moral Sentiments*, ed. Knud Haakonssen (Cambridge: Cambridge University Press, 2002), pp. vii–xxiv, at p. xi.

I judge of your sight by my sight, of your ear by my ear, of your reason by my reason, of your resentment by my resentment, of your love by my love. I neither have, *nor can have*, any other way of judging about them.[101]

And again:

when we judge in this manner of any affection ... it is scarce possible that we should make use of any other rule or canon but the correspondent affection in ourselves.[102]

On Smith's description, spectators do not judge others with abstract criteria, with a "view from nowhere." Spectators employ a *self-referential* standpoint, which means that we judge the actions and opinions of others "as right, as accurate, as agreeable to truth and reality ... for no other reason but because we find that it agrees with our own."[103] He couldn't be clearer about this. But the question of where *our own* perspectives come from is less obvious, and unfortunately not addressed by Smith in this context. But the source should be obvious to anyone familiar with Smith's central account of the sympathy process. In a well-known passage that I discussed at length earlier Smith speculated that a person who grew up in solitude "could no more think of his own character, of the propriety or demerit of his own sentiments and conduct, of the beauty or deformity of his own mind, than of the beauty or deformity of his own face."[104] Along these lines, I have argued that a spectator comes to know who he is, what he believes, and the standards by which he will judge others, through a lifetime of gazing into the "mirror of society," participating repetitively in sympathetic exchange over time with those around him. Our desire for love and approval motivates us to accommodate ourselves to what we believe spectators will indulge, to what Smith called a "point of propriety." We come to know what this point is, what our world generally approves and disapproves of, through our experiences moving through it. Compounded over time, these experiences progressively constrain my understanding of myself and others, and serve to condition the moral criteria ("my ear," "my reason," "my resentment," and so on) that I will deploy when I inevitably find myself in the position of spectator. Society thus provides the mirror of self-knowledge, and engenders – indeed, disciplines – the criteria by which the self will come to mirror and judge others.

This is what I mean when I say that Smith provided a rich account of culture formation. He described how what "we" know is engendered and transmitted through the process of sympathetic exchange: I absorb moral

---

[101] *TMS* I.i.3.10 (p. 19), emphasis added.   [102] *TMS* I.i.3.9 (p. 18).   [103] *TMS* I.i.4.4 (p. 20).
[104] *TMS* III.1.3 (p. 110).

culture as I gaze into the mirror of society, draw judgment upon myself, and adjust to what my society expects of me as a member of it. In turn, I generate culture as I become a mirror for others who gaze at me and are judged and disciplined by me. What emerges is a moral culture that is particular to those of us who participate in it. We share a language, shared understandings and expectations. A central theme in this book is that Smith's sociological account of our moral criteria culminates in a culturally insular portrait of the moral life. I agree with Samuel Fleischacker's claim that Smith's "procedure of moral judgment" makes "the standards of one's society largely determinative of one's moral judgments."[105] And because this procedure is a universal one for Smith, based in "Nature" and therefore a description of how all moral cultures unfold, we are left with a picture of deep moral diversity[106] – moral cultures particular to their participants, overlapping and communicable in some ways *perhaps*, but profoundly and deeply pluralistic.[107]

The consequence of cultural plurality for moral judgment, of course, is that the criteria we deploy will be more appropriate when we judge those who share our cultural experiences, and less appropriate with those who don't – indeed, that we may be woefully imprecise when judging a person just before our eyes, or on our television screens, clearly as our eyes may receive the "facts." In the case of affective bias, we recall, Smith had invoked the impartial spectator to help enlarge our perspective and refine our judgments; but I will argue here that this transitory sort of enlargement that Smith achieved with his spectator model is not the sort of enlargement that is required to facilitate cross-cultural intelligibility and judgment.

Smith seems to have acknowledged this when he drew on Stoic *oikeiōsis* and observed that a spectator will always sympathize more "precisely" with members of his family than with his neighbors, and with his neighbors than with his fellow citizens:

He is more habituated to sympathize with them. He knows better how everything is likely to affect them, and his sympathy with them is more precise and determinate, than it can be with the greater part of other people. It approaches nearer, in short, to what he feels for himself.[108]

---

[105] Fleischacker, "Smith and Cultural Relativism"; also Fleischacker, *Wealth of Nations*, pp. 52–54.
[106] See the connection that Fleischacker draws between the mirror of society in which we come to know ourselves and Smith's acknowledgment of cultural diversity: in *Wealth of Nations*, p. 81: "if Smith understands human nature to depend so heavily on viewing ourselves through the eyes of others, it would be extremely surprising if he overlooked the degree to which differences among different groups of those others will lead people to have different characters and aspirations." He then correctly points us to *TMS* V.
[107] The possibility of overlap renders Smith a pluralist to my mind, rather than a relativist.
[108] *TMS* VI.ii.1.2 (p. 219).

Because we share a history, and have cultivated shared sources of meaning through habitual intercourse over time, I am likelier than a stranger is to make "precise and determinate" judgments about my family, friends, co-workers and fellow citizens (in this concentric order). I already understand their worlds of meaning and "how everything is likely to affect" them. As Richard Rorty put it:

> You know more about your family than your village, more about your village than your nation, more about your nation than humanity as a while, more about being human than about simply being a living creature. You are in a better position to decide what differences between individuals are morally relevant when dealing with those whom you can describe thickly, and in a worse position when dealing with those whom you can describe only thinly.[109]

Note that *historical familiarity* works independently of *affective connection*. The subjects of affective and historical proximity will frequently overlap (I usually understand better those whom I care for), but they need not. Opposites sometimes attract; and sometimes people feel contempt for their own precisely because they understand them so well or tire of their annoying predictability.

That Smith invokes the faculty of "imagination" as the vehicle by which spectators "enter into" the motivations of others does not entail that imagination is boundless, or even that all people (such as the well-groomed nobleman *vis-à-vis* his servant) wish to exercise their imaginations. For Smith, moral imagination is bounded by familiarity. To put it differently: we are biased in historical space toward the proximate, just as we are biased in both physical and affective space. This would seem to entail that when the moral imagination is thrust beyond the sphere of the spectator's experience and understanding, it can misfire and yield judgments that are at best "*im*precise" and "*in*determinate" (to invert Smith's language in the passage cited above) and at worst based on narrow criteria foisted presumptively onto a reified other (to use language entirely anachronistic and foreign to Smith). Today we call this "misrecognition."[110]

[109] Richard Rorty, "Justice as a Larger Loyalty," in *Cosmopolitics: Thinking and Feeling beyond the Nation*, ed. Pheng Cheah and Bruce Robbins (Minneapolis, MN: University of Minnesota Press, 1998), pp. 45–58, at p. 48.

[110] See, for example, Patchen Markell, *Bound by Recognition* (Princeton, NJ: Princeton University Press, 2003), who defines misrecognition as the "failure, whether out of malice or out of ignorance, to extend people the respect or esteem that is due to them in virtue of who they are" (p. 3).

CULTURE, PERSPECTIVE AND REFLEXIVITY

Still, some have suggested that Smith's spectator model in fact enables impartial judgment of others, culturally recognizable or not. With this, we return to Smith's idea of the "impartial spectator," a faculty he invoked throughout the *Moral Sentiments* to overcome the near-sightedness of our passive sentiments. Most claims about the transcultural or cosmopolitan potential of Smith's thought focus on the impartial spectator, for obvious reasons. Smith argued that this ideal "third person," whom he sometimes called "reason," "principle," "conscience," "the man within," helps us to become impartial judges, to rise above the natural consequences of having private desires and interests, of living in families and communities and thus feeling more affection and concern for some people than others. As such, the impartial spectator has struck some interpreters as the perfect cosmopolitan device for getting us beyond ourselves, permitting access into the worlds of others and generating an impartial vantage from which to judge their practices.

Martha Nussbaum for instance draws parallels between Smith's spectator model and John Rawls' device of the original position.[111] She observes that the spectator's position in Smith's theory "is designed to model the rational moral point of view by ensuring that he will have those, and only those, thoughts, sentiments, and fantasies that are part of a rational outlook on the world."[112] No doubt Smith would have balked at Rawls' proposition of a stripped-down spectator, one ignorant of who he himself is, but since Smith too sometimes strung "reason" together with "conscience," he might have granted the observation that his own impartial spectator model, in the words of F. L. von Holthoon, "put reason on the throne again as the arbiter of moral sentiments"; or at least, as Knud Haakonssen put it, showed that "moral ideals can detach themselves from social morality."[113]

---

[111] Martha Nussbaum, *Poetic Justice*, p. 134, n. 23. But surely there is a crucial difference. Impartial judgment for Smith did not entail a "standing back," a "veiling" of self, but the imaginative insertion of a fully developed self into the circumstances of another. Rawls himself noted the crucial "contrast": for Smith, he wrote, spectators "possess all the requisite information" and "relevant knowledge" of their "natural assets or social situation," while in the original position, parties are "subject to a veil of ignorance" (John Rawls, *Theory of Justice* (Cambridge, MA: Belknap Press, 1971), pp. 183–187). Campbell, *Science of Morals*, pp. 127–141; Raphael, "Impartial Spectator," pp. 96–97; and Knud Haakonssen, "Kantian Themes in Smith," pp. 151–152. For an excellent recent discussion of Smith and Rawls that addresses the issue of Smith's "contextualism," see Carola von Villiez, "Double Standard – Naturally! Smith and Rawls: A Comparison of Methods," in *New Voices on Adam Smith*, ed. Leonidas Montes and Eric Schliesser (London: Routledge, 2006), pp. 115–139. For a reading that does the inverse, contrasting Rawls' ultimate "parochialism" with Smith's novel "universalism," see Sen, "Impartiality."

[112] Nussbaum, *Poetic Justice*, p. 73.

[113] Von Holthoon, "Adam Smith and David Hume," p. 47; Haakonssen, *Science of a Legislator*, p. 56.

Though Charles Griswold emphasizes Smith's skepticism and his resistance to using reason in this sense, he nevertheless agrees with Nussbaum and Haakonssen that Smith's impartial spectator is in some degree capable of "detaching" itself from "ordinary experience," that it employs "standard of right … over and above the judgments of the moment" and that it therefore succeeds in getting us beyond the trap of relativism and cultural perspectivism.[114] So too Jennifer Pitts more recently, who argues that for Smith our judgments are "formed in social contexts, but they are also independent of such contexts."[115] Perhaps most extreme in this sense are Luc Boltanski who claims that Smith's impartial spectator is "aperspectival" and can therefore sustain a humanitarian "politics of pity,"[116] and Amartya Sen who argues that Smith's spectator model enables "adequately objective scrutiny of social conventions and parochial sentiments."[117] But we need to ask Smith and those today who are persuaded of the cross-cultural implications of his theory: how do Smithian spectators do this? How do they detach themselves from their own experiences as agents disciplined in a world of values and overcome cultural bias? How, within the terms of Smith's thick description of the disciplinary process through which spectators in historical space come to be proper members and gatekeepers of social morality, do they now become critical of and able to transcend historical space when they imaginatively enter into the conditions and motivations of others with potentially very different histories? How does sympathy avoid assumption and speculation, avoid becoming an arrogant, smothering intrusion?

Griswold was first rigorously to pursue these sort of questions about self-knowledge and knowledge about others in a discussion of Smith's thought, and his orientation to the impartial spectator's independence has had a profound influence on the way moral philosophy thinks and talks about Adam Smith today.[118] In *Adam Smith and the Virtues of Enlightenment*, Griswold begins by dispelling a pervasive assumption in the humanities and the social sciences that grounding moral knowledge in ordinary human experience deprives us of foundations and condemns us to a relativist account of moral life. For Griswold, Smith demonstrated that morality could do

---

[114] Griswold, *Virtues of Enlightenment*, p. 281. [115] Pitts, *Turn to Empire*, pp. 43–52, at p. 43.
[116] Boltanski, *Distant Suffering*, p. 49. Boltanski borrows the formulation "politics of pity" from Hannah Arendt's discussion in *On Revolution* of Jean-Jacques Rousseau and his Revolutionary disciples.
[117] Sen, "Impartiality," p. 459.
[118] I have addressed some of these issues at length in two reviews of Griswold's *Adam Smith and the Virtues of Enlightenment*. See Fonna Forman-Barzilai, "Book Review," *Political Theory*, vol. 28, no. 1 (2000), pp. 122–30; and Fonna Forman-Barzilai, "Whose Justice? Which Impartiality?: Reflections on Griswold's Smith," *Perspectives on Political Science*, vol. 30, no. 3 (2001), pp. 146–150.

without a "philosophical" or "theoretical" apparatus precisely because ordinary human experience contained *within itself* a sufficient capacity for reflexivity and self-understanding. This reflexivity was based in ordinary moral psychology, which Smith described in the *Moral Sentiments* through his account of sympathy and the impartial spectator. Griswold praises Smith for demonstrating that moral psychology can steer a course between the empirical and the philosophical, that it can "preserve the integrity of the prephilosophical" without surrendering "its own character and aims as philosophy."[119] Smith struck this balance, we learn, by offering an account of moral psychology that "in one crucial respect" was *not* simply "continuous with ordinary experience."[120]

This balance rests, for Griswold, on the impartial spectator's ability to "detach" itself from ordinary experience. For Griswold, the impartial spectator was "rooted in time and place"[121] – this rootedness bases his claim that Smith privileged the prephilosophical. Its standpoint, however, was not fixed to this place but was rather "a reflexive refinement of the exchanges of ordinary moral life."[122] The impartial spectator's ability to reflect on the norms and practices of its own world was the basis of its "objectivity" – what Griswold also sometimes refers to as its "superior grasp of truth and reality."[123] That Smith demonstrated the possibility of genuine critical reflection within the "cave" of ordinary experience, constitutes the "virtue" and "humanity" of *his* Enlightenment – hence the title of Griswold's book.[124] No ascent into the light was required, for the cave could be enlightened from within.[125]

But how does Smith's impartial spectator in fact "stand at a critical distance from the mores of his own time"?[126] How does it become reflexive? How does it simultaneously emerge from "us" yet objectively evaluate "us"? Griswold describes a "form of moral self-awareness," that we acquire "over time" and "by degrees" through the experience of "moral education."[127] "Only through practice do we learn to feel what is appropriate to feel and, correspondingly, what is appropriate to praise and blame."[128] With experience we learn to detach ourselves from prejudice and to judge the world in light of a "reasonable standard extrapolated from the thoughtful observations governing how individuals may be expected to behave or respond in just this or that sort of situation."[129] This is how we become "responsible," "self-determining moral agents."[130] Thus, Griswold concludes that the impartial spectator is "all we really need for moral life."[131] It brings sufficient objectivity to our moral judgments

[119] Griswold, *Virtues of Enlightenment*, p. 63.   [120] *Ibid.*, p. 362.   [121] *Ibid.*, p. 349.
[122] *Ibid.*, p. 146.   [123] *Ibid.*, p. 371.   [124] *Ibid.*, p. 174.   [125] *Ibid.*, p. 247.   [126] *Ibid.*, p. 350.
[127] *Ibid.*, pp. 210–212.   [128] *Ibid.*, p. 211.   [129] *Ibid.*, pp. 131 and 136.   [130] *Ibid.*, p. 131.
[131] *Ibid.*, p. 138.

without any of the problematic claims about the transcendental status of reason, the reduction of emotions to "incentives" or "inclinations," the meshing of "maxims" with the *a priori* machinery of the categorical imperative, or claims about the mysterious noumenal status of freedom.[132]

Sounds like a magic key. And maybe Smith thought he had one. But does Smith's moral philosophy actually get us where Griswold says it does? In one breath Griswold admits freely that the impartial spectator "defines the moral point of view *already latent* in ordinary life"[133] – he even calls it a "personification of the public"[134] – but then he denies that it is a "function of any given social consensus."[135] He admits that it is "a logical development ... of traits of *actual* spectators,"[136] but then insists on its detachment and reflexivity and denies that it is a "sociological concept."[137] In another essay, he asserts that morality "is something we communally determine for ourselves" but then characterizes it as "metaphysically constitutive."[138] He seems to want it both ways: insisting on the impartial spectator's sociality primarily to establish its "reality," to avoid charges that its standpoint is either merely subjective, a "fantasy," an "illusion in the mind," something we each construct willy-nilly on our own, or else "an independent order of moral facts";[139] but then emphasizing the impartial spectator's reflexivity and objectivity to overcome the contextuality and historicity that its reality entails. Griswold moves back and forth between these claims with such rhetorical ease, and elaborates both so remarkably well, that it is sometimes easy to forget the point: that the two are very much in tension.[140]

But the questions remain: can Smith's impartial spectator stand at a critical distance from its own experience, or does it perceive only the shadows? Has Smith enlightened the cave from within, "redeemed" the ordinary?[141] Griswold poses the decisive question himself, but insists that the impartial spectator need not be "blinded" or "unalterably cooped up in its particular historical milieu."[142] Situatedness need not undermine our ability to "grasp the truth" about ourselves or even about different societies.[143] This may well be. But does Adam Smith's thought bring us to this appealing

---

[132] *Ibid.*, p. 139.   [133] *Ibid.*, p. 145.   [134] *Ibid.*, p. 135.   [135] *Ibid.*, p. 143.   [136] *Ibid.*, p. 138.
[137] *Ibid.*, p. 143.
[138] Charles L. Griswold, Jr., "Imagination: Morals, Science, and Arts," in *The Cambridge Companion to Adam Smith*, ed. Knud Haakonssen (Cambridge: Cambridge University Press, 2006), pp. 22–56, at pp. 40 and 50.
[139] Griswold, *Virtues of Enlightenment*, pp. 340–342.
[140] Fleischacker observes that Smith *himself* was caught in this trap between anthropological and philosophical approaches to morality. Fleischacker, "Smith and Cultural Relativism," p. 15.
[141] Griswold, *Virtues of Enlightenment*, p. 14.   [142] *Ibid.*, pp. 349–351.   [143] *Ibid.*, p. 350.

conclusion? Does he pave the likeliest route to intelligibility? If the impartial spectator is, as I have argued, a "socialized conscience" or, what Griswold himself calls, a "personification of the public,"[144] how is it capable of making ordinary experience intelligible? How does it cultivate the "superior grasp of truth and reality" that Griswold attributes to it?[145]

Griswold's argument about the impartial spectator's "reflexivity" and "superior grasp of truth and reality" has important implications for how a spectator judges others, and particularly those beyond his own historical space. It is here that the most troubling implications of Griswold's argument reveal themselves. He insists on a "basic transparency of human beings to each other."[146] Surely imagination cannot carry us completely beyond ourselves and into the worlds of others, he admits. This is an inevitable fact about our physical separateness. But this does not mean that we lose all capacity to understand those who are quite differently placed, and to "evaluate" their unique experiences from a "moral point of view."[147] One need not *be* an American slave or a starving person or a refugee to grasp the truth of their suffering. This obviously sounds right. Smith gives the example of a man sympathizing with a "woman in child-bed" though "it is impossible that he should conceive himself as suffering her pains in his own proper person and character."[148] As I write these words in San Diego, wildfires are raging uncontrolled just miles from where I sit. A half-million of my neighbors have been evacuated from their homes and sleep in shelters tonight. With the thick stench of destruction hanging in the air, and soot gathering on my window sill, I can sympathize, grasp the truth of their suffering, though I am "here" safe writing and they are "there" refugees suffering, perhaps homeless tomorrow. Griswold has recently carried this Smithian way of bridging perspectives into a discussion about forgiveness – how injured parties, through recognition of their shared humanity with their injurer, and acquaintance with the injurer's story, might come to cultivate forgiveness toward the injurer.[149]

Ultimately, Griswold wants to emphasize the accessibility of others' experiences to avoid the perspectivist trap of identity politics. Making "shared

---

[144] *Ibid.*, p. 135.
[145] *Ibid.*, p. 371. Again, I do argue that there are other resources in Smith's thought, which will be addressed later.
[146] *Ibid.*, p. 350.   [147] *Ibid.*, pp. 95–96.
[148] *TMS* VII.iii.1.4 (p. 317). Smith used this example when discussing the problems of conceiving of sympathy as a selfish act, but I draw on the example here since it demonstrates Smith's belief in the bridgeability of perspective quite well.
[149] Charles L. Griswold, Jr., *Forgiveness: A Philosophical Exploration* (Cambridge: Cambridge University Press, 2007), esp. ch. 2.

experience" a criterion for sympathy would amount to, what Griswold calls, an "actor-centered" or "expressivist" morality that devolves quickly into the "irrationalism," "relativism," "vulgarized skepticism" and "group narcissism," all so prevalent in contemporary thought.[150] "The subversion of the standpoint of the spectator into that of the actor" has the result that "individuals and groups see themselves as beholden only to their own standards"[151] and that it is therefore "impossible for those who are not members to understand the group in question."[152]

Luc Boltanski agrees about the pit of perspectivism. In *Distant Suffering* he draws on Smith's thought to overcome what he calls a contemporary "crisis of pity" in which so many of us have become cynical and suspicious of "any form of political action oriented towards a horizon of moral ideals."[153] Boltanski regrets that contemporary debate over humanitarian action tends to get stuck in the binary languages of "abstract universalism" and "narrow communitarianism":

the first siding with global solidarity against national particularisms and preferences, while the second unmasks the hypocrisy or, at best, naive eirenic idealism which ignores the primacy of interests and ties forged by history.[154]

Boltanski maintains that Smith's theory of spectatorship sustains a twenty-first-century humanitarian theory of political commitment that is unburdened by this tension since it provides an "apparatus" capable of unifying sentiment from a distance, of establishing and nourishing genuine connections between people quite differently situated, "without force"[155] and "without recourse to communal identification or to an Edenic fusion."[156] Because Smith emphasized the "radical distinction" between a detached, impartial observer and the individual whom he or she is observing, and did not seek to impose "the same ethical values" upon them, his theory helps demonstrate that humanitarian impulses need not be censured as an arrogant, Western assertion of partial understandings and preferences, a "smug celebration of the return of kindness," a sort of narcissistic declaration of moral superiority.[157]

For both Boltanski and Griswold, Smith's theory helps us to avoid the messy, fragmented plurality and particularity of identity politics. But as life goes, avoiding messiness often creates new messes. To make his point, Griswold emphasizes a pervasive and (from an egalitarian perspective) somewhat troubling "asymmetry" in Smith's thought between spectators and agents which, he says, establishes the "normative superiority" of the

---

[150] Griswold, *Virtues of Enlightenment*, pp. 85–86 and 371.   [151] *Ibid.*, p. 265.   [152] *Ibid.*, p. 96.
[153] Boltanski, *Distant Suffering*, p. xvi.   [154] *Ibid.*, p. xiii.   [155] *Ibid.*, p. 36.   [156] *Ibid.*, p. 38.
[157] *Ibid.*, p. 54.

spectator's standpoint. He describes sympathy as "spectator-centered" rather than "agent-centered" and states that this "asymmetrical relation of actor and spectator becomes lexical insofar as judgments of value and truth are concerned."[158] This is where the problem really emerges for me. One can accept fully Griswold's resistance to moral perspectivism and the basic claim he shares with Nussbaum, Sen, Boltanski and many others in the cosmopolitan debates that human suffering is fundamentally communicable without embracing perspectival "asymmetry" and making so decisive a move into *prioritizing* standpoints. If he is right here, this "prioritization" pierces the egalitarian heart of Smith's sympathy model which Stephen Darwall has developed so convincingly.[159]

The evidence Griswold uses to establish the spectator's priority has troubling implications, particularly when applied in multicultural and global contexts, where power is often distributed in such radically unjust ways. Griswold claims that Smith asserted a lexical "asymmetry" of standpoints when he described the moralizing impact that spectatorship has upon agents. In other words, the fact that spectatorship produces a change in the behaviour of agents on Smith's description establishes for Griswold the moral priority of the force that produced the change – dare I say, that might is right. No doubt, Smith argued that sympathy disciplines. I spent a great deal of time exploring the disciplinary dimension of sympathetic activity in Chapter 3. Its power to discipline is what gave sympathy its moral teeth in Smith's thought, for sure. But does this mean that spectators are always right? If this is Smith's argument, then egalitarians should reject it *tout court*. But even Smith acknowledged in countless places that spectators were sometimes terribly misguided, deluded and corrupt. Indeed, I have argued here that the corruptibility of our moral sentiments is a central theme in Smith's book, and largely responsible for inspiring Smith's obsessive revisions over thirty-one years. Nevertheless, Griswold argues that since agents in Smith's theory adjust their passions to the spectator's standpoint, while the spectator's standpoint "does not undergo any great modification," the agent's standpoint is therefore merely contingent, malleable, a "social artifact" – and thus, normatively inferior.[160]

[158] Griswold, *Virtues of Enlightenment*, pp. 92 and 96–99.
[159] Darwall, "Sympathetic Liberalism"; and Darwall, "Equal Dignity."
[160] Griswold, *Virtues of Enlightenment*, pp. 103–106. In a symposium on Griswold's *Adam Smith and the Virtues of Enlightenment* convened at the American Political Science Association in 2000, and later published in *Perspectives on Political Science*, Griswold argued that I deny the textual evidence that Smith normatively prioritized the spectator's standpoint. I do not deny the textual evidence at all. Indeed, the essential point in my account of sympathy (and the reason I used Foucault in earlier chapters) is that spectator's have extraordinary power in Smith's theory to motivate conformity. So, I

Asserting the spectator's normative priority, as Griswold does, confuses truth with power – an absolutely impermissible move if we are to believe that sympathy for Smith was situated in a "moral community among independent equal persons," as Darwall presses[161] – and to my mind a perilous move after the horrors of the twentieth century. Establishing the objectivity or truth of a standpoint, requires far more than noting the situational power that spectators have to discipline and extract conformity from agents. Again, if this was Smith's claim, we should reject it. If through my judgment (as an individual, as a moral community) I should happen somehow to change or through shame to repress the behavior of an Amish woman home educating her child, or a man engaging in consensual homosexual acts, or a Muslim schoolgirl in France wearing her headscarf, or a mohel carving off an infant's foreskin, or those who sleep in a family bed, or an African American speaking Ebonics, or a polygamist – does that mean my standpoint embodies truth and reality; or does it simply mean that I have the power to coerce, motivate, or shame change? Surely there may be good reasons for my standpoint. I am not denying that at all. As a political theorist committed to the values of democratic equality and human dignity I have strong positions on many, many things. We all do. But asserting these positions requires additional arguments – arguments that I am eager to make. That I judge, even that I motivate and change behavior through my judgment, implies nothing whatsoever about the truthfulness of my standpoint.

How, for Griswold, do spectators in Smith's theory know more or better than the agents they are judging? From where do they derive this knowledge? Griswold himself asserts that spectators are situated in the world – again, this rootedness bases his claim that Smith privileged the prephilosophical. But he often dodges the implications that this being-in-the-world has for the spectator's standpoint. In fact, if we are at all persuaded by Smith's typically Scottish argument about the sociological basis of morals, then we *already know* that the spectator's "superior" standpoint is no less contingent and malleable, no less a "social artifact" than the "inferior" standpoints of agents. A spectator will approve of behavior in others that is consistent with whatever he has

---

don't at all deny the textual evidence. But I am troubled by the implications of this dimension of Smith's thought in contexts characterized by unjust gaps in power and influence. Smith may correctly have described how perspectives are "harmonized," and how social order is achieved. But this sort of success has nothing to do with "truth." I simply wish to emphasize here the historicity of the spectator's standpoint, a subject Griswold himself has elaborated with more grace and lucidity than any other interpreter of Smith's thought. Does it not follow that normative priority, in this sense, would seem to rest on a moving foundation? See Griswold, "Reply to My Critics," pp. 164–165.
[161] Darwall, "Equal Dignity," p. 132.

learned to esteem. In an anthropological key, Fleischacker nicely refers to the
spectator's standpoint as a "taboo."[162] Spectators learn what they know and
derive the criteria they deploy *by being agents themselves*, observed and judged
by other spectators who, in turn, are simply agents. In the *Enquiry*, Hume
understood well the sociological origins of our "standards." He observed:

> The more we converse with mankind, and the greater social interaction we
> maintain, the more shall we be familiarized to these general preferences and
> distinctions without which our conversation and discourse could scarcely be
> rendered intelligible to each other.[163]

And again, noting the intransigence of these "preferences and distinctions":

> The intercourse of sentiments ... in society and conversation, makes us form some
> general unalterable standard by which we may approve or disapprove of characters
> and manners.[164]

This way of thinking about the origins of moral judgment was a commonplace in eighteenth-century Scottish social thought. We see it come through
clearly in the work of Smith's student, John Millar in his treatise, *An
Historical View of the English Government*. Note how he echoed the master's
observations regarding the origins of propriety:

> individuals form their notions of propriety according to a general standard, and
> fashion their morals in conformity to the prevailing taste of the times.[165]

Like his friend and like his student, Smith argued that moral knowledge is
intersubjectively produced, that our standards (the *content* of "my ear," "my
love" "my resentment" and so on) are disciplined though sympathetic
exchange with those around us. This means that we are all agents sometimes, all spectators sometimes – receptacles as well as producers of culture.
This is how we learn and teach others what it means to be "us." There is no
static *class* of spectators or agents, no lexical ordering of standpoints.
Spectators are not an elite class of impartial citizens with special access to
some self-standing reality.[166] As David Levy and Sandra Peart put it "there is
no outside vantage from which to judge the universe. There is no external
vantage to which a philosopher might escape and obtain god's view of the

---

[162] See Fleischacker, "Smith and Cultural Relativism," p. 3.
[163] Hume, *Enquiry*, p. 48.   [164] *Ibid.*, p. 49.
[165] John Millar, *An Historical View of the English Government (1803)*, 4 vols. (London, 1812), vol. IV,
p. 246; discussed in Christopher J. Berry, *Social Theory of the Scottish Enlightenment* (Edinburgh:
Edinburgh University Press 1997), pp. 74–90, at p. 75.
[166] Griswold insists that the impartial spectator is not a philosopher (see *Virtues of Enlightenment*,
pp. 136, 147 and 369), but the distinction seems to blur sometimes.

universe."[167] Spectators are just "us"; their standpoint is "ours," a product of ordinary moral experience, a representation of what "we" already know.

And I'm not convinced that Charles Griswold wouldn't ultimately agree here. Why else would he turn to Socrates in the epilogue of *Adam Smith and the Virtues of Enlightenment*, and conclude that a "completion" of Smithian moral philosophy would require the radical "disruption" of Socratic examination?[168] Socratic dialogue, he says, might "clear a space for discerning judgment" to help us distinguish "reality" from "received social practice," from that which is "intersubjectively" made.[169] This is no small concession in a book committed to demonstrating the adequacy of Smithian "therapy."[170] Griswold's final appeal to a "pared-down Platonism" might just suggest that the impartial spectator's autocritique was not critical enough, that the cave was still too dark.[171]

TRANSCENDENT FRAMES

Stephen Darwall was correct that *Adam Smith and the Virtues of Enlightenment* "may be the first truly comprehensive and philosophically probing account of Smith's moral and political thought ever written. To read it is to understand why Smith deserves such a treatment."[172] I agree absolutely; Griswold is obviously my most important interlocutor here. There is no book from which I have learned more about Smith, and to which I return more often to sharpen my own interpretation. And yet, I believe he underestimates the historical and cultural implications of Smith's moral psychology when he links the "impartial spectator" with truth. In fact it is Griswold's remarkably rich and sensitive account of ordinary morality in Smith's thought that provides us with every reason *not* to accept the reconciliation he offers. As a good student I believe I have taken Griswold's interpretation to its logical limits. A key theme in my account here is that the tension Griswold illuminates so well between ordinary experience and reflective transcendence remains productively unresolved in Smith's thought, and that we stand to learn much about ourselves,

---

[167] Levy and Peart, "Adam Smith and His Sources," p. 60.
[168] Griswold, *Virtues of Enlightenment*, pp. 372–375.   [169] *Ibid.*, p. 373.   [170] *Ibid.*, p. 20.
[171] In "Reply to My Critics," Griswold resists the claim I am making here. He insists that his gestures at the end of the book "are not meant to suggest that Smith's moral theory is a failure." I also do not believe that Smith's moral theory is a failure if it is understood in an affective key, as a technique for bridging self and society. When applied in historical space, however, I believe it runs into more difficulties – though potentially not insurmountable ones, as I will suggest in Chapter 7.
[172] Darwall, "Sympathetic Liberalism."

our limitations, and our relations with others by accepting the irresolution and living with the tension. Much as the perfectionist urge in me aligns with Griswold's philosophical desire for something firmer, something larger, the anthropologist/historian in me has come to terms that Smith's moral psychology doesn't get us there. It doesn't within its own logic provide a way to transcend itself. Any progress in that regard is left to chance, fortuitous.

My central argument here might be restated productively as such: different sorts of impartiality are required for different sorts of judgment, and I believe Griswold and others have conflated them. The sort of impartiality Smith achieves with his impartial spectator model might be effective in adjusting physical and affective shortsightedness (in other words, enlarging bias in the first two spaces I discussed in this chapter). But it is *not* the sort required to render unbiased cross-cultural judgments.[173] Note, I am not denying the general possibility of self-distancing. I too resist postmodern assertions about the absolute impenetrability of otherness, and that historical variability renders knowledge about self inaccessible and illusory. In this, I share what Amanda Anderson characterizes as a commitment to cosmopolitan self-distancing in an "aspirational" sense, envisioned as an "ambivalent, hesitant, uneasy, and sometimes quite thoughtfully engaged … complex process of self-interrogation and social critique."[174] But I am less convinced than Griswold and others that Adam Smith's theory of conscience is the most plausible or compelling way to initiate in such a process. Smith's spectator model surely generates a highly effective, transitory sort of coolness – for example, restraining someone who in the heat of passion or group fanaticism is tempted to act aggressively toward a stranger or group of strangers. Observe the following passage, in which Smith invokes the impartial spectator to "temper" the "vehemence" of group attachment:

Should those passions be, what they are very apt to be, too vehement, Nature has provided a proper remedy and correction. The real or even the imaginary presence of the impartial spectator, the authority of the man within the breast, is always at hand to overawe them into the proper tone and temper of moderation.[175]

---

[173] I will argue in Chapter 7 that Smith's idea of negative justice may do more work in this regard.

[174] See the introductory chapter in Amanda Anderson, *The Powers of Distance: Cosmopolitanism and the Cultivation of Detachment* (Princeton, NJ: Princeton University Press, 2001), pp. 3–33, at p. 33.

[175] *TMS* VII.ii.1.44 (p. 292).

The impartial spectator "overawes" our emotions, tempers and moderates the "vehemence" of our affective attachments here. This was its role in Smith's theory. On its own terms, Smith's model succeeds in mediating our self-regarding and other-regarding tendencies, disciplining propriety, and ensuring relatively stable and sociable communities. But rendering cross-cultural judgments that don't simply reduce the other to oneself requires something much different: that a spectator be able to transcend not merely the vehemence of his *physical* and *affective* "connexions" to self and specific others, but more fundamentally, to interrogate and sometimes to subvert the *very measure* by which he has become accustomed to judging himself and the world. These are two very different sorts of activities. In other words, while Smith is primarily concerned with social coordination, the problem of historical self-consciousness and critique is an epistemic one and in many respects beyond the scope of his theory.[176]

Therefore, to say that moral judgment is "an ongoing process of adjustment, a continual search for equilibrium," as Griswold, Haakonssen, Hope, Pitts and others correctly do – or as a "refinement" as Karen Valihora does (in a particularly fine essay on Smith's Kantian aesthetic model of moral judgment), or as Emma Rothschild describes as an "oscillation ... from the world to the mind, and from the mind to the world" – does not get us any closer to an explanation of how Smithian spectators might transcend historical bias.[177] Jennifer Pitts in *A Turn to Empire* and Amartya Sen in his recent work on justice have made perhaps the most progress in this regard. Pitts, for example, argues that "our moral judgment is likely to improve as our circle of comparison broadens."[178] She is admirably attuned to the particularity of moral judgment in Smith's thought – "that morality is developed necessarily within the context of a particular group or society,"[179] that "our moral judgments are formed within particular social contexts," and so forth.[180] Her account of cultural/moral diversity in Part V of the *Moral Sentiments* is wonderfully rich and insightful, an important contribution to scholarship on Smith. One particularly textured dimension of her presentation is the way she distances herself from "relativist" readings of Smith's system, like that of T. D. Campbell (which equates relativism with a resistance to speaking in overtly universalist terms), and ultimately

---

[176] That Smith was concerned more with moral action than with moral epistemology see Samuel Fleischacker, "Kant and Adam Smith," pp. 255–256.

[177] Griswold, *Virtues of Enlightenment*, p. 102; Haakonssen, *Science of a Legislator*, pp. 58–59; Hope, *Virtue by Consensus*, p. 87; Pitts, *Turn to Empire*, p. 43; Karen Valihora, "The Judgment of Judgment: Adam Smith's *Theory of Moral Sentiments*," *British Journal of Aesthetics*, vol. 41 (2000), pp. 138–159. Emma Rothschild's reference to "oscillation" comes from "Dignity or Meanness," p. 154.

[178] Pitts, *A Turn to Empire*, p. 43.   [179] *Ibid.*, p. 43.   [180] *Ibid.*, p. 45.

turns to Smith's jurisprudence to save him from this fate – a move that I am sympathetic with and will address at greater length myself in Chapter 7.[181] The problem emerges with Pitts' second argument against a relativist reading that seems to conflate the very affective and historical spaces that I am trying to keep distinct here. She argues that cross-cultural judgments are "possible" for Smith, that an impartial spectator can judge unfamiliar practices morally from within a particular social context, since moral judgment is a "process by which we continually revise our opinions in response to new experiences and new opportunities for comparison with the views of others."[182] Again, we see the idea of "process" and "reflective refinement" that Haakonssen and Griswold so emphasize, but given here a multicultural twist. Pitts goes on to include in her depiction of these "new experiences and new opportunities" interaction with "broader circles," with unfamiliar others, with less partial spectators (which she transforms into those who are culturally remote, and not just affectively remote as I believe Smith suggested), and concludes that Smith's theory encourages "openness toward unfamiliar values and practices."[183] No doubt, this is an ingenious and intuitively appealing argument. I am deeply drawn to the sort of openness Pitts describes here. But this claim that the spectator can refine his judgments by "broadening" his "circle of comparison" to (presumably) cultural strangers strikes me as a wishful addendum to Smith's thought, resonant with contemporary multicultural theory, but really quite alien to what I have been describing here as Smith's preoccupation with overcoming affective bias, and relatedly his preoccupation with local social order.[184] Surely he argued that "impartial" spectators help us cool our self-preference, individually and in groups, as Pitts correctly notes. Like his friend Edmund Burke, Smith was a notorious critic of fanaticism and faction, and he encouraged people in the grip of group frenzy to cool off by surrounding themselves with less partial observers. I will have more to say about this in my discussion of Smith's international political thought in the next chapter. But note for now that in such passages, Smith recommended situating oneself among spectators that are less partial *affectively*, who cool us down precisely because they are uninvolved, untouched by the heat of our frenzy.

[181] *Ibid.*, pp. 45–52. If any method of enlarging historical perspective exists in Smith's thought, I believe it emerges in his jurisprudence as Pitts (citing Haakonssen) ultimately argues convincingly, and not, as I argue, from within his moral psychology, which is inescapably particularistic, and yet highly instructive for that very reason. I will address Smith's jurisprudence in this context later in Chapter 7.

[182] Pitts, *A Turn to Empire*, p. 45.   [183] *Ibid.*, p. 45.

[184] For more on this theme, see Fonna Forman-Barzilai, Book Review of Jennifer Pitts, *A Turn to Empire: The Rise of Imperial Liberalism in Britain and France* (Princeton, NJ: Princeton University Press, 2005), in *Ethics and International Affairs*, vol. 21, no. 2 (2007), pp. 265–267.

Surely this group of affectively impartial observers might coincide or overlap with those who are less partial culturally, but Smith's focus here was clearly on cooling affective fanaticism – and I am not persuaded that this has anything to do in Smith's argument with "broadening" our cultural sensibility and helping us make "moral" judgments about others beyond our historical space. Certainly Smith never thought about "cooling down" in these terms. Surrounding ourselves with impartial spectators enables a person or group to overcome *affective* bias, to become less fanatically self-absorbed, and perhaps to cultivate some awareness and concern for broader circles (circles which in Smith's time were incidentally generally very narrow, and close to home). But these affective acts of cooling self-preference, augmenting concern for others, or even cultivating a tolerant, open-minded stance toward others, are entirely different sorts of activity, different sorts of enlarging, than the act of judging the values and practices of unfamiliar others *with unbiased criteria*. This is *precisely* why I have differentiated affective and historical bias in this chapter. The process of refining and enlarging our perspective works very differently in each space.

Amartya Sen offers an argument very similar to Pitts' – and equally appealing on an intuitive level – concluding that Smith's theory has resources for "scrutinizing ... the impact of entrenched tradition and custom."[185] Because he links his interpretation of Smith explicitly to a twenty-first-century humanitarian agenda, I would like to explore it in some detail. Sen's essay differentiates what he calls "closed" and "open" variants of impartiality – the first of which attempts to "eliminate partiality toward the vested interests or personal objectives of individuals in the focal group"; the second of which seeks "to address the limitations of partiality toward the shared prejudices or biases of the focal group itself."[186] This distinction maps quite exactly onto the distinction I have asserted in this chapter between affective and historical bias. Sen characterizes Rawls' contractarianism as a prime illustration of closed impartiality, a device that claims universality and objectivity for itself, but erroneously so since its "program of impartial assessment [is] confined only to members of the focal group," and is thus "parochial" and "polity-prioritized" in scope.[187] Smith, on the other hand, offers a theory of open impartiality through his device of the impartial spectator, which Sen believes has more solid claims to universality and objectivity because it reaches beyond the focal group to "outsiders," to those both "far and near," to "real spectators at a distance."[188]

---

[185] Amartya Sen, "Open and Closed Impartiality," *Journal of Philosophy*, vol. 99, no. 9 (2002), pp. 445–469.
[186] Sen, "Impartiality," p. 447.   [187] *Ibid.*, pp. 440 and 447–448.
[188] *Ibid.*, pp. 449–451 and 458–459.

Echoing Pitts' argument that the spectator refines his judgments as he comes into contact with "broader circles," Sen observes that Smith "saw the possibility that the impartial spectator could draw on the understanding of people who are far as well as those who are near."[189] Thus, he asserts that Smith's open view of impartiality is likelier than Rawls' closed view to instigate a "forceful scrutiny of local values," to "guarantee an adequately objective scrutiny of social conventions and parochial sentiments."[190]

I find Sen's distinction between closed and open impartiality very helpful, for it resonates significantly with the distinction I have drawn in this chapter between two sorts of self-distancing – from bias that is affective in nature (what Sen in his formulation would call "interested" or "personal" partiality) and from bias that is historical or cultural in nature (what Sen would characterize as focal group partiality). But for reasons I have explored at length in this chapter, I am not convinced by Sen that Smith's impartial spectator model amounts to a theory of open impartiality. I have been characterizing Smith's theory as distinctively closed, in Sen's sense. I believe Sen's interpretation is noble and hopeful, but flawed for two related reasons. He both overplays Smith's use of the distant spectator; and under-emphasizes the importance in Smith's theory of intimacy and proximity for accurate and well-informed judgments. A word now about each. First, one mustn't forget that Smith's account of spectatorship was primarily a descriptive one. When he referred to the "eyes of other people" – a formulation Sen seizes on repeatedly as the key to Smith's "openness" – Smith was primarily concerned with describing the effects of spectatorship on moral sentiment in relatively close quarters. The "eyes of other people" tended most often to be the eyes of those with whom an individual came into contact most frequently – those he already knew, those he already loved, those with whom he was already most inclined to agree on a variety of subjects. Spectatorship was primarily a local, visual affair for Smith; he valued it in a distinctively modern way for producing social harmony and moral consensus without traditional forms of coercion. Therefore, although Smith's impartial spectator model is not procedurally contractarian like Rawls' "veil of ignorance," the consensus it yields tends to share the same "parochial" and "polity-prioritized" scope that Sen rejects in Rawls. Certainly Sen is accurate that Smith spoke occasionally in the *Moral Sentiments* about the usefulness of the distant, stranger-spectator. But he places far too much emphasis on it. And like Pitts, he doesn't adequately contextualize Smith's use of the stranger-spectator, and therefore fails to notice that Smith invokes this figure very specifically in the case of

[189] *Ibid.*, p. 457.   [190] *Ibid.*, pp. 458–459.

subduing intense factional (read: affective) prejudice. Smith does not in any sense invoke the stranger-spectator for purposes of cultural self-awareness, or in Sen's words, to scrutinize "the impact of entrenched tradition and custom."[191] Whatever we might wish to make of it for present purposes, distant spectatorship served *for Smith* as a coolant of fanatical passion – of course, not in itself an altogether unimportant contribution in light of today's most vexing global problems.

The second shortcoming of Sen's interpretation is that he de-emphasizes the importance in Smith's theory of intimate spectatorship for well-informed judgments, a subject of profound importance when attempting to engage unfamiliar cultures with openness and respect, and which I have explored at length earlier in this chapter.

In the end, I believe Smith's version of impartiality was far less "open" on Sen's own terms, and that, in fact, the moral "progress" entailed by the Smithian view of self-correction, of "reflective refinement," of moral matur-ity, of making more objective judgments, may actually entrench the spec-tator *more deeply* in his own world of meanings. Haakonssen is very helpful here when he observes that the "process" of refining our judgments for Smith "is a continual weeding out of behaviour which is incompatible with social life."[192] Moral maturity for Smith seems to entail that we become even more disciplined, in "command" of ourselves, proper, sociable, polite – whatever these things mean in our particular moral universe. With matur-ity, in other words, we enlarge our affective scope beyond our little selves by attuning ourselves more closely to our own society's particular expectations of us. We become better and better interpreters of our own cultural signals. Again, this all reinforces my argument that Smith was concerned primarily with social coordination. But how does this process of becoming a more mature, proper and congenial member of my society help me to better know myself, or better understand someone who has learned (through the same process as I have, for sympathy is a universal process) what it means *in her world* to be "in command" of herself, proper, sociable, polite? In fact, it seems that as my capacity for sympathetic judgment "progresses" and "matures" in Smith's theory, I become *more* deeply entrenched culturally, more docile, less critical, less inclined to understand myself and others. Fleischacker put it well, capturing my distinction between affective and cultural space: Smith's "focus is on self-correction and not on the reform of social standards of morality."[193] Moral maturity for Smith seems to function

---

[191] *Ibid.*, p. 459.   [192] Haakonssen, *Science of a Legislator*, p. 58.
[193] Fleischacker, "Smith and Cultural Relativism," p. 20, n. 16.

without the reflective space that is necessary for critical self-awareness and cross-cultural judgment. Surely some might find ways to reach beyond, but as Fleischacker notes, "this will be fortuitous, not built into the very nature of Smith's moral method."[194]

Critics of course will point to Smith's thoughts on praise-worthiness in Part III of the *Moral Sentiments*. At various points, no doubt, Smith argued that a mature spectator will learn to distinguish what is inherently "praise-worthy" from that which is conventional, merely praised, and therefore less worthy.[195] I spent considerable time in Chapter 3 discussing this perfection-ist amalgam of Stoic, Rousseauian and Kantian elements that Smith grafted onto his empirical description of moral judgment, spurred by a letter Smith had received from his old friend Sir Gilbert Elliot of Minto soon after the *Moral Sentiments* was published in 1759. Smith's distinction between praise and praise-worthiness would seem to provide the spectator with some measure of critical distance from his own history, and a capacity for cultivating a more impartial, less insular view of the world. Since it is easy to see why one might wish to hang one's cosmopolitan hat on this perfec-tionist evolution in Smith's thought, let's explore it further.

Smith believed he had advanced on the conventionalism of Humean common sense when he proposed an impartial spectator that could improve itself by learning to distinguish praise-worthiness from mere praise. Surely they agreed on much: Hume and Smith both observed that affective bias can wreak havoc on our morals, leading us to exaggerate the importance of that which affects us and to underestimate that which does not. Accordingly they both asserted that moral judgment demands a firmer, more impartial foundation than our sentiments can provide. Hume discovered this foun-dation in the "general unalterable" standards that emerge through social intercourse:

it is necessary for us, in our calm judgments and discourse concerning the characters of men, to neglect all these differences, and render our sentiments more public and social ... The intercourse of sentiments, therefore, in society and conversation, makes us form some general unalterable standard, by which we may approve or disapprove of characters and manners.[196]

At first, this looks much like Smith's account of ordinary moral life, which we explored in Chapter 2. Indeed, it was a staple in Scottish social theory that convention was efficient in diverting us from ourselves and enlarging

---

[194] *Ibid.*, p. 20, n. 15.   [195] *TMS* III.2.7 (p. 117); *TMS* 2.32 (pp. 130–131).
[196] Hume, *Enquiry*, pp. 48–50.

the natural bias of our passive feelings. As such, Smith's account of sympathetic exchange greatly resembled Hume's "intercourse of sentiments." But one of the most interesting differences between them, from the perspective of this chapter, is that Smith was troubled by the "unalterable" quality of Humean common sense, which comes through nicely in the passage cited above. As we saw in Chapter 3, Smith ached over the problem of conventionalism. Humean efficiency was not reason enough to surrender our moral judgments to convention, to what is merely praised. What if convention happens to be corrupt, profane, bellicose – or today, say, racist, sexist, antisemitic, homophobic? Corrupt societies are often very successful in socializing their members, and highly efficient in this sense (think here of Bettelheim's account of totalitarian obedience[197]), but they nevertheless inevitably cultivate deeply disturbing judgments – for example, when a slaveholder is affirmed by the values of his slaveholding society,[198] or when a Hitler youth is celebrated as courageous and patriotic for surrendering his parents to the Gestapo. This phenomenon was not lost on Smith who spoke at length in Part V of the *Moral Sentiments* about:

> Those … who have had the misfortune to be brought up amidst violence, licentiousness, falsehood, and injustice; lose, though not all sense of the impropriety of such conduct, yet all sense of its dreadful enormity, or of the vengeance and punishment due to it. They have been familiarized with it from their infancy, custom has rendered it habitual to them, and they are very apt to regard it as, what is called, the way of the world.[199]

"Custom reconciles us to everything," Edmund Burke observed, in an oft-cited passage from the *Philosophical Inquiry into the Origin of Our Ideas of the Sublime and Beautiful*.[200] Corrupt moral cultures as all moral cultures function as habits, and do not require for their success a critical space for reflection and analysis of their assumptions, beliefs and the practices they sustain. In fact one can see precisely how such a critical space might become offensive and annoying to members of a moral culture who are invested, self-consciously or not, in sanctioning, propagating and protecting it. Think here of Socrates as gadfly nipping at the corrupt and self-righteous ass of

---

[197] Bruno Bettelheim, "Remarks on the Psychological Appeal of Totalitarianism," *American Journal of Economics and Sociology*, vol. 12 (1952), pp. 89–96; reprinted in Bruno Bettelheim, *Surviving and Other Essays* (New York: Alfred A. Knopf, 1979), pp. 317–332.

[198] Smith uses this example himself at *WN* IV, vii, b (p. 54); *LJ* (A) iii (pp. 101–105 and 114–117); and *LJ* (B) (pp. 134–136). See Haakonssen's discussion of Smith's argument here in Haakonssen, *Science of a Legislator*, p. 132.

[199] *TMS* V.2.2 (pp. 200–201).

[200] Edmund Burke, *Philosophical Inquiry into the Origin of Our Ideas of the Sublime and Beautiful*, in *The Works of the Right Honorable Edmund Burke*, 12 vols. (Boston: Little Brown, 1881), vol. II, p. 231.

Athenian moral culture – and his fate. Smith spoke explicitly about "just" individuals who brave the "general contagion" of groupthink, and "incur" the "contempt, and sometimes even the detestation of his fellow citizens" – and particularly so in times of public turbulence:

> there are, no doubt, always a few, though commonly but very few, who preserve their judgment untainted by the general contagion. They seldom amount to more than, here and there, a solitary individual, without any influence … All such people are held in contempt and derision.[201]

That Smith was troubled by the relativity of Hume's conventionalist approach to coordinating our sentiments seems to be one key reason he attempted to locate a more stable foundation for moral judgment in the "impartial spectator" and its ability to identify corruption within its own very constitution.

But there are two fundamental problems with believing that Smith succeeds in achieving cultural reflexivity and sustaining unbiased cross-cultural judgments through his attempt to further stabilize judgment by positing an impartial spectator capable of identifying its own perversion. The first is historical, and relates to the *reason* Smith first began to differentiate praise from praise-worthiness. Concerns about moral relativity have a distinctly contemporary ring to them; mine are driven by discomfort with many culturally sanctioned violations of human liberty and dignity. To the extent that Smith was troubled by moral relativity, he was motivated not by humanitarian or cosmopolitan concerns, but by the very local corruption of European moral culture. As I argued in Chapter 3, Smith wanted to stabilize moral judgment, to locate something firmer, because he was revolted by the vulgar displays of wealth and power that had disguised themselves as virtue in eighteenth-century European life. Corrupt people (Smith singled out "profligates" and politicians) too often paraded themselves as "virtuous" and succeeded in deluding a pliable and envious public into esteeming and emulating them.[202] The corrupt few, in other words, tended to set the standards of taste and value for the many. This cultural elevation of profligacy is one way Smith believed common sense – "the way of the world" – can very easily become corrupted. For Smith, the sympathy process (notably our desire "to assimilate and to accommodate … our own sentiments, principle, and feelings to those which we see fixed and rooted in the persons with whom we are obliged to live and converse a great deal with") is the very "cause of the contagious effects of both good and bad company":

---

[201] *TMS* III.3.43 (p. 155).   [202] *TMS* I.iii.2–3 (pp. 50–66).

The man who associates chiefly with the wise and virtuous, though he may not himself become either wise or virtuous, cannot help conceiving a certain respect at least for wisdom and virtue; and the man who associates chiefly with the profligate and dissolute, though he may not himself become profligate and dissolute, must soon lose, at least, all his original abhorrence of profligacy and dissolution of manners.[203]

Thus, when Smith drew a perfectionist line between praise and praise-worthiness, or relatedly between "ordinary perfection" and "exact propriety and perfection," or between the ends of "wealth and greatness" and "wisdom and virtue," he was not interested in "universalizing" the standards of moral judgment, the way a cosmopolitan today might conceive of such an activity. In fact, Smith's obsession with social order and his focus on the moral capacities of "middling men" rather than exceptional ones, on the "tolerably good soldier" rather than the "saint" (which I explored at length in Chapter 4 in the context of his resistance to Christian and Stoic perfectionism), would have made him more concerned with *avoiding* the corrosive effects of praise in corrupt contexts than with *elevating* the perfection of praise-worthiness as a universal moral standard. In other words, Smith was a localist, and his discussion of praise-worthiness was driven by his local anxieties. In this sense, I depart somewhat from Donald Winch, who suggested that Smith had adopted a "cosmopolitan standpoint," in which his overall "method" and "rationale" were oriented around "being part of a much larger political unit."[204] I tend instead to agree with Jennifer Pitts that Smith was preoccupied primarily with social order and "metropolitan" prosperity.[205] Exaggerating here perhaps, but only a little, I suspect that conventionalism would not have troubled Smith, might not even have crossed his mind, had he lived in a society that esteemed what he believed was properly estimable.

The second, and from a moral philosophic perspective more fundamental problem with believing that Smith succeeds in achieving cultural reflexivity and sustaining unbiased cross-cultural judgments through his attempt to further stabilize judgment by positing an impartial spectator capable of identifying its own perversion, is that Smith asserted the distinction between praise and praise-worthiness without saying a word about how

---

[203] *TMS* VI.ii.1.17 (p. 224).

[204] Donald Winch, "Adam Smith's 'Enduring Particular Result': A Political and Cosmopolitan Perspective," in *Wealth and Virtue*, ed. Istvan Hont and Michael Ignatieff (Cambridge: Cambridge University Press, 1983), pp. 253–269, at p. 267.

[205] See Pitts' excellent discussion of Smith's "metropolitan" orientation – and its relation to universalist dimensions of his thought in *Turn to Empire*, pp. 25–58.

ordinary people within his empirical description come to know the difference, how they differentiate these standards. Surely he argued that the
distinction exists, that there is indeed a form called "the praise-worthy" –
a perfectionist moment in his thought no doubt – but we need to address
the plausibility of asserting such a distinction within the logic of Smith's
moral method. The distinction seems to be an epiphenomenal assertion,
divorced from Smith's description of the sociological process through which
the standards of judgment are formed. Understanding when common sense
is perverted, understanding the difference between what is praise-worthy
and what is merely praised, requires a critical distance that Smith's moral
psychology, on its face, fails to supply. As Samuel Fleischacker notes:

> There is little in Smith's construction of the idealized spectator to correct for the
> surrounding society's standard of judgment; the idealized figure takes over those
> standards and corrects merely for their partial or ill-informed *use*. If the moral
> standards, the basic moral sentiments, of a society are profoundly corrupt – if a
> feeling of contempt for Africans or hatred for Jews or homosexuals, say, has become
> confused with a moral feeling, and a society's judgments of these people's actions
> have been comprehensively skewed as a result – the impartial spectator within each
> individual will share in, rather than correcting for, that corruption.[206]

Smith's foray into "is" and "ought," his distinction between that which is
praise-worthy and that which is merely praised, never explained *how* the
impartial spectator comes to know the difference, how he knows that his
standards have become perverted, or *where* this new knowledge about the
world might come from. As Fleischacker asks, "How are we supposed to tell
whether our society is bigoted or not?"[207] To maintain that the impartial
spectator is like an Aristotelian *phronimos*, as Griswold does – or a "public
purged of defects," as John Durham Peters does[208] – is not the same thing as
saying that Smith's theory has the *resources* to transform ordinary spectators
into *phronimoi*.[209] Smith tried to finesse the problem by crafting a deistic
argument about the divinity of praise-worthiness – recall the 1790 argument
that conscience is best understood as a "demigod" residing in the breast –
but he never explained to a secular audience where its knowledge comes
from. Surely some people find a way beyond. As I said earlier, I tend to take
an aspirational, process-oriented approach to self-critique. I certainly am

---

[206] Fleischacker, "Smith and Cultural Relativism," p. 8.
[207] *Ibid.*, p. 13.   [208] Peters, "Publicity and Pain," p. 663.
[209] In "Reply to My Critics," Griswold argues that I have "conflated the standpoint of the spectator with
that of the impartial spectator" in Smith's thought. He insists that the impartial spectator becomes, for
Smith, an Aristotelian *phronimos* who can resist social convention, and that his theory has the
"resources" to do so. I still believe this needs analysis. See Griswold, "Reply to My Critics," pp. 164–166.

not suggesting that people cannot adopt a critical stance toward their own moral cultures. Smith himself acknowledged that even in the worst, most corrupted of times, a few – "though commonly but a very few" – will manage "to preserve their judgment untainted by the general contagion."[210] Indeed, Smith did so with regard to British prejudices in favor of slavery and empire.[211] The sober point, however, is that most people do not. And Smith knew this. Most people conform, often times even when asked to do something that overtly violates a deeper gut sense of wrongfulness. How else can we make sense of the horrors of the last century? Studies of genocide in the twentieth century – perhaps the most extreme case of social conformity running afoul of the instincts of basic human inhibition – affirm again and again that this question about human motivation is settled.[212] Smith tried to address the problem by temporarily suspending the thick empiricism which generated his sociological account of moral life and by shrouding the impartial spectator in theological garb – which may have settled the matter for some. But I believe we learn more about the depth of the problem through Smith's struggles than about resolving it through his solutions.

Given the complicity of the impartial spectator in reinforcing "the way of the world," how do we "enter into" contexts of meaning that are unfamiliar to us without speculating about the other, and forcing their practices into our own frames of reference, demanding that they conform to "my sight," "my ear," "my reason," and so on? Modern social science traditionally sends us into the field, to do "fieldwork in unfamiliar places," to come to know who inhabits these places by observing them, talking with them, being among them. The Renaissance skeptic Michel de Montaigne, who generated some frenzy for defending the integrity of Amerindian cannibalism, was probably first rigorously to pursue this mode of thinking about cultural bias and how to overcome it:

---

[210] *TMS* III.3.43. This passage comes from Smith's remarks about faction, and difficulties of resisting it.

[211] For Griswold this resistance to prejudice is evidence that Smith's theory has "critical punch." "Reply to My Critics," p. 165. Jennifer Pitts' rich and insightful discussion of Smith's critical reaction to many social practices in *Turn to Empire* strikes me as potentially more convincing. She does not attribute such judgment to the "impartial spectator's" ability to distance itself from social convention, as Griswold does, or that a practice is "self-evidently immoral." But she describes Smith's more "modest and careful" attempt to "contextualize" a practice in the very reasons that a particular society first adopted it. All practices are adaptations for Smith, "reasonable responses to circumstance," she suggests. Judgment, then, consists in an assertion that a given practice "persist(s) long after circumstances have stopped justifying them." Pitts, *A Turn to Empire*, pp. 48–52. See also Haakonssen, *Science of a Legislator*, pp. 59–61; and Shaver, "Virtues," p. 200.

[212] See, for example, James Waller, *Becoming Evil: How Ordinary People Commit Genocide and Mass Killing* (New York: Oxford University Press, 2002).

This great world which some do yet multiply as several species under one genus, is the mirror wherein we are to behold ourselves, to be able to know ourselves as we ought to do in the true bias. In short, I would have this to be the book my young gentleman should study with the most attention. So many humours, so many sects, so many judgments, opinions, laws, and customs, teach us to judge aright of our own, and inform our understanding to discover its imperfection and natural infirmity, which is no trivial speculation.[213]

So too René Descartes, who managed to render Montaigne's insights compatible with a rationalist critique of prejudice – that of others as well as our own:

It is a good thing to know something of the customs and manners of various people in order to judge of our own more objectively and so not think everything which is contrary to our ways is ridiculous and irrational, as those who have seen nothing are in the habit of doing.[214]

The idea that encountering the other might help us better to know ourselves and others became a touchstone for modern skeptics, and remains central for those today who wish to navigate beyond relativism while acknowledging deep cultural diversity. Observe for example Richard Madsen and Tracy Strong's recent claim in their introduction to a collection of essays on ethical pluralism:

one needs to strive for a full understanding of the other, because without such an understanding, one cannot truly know oneself. Full self-understanding is initially restricted by our horizon of unexamined assumptions. The attempt to understand other cultures and systems of morality leads to a "fusion of horizons" in which we gain a broader set of terms to reflect critically on our identity.[215]

This all seems to resonate with the claim Sen shares with Pitts that for Smith "our moral judgment is likely to improve as our circle of comparison broadens."[216] And indeed this is very likely the best we can do. But we also must acknowledge that encountering unfamiliar and perplexing things – without something more – need not produce openness. Coming

[213] Michel de Montaigne, *Essays*, I, 25.
[214] René Descartes, *Discourse on the Method of Properly Conducting One's Reason and of Seeking the Truth in the Sciences*, trans. F. E. Sutcliffe (London: Penguin, 1968), pp. 25–91, at pp. 30–31.
[215] Richard Madsen and Tracy B. Strong, "Introduction: Three Forms of Ethical Pluralism," in Richard Madsen and Tracy B. Strong, *The Many and the One: Religious and Secular Perspectives on Ethical Pluralism in the Modern World* (Princeton, NJ: Princeton University Press, 2003), pp. 1–21, at p. 11. For further discussion of the various possible outcomes of cultural contact, see Chan Kwok-Bun, "Both Sides, Now: Culture Contact, Hybridization and Cosmopolitanism," in *Conceiving Cosmopolitanism: Theory, Context, and Practice*, ed. Steven Vertovec and Robin Cohen (Oxford: Oxford University Press, 2002), pp. 191–208, esp. pp. 192–196.
[216] Pitts, *A Turn to Empire*, p. 43.

upon something strange or ugly without a predisposition of openness, without a suspension of certitude, without a willingness to learn and broaden oneself, may actually reinforce one's prejudices, lead one to "dig in one's heels" so to speak, even to transform or destroy what one encounters. One need look no further than European encounters in the "New World," a subject Smith himself discussed at some length in Part V of the *Moral Sentiments*, which he devoted to the subject of custom. Smith described the Europeans' sense of astonishment when encountering Amerindian practices that rubbed hard against their more delicate civilized sensibilities.[217] He castigated the hypocrisy of European civility for condemning the barbarity of such practices while Europeans themselves engaged in a host of barbarities, including slavery, imperialism and the corsetting of women. In Part V, Smith clearly did not believe that encounter will lead necessarily to openness and a broadening of one's perspective. I will have more to say about Part V later.

For the moment, consider the old Hasidic tale attributed to the Baal Shem Tov that tells of a gentile standing before a window through which he sees a group of Hasidim dancing in circles, sweaty and red-faced, extremities and talit flailing fast, furious and in every direction, and assumes he has come upon a den of madmen. That I have difficulties understanding the sense of liberation that some Muslim women report living life with their faces covered has much to do with the particular Western understanding of agency and expression that I have been disciplined to value. When we encounter the unfamiliar, especially when it rubs hard against deeply entrenched beliefs, "something will have to stay behind the lens."[218] As Thomas Nagel put it: "However often we may try to step outside of ourselves … something in us will determine the resulting picture, and this will give grounds for doubt that we are really getting any closer to reality."[219] Engaging in a dialogue with my shrouded sister, allowing her "identity story" to unfold,[220] I might acquire a new respect for her resolve and the worldview that sustains it. But physical proximity might actually serve to reinforce my biases and presuppositions, substantiating my sense of the sheer discomfort and humiliation of wearing a *hijab*, confirming what I *already knew* about the woman who does and the culture that forces her to accept and defend her conditions. How do we "enter into" contexts and worlds of meaning that are unfamiliar to us without

[217] *TMS* V.I.9 (p. 199).   [218] Nagel, *View from Nowhere*, p. 86.   [219] *Ibid.*, p. 68.
[220] The phrase I borrow from Michael J. Shapiro, "The Ethics of Encounter: Unreading, Unmapping the Imperium," in *Moral Spaces: Rethinking Ethics and World Politics*, ed. David Campbell and Michael J. Shapiro (Minneapolis, MN: University of Minnesota Press, 1999), pp. 57–91, at pp. 59–63.

speculating or reifying, *museumizing*,[221] the other, and forcing their practices into our own frames of reference? Smith seems to be very right when he asserted that we have no other way of judging others than by assimilating them to ourselves (to "my sight," "my ear," "my reason," "my resentment," "my love"). Does assimilating the other to myself in this fashion bring me any closer to understanding others – or, for that matter, understanding myself?

In this sense the Stoic cosmopolitan project of assimilation, of collapsing the circles inward toward the self, seems highly presumptuous. Uday Singh Mehta in *Liberalism and Empire*, a book that addresses the prevalence of this phenomenon in nineteenth-century European thought, differentiates what he calls a "cosmopolitanism of reason" from a "cosmopolitanism of senti-ment."[222] The first, which is endemic to the liberal imperial mindset on Mehta's reading, is exercised through practices of "fusion" and "assimila-tion" and is premised on the assumption "that the strange is just a variation on what is already familiar" – "only spots on a map or past points on the scale of civilizational progress, but not *dwellings* in which peoples lived and had deeply invested identities."[223] I do not always agree with Mehta's sweeping indictments of liberalism and the Enlightenment, though his ire is sometimes understandable given that his primary case is British atrocity in India, surely one of liberalism's darkest hours.[224] What I value most about Mehta's narrative for my purposes here is his emphasis on a second variant of cosmopolitanism that he believes opens itself to "wider bonds of sym-pathy."[225] In other words, as vivid as his account of British arrogance in India may be, he does not preclude the possibility of knowledge and care across cultural boundaries. Instead he emphasizes humility, and the ago-nistic and processual dimensions of learning through encounter. In this light he draws on Edmund Burke to develop the idea of a "cosmopolitanism of sentiments" which is exercised through "dialogue with the unfamiliar" and is willing to "risk ... being confronted with utter opacity – an intran-sigent strangeness, an unfamiliarity that remains so, an experience that

[221] I borrow the museum metaphor from Pheng Cheah, "Given Culture: Rethinking Cosmopolitical Freedom in Transnationalism," in *Cosmopolitics: Thinking and Feeling beyond the Nation*, ed. Pheng Cheah and Bruce Robbins (Minneapolis, MN: University of Minnesota Press, 1998), pp. 290–328, at p. 290.
[222] Uday Singh Mehta, *Liberalism and Empire: A Study in Nineteenth-Century British Liberal Thought* (Chicago: University of Chicago Press, 1999), pp. 17–23.
[223] *Ibid.*, pp. 20–21.
[224] I am inclined to read large swathes of eighteenth-century thought more generously on these issues, in line with various insights in Muthu, *Enlightenment Against Empire* (Princeton, NJ: Princeton University Press, 2003); and Pitts, *Turn to Empire*.
[225] Mehta, *Liberalism and Empire*, p. 22.

cannot be shared, prejudices that do not really fuse with a cosmopolitan horizon, a difference that cannot be assimilated."[226] On Mehta's reading collapsing the Stoic circles would amount to a violent assimilation of the other into the worldview of the conqueror (though of course cosmopolitans would fiercely deny the imperialistic nature of their project). In a similar vein Margaret Chatterjee, who discusses cosmopolitan linkages between Hierocles, Smith and Gandhi notes that the act of collapsing the circles inward must be conceived as a "mutual matter," and that the outer circles may in fact resist being drawn in – that there might be a "question mark about willingness."[227] Like Mehta, Chatterjee helps us think about the resistance of the "periphery" to being collapsed into a regime of cosmopolitan judgment and care.

Reflecting on the contemporary problems of cultural insularity and chauvinism, proponents of "multicultural education" today advocate exposing children early to cultural diversity. This is a rich and contested field that crosses many disciplines, but the overall thrust is that early exposure to a variety of cultural practices and belief systems – what we might think of, for our purposes, as a sort of simulated physical proximity, a simulated encounter – ultimately makes a difference in how children understand themselves and others, their similarities and differences with others both near and far, and their relative place in a deeply diverse and interconnected world.[228] If we deliberately add multicultural sensitivity to the "curriculum" of beliefs and conventions already in circulation, which children inevitably internalize through the education of social experience,[229] perhaps it might engender humility and a stance of genuine openness toward others. Surely this was not Adam Smith's agenda – not at all. But I find it plausible and intuitively appealing that the moral life he so richly described might become more reflexive, ultimately more conscious of itself, if supplemented by exogenous encounters through ideas, narratives, and images *during childhood*, as the young and malleable conscience

[226] *Ibid.*, p. 22.   [227] Chatterjee, "Oceanic Circle," p. 152.

[228] A very useful summary of the debates on multicultural education is found in Kevin McDonough, "Cultural Recognition, Cosmopolitanism and Multicultural Education," in *Philosophy of Education 1997*, ed. L. Stone (Urbana, IL: Philosophy of Education Society, 1998). For more, see the essays in Kevin McDonough and Walter Feinberg, eds., *Citizenship and Education in Liberal-Democratic Societies: Teaching for Cosmopolitan Values and Collective Identities* (Oxford: Oxford University Press, 1993).

[229] Peters calls Smith's ordinary morality a "school of virtue": "Publicity and Pain," p. 662. Knud Haakonssen similarly described the education of ordinary morality in Smith as such: "From the hand of nature all men are basically alike, but education can make them different for education consists in exposure to a variety of situations from which new lines of behaviour and thinking are picked up through mutual sympathy with other participants in the educational process." Haakonssen, *Science of a Legislator*, pp. 59–60.

is developing.[230] Indeed, as Plato put it, "the beginning of any process is most important, especially for anything young and tender."[231]

Of course from a cosmopolitan or multicultural perspective, Smith himself provided a woefully insular account of education in the *Moral Sentiments*.[232] As a localist preoccupied with social order, he was suspicious of sending children to foreign schools, or supplementing university education with foreign travel, since these practices tended to "hurt most essentially the domestic morals."[233] A cosmopolitan education might have helped a spectator in Smith's theory contextualize a curious foreign spectacle before him, and anchor his judgment more firmly on "the whole case of his companion with all its minutest incidents," as Smith put it elsewhere.[234] But this sort of thinking is entirely absent from Smith's narrative on education because, again, he was primarily concerned with maintaining "domestic morals." And in this light, he believed that the best education is the one we receive from the physically near and familiar. Only when you "educate them in your own house" and "let their dwelling be at home," Smith warns, will you have children who are "dutiful, kind and affectionate."[235]

A WORLD WITHOUT SYMPATHY?

After the original publication of the *Moral Sentiments* in 1759 Smith attempted to refine and stabilize his theory of moral judgment in a variety of ways. In Chapters 3 and 4, I examined some of the more substantial ones: his further conceptualization and refinement of his impartial spectator theory, amplification of Stoic themes of self-command and moral maturity, the characterization of conscience as a "demigod," a rather anxious discussion about fortifying judgment with "moral rules" that reflect the "Infinite Wisdom and Infinite Power!" of God's will. I have argued that all of these adjustments and enhancements were motivated by Smith's preoccupation with maintaining "the very existence of human society," the "fabric of human society" – to ensure that it would not "crumble into nothing."[236] The *Moral Sentiments* is primarily a description of how the self learns to calm passionate self-preference and harmonize with the other selves that it

---

[230] See Martha Nussbaum's defense of cosmopolitan education in *Cultivating Humanity*.
[231] Plato, *Republic* 377a (p. 52).   [232] *TMS* VI.ii.1.10 (p. 222).   [233] *TMS* VI.ii.1.10 (p. 222).
[234] *TMS* I.i.4.6 (p. 21).
[235] *TMS* VI.ii.1.10 (p. 222). For this reason, I am uncomfortable with attempts to enlarge the spectator's perspective from within Smith's theory of education. See, for example, Jack Russell Weinstein, "Sympathy, Difference, and Education: Social Unity in the Work of Adam Smith," *Economics and Philosophy*, vol. 22, no. 1 (2006), pp. 1–33.
[236] *TMS* III.5.2 (p. 163); *TMS* II.ii.3.4 (p. 86).

most often comes into contact with. This the role that sympathy and the impartial spectator play in Smith's moral philosophy as a whole. Smith sought to demonstrate that people could live together peaceably and pro-ductively without coercive forms of moral policing long associated with religious authority, the "laws of the magistrate," and casuistic moral educa-tion and consensus on moral foundations. The first two Parts of the *Moral Sentiments* describe a self-regulating process of sympathetic exchange through which ordinary people in their daily interactions coordinate their sentiments and generate social norms. In short, Smith believed that our sentiments were capable of ordering our moral lives. They coordinate and unify.

They also, however, engender moral culture as a by-product of this coordination, which can sometimes go awry, yield disturbing conventions, and creating serious problems for the stability Smith sought. Despite his general faith in the moral capacities of ordinary people, Smith was a perceptive analyst of human behavior, and observed that sentiment was inherently unstable, susceptible to a variety of irregularities, distortions and delusions that threatened to compromise our moral judgments, producing unsociable and even violent outcomes. Thus, when Smith sought to adjust his theory of the impartial spectator theory in subsequent editions of the *Moral Sentiments*, he did so very deliberately with an eye to this fundamen-tal problem of social coordination.

This preoccupation with social order helps explain Smith's localism, which is evident throughout the *Moral Sentiments* – from his description of moral culture to his emphasis on caring for one's own, to his sharp rejection of Stoic cosmopolitanism. I believe that the *Moral Sentiments* was ultimately dedicated to addressing this problem of social coordination among those who lived in relatively close proximity with one another; who tended *already* in varying degrees to care for one another as neighbors, fellow citizens, Christians, moderns; and who tended *already* in varying degrees to be unified by shared views and beliefs about many fundamental things. But our focus in this chapter has shifted ultimately away from Smith's concerns with social coordination among those who tend to share physical, affective and historical space, and toward coordination in realms that are spatially far more complicated. How did Smith conceptualize a society that might exist beyond the narrow spaces that in past ages limited our physical contact with distant strangers, our knowledge and understand-ing about their condition, our efficacy in assisting them, and ultimately any conventional moral duty we had towards them?

Obviously we cannot know whether Smith might have paid his Oxfam dues – whether he might have expanded the duty to commiserate beyond the proximate had he known of the power of the media to bring the faces of suffering people into our living rooms, or about the variable successes of international and transnational institutions like the World Health Organization, the United Nations, and what Alex de Waal has memorably referred to as the "humanitarian international" of NGOs such as Amnesty International and the Red Cross.[237] But after examining Smith's moral psychology in the first five chapters of this book, we seem to be left with a strikingly parochial ethics.

But is Smith ultimately a radical localist and particularist, who believed that our moral horizon fades out at the edges of physical immediacy, affective "connexion" and historical familiarity? Did Smith's *oikeiōsis* remain intact "all the way down," so to speak? Such an assertion would make his thought seriously uninteresting, isolationist communitarianism at its absolute worst, relativist at its core, and of no help in thinking through the most salient issues today in ethical and political thought. Was his notorious belief in a divine *œconomy* Smith's final word about the cosmopolis – a system in which God minds the happiness of the universe, leaving each of us free to indulge ourselves, blind to the world we harm through our actions or neglect? Some would have us believe this. But I join the wave of scholarship in recent decades that rejects the claim that Smith celebrated avarice. The interesting observation for contemporary thought is how Smith ultimately addressed larger and broader circles in light of the localism and particularism inevitably generated by his moral psychology. We might characterize Smith's orientation here as *troubled* or perhaps *conflicted* for he was well aware that localism and particularism often provoke suspicion, jealousy and conflict in the international sphere (or at least supply little incentive against them), and thus continually threaten to undermine international peace and harmony, which Smith sincerely wished for.

I shall argue in the next two chapters that unlike many localist and particularist reactions to cosmopolitan and universalist thinking today, Smith did not abandon his international political thought to anarchy nor his moral philosophy to relativism. Though I have argued to this point that Smith's moral psychology exposes serious practical problems for any cosmopolitan agenda, I will suggest that Smith ultimately gestures toward the possibility of just such a cosmopolitan frame in different and (in this context) comparatively neglected dimensions of his thought, making him an interesting and salient voice in contemporary debates about international

---

[237] Alex de Waal, "The Humanitarian Juggernaut," *London Review of Books*, June 22, 1995, p. 10.

and cross-cultural ethics.[238] In the final two chapters, I will disentangle two "strands" of modern cosmopolitanism in Smith's thought, each largely independent of his moral psychology, that cogently confront the dangers of localism and particularism. The first strand, to be discussed in Chapter 6, is Smith's international political economy, which might be described in this context as a theory of commercial cosmopolitanism that produces good effects without good intentions, thus challenging an assumption in realist international political thought that the world is anarchic and fundamentally conflictual. The second strand, to be discussed in Chapter 7, is Smith's theory of justice conceived "negatively" as the avoidance of human cruelty, which Smith himself described as "universal" and independent of positive institution. If Smith's commercial cosmopolitanism in Chapter 6 addresses the problems of physical and affective bias in the international realm, his negative justice in Chapter 7 addresses the problem of cultural bias.

Ultimately I will resist the argument that a spectator's situatedness definitively closes the possibility of understanding and judging the beliefs and practices of cultural "others," or of adopting what Pheng Cheah has called a "cosmopolitical frame of analysis."[239] If that were the case, only historical curiosity would justify reading Smith's book today. We would simply dismiss him as a relativist, and place his book on display alongside the cultural artifacts that his theory refuses to let us discuss or touch. What I have suggested here is that Smith's moral psychology in the *Theory of Moral Sentiments* cannot easily generate such a cosmopolitical frame of analysis. Sympathy and the impartial spectator are far too contingent. Those of us who are interested in cultivating such a frame need to look elsewhere. I suggest next that we might look to other dimensions of Smith's thought.

---

[238] For lively discussion of this important new direction in contemporary discourse, see the essays in *Cosmopolitics*, ed. Cheah and Robbins. See also *International Society: Diverse Ethical Perspectives*, ed. David R. Mapel and Terry Nardin (Princeton, NJ: Princeton University Press, 1998); *Moral Spaces: Rethinking Ethics and World Politics*, ed. David Campbell and Michael J. Shapiro (Minneapolis, MN: University of Minnesota Press, 1999); and several of the essays in *Pluralism: The Philosophy and Politics of Diversity*, ed. Maria Baghramian and Attracta Ingram (New York: Routledge, 2000).

[239] Cheah, "Given Culture," p. 290.

CHAPTER 6

The commercial cosmopolis

Sometimes I am jostled among a Body of Americans; sometimes I am
lost in a Crowd of Jews, and sometimes in a Group of Dutch-men.
I am a Dane, a Swede, or Frenchman at different times, or rather fancy
myself like the old Philosopher, who upon being asked what country-
man he was, replied that he was a Citizen of the World.
                    Joseph Addison, *The Spectator* (19 May 1711), on a visit
                                         to the Royal Exchange in London

Throughout I have emphasized Smith's focus on social order, and his desire
to harmonize tensions between self and others. I ultimately argued that
Smith's reconciliation of this tension through the apparatus of moral
psychology yielded an acute localism that is bound to strike twenty-first-
century interpreters reflecting on global interconnectedness as an insightful
and finely textured theory of social coordination, but also an unsatisfying
theory of, even an obstacle to, society in broader spaces.

In this chapter I shall extend my argument in two related ways. First, I will
economize the tension Smith described throughout the *Moral Sentiments*
between self and society, describing it here as a tension between economy
and ethics. Clearly, this is an old subject. The tension between Adam Smith's
ethical and economic thought first became a "problem" for European scholarship in the closing years of the nineteenth century, and turned on the extent
that Smith's *Wealth of Nations* (1776) arose conceptually from the ethical
framework developed in the *Moral Sentiments*? (1759). This chapter contributes
to a tradition of scholarship within this long debate that tends to see this tension
as putatively artificial since Smith was manifestly clear that his political economy was contained within his larger project of moral philosophy.[1] The debate
on this is to my mind settled; there is no point in rehearsing it here again.

But here I am registering a different kind of response to the "Adam Smith
Problem," one that accepts the general contours of a conceptual tension

---

[1] See my discussion in Chapter 1.

between "self and society" – economized here as "economy and ethics" – but expands this tension spatially to the international realm, a sort of "globalization" of the "Adam Smith Problem." So in this chapter I am both "economizing" the tension between self and society which I have explored at length in this book, as well as "globalizing" its scope. Here I examine portions of the *Moral Sentiments* in which Smith discussed international themes, portions which have received surprisingly little attention among political and moral theorists reflecting on globalism and cosmopolitanism today. In Chapter 4, I already discussed at length Smith's rejection of Christian and Stoic cosmopolitanism, the reasons for which remain central to the argument I will make here. In this chapter I revisit this break between Smith and traditional cosmopolitan theory, and explore Smith's attempt to replicate ends traditionally understood as "cosmopolitan" through the apparatus of international commerce.

In short, I demonstrate here that Smith's international political economy was not simply an economist's unmitigated celebration of selfishness and the triumph of national and corporate self-interest – as it is still today so often interpreted by devotees and detractors alike. Rather, I argue that we should understand it, in good measure, as a moral philosopher's reluctant concession to living in a world highly resistant to cosmopolitan aspirations. A notorious lover of harmony and equilibrium, Smith detested war, and all things that contributed to it.[2] He never suggested that nations were continually at war with each other. But he seems to have adopted Hobbes' view, called "realism" today in the field of international relations, that conflict exists when there is "no assurance to the contrary":

For as the nature of Foul weather, lyeth not in a showre or two of rain, but in an intention thereto of many dayes together: So the nature of War, consisteth not in actual fighting; but in the known disposition thereto, during all the time there is no assurance to the contrary.[3]

Note similarities in Smith's account of "uncertainty and irregularity" in international relations:

for where there is no supreme legislative power nor judge to settle differences, we may always expect uncertainty and irregularity.[4]

---

[2] See Samuel Fleischacker's discussion of Smith's hatred of war in *Wealth of Nations*, pp. 250–257.
[3] Thomas Hobbes, *Leviathan* (1651), ed. Richard Tuck (Cambridge: Cambridge University Press, 1991), pp. 88–89.
[4] *LJ* (B), p. 339. For discussion of international instability in Smith's thought, see Haakonssen, *The Science of a Legislator*, pp. 133–134.

My Hobbesian reading of Smith here may strike some as counterintuitive, given all that he said in the *Moral Sentiments* about our general tendency to "sympathize" with others. Indeed, as we have seen, he regularly condemned "Hobbes and his followers" for "deducing all our sentiments from certain refinements of self-love" – for arguing that "man is driven to take refuge in society, not by any natural love which he bears to his own kind, but because without the assistance of others he is incapable of subsisting with ease or safety."[5] Nevertheless, Smith's emphasis on international conflict, and on the absence of "any assurance to the contrary" was central to his attempt to discover alternative paths toward cooperation and peace. In this light, he characterized free commercial intercourse among self-interested nations as a new cosmopolitan trope suited to the eighteenth century and its commercial aspirations, one that promised to mitigate conflict among spatially disparate entities, and to generate a tolerable peace in the absence of better motives. One commentator has usefully called this sort of argument a "self-centered cosmopolitanism."[6]

More than two centuries of scholarship have been devoted to applying or rejecting Smith's political economy in the *Wealth of Nations*. It is not my intention here to engage in that sort of activity. Instead, I ask why Smith believed the world was so conflictual and how he intended to confront the problem, given the various constraints that his moral philosophy revealed to him. With Smith's orientation to distance and proximity as our backdrop, I argue here that at least part of what motivated him to embrace and not bewail national self-interest was its remarkable ability, when enlightened, to emulate the effects of cosmopolitan good-will on a global scale. Understood in this way, Smith's commercialism was not simply an Enlightenment optimist's blind celebration of wealth and historical progress, but a moral philosopher's humbler attempt to replicate moral sentiment in the international sphere. The idea of concession is captured in the very conceptual formulation of commercial cosmopolitanism: a cosmopolitanism that is not grounded ethically (as traditional cosmopolitanism was) but produced effectively through the practices of commercial exchange.

I begin my discussion with some preliminary thoughts on the relation between political economy and moral philosophy in Smith's understanding of modernity, describing what some have referred to as his reconciliation of "wealth and virtue." I then argue that this reconciliation sheds much light on Smith's turn toward the commercial cosmopolis. Finally I introduce Smith's thoughts on national self-interest and its function in the

---

[5] *TMS* I.i.2.1 (p. 13); and *TMS* VII.iii.1.1 (p. 315).   [6] Gordon, *Citizens without Sovereignty*, pp. 73–76.

cosmopolis, relying primarily on passages from the *Moral Sentiments* and not the *Wealth of Nations* as interpreters generally do when discussing Smith's international political economy. An interpretive premise here is that the relation between Smith's political economy and his moral philosophy in the international sphere – and particularly the way that the former was invoked to compensate for deficiencies in the latter – will be revealed most vividly when we note exactly where Smith integrated economic themes into his treatise on morals.

WEALTH AND VIRTUE

Analysis of Smith's thought today must engage the work that has been done in recent decades by intellectual historians on the evolution of seventeenth- and eighteenth-century European political economy. The essential insight is that no modern commercial thinker, including Smith, was developing a theory of economic progress under the assumption that economics rendered ethics and politics meaningless or unnecessary. Such a reading is the product of ideology. Scholars who read history through a lens of dissatisfaction with the triumph of Anglo capitalism too often reify liberal theory's historical endorsement of self-regulating markets and its purported resistance to central planning. Neo-classical economists and capitalists looking for historical justifications fare no better. Moreover, contextual intellectual historians have demonstrated the anachronism in saying that modern political economy embraced anything like what Michael Sandel has called "stripped-down individualism"[7] or what C. B. MacPherson decried as "possessive individualism."[8] Scholarship on Smith has benefitted enormously from all of this.

---

[7] This is Michael Sandel's description of liberalism in *Liberalism and the Limits of Justice* (Cambridge: Cambridge University Press, 1982), *passim*; and especially in "The Procedural Republic and the Unencumbered Self," *Political Theory*, vol. 12, no. 1 (1984), pp. 81–96.

[8] Macpherson, *Possessive Individualism*. For a critique of Macpherson along "contextualist" lines, see John Dunn, "Democracy Unretrieved, or the Political Theory of Professor Macpherson," *British Journal of Political Science*, October (1974); reprint in Dunn, *Political Obligation in Its Historical Context* (Cambridge: Cambridge IV, 4 University Press, 1980), pp. 206–216; and J. G. A. Pocock, *The Political Works of James Harrington* (Cambridge: Cambridge University Press, 1977), pp. 43–76; J. G. A. Pocock, "Authority and Property: The Question of Liberal Origins," in *After the Reformation: Essays in Honor of J. H. Hexter*, ed. Barbara C. Malament (Philadelphia: University of Pennsylvania Press, 1980), pp. 331–354. For an excellent summary of the variety of contextual and other historiographical responses to Macpherson's thesis, and to the generation of scholars that it influenced, see James Tully, *An Approach to Political Philosophy: Locke in Contexts* (Cambridge: Cambridge University Press, 1993), pp. 71–95.

In the past thirty years or so, a community of intellectual historians associated with Cambridge University has identified a "language" – the so-called language of "wealth and virtue" paradigm – to help us grasp the ethical and political dimensions of seventeenth- and eighteenth-century political economy.[9] To describe "wealth and virtue" as a language, or as a paradigm is to say that modern commercial thinkers were participating in a debate about the teleological compatibility of economics and ethics, of wealth and virtue. What distinguished thinkers under the rubric of "wealth and virtue" were the various theoretical and institutional solutions through which they sought to balance these two historically divergent human "ends," the means by which they sought to save "virtue" and stave off the Polybian cycle of civilizational decline that always follows when a nation becomes "opulent."[10]

John Pocock was perhaps most influential initially in refining our understanding of the "wealth and virtue" paradigm. Pocock situated the intellectual development of English and Scottish political economy in the context of an eighteenth-century tension between "natural/civil jurisprudential" and "civic humanist/republican" traditions of discourse – what Pocock called the "Cambridge paradigms."[11] Several years earlier in *The Machiavellian Moment*, Pocock had traced the origins of "civic virtue" from its development in the declining years of the Florentine republic[12] to its reception in post-Tudor England, where opponents to the new political order began to employ "republican" or "civic humanist" language to

[9] Two influential books organized around the paradigm of "wealth and virtue" are J. G. A. Pocock, *Virtue, Commerce and History: Essays on Political Thought and History, Chiefly in the Eighteenth Century* (Cambridge: Cambridge University Press, 1985); and Istvan Hont and Michael Ignatieff, eds., *Wealth and Virtue: The Shaping of Political Economy in the Scottish Enlightenment* (Cambridge: Cambridge University Press, 1985).

[10] For an excellent introduction to a tradition of discourse that attempted to balance national wealth and virtue in this sense, see Istvan Hont's discussion of Charles Davenant, the late-seventeenth-century English theorist of trade who, mindful of Polybius, attempted to balance national wealth and virtue through the "Practical Ethicks [*sic*]" of "modern prudence." "Free Trade and the Economic Limits to National Politics: Neo-Machiavellian Political Economy Reconsidered," in *The Economic Limits to Modern Politics*, ed. John Dunn (Cambridge: Cambridge University Press, 1990), pp. 41–120, at pp. 57–95. See also Laurence Dickey's discussion of Adam Smith's predecessors in "Appendix IV," in Adam Smith, *An Enquiry into the Nature and Causes of the Wealth of Nations*, ed. Laurence Dickey (Indianapolis, IN: Hackett Publishing, 1993), pp. 246–254. From Sallust, Lucretius and Seneca through Bodin and Botero to Bacon, Berkeley and Hutcheson, Dickey traced the development of the idea that the "mediocrity of money" allowed nations to be "wealthy and strong" without sliding into "corruption and luxury."

[11] For Pocock's clearest statement on the subject, see "Cambridge Paradigms and Scotch Philosophers: A Study of the Relations between the Civic Humanist and Civil Jurisprudential Interpretation of Eighteenth-Century Social Thought," in *Wealth and Virtue*, ed. Hont and Ignatieff, pp. 235–252.

[12] J. G. A. Pocock, *The Machiavellian Moment: Florentine Political Thought and the Atlantic Republican Tradition* (Princeton, NJ: Princeton University Press, 1975), Part II.

challenge the rise of new commercial exchange relationships that under-mined the role that "real property" (land) had played in assuring the perpetuation of a "martial" and "virtuous" citizenry dedicated to the public good.[13] Defenders of the new order, pressed by these republican critics of corruption and luxury to explain how commercial wealth was to be com-patible with virtue, tried to nuance the question by "redefining" both wealth and virtue.[14] That is, as apologists for wealth and progress, they attempted to save virtue as a concept by shifting its content. And they did this, Pocock tells us, by constructing a socio-economic *substitute* for the old Gothic civic virtue, which they believed was too "rigid and austere" in its condemnation of individual personality, commercial wealth and historical progress.[15]

We saw in Chapter 4 that Adam Smith rejected various rigoristic ethical systems along these very same lines. Eighteenth-century defenders of com-merce like Smith who redefined virtue in this modern way, Pocock tells us, placed their "faith" in an unhistorical, specifically non-political form of virtue that would spring "spontaneously" and sociologically through the pursuit of wealth in the commercial process.

To put it another way, modern virtue sprung up from within a newly created "space" – a realm of private activity within which individuals bearing natural rights could engage energetically in commercial activity to realize their full potential as human beings free from any political coercion whatsoever.[16] Pocock explains how "manners" and "politeness" cultivated in this new space during the "leisure" time that commercial wealth

---

[13] *Ibid.*

[14] Some who have organized their thoughts on this period by contrasting classical critiques of luxury with eighteenth-century "redefinitions" are John Sekora, *Luxury: The Concept in Western Thought, Eden to Smollett* (Baltimore, MD: Johns Hopkins Press, 1977), pp. 110–131; and Berry, *Idea of Luxury*, esp. pp. 101–125, which conceptualizes the "transition to modernity" as the "demoralization of luxury" that began with Thomas Munn, Nicholas Barbon and the late-seventeenth-century "Balance of Trade" literature in England. For a similar formulation, see also J. A. W. Gunn's classic, *Politics and the Public Interest in the Seventeenth Century* (London: Routledge & Kegan Paul, 1969). A very early "apology for luxury" can be found in Poggio Bracciolini's 1229 *De Avaritia*. On the importance of Poggio to the tradition of redefinition, see Quentin Skinner, *The Foundations of Modern Political Thought*, vol. I: *The Renaissance* (Cambridge: Cambridge University, Press, 1978), pp. 73–74; and Quentin Skinner, "Rhetoric and the Constitution of Reality," *Proceedings of the British Academy*, vol. 76 (1990), pp. 1–63. Teichgraeber has identified a connection along these lines between Poggio and Smith in "Rethinking," p. 41.

[15] Pocock, *Virtue, Commerce and History*, pp. 37–50 and 103–123.

[16] For other influential discussions of the rise of the social and the decline of the political, in this sense, see T. H. Marshall, *Citizenship and Social Class* (Cambridge: Cambridge University Press, 1950; reprint London: Pluto, 1992); Hannah Arendt, *Between Past and Future: Eight Exercises in Political Thought* (New York: Viking Press, 1960; reprint New York: Penguin, 1977); Wolin, *Vision*; and Nicholas Xenos, "Classical Political Economy: The Apolitical Discourse of Civil Society," *Humanities in Society*, vol. 3 (1980), pp. 229–242.

provided, constituted the scene of a new sort of practical morality in the eighteenth century, shifting the locus of virtue from the "civic" realm to the "civil" – from politics to society. The point is that virtue in the modern world had become a "sociological" rather than a "civic" principle. When this happened, a wedge was driven between society and politics, which over the next 200 years opened into an irreconcilable divide. Nation-states continued the project of de-politicizing and commercializing this new private space, expanding freedoms in the name of individualism in order to support their burgeoning bureaucracies and militaries with the tax and tariff revenues generated by a vigorous commercial culture. Indeed, the modern state was compensated "plenty," in Jacob Viner's sense of that word, for its remarkable new "faith" in natural man's modern commercial reincarnation.[17]

Though Smith was a notorious critic of the mercantilist implications of this shift – the fact that nation-states now perceived that military power was most effectively aggregated through protectionist trade policies, a tradition of thinking that Istvan Hont calls "economic neo-Machiavellianism"[18] – he must be seen as a key figure in this eighteenth-century reinterpretation of politics, and its corresponding, distinctively modern, conception of virtue. Smith's Scottish sensibility makes clear why this is so. Smith wanted to pull Scotland from her clannish backwardness, and in this sense was attracted to the infinite benefits of commercial development, though he well understood the costs. Ultimately he resisted Andrew Fletcher's "civic" discourse which, since Scotland's standing army debate, had become the linguistic core of Scottish opposition to commercial development, the "effeminacy" of commercial values, and the "dependency" of a union with England.[19]

Smith's thought in its Scottish context seems to exemplify the Enlightenment's aim to liberate mankind from every imaginable

---

[17] To understand why the taxation of vigorous market actors was significant politically in the eighteenth century, see Viner's classic discussion in "Power versus Plenty."

[18] See especially the introductory essay in Istvan Hont, *Jealousy of Trade: International Competition and the Nation-State in Historical Perspective* (Cambridge, MA: Harvard University Press, 2005), pp. 5–156.

[19] For background, see John Robertson, *The Scottish Enlightenment and the Militia Issue* (Edinburgh: John Donald Publishers Ltd, 1985), pp. 212–225. See also the following essays in Hont and Ignatieff, eds., *Wealth and Virtue*: Istvan Hont and Michael Ignatieff, "Needs and Justice in the *Wealth of Nations*: An Introductory Essay," pp. 1–44 at pp. 7–8 and pp. 43–44; Istvan Hont, "The Rich Country–Poor Country Debate in Scottish Classical Political Economy," pp. 271–315, at pp. 298–306; and Nicholas Phillipson, "Adam Smith as Civic Moralist," pp. 179–202, at p. 20. Also Nicholas Phillipson, "Politics and Politeness in the Reigns of Anne and the Early Hanoverians," in *The Varieties of British Political Thought, 1500–1800*, ed. J. G. A. Pocock with assistance from Gordon J. Schochet and Lois G. Schwoerer (Cambridge: Cambridge University Press, 1993), pp. 211–245, at pp. 236–238; and J. G. A. Pocock, "Political Thought in the English-speaking Atlantic, 1760–1790 (ii): Empire, Revolution and an End of Early Modernity," in *Varieties*, ed. J. G. A. Pocock, pp. 283–317, at pp. 293–294.

contingency: from rusticity and Gothic ignorance, from the shackles of superstition and custom, nature and fortune, from theology, ontology, metaphysics and "pneumaticks." Smith celebrated "civilization," refinement and the triumph of the arts and sciences. He condemned war and faction. He was committed to moral equality, autonomy and self-sufficiency; and he insisted that a neutral state with a standing army was the best guarantee for modern freedom and general well-being. Insofar as we might characterize the Enlightenment as a unified movement, Smith by and large seems to have supported every one of its aims for Scotland.[20]

And yet, the Scottish context adds a sort of gradualism that we do not always find in continental or even British Enlightenment thought. Despite Smith's general commitment to the project of Enlightenment, and his firm commercial commitments in eighteenth-century Scottish political debates, he never simply leaped without hesitation from the "Gothic" world of "virtue" to the "commercial" world of "wealth," as posterity would have it.[21] As John Robertson and Nicholas Phillipson have argued, when we look carefully at Smith's language, he seems to be lying at the "limits" of civic political discourse itself. His language frequently conveys a certain admiration for the "civic humanism" of the Country Party, of Fletcher, and of the opponents to standing armies in the early 1750s.[22] Smith gave voice to classical republican themes that still dwelled more or less overtly in Scottish Enlightenment thought, despite the diminished appeal of republican sentiment for moderns elsewhere. Though he was fully committed to commerce as the engine of historical progress, Smith's modernity was articulated in a distinctively Scottish key.

Committed to the eighteenth-century ideal of civilizational progress, yet mindful of various classical warnings about the dangers of wealth and corruption, Smith was keen to "embed" modernity in a new ethical foundation that would assume the function that waning "Gothic" institutions and ideas once played. The author of the four-stage conjecture on civilizational progress clearly did not regret the decline of these retrogressive feudal forms – far from it. But he also did not "detach" himself "from everything that all previous experiences had to offer," as Reinhart Koselleck argued the eighteenth century, in its linear drive toward the future, tended to do.[23] And so, there are two historiographical

[20] See Jerry Muller's discussion of Smith as a "cosmopolitan provincial" in *Adam Smith*, pp. 16–27.
[21] See Clark's argument about Smith's "moderate virtue" in this context in "Conversation."
[22] See the two following essays in Hont and Ignatieff, eds., *Wealth and Virtue*: John Robertson, "The Scottish Enlightenment at the Limits of the Civic Tradition," pp. 137–179; and Nicholas Phillipson, "Adam Smith as Civic Moralist," pp. 179–202.
[23] Koselleck, *Futures Past*, p. 220. For an interesting argument that Smith manipulated history by turning the decline of the barons into a modern "lesson" about the consequences of indulging in

reasons for focusing here on Smith's hesitation: first, it enables us clearly to distinguish his thought from what posterity too often has reduced to an eighteenth-century "celebration of avarice."[24] Second, relatedly, it helps us better to appreciate the place of Smith's thought about international political economy within his larger project of moral philosophy.

SMITH'S COLD WORLD

Smith's meditations on international conflict are contained in two sections of the *Moral Sentiments*, both added to the 1790 revision of the text: Section III.3.42 (pp. 154–155) and Section VI.ii.2 (pp. 227–234). In these passages Smith identified grounds for *realism* in eighteenth-century international relations, which are remarkably compelling from a twenty-first-century perspective. He explored the intransigence of national "prejudice," described in moral psychological terms as a "noble love of country" that has become distorted and ugly through practices of socialization within narrow spatial boundaries. This is a profoundly interesting phenomenon given what I have described in this book as the essentially *local* texture of Smith's moral thought as a whole. Recall, I argued in Chapter 5 that Smith's ultimate purpose in the *Moral Sentiments* was to describe the process through which individuals enlarge physical and affective bias by attuning their judgments to something larger, notably the particular society in which they live. Moreover, recall as well Smith's arguments against Stoic and Christian cosmopolitanism, in which he directed man's attention and energies to local events:

By Nature the events which immediately affect that little department in which we ourselves have some little management and direction, which immediately affect ourselves, our friends, our country, are the events which interest us the most, and which chiefly excite our desires and aversions, our hopes and fears, our joys and sorrows.[25]

In every dimension of Smith's moral thought, in other words, the social realm sits in a sort of privileged middle space between myopic self-preference and elusive cosmopolitan fluff, confirming my assertion throughout this book that Smith's was primarily concerned in the *Moral Sentiments* with preserving local social order. Society, for Smith, was most often the solution to whatever problem he happened to be considering. But then, of course, he needed to come to terms with the tendencies of humbler

luxury, see Dickey, "Appendix II," *WN*, pp. 220–225. For an excellent recent account of Smith's stadial theory of development that is sensitive to his distance from the chauvinistic and "triumphalist" view of European progress, see Pitts, *Turn to Empire*, pp. 25–58.

[24] See Holmes, "Secret History," on the problems with interpreting modernity as such.

[25] *TMS* VII.ii.1.44 (p. 292).

departments – of societies, parties, factions and nations – to *themselves* become myopic and fanatical, to fall sway to the eloquent manipulations of zealots, creating profound instabilities inside of nations and among nations. In the discussion that follows I am concerned less with Smith's description of civil and ecclesiastical factions than with larger-scale national partiality and its implications for international stability – though clearly most of what Smith said about the psychology of nationalism is perfectly applicable to sub-national group pathologies as well. Smith's psychological diagnosis of group sentiment is highly transportable, deriving in every application from his foundational description of affective bias in individuals.

In the discussion that follows, I consider the problem of national prejudice in greater detail, dividing my presentation into two parts. First I address Smith's description of national prejudice, noting significant parallels with his account of affective bias in individuals. Second, I discuss Smith's concerns about national insularity, which served to intensify national prejudice and further destabilize international relations. Echoing his general claim that solitude leads individuals to "feel too strongly whatever relates to ourselves" and that the presence of spectators composes us,[26] Smith was distressed by the absence of an overarching power among nations to enforce universal compliance with the "laws of nations." Exploring these two related phenomena – national prejudice and national insularity – will give us a better grasp of the bleak international setting that Smith identified and sought to remedy with his commercial cosmopolitanism. Indeed, Smith was a *troubled realist*, and in 1790 turned his attention explicitly to these sorts of tensions.

NATIONAL PREJUDICE

Smith observed that "the mean principle of national prejudice is often founded upon the noble one of the love of our own country."[27] That love of country is "noble" here does not mean that it is somehow benevolent for Smith, or "derived from the love of mankind."[28] On the contrary, Smith argued that we love our own country for more or less partial reasons. He noted two:

The love of our country seems, in ordinary cases, to involve in it two different principles; first, a certain respect and reverence for that constitution or form of

[26] *TMS* III.3.38 (p. 153).   [27] *TMS* VI.ii.2.3 (p. 228).   [28] *TMS* VI.ii.2.4 (p. 229).

government which is actually established; and secondly, an earnest desire to render the condition of our fellow-citizens as safe, respectable, and happy as we can. He is not a citizen who is not disposed to respect the laws and to obey the civil magistrate; and he is certainly not a good citizen who does not wish to promote, by every means in his power, the welfare of the whole society of his fellow-citizens.[29]

Smith's formulation here resonates with Judith Shklar's well-known distinction between obligation and loyalty – essentially that obligation is reason-based and motivates through rules; while loyalty is primarily affective.[30] Obligation, she wrote, refers to "rule-immersed" activity grounded in "rule-like" principles. Regardless of whether the rule following was recommended by consent, utility, natural law or deontology, for Shklar these are all examples of "rational, rule-immersed thinking."[31] Similarly, Smith argued that the first "principle" of "love of our country" consists in obedience to the law, in a "certain respect and reverence for that constitution or form of government which is actually established."[32] Why do people obey established law? What recommends it to them? In his *Lectures on Jurisprudence* of 1766, Smith noted a variety of reasons, all "rule-like principles" in Shklar's sense:

Ask a common porter or day-laborer why he obeys the civil magistrate, he will tell you that it is right to do so, that he sees others do it, that he would be punished if he refused to do it, or perhaps that it is a sin against God not to do it.[33]

Smith observed in the *Moral Sentiments* that most people, even the most partial and factious, tend ultimately to respect their government and its established constitution and laws, essentially because these institutions provide "security and protection" for all: "All those different orders and societies are dependent upon the state to which they owe their security and protection."[34] At least this holds true, he said, in "peaceable and quiet times."[35]

On the other hand, Shklar described loyalty as "deeply affective" and not "primarily rational."[36] We feel loyalty toward those groups into which we have been born and nurtured – those with which we identify ourselves when asked the question: "Who are you?" Political loyalty in particular is "evoked by nations, ethnic groups, churches, parties, and by doctrines, causes,

---

[29] *TMS* VI.ii.2.11 (p. 231).
[30] Judith N. Shklar, "Obligation, Loyalty and Exile," *Political Thought and Political Thinkers*, ed. Stanley Hoffman (Chicago: University of Chicago Press, 1998), pp. 38–55, and Judith N. Shklar, "The Bonds of Exile," in *Political Thought*, ed. Stanley Hoffman, pp. 56–72, at pp. 58–60.
[31] Shklar, "Obligation," pp. 40–41.   [32] *TMS* VI.ii.2.11 (p. 231).   [33] *LJ* (B) 15 (pp. 402–403).
[34] *TMS* VI.ii.2.10 (p. 231).   [35] *TMS* VI.ii.2.11 (p. 231).   [36] Shklar, "Obligation," p. 41.

ideologies, or faiths that form and identify associations."[37] Smith's second "principle" of "love of country" coincides precisely with Shklar's description of affective loyalty. It consists in the "earnest desire to render the condition of our fellow-citizens as safe, respectable, and as happy as we can":

Not only we ourselves, but all the object of our kindest affections, our children, our parents, our relations, our friends, our benefactors, all those whom we naturally love and revere the most, are commonly comprehended within it [the "state or sovereignty"]; and their prosperity and safety depend in some measure upon its prosperity and safety. It is by nature, therefore, endeared to us, not only by all our selfish, but by all our private benevolent affections.[38]

Of course, if Shklar was often ambivalent about rule-following, she was consistently troubled by the unreflective, xenophobic tendencies of political loyalty. "No one in our horrible century," she insisted, "can be unaware of the passion that is invested in such attachments."[39] Smith too was hardly ambivalent about it: "Of all the corrupters of moral sentiments … faction and fanaticism have always been by far the greatest."[40] Love of country, which is "noble" in its foundations, inspired by a genuine care and concern for those whom habit has taught us to love, is nevertheless frequently whipped into group hatred through a socializing process that greatly resembles Smith's moral psychology in narrower spaces, in which norms are disciplined through the surveillance of local spectators, and solidified through habit and experience into conscience. As we saw earlier, an agent in Smith's moral theory adjusts his conduct to obtain the approbation of the spectators about him. This very same process is at work in Smith's description of the fomentation of nationalism among citizens:

His whole ambition is to obtain the approbation of his own fellow-citizens; and as they are all animated by the same hostile passions which animate himself, he can never please them so much as by enraging and offending their enemies.[41]

A citizen who would brave the "general contagion" would meet an unhappy fate indeed:

The ambassador who dupes the minister of a foreign nation, is admired and applauded. The just man who disdains either to take or to give any advantage,

[37] *Ibid.*, p. 41. [38] *TMS* VI.ii.2.2 (p. 227). [39] Shklar, "Bonds," p. 59.
[40] *TMS* III.3.43 (p. 156). For this reason Rebecca Kingston is absolutely right to observe that Smith was hesitant about cultivating "collective" or "public passions." See her argument in "The Political Relevance of the Emotions from Descartes to Smith," in *Bringing the Passions Back In: The Emotions in Political Philosophy*, ed. Rebecca Kingston and Leonard Ferry (Vancouver, BC: University of British Columbia Press, 2008), pp. 108–125, at pp. 121–124.
[41] *TMS* III.3.41 (p. 154).

but who would think it less dishonourable to give than to take one; the man who in all private transactions, would be the most beloved and the most esteemed; in those public transactions is regarded as a fool and an idiot, who does not understand his business; and he incurs always the contempt, and sometimes even the detestation of his fellow-citizens.[42]

Smith spends several pages describing the sociological processes through which a sense of national "superiority" and "public spirit" are cultivated through the vilification of enemies, and the mythic elevation of patriots, heroic warriors, statesmen, poets, philosophers, and men of letters. "We are disposed to view [them] with the most partial admiration, to rank them (sometimes most unjustly) above those of all other nations."[43]

The result of this process is a lively "prejudice" that "disposes us to view, with the most malignant jealousy and envy, the prosperity and aggrandizement of any other neighboring nation."[44] For Smith this seems to be the natural course of events for all nations, though it emerges most vividly during times of turbulence, and is "almost always more pure and more splendid" during a "foreign war."[45] Thus for Smith the portrait of Cato the elder embodied the phenomenon of "savage patriotism" in its purest form:

The sentence with which the elder Cato is said to have concluded every speech which he made in the senate, whatever might be the subject, "*It is my opinion likewise that Carthage ought to be destroyed*," was the natural expression of the savage patriotism of a strong but coarse mind, enraged almost to madness against a foreign nation from which his own had suffered so much.[46]

NATIONAL INSULARITY

Although realists today insist on the essential predictability of state action under conditions of anarchy,[47] Smith emphasized the "uncertainty and irregularity" of international relations in the absence of a supreme legislative power with the authority to settle differences and to enforce "the laws of nations." I spent time in Chapter 4 exploring Smith' description of delusive self-preference in individuals. He argued that self-love tends to become exaggerated and delusive in solitude or when the self is surrounded only by indulgent, "partial" spectators. His account of national prejudice works very

---

[42] *TMS* III.3.42 (p. 154). "General contagion" comes in the next paragraph: *TMS* III.3.43 (p. 155).
[43] *TMS* VI.ii.2.2 (pp. 227–228); *TMS* VI.ii.2.13 (p. 232).   [44] *TMS* VI.ii.2.3 (p. 228).
[45] *TMS* VI.ii.2.13 (p. 232).   [46] *TMS* VI.ii.2.3 (p. 228).
[47] Most famously, Kenneth Waltz, *Man, the State and War* (New York: Columbia University Press, 1959).

much the same way. Isolationism was as dangerous for a nation, as solitude was for the moral agent who found himself in the grip of self-delusion:

The propriety of our moral sentiments is never so apt to be corrupted, as when the indulgent and partial spectator is at hand, while the indifferent and impartial one is at a great distance.[48]

Smith regretted the absence of a "common superior" among nations,[49] what he also referred to elsewhere as a "supreme legislative power,"[50] a "neutral … indifferent and impartial spectator"[51] that might help deflate national prejudice, alleviate suspicion and pre-emptive activity among neighboring nations, and enforce universal compliance with the "laws of nations" – much like the impartial spectator in Smith's moral psychology oversees and disciplines the conventions of sociable living within narrower boundaries, as we have seen. The result was a complete lack of trust and good-will among nations. There was indeed such a recognized thing as international law in the eighteenth century; but the language Smith regularly used to describe it conveys how impotent and corruptible he believed it was. At one point he described the "laws of nations" as "those rules which independent states profess or pretend to think themselves bound to."[52] Like laws, international treaties too were meaningless without stable consequences for defection. "Statesmen," Smith observed, occasionally "form alliances among neighboring or not very distant nations, for the preservation either of, what is called, the balance of power, or of the general peace and tranquility of the states within the circle of their negotiations."[53] Such is "the most extensive public benevolence which can commonly be exerted with any considerable effect," Smith noted. But these alliances were not credible commitments. They were always highly unstable since "the statesmen … who plan and execute such treaties, have seldom any thing in view, but the interest of their respective countries." Unconstrained by consequence voluntary treaties were readily abandoned at the smallest provocation. Clearly, for a thinker like Smith, whose moral thought generally was based on the effects of surveillance on judgment and choice, the spectatorial vacuum in international affairs was devastating:

Truth and fair dealing are almost totally disregarded. Treaties are violated; and the violation, if some advantage is gained by it, sheds scarce any dishonour upon the violator … [T]he laws of nations, are frequently violated, without bringing (among

---

[48] *TMS* III.3.41 (p. 154).   [49] *TMS* VI.ii.2.3 (p. 228).   [50] *LJ* (B), p. 339.
[51] *TMS* III.3.42 (pp. 154–155).   [52] *TMS* VI.ii.2.3 (p. 228).   [53] *TMS* VI.ii.2.6 (p. 230).

his own fellow-citizens, whose judgments he only regards) any considerable dishonour upon the violator.[54]

And later:

Independent and neighboring nations, having no common superior to decide their disputes, all live in continual dread and suspicion of one another. Each sovereign, expecting little justice from his neighbors, is disposed to treat them with as little as he expects from them. The regard for the laws of nations, or for those rules which independent states profess or pretend to think themselves bound to observe in their dealings with one another, is often very little more than mere pretense and profession. From the smallest interest, upon the slightest provocation, we see those rules every day, either evaded or directly violated without shame or remorse.[55]

Similarly, in a lecture entitled "Of the Laws of Nations" delivered in his course on Jurisprudence at the University of Glasgow in 1766, Smith observed that "where there is no supreme legislative power to settle differences, we may always expect uncertainty and irregularity."[56] The absence of a common superior to regulate international affairs was central to Smith's realism.

Today we think of such institutions as Nuremberg, the Hague, the United Nations and NATO. But Smith never conceived of such an intricate network of international cooperation. At one point he speculated that "neutral nations" might assume such a mediating function, but concluded that they were essentially without teeth and easily ignored:

Of the conduct of one independent nation towards another, neutral nations are the only indifferent and impartial spectators. But they are placed at so great a distance that they are almost quite out of sight. When two nations are at variance, the citizens of each pays little regard to the sentiments which foreign nations may entertain concerning his conduct. His whole ambition is to obtain the approbation of his fellow-citizens … The partial spectator is at hand: the impartial one at a great distance.[57]

Reflecting on these problems in 1790, just as accounts of the French Revolution were beginning to trickle their way into the English consciousness, Smith never imagined a technological era in which massacres like My Lai, Tiananmen Square, September 11, 2001 and Burma/Myanmar in the Fall of 2007 could be broadcast live in bloody, fiery technicolor to observers half a world away, often as they are taking place. He never imagined a world in which, as Pramoeda Ananta Toer described it, "the entire world can now

[54] *TMS* III.3.42 (pp. 154–155).   [55] *TMS* VI.ii.2.3 (p. 228).
[56] *LJ* (B) 339 (p. 545).   [57] *TMS* III.3.42 (p. 154).

observe the actions of any person. And people can observe the actions of the entire world."⁵⁸ We are living in very different times.

But we should resist consigning Smith to irrelevancy here, for his underlying point is perfectly compatible with our new reality. In claiming that distant nations were "out of sight" he was simply affirming his insight throughout the *Moral Sentiments* that *seeing* something arouses our imagination and triggers our sympathetic self-projection into action in a way that merely thinking about it cannot. This insight remains valid. The difference is that we *see* more today and thus know more, and it rouses our indignation. We see the images of African-American motorists bloodied by the batons and boot heels of the LAPD, the bits of Israeli flesh scattered across the pavement after being blown apart in a city bus, a Palestinian child dying in the protective arms of his father after being struck by a bullet in a sniper's crossfire, the torsos of slain monks floating in a Burmese river, hurricane victims stranded on rooftops. Indeed, television and the Internet have mediated sight in a way that Smith could not have imagined. Technology now helps to shape and unify our collective sentiments, even from a distance, though perhaps it does no more to stimulate beneficent action among most of us.⁵⁹

THE COMMERCIAL COSMOPOLIS

Smith, a notorious lover of harmony and equilibrium, was confronted with a dilemma. There was no natural affection against which to balance "national prejudice" and to cultivate a stable sense of international goodwill. And there was no "common superior" to constrain behavior or enforce compliance with laws or treaties. What was a moral philosopher to do? He could either surrender to the realism that his moral philosophy suggested, or he could strive for another solution. Smith pursued the latter, believing he had discovered a solution in commerce – a solution I call here his *commercial cosmopolitanism*.⁶⁰

Suddenly, at the center of a moral philosophical dilemma, Smith invoked the civilizing effects of international political economy, providing us with a new way of thinking about the coherence and unity of economics and ethics

---

⁵⁸ Translated and cited by Pheng Cheah in "The Cosmopolitical – Today," in *Beyond the Nation*, p. 20.
⁵⁹ See Boltanski, *Distant Suffering*, which uses Smith's moral psychology to advance a contemporary humanitarian "politics of pity."
⁶⁰ For similar formulations, see Nieli, "Spheres of Intimacy"; and Lisa Hill and Peter McCarthy, "On Friendship and *Necessitudo* in Adam Smith," *History of the Human Sciences*, vol. 17, no. 4 (2004), pp. 1–16.

in his thought. Truth and fairness were unlikely in international affairs, where interest ruled and no impartial spectator was present to enforce compliance with the "law of nations" or international treaties. But Smith observed that free, self-interested commercial intercourse among nations might mitigate aggression and cultivate international peace without goodwill or coercion, produce cosmopolitan ends without cosmopolitan intentions, balance national wealth with global "virtue." Smith conceived of a new cosmopolis that could replicate the harmony born of familiarity and habitual fellow-feeling, and could even replicate the effects of law and coercion without stifling modern commercial aspirations.[61]

Smith's commercial cosmopolitanism rested on what we might refer to as the "unintended consequences" of national self-interest. "The love of our own nation," Smith insisted, should not lead us "to view with the most malignant jealousy and envy, the prosperity and aggrandizement of any other neighboring nation."[62] On the contrary, the prosperity of others should be embraced as a stimulant to our own prosperity. A passage from the *Wealth of Nations* elaborates Smith's assertion here:

The wealth of a neighboring nation ... though dangerous in war and politicks, is certainly advantageous in trade. In a state of hostility it may enable our enemies to maintain fleets and armies superior to our own; but in a state of peace and commerce it must likewise enable them to exchange with us to a greater value, and to afford a better market.[63]

In this key, he then shamed France and England for their "mercantile jealousy" and "national animosity."[64] This "jealousy of trade" theme in

---

[61] That Smith, in this sense, was participating in an eighteenth-century discourse in which free trade was linked conceptually to the growth of humanitarian values, see Laurence Dickey, "*Doux-Commerce* and Humanitarian Values: Free Trade, Sociability and Universal Benevolence in Eighteenth-Century Thinking," in *Grotius and the Stoa*, ed. Hans W. Blom and Laurence C. Winkel (Assen: Van Gorcum, 2004), pp. 271–318. I agree that Smith was participating in a discourse that linked commerce with cosmopolitanism, but I tend to see them in a relation of replication and substitution, rather than a progressive one of cultivation. Commercial cosmopolitanism, on my interpretation, is not motivated by anything we can describe in ethical terms as "humanitarian," but is rather the sociable by-product of selfish activity. For an interpretation compatible with Dickey's – that commercial society in Scottish thought *enables* something like genuine friendship – see two essays by Allan Silver, "Friendship in Commercial Society: Eighteenth-Century Social Theory and Modern Sociology," *American Journal of Sociology*, vol. 30 (1990), pp. 274–297; and "'Two Different Sorts of Commerce' – Friendship and Strangership in Civil Society," in *Public and Private in Thought and Practice: Perspectives on a Grand Dichotomy*, ed. Jeff Weintraub and Krishan Kumar (Chicago: University of Chicago Press, 1997), pp. 43–74.

[62] *TMS* VI.ii.2.3 (p. 228); cf. *WN* IV.iii.c.9 (p. 493): "Commerce, which ought naturally to be, among nations, as among individuals, a bond of union and friendship, has become the most fertile source of discord and animosity."

[63] *WN* IV.iii.c.11 (p. 494).   [64] *WN* IV.iii.c.12 (p. 495).

the *Wealth of Nations* carried over into the 1790 edition of the *Moral Sentiments*. Contrasting the elder Cato's "savage patriotism" with the "more enlarged and enlightened mind" of Scipio Nascia "who felt no aversion to the prosperity even of an old enemy," Smith censured the "weak" and "foolish" jealousies of France and England:

France and England may each of them have some reason to dread the increase of the naval and military power of the other; but for either of them to envy the internal happiness and prosperity of the other, the cultivation of its lands, the advancement of its manufactures, the increase of its commerce, the security and number of its ports and harbours, its proficiency in all the liberal arts and sciences, is surely beneath the dignity of two such great nations. These are all real improvements in the world we live in. Mankind are benefited, human nature is ennobled by them. In such improvements each nation ought, not only to endeavour itself to excel, but from the love of mankind, to promote, instead of obstructing the excellence of its neighbors. These are all proper objects of national emulation, not of national prejudice or envy.[65]

This view that prosperity was infectious, and that the suspicion and jealousy of modern states was parochial and self-destructive, was common among Enlightenment thinkers in both France and England. Hume proclaimed: "I shall therefore venture to acknowledge, that, not only as a man, but as a BRITISH subject, I pray for the flourishing of commerce of GERMANY, SPAIN, ITALY, and even FRANCE itself."[66]

Smith attributed the infectiousness of prosperity to what he called an "œconomy of nature" or sometimes a vast "machine." For some interpreters this is an obvious application of Newton's atomistic-mechanistic philosophy to political economy. Surely there is something in this, given Smith's life-long fascination with Newton.[67] But the providentialism in his political economy seems to me to resonate more plausibly with Stoic themes that run through the *Moral Sentiments* – that God ordered everything in nature to produce the greatest quantity of human happiness:

[65] *TMS* VI.ii.2.3 (p. 229); cf. *WN* IV.iii.c.12–13 (pp. 495–496). "Weak and foolish" comes from *TMS* VI. ii.2.5 (p. 230).

[66] David Hume, "Jealousy of Trade," in *Political Essays*, ed. Knud Haakonssen (Cambridge: Cambridge University Press, 1994). For discussion, see Schlereth, *Cosmopolitan Ideal*, ch. 5; and Hont, *Jealousy of Trade*.

[67] See Smith's early essay, "The History of Astronomy," in *Essays on Philosophical Subjects*, ed. W. L. D. Wightman, as vol. III of *The Glasgow Edition of the Works and Correspondence of Adam Smith* (Oxford: Oxford University Press; reprint Indianapolis, IN: Liberty Press, 1982), pp. 256–332. For an alternative reading of Newton's influence on Smith and general economic equilibrium theory, see Vernard Foley, *The Social Physics of Adam Smith* (West Lafayette, IN: Purdue University Press, 1976); and Montes, *Smith in Context*, pp. 130–164.

The ancient stoics were of opinion, that as the world was governed by the all-ruling providence of a wise, powerful, and good God, every single event ought to be regarded, as making a necessary part of the plan of the universe, and as tending to promote the general order and happiness of the whole.[68]

In this passage, as in many others, Smith describes nature as an "immense machine," as an "œconomy," as a plan divined by "Providence."[69] Just as the "wheels of the watch turn" when "put into motion by a spring," just as "blood circulates" and "food digests" according to an "artifice" in nature, so too are we led without intention or will to those "ends" which God has "proposed for Mankind."[70] Because human life was situated in a natural order imprinted with God's purpose for mankind, it worked just as automatically, just as mechanically and predictably as the cosmos. "Human society, when we contemplate it in a certain abstract and philosophical light, appears like a great, an immense machine, whose regular and harmonious movements produce a thousand agreeable effects."[71] Viewing international society in this same light, God had arranged everything in nature to ensure that "the great society of mankind" could flourish materially in a context of peace without onerous and unnatural sacrifices by individuals or nations. Smith wrote:

That wisdom which contrived the system of human affections, as well as that of every other part of nature, seems to have judged that the interest of the great society of mankind would be best promoted by directing the principal attention of each individual to that particular portion of it, which was most within the sphere both of his abilities and of his understanding.[72]

From the perspective of this chapter, and my claim that Smith developed a theory of commercial cosmopolitanism in good measure to soothe his troubled realism, this is the single most important passage in the *Moral Sentiments*. It links Smith's moral psychological rejection of Stoic cosmopolitanism with his claim that mankind benefits by seizing on human

[68] *TMS* I.ii.3.4 (p. 36).
[69] *TMS* III.5.7 (p. 166). See also *TMS* II.ii.5.10 (p. 77); *TMS* IV.1.1–5 (pp. 179–180); *TMS* IV.1.9 (p. 183); *TMS* IV.2.12 (p. 192); *TMS* VII.iii.1.2 (p. 316); *TMS* VII.iii.3.15 (p. 326). See Viner, *Providence*; and Hill, "Hidden Theology." For a recent interpretation of "unintended consequences" and "spontaneous order" in various dimensions of Smith's thought, see Craig Smith, *Adam Smith's Political Philosophy* (London: Routledge, 2006). On the secularization of providence in modern ethical systems generally, see J. B. Schneewind, "The Divine Corporation and the History of Ethics," in *Philosophy in History: Essays on the Historiography of Philosophy*, ed. Richard Rorty, J. B. Schneewind and Quentin Skinner (Cambridge: Cambridge University Press, 1984), pp. 173–191. See also Charles Taylor, "The Providential Order," in *Sources of the Self: The Making of Modern Identity* (Cambridge, MA: Harvard University Press, 1989).
[70] Compare *TMS* II.i.5.10 (p. 77); and *TMS* II.ii.3.5 (p. 87).   [71] See *TMS* VII.iii.1.2 (p. 316).
[72] *TMS* VI.ii.2.4 (p. 229).

limitations and permitting man vigorously to pursue his own partial interests in the "sphere both of his abilities and of his understanding."

Smith refused to collapse the Stoic circles here since *oikeiōsis* (familiarity) remained for him the most appropriate index of our duties: "To man is allotted a much humbler department," he wrote, "but one much more suitable to the weakness of his powers, and to the narrowness of his comprehension; the care of his own happiness, of that of his family, his friends, his country."[73] Smith's commercial cosmopolitanism entrusts people to their own affections and abilities, to that which naturally most interests and directly benefits them. The good of mankind is promoted without asking people to become something that Smith insisted they were not – and, indeed, ought not waste their time, their efforts and their good spirits striving to become.

Smith was hardly unconcerned about the moral dangers of parochialism and the narrowing of one's moral concern to one's own, as we have seen. Indeed, he characterized the tendency of groups to become factious and fanatical as the worst "corrupters" of our moral sentiments. But he also believed that ordinary moral life, most often, adequately contained these dangers. Should partial attachments become too passionate, Smith's moral psychology intervened to temper them into a more proper and sociable balance:

Should those passions be, what they are very apt to be, too vehement, Nature has provided a proper remedy and correction. The real or even the imaginary presence of the impartial spectator, the authority of the man within the breast, is always at hand to overawe them into the proper tone and temper of moderation.[74]

In this passage we have a perfect illustration of Smith's providentialism, his "œconomy of nature" at work, here arranged with a capacity to contain its own excesses.

Obviously Smith had explicit economic and political reasons for advocating international commerce, aside from the moral philosophic ones I identify here. To suggest otherwise would be absurd. My purpose here is not to apologize for those dimensions of Smith's economic and political thought that have been dismissed all too often correctly as an extravagant ruse. Indeed, in the last two centuries, variants of Smith's solution have had moments of undeniable success for many people fortunately situated – but arguably just as many dismal failures.[75] But the purpose of this book is not

---

[73] *TMS* VI.ii.3.6 (p. 237).   [74] *TMS* VII.ii.1.44 (p. 292).

[75] For discussion of Smith's own ambivalence about global commerce, in light of the ascendance and power of international trading companies, see Sankar Muthu, "Adam Smith's Critique of International Trading Companies: Theorizing 'Globalization' in the Age of Enlightenment,"

to engage in these sorts of polemic. Instead, I want to situate Smith's faith in the commercial cosmopolis within the complex of the moral philosophical quandaries with which he was struggling – in other words, to contextualize it *within* his moral philosophy. Once so contextualized, Smith's commercialism can no longer be interpreted in a vacuum – as an Enlightenment commercialist's bacchanal pursuit of wealth, come what may – but must be understood as a moral philosopher's attempt to emulate good-will on a global scale, to locate a plausible substitute for moral sentiment in the international sphere.

Understood in this light, Smith helped to redefine cosmopolitan thinking in the eighteenth century. For him, free commercial intercourse among nations was a new way to talk about the cosmopolis. Of course it must be noted that Smith meant something very specific when he referred here to "free" commercial intercourse. In this sense Smith's commercial cosmopolitanism is linked conceptually with his 900-page assault on mercantilism and its faulty assumptions about the nature and causes of national wealth, contained in the *Wealth of Nations*. While mercantilists believed that national wealth consisted in the accumulation of precious metals, achieved by manipulating the balance of trade through protectionist policies and punitive tariffs, Smith located national wealth in the annual flow of goods and services, which was stimulated most effectively under conditions of free trade. Smith described this as a "system of natural liberty and perfect justice" in which the proper function of government was to stabilize market conditions, primarily by maintaining a standing army to defend the society from invasion and by maintaining a system of justice, understood commutatively as the protection of property. When left to unfold freely without government intrusion (which was regularly commandeered in the eighteenth century by the interests of international trading companies[76]) Smith insisted that international trade would not only generate wide-scale wealth, but that it would mitigate conflict and stimulate peace in the absence of good-will or coercion. This is ultimately what *commercial cosmopolitanism* was about for eighteenth-century thinkers like Hume, Smith, Benjamin Franklin and Jacques Turgot who promoted it.[77]

Smith's commercial cosmopolitanism broke with Stoic morality by easing cosmopolitan teleology from human reason and intention, placing it instead in the invisible hand of national self-interest. Because of the

---

Political Theory, vol. 36, no. 2 (2008), pp. 185–212. There he emphasizes that Smith was painfully aware of the "gross imbalances of power, destructive economic inefficiencies, and horrific cruelties" hastened by the institutions of global commerce in Smith's own day (p. 188).

[76] See Muthu, "International Trading Companies."   [77] See Schlereth, *Cosmopolitan Ideal*, ch. 5.

providential strain in his thought, he never imagined he had abandoned the poor to the caprice of the rich and powerful. He never fully envisioned what might become of international commerce in Western imperial hands, though surely he had good evidence to speculate.[78] Smith already observed in the eighteenth century the extent that national policy was being hijacked by international trading companies whose corporate interests and violent tactics were antithetical to the interests of their respective nations, profoundly disrupting the international harmony and prosperity he envisioned. As Sankar Muthu put it: "The institutions of global commerce were now helping to fuel global wars, hardly the enlightened *doux-commerce* that transnational trade was sometimes said to produce."[79]

[78] See Pitts, *Turn to Empire*, pp. 25–58, on Smith's resistance to the European imperial project.
[79] Muthu, "International Trading Companies," p. 199.

CHAPTER 7

Negative justice

> It happened that a certain heathen came before Shammai and said to
> him, "Convert me to Judaism on condition that you teach me the
> whole Torah while I stand on one foot." Shammai chased him away
> with the builder's rod in his hand. When he came before Hillel, Hillel
> converted him and said, "What is hateful to you, do not do to your
> neighbors ... The rest is commentary."
>
> Babylonian Talmud, Shabbat 31a

I begin with several assumptions. First, let's assume that Smith was right
about our moral sentiments – that, as we discovered in Chapter 5, we are
likelier to sympathize with the physically proximate, with the familiar, and
with the beloved and "peculiarly connected"; and that we generally have
difficulty sympathizing with that which is distant and unfamiliar without
assuming facts and foisting alien criteria upon them by assimilating them to
very particular, incomplete meanings and frames. Second, let's invert
Pascal's wager, and assume that there is no God intervening in the world,
invisibly directing human happiness through a "divine œconomy." For
Smith, "the very suspicion of a fatherless world" was "the most melancholy
of all reflections."[1] But let's be melancholy and assume such a world.
Relatedly, third, let's assume that Smith's commercial cosmopolitanism,
which we characterized in Chapter 6 as a moral philosophic attempt to
harmonize relations among distant peoples in a world that lacked an
effective apparatus to enforce good-will, failed to hit its mark – that we
still observe deep mistrust and horrific conflict among nations, among
peoples, among peoples within nations, and so on; and that many people
are not made "happier" (however we might conceive that) through the
commercialization of modern life.

Given such assumptions, that Smith was right about sympathy but
wrong about commerce, might anything remain for us in Smith's thought

---

[1] *TMS* VI.ii.3.2 (p. 235).

as we struggle to understand the moral texture of our new global reality? In this chapter, I tease out a theory of universal understanding in Smith's *Moral Sentiments* that he never fully developed or defended. I will argue that despite the particularism of Smith's moral psychology, which we examined at length in terms of its physical, affective and historical contingencies, the Smithian spectator always retained a fundamental, visceral access to the suffering of others, even those at great physical distances and/or with very different histories. This method of access, I argue, works *independently* of the sympathetic apparatus that grounds Smith's general description of our moral sentiments and where they come from. I focus here on Smith's theory of justice – and particularly his claim that justice is a "negative virtue" grounded not in ordinary morality which, as we've seen, was subject to great cultural variation and corruption, but in what Smith described as a human aversion to cruelty, which struck him as universal. To function in the way Smith hoped it could, justice needed to be outside of history, independent of the ebb and flow of ordinary moral life with its delusions and corruptions. Here I will explore the reasons Smith believed our visceral reaction to cruelty has the positive effect of opening a "critical" space for detached judgment about ourselves and others.[2] Whether Smith succeeds is another question for us, which I will address in due course.

SMITH ON JUSTICE

In this chapter I pursue Smith's idea of "justice," what he sometimes referred to, following Hugo Grotius, as "natural jurisprudence" or "the natural rules of justice independent of all positive institution."[3] Overall, Smith had relatively little to say about justice in the *Moral Sentiments*, and what he did say was sporadic and uncharacteristically unsystematic – Fleischacker calls it "anomalous" to the rest of the book.[4] He made frequent references to the "plainest and most obvious rules of justice," to the "most sacred laws of justice," to "what justice demands," to the attempt of "all well-governed states" to prescribe positive laws that "coincide with those of natural justice," to "the natural rules of justice independent of all positive institution," to "the general

---

[2] I borrow the designation "critical" from Knud Haakonssen's study of Smith's jurisprudence, *Science of a Legislator*, ch. 6. Haakonssen was the first rigorously to examine Smith's "negative justice," its universal significance, and its "critical" capacity. See also Samuel Fleischacker in *Wealth of Nations*, ch. 8, who takes a very different view. I will have more to say later about Haakonssen's and Fleischacker's interpretations of Smith's negative justice.

[3] *TMS* VI.ii.intro.2 (p. 218); *TMS* VII.iv.7–14 (pp. 329–333); *TMS* VII.iv.37 (pp. 341–342).

[4] For discussion see Haakonssen, *Science of a Legislator*; Griswold, *Virtues of Enlightenment*, ch. 6; and Fleischacker, *Wealth of Nations*, ch. 8, p. 147.

principles which ought to run through and be the foundation of the laws of all nations ... without regard to the particular institutions of any one nation," and so on.[5] In other words, he frequently gestured toward the universality of justice – but about content he said very little.[6] In the *Moral Sentiments* he acknowledged that "natural jurisprudence" is "of all the sciences by far the most important, but hitherto, perhaps the least cultivated."[7] But he quickly relieved himself of the difficulties of elaborating, asserting that "it belongs not to our present subject to enter into any detail." In the closing paragraph of the *Moral Sentiments* he promised his readers a more "complete" account in future work:

Grotius seems to have been the first who attempted to give the world anything like a system of those principles which ought to run through, and be the foundation of the laws of all nations: and his treatise of the laws of war and peace, with all its imperfections, is perhaps at this day the most complete work that has yet been given upon this subject. I shall in another discourse endeavour to give an account of the general principles of law and government, and of the different revolutions they have undergone in the different ages and periods of society.[8]

But his promise remained unfulfilled for thirty years and his notes on the subject were famously consigned to the flames upon his death. Charles Griswold and Ian Simpson Ross have debated the reasons for this. Griswold attributed Smith's failure to write a jurisprudence, in the terms he had promised, to the fact that it simply could not be written given the nature of his system: "To pursue questions about first principles is to seek a standpoint external to the human spectacle, and he thinks that that is unavailable" (p. 258). Ross vigorously disagreed with Griswold's account of Smith's "aporia" and drew mainly on personal correspondence to characterize Smith's hesitance to finish his jurisprudence as a function of perfectionism and advanced age.[9]

---

[5] See, for example, *TMS* VI.ii.intro.2 (p. 218); *TMS* II.ii.2.2 (p. 84); *TMS* III.3.41 (p. 155); *TMS* VII.iv.7–114 (pp. 329–333); and *TMS* VII.iv.37 (pp. 341–342).

[6] On the "content" problem, see Fleischacker, *Wealth of Nations*, ch. 8. For Fleischacker, the problem is not merely that Smith was hesitant to articulate content, but that precisely defining content would have been antithetical to the historical nature of his project.

[7] *TMS* VI.ii.intro.2 (p. 218).

[8] *TMS* VII.iv.37 (pp. 341–342). See Smith's discussion of the natural jurisprudence of Grotius, Hobbes and Pufendorf in *Lectures on Jurisprudence (1762–1766)*, ed. R. L. Meek, D. D. Raphael and P. G. Stein, as vol. V of *The Glasgow Edition of the Works and Correspondence of Adam Smith*. Oxford: Oxford University Press; reprint Indianapolis, IN: Liberty Press, 1982.; *LJ* (B) 1–3 (pp. 397–398).

[9] Griswold, *Virtues of Enlightenment*, p.258. Ian Simpson Ross, "'Great Works upon the Anvil' in 1785: Adam Smith's Projected Corpus of Philosophy." *Adam Smith Review*, vol. 1 (2004), pp. 40–59. See Griswold's reply: "On the Incompleteness of Adam Smith's System," *Adam Smith Review*, vol. 2 (2006), pp. 181–186. Fleischacker takes essentially the same position as Griswold in *Wealth of Nations*, ch. 8. See also Sergio V. Cremaschi, "Adam Smith: Skeptical Newtonianism, Disenchanted Republicanism, and the Birth of Social Science," in *Knowledge and Politics: Case Studies in the Relationship between Epistemology and Political Philosophy*, ed. Marcelo Dascal and Ora Gruengard

Fortunately Smith's students at the University of Glasgow preserved his lectures on jurisprudence, and their notes are now available to us in the posthumously published *Lectures on Jurisprudence*. On balance, however, Smith's *Lectures* were devoted primarily to a dry, academic enumeration of public, domestic and private laws.[10] But he did deliver one revealing lecture entitled "Of the Laws of Nations"[11] in which we get some access to what he might have meant when he referred in the *Moral Sentiments* to "those principles which ought to run through, and be the foundation of the laws of all nations" – a "philosophy of law," "rules of justice" articulated "without regard to the particular institutions of any one nation."[12]

ORNAMENTS AND FOUNDATIONS

In an early unpublished manuscript written before the 1759 appearance of the *Moral Sentiments*, Smith asserted that "Natural Jurisprudence, or the Theory of the general principles of Law ... *make a very important part of the Theory of moral Sentiments*."[13] Although he never pursued the connections between jurisprudence and moral sentiment in future work, offering surprisingly few words on the subject in the *Moral Sentiments* itself, he did assert there quite explicitly that "no social intercourse can take place among men who do not generally abstain from injuring one another."[14] And even more boldly:

Justice ... is the main pillar that upholds the whole edifice. If it is removed, the great, immense fabric of human society, that fabric which to raise and support seems in this world, if I may say so, to have been the peculiar and darling care of Nature, must in a moment crumble into atoms.[15]

Nowhere do we learn more about Smith's idea of justice than in a modest section of the *Moral Sentiments* devoted to a distinction between "justice" and "beneficence."[16] Here we learn several important things about Smithian justice: that it is what Smith calls, the "foundation" of social life and is therefore unique among the virtues; that it cannot be guaranteed through ordinary morality or through utility calculations; that Nature has thus ensured its observance by implanting in "the human breast" an instinctive and immediate "appetite" both for it and for the means necessary to obtain

---

(Boulder, CO: Westview Press, 1989), pp. 83–110, at pp. 100–101. For interesting discussion of Smith's lapse from a literary perspective, see Maureen Harkin, "Adam Smith's Missing History: Primitives, Progress and Problems of Genre," *English Literary History*, vol. 72 (2005), pp. 429–451.

[10] *LJ* (A) i.1-iii.147 (pp. 5–199); *LJ* (B) 1–201 (pp. 397–485). [11] *LJ* (B) 341–358 (pp. 545–554).

[12] *TMS* VII.iv.37 (pp. 341–342).

[13] *TMS* Appendix II (p. 389): Glasgow University Library, MS Gen. 1035/227. These were most likely lecture notes for his ethics course in the University of Glasgow.

[14] *TMS* II.ii.3.6 (p. 87).   [15] *TMS* II.ii.3.4 (p. 86).   [16] *TMS* II.ii (pp. 78–91).

it; that justice is a "negative virtue," which means that it consists in refraining from doing things that are unjust, rather than in doing "good" things; that it is precise and easily codified; relatedly, that it is what we might call today "minimal" but also absolutely imperative; that while it doesn't merit praise its violation produces "resentment" in every impartial spectator; and that it is subject to legitimate coercion by the state.

How did all of these characteristics hang together for Smith? He began by contrasting a stable society that is grounded in justice with a happy one that coheres through genuine affection. He maintained that "society flourishes and is happy" when

necessary assistance is reciprocally afforded from love, from gratitude, from friendship, and esteem … [and when] all the members of it are bound together by the agreeable bands of love and affection, and are, as it were, drawn to one common centre of mutual good offices.[17]

It is important to note that beneficence is a function of ordinary morality for Smith. It quite naturally takes place among people who are familiar with one another, *oikeion* in the Stoic sense, which is why its scope tended to be quite narrow. Recall in Chapter 4, I explored the concentric pattern of Smith's account of the "distribution of our good offices" in Section VI.ii of the *Moral Sentiments*.[18] Beneficent activity is a natural consequence of the affective connection individuals feel toward those closest to them. In these narrow spaces, Smith observed, beneficence is natural and quite common. It always pleases the spectator and merits praise and gratitude; inversely "a want of beneficence" always jars the spectator and merits condemnation. Society we concur should become a "desert" to the hard-hearted:

Those whose hearts never open to the feelings of humanity should, we think, be shut out in the same manner, from the affections of all their fellow creatures, and be allowed to live in the midst of society, as in a great desert where there is nobody to care for them, or inquire after them.[19]

Yet, although hard-heartedness displeases and stimulates condemnation and disapprobation, Smith insisted that we may never legitimately coerce beneficence. Moreover, he said that it is inappropriate to feel "resentment" toward or to punish someone who has committed no affirmative act of harm

---

[17] *TMS* II.ii.3.1 (p. 85).
[18] It is interesting to observe that Smith began his discussion of "our very limited powers of beneficence" in *TMS* VI.ii (pp. 218–237, at p. 218) by contrasting beneficence with justice, in nearly the same terms as justice was presented here, in *TMS* II.ii.
[19] *TMS* II.ii.1.10 (p. 82).

to particular persons. "Beneficence is always free, it cannot be extorted by force, the mere want of beneficence tends to do no real positive hurt."[20]

When a man attacks, or robs, or attempts to murder another, all the neighbors take the alarm, and think that they do right when they run, either to revenge the person who has been injured, or to defend him who is in danger of being so. But when a father fails in the ordinary degree of affection towards a son; when a son seems to want that filial reverence which might be expected to his father; when brothers are without the usual degree of brotherly affection; when a man shuts his breast against compassion, and refuses to relieve the misery of his fellow creatures, when he can with the greatest ease; in all these cases, though everybody blames the conduct, *nobody imagines that those who might have reason, perhaps, to expect more kindness, have any right to extort it by force.*[21]

Beneficence is "always free," "left to the freedom of our own wills."[22] Note, however, in the following passage, the way Smith uses "hatred" to characterize the social regulation of heartless behavior.

The man who does not recompense his benefactor, when he has it in his power, and when his benefactor needs his assistance, is, no doubt, guilty of the blackest ingratitude. The heart of every impartial spectator rejects all fellow-feeling with the selfishness of his motives, and he is the proper object of the highest disapprobation. But still he does no positive hurt to any body. He only does not do that good which in propriety he ought to have done. He is the object of hatred, a passion which is naturally excited by impropriety of sentiment and behaviour; not of resentment, a passion which is never properly called forth but by actions that do real and positive hurt to some particular persons.[23]

Smith's distinction here between resentment and hatred is very important, particularly when considering the cosmopolitan significance of Smith's theory of justice. Resentment is a passion ignited at the sight of suffering victims: the "sympathetic indignation which naturally boils up in the breast of the spectator" prompts "fellow-feeling with their just and natural resentment."[24] For Smith, thus, resentment is closely connected with justice:

Resentment seems to have been given us by nature for defence, and for defence only. It is the safeguard of justice and the security of innocence.[25]

Resentment "must be reserved therefore for these purposes; nor can the spectator go along with it when it is exercised for any other."[26] However, it is perfectly appropriate to feel "hatred," "dislike" and "the highest disapprobation" toward those who shock us with their hard-heartedness. The

[20] *TMS* II.ii.1.3 (p. 78).   [21] *TMS* II.ii.1.7 (p. 81), emphasis added.   [22] *TMS* II.ii.1.1–5 (pp. 78–81).
[23] *TMS* II.ii.1.3 (pp. 78–79).   [24] *TMS* II.i.5.6 (p. 76).   [25] *TMS* II.ii.1.4 (p. 79).
[26] *TMS* II.ii.4 (p. 79).

point here is that Smith left beneficence and all of the softer virtues like friendship, generosity, and charity to the ordinary governance of the sympathy process. He argued that it needed no additional support.[27] Indeed, beneficence is a function of ordinary morality, for Smith:

> Though Nature ... exhorts mankind to acts of beneficence, by the pleasing consciousness of deserved reward, she has not thought it necessary to guard and enforce the practice of it by the terrors of merited punishment in case it should be neglected ... [I]t was, therefore, sufficient to recommend, but by no means necessary to impose.[28]

Moreover, beneficence is often effectively substituted by enlightened self-interest, rendering coercion unnecessary for yet another reason:

> But though the necessary assistance should not be afforded from such generous and disinterested motives, though among the different members of the society there should be no mutual love and affection, the society, though less happy and agreeable, will not necessarily be dissolved. Society may subsist among different men, as among different merchants, *from a sense of its utility*, without any mutual love or affection; and though no man in it should owe any obligation, or be bound in gratitude to any other, it may still be upheld by a mercenary exchange of good offices according to an agreed valuation.[29]

When pressed on the lack of good-will among men, Smith frequently turned to the invisible hand of enlightened self-interest. I have argued already in Chapter 1 that we should not inflate this dimension of Smith's thought beyond proper bounds. In the *Moral Sentiments*, enlightened self-interest served to supplement our moral sentiments when self-love spoke too loudly and threatened to corrupt our judgments and actions, a sort of insurance policy through which the benevolent hand of Nature guaranteed her "favorite ends."

But Smith was less cavalier with justice, for it was foundational to his primary concern in the *Moral Sentiments*: to guarantee modern social order. "Society may subsist, though not in the most comfortable state, without beneficence," he observed, "*but the prevalence of injustice must utterly destroy it.*"

> Society ... cannot subsist among those who are at all times ready to hurt and injure one another. The moment that injury begins, the moment that mutual resentment and animosity take place, all the bands of it are broken asunder, and the different members of which it consisted are, as it were, dissipated and scattered abroad by the violence and opposition of their discordant affections.[30]

---

[27] *TMS* II.ii.1–5 (pp. 78–80).　　[28] *TMS* II.ii.3.4 (p. 86).
[29] *TMS* II.ii.3.2 (pp. 85–86), emphasis added.　　[30] *TMS* II.ii.3.3 (p. 86).

While "beneficence" is an "ornament which embellishes" social life, making it lovelier and perhaps more fulfilling for its members, "justice" is the "foundation of the building." It is

the main pillar that upholds the whole edifice. If it is removed, the great, the immense fabric of human society must in a moment crumble into atoms.[31]

Because of the foundational role of justice in the maintenance of society, Nature ensured that injustice will always stimulate immediate resentment in the spectator, as well as a poignant sense that punishment is appropriate. The following passage is central to the interpretation that follows, so I cite it here at length:

There is, however, another virtue, of which the observance is not left to the freedom of our wills, which may be extorted by force, and of which the violation exposes to resentment, and consequently to punishment. This virtue is justice: the violation of justice is injury: it does real and positive hurt to some particular persons, from motives which are naturally disapproved of. It is, therefore, the proper object of resentment, and of punishment, which is the natural consequence of resentment. As mankind go along with, and approve of the violence employed to avenge the hurt which is done by injustice, so they much more go along with, and approve of, that which is employed to prevent and beat off the injury, and to restrain the offender from hurting his neighbors … And upon this is founded that remarkable distinction between justice and all the other social virtues, which has of late been particularly insisted upon by an author of very great and original genius, that we feel ourselves to be under a stricter obligation to act according to justice, than agreeably to friendship, charity, or generosity; that the practice of these last mentioned virtues seems to be left in some measure to our own choice, but that somehow or other, we feel ourselves to be in a peculiar manner tied, bound, and obliged to the observation of justice.[32]

Again, we learn several important things here about justice: that it is obligatory (not discretionary); that its violation does real injury (and not mere insult or affront); that it always naturally stimulates resentment and consequently a desire to punish; and that it is therefore unique among the virtues.

And yet, note that justice merits "very little gratitude."[33] I feel no gratitude toward someone who allows me to pass on the street unharmed or who refrains from taking my child's lunch money. The man who "merely abstains from hurting his neighbors" merits no praise.[34] Indeed, justice most often requires very little of us. In a passage that has become red meat for libertarians,

[31] *TMS* II.ii.3.4 (p. 86).   [32] *TMS* II.ii.1.5 (p. 79).   [33] *TMS* II.ii.1.9 (pp. 81–82).
[34] *TMS* II.ii.1.10 (p. 82).

Smith asserted that "we may often fulfill all the rules of justice by sitting still and doing nothing":

Mere justice is, upon most occasions, but a *negative virtue*, and only hinders us from hurting our neighbor.[35]

Similarly in Section VI.ii, the most overtly anti-cosmopolitan portion of the *Moral Sentiments*, as we saw earlier, Smith contrasted the absolute commands of justice, which are codified in law and subject to state coercion, with "our very limited powers of beneficence," which are sufficiently regulated by human connection, interest and capacity. There Smith defined justice as follows:

The wisdom of every state or commonwealth endeavours, as well as it can, to employ the force of the society to restrain those who are subject to its authority, from hurting or disturbing the happiness of one another. The rules which it establishes for this purpose, constitute the civil and criminal law of each particular state or country. The principles upon which those rules either are, or ought to be founded, are the subject of a particular science, of all sciences the most important, but hitherto, perhaps, the least cultivated, that of natural jurisprudence; concerning which it belongs not to our present subject to enter into any detail. A sacred and religious regard not to hurt or disturb in any respect the happiness of our neighbor, even in those cases where no law can properly protect him, constitutes the character of the perfectly innocent and just man ... It is a character sufficiently understood, and requires no further explanation.[36]

JUSTICE AS A "NEGATIVE VIRTUE"

In his description of justice as a "negative virtue," Smith was resuscitating an ancient legal distinction between what Aristotle called "commutative justice" and "distributive justice" and what Hugo Grotius later called "the *justicia expletrix*" and "the *justicia attributrix*." Smith described these two senses of law both in his *Lectures on Jurisprudence* and in section VII of the *Moral Sentiments*, distinguishing "perfect rights" from "imperfect rights," and aligning the former with commutative justice, and the latter with distributive justice:

Perfect rights are those which we have a title to demand and if refused to compel an other to perform. What they [Pufendorf, Hutcheson] call imperfect rights are those

---

[35] *TMS* II.ii.1.9 (pp. 81–82).

[36] *TMS* VI.ii.intro.2 (p. 218), emphasis added. Here we see Smith overtly side-stepping the subject of the "principles" of natural jurisprudence – something he frequently did – and so essential to claims today about the incompleteness (and likely incompletability) of Smith's jurisprudence which I alluded to earlier. At the end of this passage, exploration of the just man requires "no further explanation" presumably because Smith had already given extensive attention to the subject in *TMS* II.ii.

which correspond to those duties which ought to be performed to us by others but which we have no title to compel them to perform; they having it intirely [*sic*] in their power to perform them or not. Thus a man of bright parts or remarkable learning is deserving of praise, but we have no power to compel any one to give it him. A beggar is an object of our charity and may be said to have a right to demand it; but when we use the word right in this way it is not in a proper but in a metaphorical sense.[37]

Smith confined his reflections to perfect rights, since "the latter do not belong properly to jurisprudence, but rather to a system of moralls as they do not fall under the jurisdiction of the laws."[38] Accordingly in Part VII of the *Moral Sentiments*, Smith embraced the former sense of justice over the latter since he believed Grotius' *justitia attributrix* had conflated justice with beneficence – which meant essentially, for Smith, that Grotius was developing a "system of moralls" and not of "jurisprudence":

we are said not to do justice to our neighbor unless we conceive for him all that love, respect, and esteem, which his character, his situation, and his connexion with ourselves, render suitable and proper for us to feel, and unless we act accordingly. It is in this sense that we are said to do injustice to a man of merit who is connected with us, though we abstain from hurting him in every respect, if we do not exert ourselves to serve him and place him in that situation in which the impartial spectator would be pleased to see him ... [T]he *justitia attributrix* of Grotius ... consists in proper beneficence, in the becoming use of what is our own, and in the applying it to those purposes either of charity or generosity, to which it is most suitable, in our situation, that it should be applied. In this sense justice comprehends all the social virtues.[39]

The *justitia attributrix* are embedded in such arguments today that sitting idle in the midst of suffering when one has resources and capacity to intervene can be as hurtful, as *unjust*, as a willful, affirmative act of harm. One thinks here about public outrage at the Kitty Genovese case. One thinks of arguments for social welfare, for Good Samaritan laws, for the reasons given by those who risked life and limb to rescue Jews from the Nazis – the examples are endless. But Smith insisted that withholding beneficence does "no positive hurt," and that the "social fabric" could "subsist" without such assistance. As such he left the imperative of "charity and generosity" to the ordinary governance of moral approbation.[40]

Smith regularly condemned ancient and modern "casuists" (among whom he included Cicero, Augustine, Pufendorf, Barbeyrac and Hutcheson) for attempting to "lay down exact and precise rules for the direction of every

---

[37] *LJ* (A) i.14–15 (p. 9).   [38] *LJ* (A) i.14–15 (p. 9).
[39] *TMS* VII.ii.1.10 (pp. 269–270).   [40] *TMS* II.ii.3.4 (p. 86).

circumstance of our behaviour" – for attempting to "prescribe rules for the conduct of a good man."[41] He declared that "justice is the *only* virtue to which such exact rules can properly be given."[42] Smith's commutative orientation to justice seems to be grounded in a belief that human ends are necessarily plural and contentious, and that codifying the good is inherently problematic – which is likely why he was never able to complete his jurisprudence, which by his own definition of the proposed project required a declaration about universal "principles." As Haakonssen puts it,

Because of the individuality and, not least, the uncertainty of human life, it is impossible to formulate a universal idea of the highest good or the good life.[43]

A modern polity that permits individuals to pursue their own ends, and tolerates the result, is prohibited from codifying the "exact and precise" demands of human conduct. At one point, Smith did acknowledge that sovereigns must sometimes "command mutual good offices to a certain degree" – for example requiring parents to maintain their children, children to maintain their elderly parents, and so forth.[44] He also referred vaguely and without elaboration to other "duties of beneficence" that promote, what he called, "the prosperity of the commonwealth" and prevent "gross disorders." But recapitulating his essential point, Smith also recognized the extreme "delicacy" involved in such legislation:

Of all the duties of a law-giver, however, this, perhaps, is that which it requires the greatest delicacy and reserve to execute with propriety and judgment. To neglect it altogether exposes the commonwealth to many gross disorders and shocking enormities, and to push it too far is destructive of all liberty, security, and justice.[45]

The heart of Smith's account of law is that it must be minimal, broadly consensual, codifying and coercing with state power only that which we can know for certain – which most often boils down to something very simple for Smith: that "injury … does real and positive hurt."[46]

---

[41] *TMS* VI.iv.7–8 (pp. 329–330).   [42] *TMS* VI.iv.7 (p. 329).
[43] Haakonssen, "Introduction," pp. 5–6.   [44] *TMS* II.ii.1.8 (p. 81).
[45] *TMS* II.ii.1.8 (p. 81). Fleischacker, *Wealth of Nations*, p. 149, notes thus that enforceability was not unique to justice for Smith. I think the hesitance Smith demonstrates when describing such legislation, however, reinforces the main point. I also think Smith's more general argument about pluralism, minimalism and coercion is still highly relevant to contemporary international ethics. The commands Smith alludes vaguely to in *TMS* II.ii.1.8 are geared toward the maintenance of local communities, whose members are already *oikeion* and likelier to agree on a wider base, as opposed to larger spaces where diversity and affective distance necessitate a thinner conception of law.
[46] *TMS* II.ii.1.5 (p. 79).

JUSTICE AS "APPETITE"

But, how did Smith believe justice recommends itself to us? How do we know and broadly agree to its terms? How does it "tie, bound, and oblige" us? The very question of epistemology that drove my interpretation of the impartial spectator earlier inevitably returns when we reflect on the source of Smith's idea of justice. Again, we must ask: from where do unchanging, universal principles of justice derive, given Smith's sociological description of the origin of our moral sentiments? For one thing, Smith took issue with Hume's well-known claim in the *Enquiry* that "public utility is the sole origin of justice"[47] – that "this virtue derives its existence entirely from its necessary use to the intercourse and social state of mankind."[48] Smith asserted that justice was *not* simply a function of its social utility, and that in saying that it was, Hume had mistaken an efficient cause for a final cause. Smith agreed that justice is useful for the maintenance of society in a foundational sort of way; but its utility does not explain *why* we initially are drawn to justice and away from injustice.

As society cannot subsist unless the laws of justice are tolerably observed, as no social intercourse can take place among men who do not generally abstain from injuring one another; the consideration of this necessity, it has been thought, was the ground upon which we approved of them and enforcement of the laws of justice by the punishment of those who violated them ... But though it commonly requires no great discernment to see the destructive tendency of all licentious practices to the welfare of society, it is seldom this consideration which first *animates* us against them. All men, even the most stupid and unthinking, abhor fraud, perfidy, and injustice, and delight to see them punished. But few men have reflected upon the necessity of justice to the existence of society, how obvious soever that necessity may appear to be.[49]

And yet, if not through a Humean sense of utility, or Hutchesonian benevolence, or Lockean reason, or Rousseau's general will, or raw coercion, how did Smith believe justice recommended itself to us? In his own words above, how did justice "animate" itself to us?

Smith believed that justice was unique among "all the other social virtues" in the following way:

---

[47] Hume, *Enquiry*, III.3.1.1 (p. 203). On the differences between Hume and Smith on justice and utility, see, for example, Haakonssen, *Science*, pp. 87–89; D. D. Raphael, "Justice and Utility"; and Eric Schliesser and Spencer Pack, "Adam Smith's 'Humean' Criticism of Hume's Account of the Origin of Justice," *Journal of the History of Philosophy*, vol. 44, no 1 (2006), pp. 47–63.
[48] Hume, *Enquiry*, III.1 (p. 206).   [49] *TMS* II.ii.3.6 (p. 87); *TMS* II.3.9 (p. 89), emphasis added.

we *feel ourselves* to be under a stricter obligation to act according to justice, than
agreeably to friendship, charity, or generosity; that the practice of these last
mentioned virtues seems to be left in some measure to our own choice, but that,
somehow or other, we *feel ourselves* to be in a peculiar manner tied, bound, and
obliged to the observation of justice.[50]

In this very important passage, Smith claimed that "somehow or other" we
"feel ourselves to be" under such an obligation, which makes the feeling
seem somewhat mystical. But Smith the sober empiricist did not go in for
such things. He established very clearly in the surrounding pages *just how*
we come to "feel" this way. As a general rule, whenever Smith in the *Moral
Sentiments* discussed the issue of social order, he always in the next breath
referred to the ways that Nature had ensured it by endowing man with
certain appetites, which he always characterized as "immediate" and
"instinctive" and "impressed by nature."[51] He explained this connection
very clearly to his readers:

Though man, therefore, be naturally endowed with a desire of the welfare and
preservation of society, yet the Author of nature has not entrusted it to his reason to
find out that a certain application of punishments is the proper means of attaining
this end; but has endowed him with an immediate and instinctive approbation of
that very application which is most proper to attain it. The œconomy of nature is in
this respect exactly of a piece with what it is upon many other occasions. With
regard to all those ends which, upon account of their particular importance, may be
regarded, if such an expression is allowable, as the favorite ends of nature, she has
constantly in this manner not only endowed mankind with an appetite for the end
which she proposes, but likewise with an appetite for the means by which alone this
end can be brought about.[52]

Smith's discussion of justice follows this very pattern. Since justice was
foundational to the "fabric of human society," and since maintaining this
fabric was the "peculiar and darling care of Nature," it was Nature *itself* that
assured our feeling.[53]

Nature has implanted in the human breast that consciousness of ill-desert, those
terrors of merited punishment which attend upon its violation, as the great safe-
guards of the association of mankind, to protect the weak, to curb the violent, and
to chastise the guilty.[54]

Moreover, as further guarantee, as an extra "precaution," nature also gave us
an instinctive sense that force is appropriate to constrain its observation.[55] In

---

[50] *TMS* II.ii.1.5 (p. 80), emphasis added.
[51] See, for example, *TMS* II.i.5.10 (pp. 77–78); *TMS* III.5.2–3 (p. 163).   [52] *TMS* II.i.5.10 (p. 77).
[53] *TMS* II.ii.3.4 (p. 86).   [54] *TMS* II.ii.3.4 (p. 86).   [55] *TMS* II.ii.1.5 (p. 80); *TMS* II.ii.3.4 (p. 86).

"well-governed states," Smith observed, this charge is handed over to "the public magistrate" who is "under a necessity of employing the power of the commonwealth to enforce the practice of this virtue."[56]

JUSTICE UNIQUE AMONG THE VIRTUES

No "end" in the *Moral Sentiments* but justice was endowed with the distinctive qualities first of being untutored and "immediate," a "natural sense," an "appetite," something that nature has "implanted in the human breast," "stamped upon the human heart in the strongest and most indelible characters"; and second, of being properly coerced by the "power of the commonwealth." Indeed, as "nature's favorite end," justice was unique. For Smith these qualities established the "remarkable distinction between justice and all the other social virtues."[57]

In his distinction between justice and beneficence, Smith acknowledged the work of "an author of very great and original genius," referring possibly to David Hume, possibly to Henry Home, Lord Kames who, in his *Essays on the Principles of Morality and Natural Religion*, noted that justice is "less free" than generosity.[58] I have no real quarrel with either hypothesis. But I submit that Smith's claim that *justice was unique among the virtues* may have been influenced as well by Joseph Butler who, in his *Dissertation Upon the Nature of Virtue* in 1726, argued in parallel fashion that *injustice was unique among the vices*. Although Smith ranked virtues and Butler vices, the criteria each used to order his rankings were nearly identical. Observes Butler:

nature has not given us so sensible a disapprobation of imprudence and folly, either in ourselves or others, as of falsehood, injustice and cruelty; I suppose, because that constant habitual sense of private interest and good, which we always carry about with us, renders such sensible disapprobation less necessary, less wanting, to keep us from imprudently neglecting our own happiness ... and also because imprudence and folly appearing to bring its own punishment more immediately and constantly than injurious behavior, it needs less the additional punishment which would be inflicted upon it by others had they the same sensible indignation against it as injustice and fraud and cruelty.[59]

Earlier, in Chapter 1, I demonstrated Smith's familiarity with Butler's sermons. All eighteenth-century Scots were familiar with them; and Smith certainly would have been attracted to Butler's reasons for distinguishing the vice cluster falsehood-injustice-cruelty from the other less destructive, less fundamental

---

[56] *TMS* VII.iv.36 (p. 340); see also *WN* V.i.b (pp. 708–723).   [57] *TMS* II.ii.1.5 (p. 80).
[58] For discussion, see the editors' note at *TMS* II.ii.1.5 (p. 80), n. 1.   [59] Butler, "Dissertation," p. 72.

vices, such as imprudence and folly. Like Butler who claimed that most vices were matters of "private interest" and therefore subjected the violator to their "own punishment," their own immediate negative consequences – as say, foolishly squandering one's money makes one poor – Smith claimed that the virtues of beneficence (love, respect, esteem, friendship, charity, generosity[60]) were not only sufficiently governed by the sympathy process, but that they could be effectively substituted in a stable (though not necessarily happy) society by a "mercenary exchange of mutual good offices."[61] Because they were *self-policing*, governed endogenously, neither Butler's ordinary vices nor Smith's ordinary virtues required additional assurances. But the similarities went deeper. Like Butler, who argued that nature had assured against the vices of injustice, falsehood and cruelty by giving to mankind a "sensible disapprobation" and "indignation" against them, Smith concurred that justice was unique among the virtues because of our natural and instinctive "appetite" for it. Neither Smith nor Butler entrusted "nature's favorite end" to utility, as Hume had. For both, *appetite, not utility, was the final cause of justice.*

Now, it makes sense to speak of an appetite for something that satisfies a physical urge. Smith himself referred to "hunger, thirst, the passion which unites the two sexes, the love of pleasure, the dread of pain," and so forth.[62] But how did he go on to include justice among these stimuli? What does it mean to have an "appetite" for an abstract thing like justice? What does an appetite for justice consist in? Smith believed that these questions could be addressed only in the *negative*.[63] Since justice was essential for even the most rudimentary degree of social intercourse, he didn't want to rest it precariously on instrumental rationality, or on a strong, positive conception of the good which was always subject to contestation. Surely Smith characterized justice as "Nature's favorite end," but nature did not fasten justice to a *summum bonum*, a positive conception of the good which always rested on local opinion. Striking a chord with pluralists today, Smith believed that positive goods make for necessarily precarious foundations. And yet, he was eager to prevail over conventionalism and relativity. So he did as so many others in the modern Western tradition before him had done, and returned to the idea of human nature – with the intention of articulating as

---

[60] This list is drawn from Smith's discussion of beneficence at *TMS* II.ii.1.3 (p. 79); and of Grotius' *justitia attributrix* at *TMS* VII.ii.1.10 (pp. 269–270).

[61] *TMS* II.ii.3.3 (p. 86). [62] *TMS* I.ii.1.9 (pp. 27–31).

[63] Haakonssen attributes this to the greater "pungency" and "universal" identifiability of pain over joy, and linked this prioritization to Smith's negative justice in *Science of a Legislator*, pp. 83–84. Similarly, Fleischacker observes that Smith resisted making positive assertions about human "happiness," preferring instead to stress "failings that take away from happiness." *Third Concept of Liberty*, pp. 144–149.

thin and minimalist an Archimedean point as he could. Smith insisted that nature had safeguarded her "favorite end" by anchoring it on something firmer than convention, and through a process more stable than ordinary morality. I believe that Smith was attempting to articulate a theory of justice more certain than Humean utility, but one that didn't require the strong, abstract foundations of Hutchesonian benevolence or a Lockean natural law that reason revealed to the attentive. The answer for Smith lay in what he described as an instinctive human aversion to *cruelty*, much like Judith Shklar's "*summum malum* of cruelty" 200 years later in the "Liberalism of Fear."[64]

A few words about Shklar and her project before establishing connections here with Smith. Shklar thought that many basic concepts in political philosophy had become lifeless moral abstractions. Throughout her work, she sought to enliven and illuminate such concepts as liberty, justice and obligation by examining "limiting cases" drawn from concrete experiences. For example, in *Faces of Injustice* she illuminated justice through an examination of various *in*justices.[65] In a well-known essay on political obligation and loyalty, Shklar discussed exile as a "particularly concrete and extreme" way of examining political obligation at its limits.[66] Most relevant for our purposes is her well-known essay "Liberalism of Fear" in which Shklar employed what she called a "negative" method to explore the idea of liberty through an examination of concrete experiences of cruelty.[67]

Shklar sought to articulate a liberalism whose primary objective was to prohibit the "deliberate infliction of physical, and secondarily emotional, pain upon a weaker person or group by stronger ones in order to achieve some end, tangible or not, of the latter."[68] She acknowledged that the "sources of oppression are indeed numerous" in modern life but she focused specifically on "agents of the modern state" who have "unique resources of physical might and persuasion at their disposal."[69] Although Smith didn't stress particular agents of cruelty in his account, he very likely would have sympathized with Shklar's preoccupation with the perils of unrestrained governmental power. But I believe the affinity between Smith and Shklar goes far deeper (than a superficial swipe at their penchant for small states), and is interesting for two less obvious reasons, both having to do with moral epistemology. First, although their language differed (Shklar "intuition,"

[64] See Judith N. Shklar, "Liberalism of Fear," in *Political Thought and Political Thinkers*, ed. Stanley Hoffman (Chicago: University of Chicago Press, 1998), pp. 3–20. Shklar noted in passing her affinity with Smith on this point in *Faces of Injustice*, pp. 117–118.
[65] Shklar, *Faces of Injustice*.   [66] Shklar, "Obligation, Loyalty and Exile."
[67] Shklar, "Liberalism of Fear," pp. 3–20.   [68] *Ibid.*, p. 11.   [69] *Ibid.*, p. 3.

Smith "appetite") both described an affective aversion to cruelty that derives
from negative human experience. Second, both asserted that our aversion to
cruelty produces knowledge that cruelty is "an absolute evil," grounding a
minimalist political morality that is intelligible across cultural space.[70]

Evidence for the uniqueness of cruelty abounds in the *Moral Sentiments*.
Like Shklar in *Ordinary Vices*, Smith frequently addressed such ordinary vices
as greed, envy, mean-spiritedness, misanthropy, vengeance, resentment –
what he labeled "the unsocial passions" – demonstrating that each tended
to repel the spectator and stimulate disapprobation in varying degrees.[71] But
he regularly referred to our aversion to cruelty as a "horror," a "repugnance,"
an "abhorrence," an "indignation," a reaction that is "immediate and instinctive."[72] Cruelty speaks to us in a different sort of language, works through
different channels, and inspires a different sort of "discord" than ordinary
vices do:

> Our horror for cruelty has no sort of resemblance to our contempt for mean-
> spiritedness. It is quite a different species of discord which we feel at the view of
> those two different vices.[73]

To understand better how our response to cruelty differs from our response
to ordinary vices, we must return momentarily to Smith's description of
sympathetic judgment, which I explored earlier in Chapter 2. Recall that
when a spectator imaginatively enters into the behavior of an agent to
determine whether or not it is "proper," Smith said that he generally seeks
to understand the *circumstances* that motivate the agent to feel as he feels,
and to act as he acts.[74] Knowledge of the agent's circumstances helps a
spectator better understand the "whole case ... with all its minutest incidents," as Smith put it.[75]

But Smith's description of our engagement with cruelty is very different.
Coming upon it, we focus instantly on consequences according to Smith;
our attention is immediately drawn away from the motivations of the brute
who committed the cruel act, and toward the *consequences* of his action: the
bloody victim, the torn flesh, "the deformed and mangled carcass of the

---

[70] *Ibid.*, p. 5.
[71] Judith N. Shklar, *Ordinary Vices* (Cambridge: MA: Belknap Press, 1984). On the "unsocial passions,"
see *TMS* I.ii.3 (pp. 34–38). Interesting in this context is that Smith included resentment, so essential to
justice, in his list of ordinary vices. For discussion of the mediocrity of proper resentment in this sense,
see Eric Schliesser, "Articulating Practices as Reasons: Adam Smith on the Social Conditions of
Possibility of Property," *Adam Smith Review*, vol. 2 (2006), pp. 69–97, at pp. 75–76.
[72] See, for example, *TMS* II.i.3.1 (p. 71); *TMS* II.i.5.6 (p. 76); *TMS* II.ii.3.9 (p. 89); *TMS* VII.iii.3.9
(p. 323); *TMS* VII.iii.3.14 (p. 325).
[73] *TMS* VII.iii.3.14 (p. 325).   [74] See esp. *TMS* I.i.3.5–10 (pp. 18–19).   [75] *TMS* I.i.4.6 (p. 21).

slain."[76] Haakonssen notes that "pain and misery" are most "pungently" felt in Smith's account, and thus most "universally" and "distinctly" sympathized with.[77] Our reaction is not an argument we make to ourselves; we do not mediate the sight through reason, "bring the case home" and reflect on how we might feel if we were the agent in the agent's circumstances – as we do with less compelling spectacles. The human heart leaps unmediated to the suffering victim. We are pulled in by the spectacle, much the way Rousseau's *pitié* pulls us in to the distress of our fellow creatures. For Smith, this visceral affinity with the victim of cruelty relates directly to our own experiences, our innate knowledge about suffering, and our own "dread of death" which he characterized as "the great restraint upon the injustice of mankind which, while it affects and mortifies the individual, guards and protects the society."[78]

Our sympathy with the sufferer's "unavoidable distress" and his "anguish" leads us simultaneously to arrive at a "fellow-feeling" with his "just and natural resentment" toward the person who caused him harm. Our sympathetic indignation "naturally boils up in the breast."[79]

When we bring home to ourselves the situation of the persons whom those scourges of mankind insulted, murdered or betrayed, what indignation do we not feel against such insolent and inhuman oppressors of the earth? Our sympathy with the unavoidable distress of the innocent sufferers is not more real nor more lively, than our fellow-feeling with their just and natural resentment. The former sentiment only heightens the latter, and the idea of their distress serves only to inflame and blow up our animosity against those who occasioned it.[80]

I have been arguing throughout that Smith was preoccupied with maintaining social order – with preventing society from "crumbling into atoms," from being "dissipated and scattered abroad by the violence and opposition of ... discordant affections."[81] Nowhere is this preoccupation more evident than in his discussion of justice, and particularly in the following passage. Here Smith explained how essential the instinctive "sense" of justice, resentment and merited punishment becomes when human temptation is unconstrained by our "particular connexion" with specific others. This affective consideration becomes important when thinking about the cosmopolitan significance of Smith's theory of justice. Note too the Hobbesian intonations:

In order to enforce the observation of justice ... Nature has implanted in the human breast that consciousness of ill-desert, those terrors of merited punishment which attend upon its violation, as the great safe-guards of the association of

[76] *TMS* II.i.2.5 (p. 71). [77] Haakonssen, *Science of a Legislator*, pp. 83–87. [78] *TMS* I.i.1.13 (p. 13). [79] *TMS* II.i.5.6 (p. 76). [80] *TMS* II.i.5.6 (p. 76). [81] *TMS* II.ii.3.3–4 (p. 86).

mankind, to protect the weak, to curb the violent, and to chastise the guilty. Men, though naturally sympathetic, feel so little for another, with *whom they have no particular connexion,* in comparison with what they feel for themselves; the misery of one, who is merely their fellow-creature, is of so little importance to them in comparison even of a small conveniency of their own; they have it so much in their power to hurt him, and may have so many temptations to do so, that if this principle did not stand up within them in his defence, and overawe them into a respect for his innocence, they would, like wild beasts, be at all times ready to fly upon him; and a man would enter an assembly of men as he enters a den of lions.[82]

In this passage, Smith described justice as an appetite that compensates for our lack of "feeling" for strangers, for all innocents, for those who are "not particularly connected" with us.[83] We are indeed sympathetic creatures, but Smith acknowledged here the narrow affective spaces in which our beneficence operates – an affirmation once again of his anti-cosmopolitan stance in Section VI.ii of the *Moral Sentiments* where he described "our very limited powers of beneficence."[84] Ordinary moral processes are largely incapable of restraining our self-love when we are confronted with "inconveniency" and "temptation"; for at such times we are inclined (to the extent we are) to refrain from harming *only* those people "particularly connected" to us, *oikeion,* in our innermost circles of sympathy. Our appetite for justice is therefore intended to protect humanity at times like these – those "innocent" and endangered "fellow-creatures" with whom we have no "particular connection."[85] Eric Schliesser suggests that Smith here articulated a thin, trans-cultural humanitarian ethic grounded in our shared human nature to resent injury done to innocents:

Our moral approval of just punishment originates in our feeling of common humanity coupled with our ability to imagine, as impartial spectators, the natural resentment and hence the propriety of retaliation by the victim.[86]

I agree here fully. The novelty in Smith's project seems to reside not so much in his description of our instinctive revulsion to human suffering – indeed, this was a staple in both ancient and modern literature and thought. Rather I believe his innovation consists in the conceptual thread that runs

---

[82] *TMS* II.ii.3.4 (p. 86), emphasis added.   [83] *TMS* II.i.5.10 (p. 77).   [84] *TMS* VI.ii.intro.2 (p. 218).

[85] Robert C. Solomon, whose work on emotion I greatly admire, and who died just as my writing was coming to a close, noted perceptively that for Smith "a sense of justice is needed to supplement sympathy, which by itself is not nearly powerful enough to counter the inevitable self-serving motives of most people." *A Passion for Justice: Emotions and the Origins of the Social Contract* (Lanham, MD: Rowman & Littlefield, 1995), p. 206.

[86] My thanks to Eric Schliesser for encouraging me to think more about resentment in this context. See Schliesser, "Articulating Practices," esp. pp. 75–79.

from suffering-revulsion to resentment-justice-law, undeveloped though it was – that the instinctive revulsion and the resentment it provokes provide grounds for a system of natural jurisprudence, which Smith described as a "system of those principles which ought to run through, and be the foundation of the laws of all nations."[87]

Surely there are important psychological questions of whether the revulsion Smith described is indeed "natural" and thus "universal" in this sense. This is an issue that I am not trained to address, though it does resonate as true for me. When we encounter an individual who appears immune to the pain and suffering of others, the coldness strikes us as deformed and unnatural; and we are led to wonder about the irregularities of mind or the corruptions of practical circumstance that produced such a disturbing orientation to the world. Experts for this reason tend to characterize such detachment as sociopathic. I am inclined to take Smith's revulsion thesis as a simple truth about human beings, perhaps because I cannot bear the thought of human reality without it. Nevertheless, there are important anthropological and legal questions about whether the *objects* of our revulsion can be universalized; indeed whether harm itself is universalizable. As this book comes to a close I will turn to the question of how Smith might have translated the instinctive revulsion he described in his account of justice into a positive, cosmopolitan international law; and the extent that this move is a plausible and desirable one for us today.

[87] *TMS* VII.iv.37 (p. 342).

Conclusion: cultural pluralism, moral goods, and the "laws of nations"

> Thus said the Lord of Hosts: I am exacting the penalty for what Amalek did to Israel, for the assault he made upon them on the road, on their way up from Egypt. Now go, attack Amalek, and proscribe all that belongs to him. Spare no one, but kill alike men and women, infants and sucklings, oxen and sheep, camels and asses!
>
> 1 Samuel 15:2–3

Judith Shklar was uncomfortable grounding liberalism on a "*summum bonum* toward which all political agents should strive" since she believed that monistic impulses are fundamentally incompatible with an individual's freedom, and by extension a political community's freedom, to chose its own ends.[1] She also insisted that positive goods make for necessarily precarious foundations since they are subject to endless contestation and violence. And yet, eager to prevail over relativity and unthinking acquiescence to culture and tradition (read: eager unequivocally to condemn Nazism and regimes that resemble it), Shklar wanted to identify a moral minimum that was incontrovertible. Instead of assuming a more conventional liberal posture and positing an abstract *summum bonum* like justice or equality, she reflected instead on human psychology and experience and identified a universal aversion to cruelty, a *summum malum* "which all of us know and would avoid if only we could."[2] Shklar insisted on the universal and cosmopolitan significance of cruelty since she believed that the intuition upon which it rests is itself universal:

Because the fear of systematic cruelty is so universal, moral claims based on its prohibition have an immediate appeal and can gain recognition without much argument … If the prohibition of cruelty can be universalized and recognized as a

---

[1] My reference to "monism" comes from Berlin, "Negative and Positive Liberty."
[2] Shklar, "Liberalism of Fear," pp. 10–11.

necessary condition of the dignity of persons, then it can become a principle of political morality.[3]

Even if the universality of her *summum malum* could not be proven to the satisfaction of cultural critics like Michael Walzer, for her it was asymptotic to truth, close enough that liberalism could proceed as if it was. A simple truth. For her, the urgency of responding to political cruelty justified it.

Knud Haakonssen suggests that Smith would likely have agreed here – that "some situations involving injury are so basic to human life that the spectator's verdicts will always be recognizably similar."[4] In what follows I would like to reflect on how Smith translated his negative view of justice into a positive conception of international law, and to think about its plausibility in light of plural moral goods.

SMITH AND THE "LAWS OF NATIONS"

Smith frequently complained that "the laws of nations" were impotent in the eighteenth century since national self-interest asserted itself largely unchecked by a coercive "common superior" in the international sphere. Recall:

Independent and neighboring nations, having no common superior to decide their disputes, all live in continual dread and suspicion of one another. Each sovereign, expecting little justice from his neighbors, is disposed to treat them with as little as he expects from them. The regard for the laws of nations, or for those rules which independent states profess or pretend to think themselves bound to observe in their dealings with one another, is often very little more than mere pretense and profession. From the smallest interest, upon the slightest provocation, we see those rules every day, either evaded or directly violated without shame or remorse.[5]

One might be inclined to dissolve Smith's interest in international law in the disappointments of his realism. Such a claim might seem to be further substantiated biographically by Smith's failure to complete his promised system of natural jurisprudence, a lapse I discussed in Chapter 6.[6] Nevertheless, we shouldn't underestimate Smith's interest in the subject, or its place in his overall system. He frequently gestured toward the

---

[3] *Ibid.*, p. 11.
[4] Haakonssen, *Science of a Legislator*, p. 148. Yet Haakonssen later noted that "what *counts* as injury is not a universal matter," that it "varies dramatically from one type of society to another" ("Introduction," Adam Smith, *Theory of Moral Sentiments*, ed. Knud Haakonssen (Cambridge: Cambridge University Press, 2002), pp. vii–xxiv, at p. ix). Samuel Fleischacker strenuously takes issue with Smith's assumptions about injury. Because "harm is an essentially *social* good", he believes that Smith's theory of justice emphatically fails as a response to cultural bias (Fleischacker, *Wealth of Nations*, p. 156).
[5] *TMS* VI.ii.2.3 (p. 228).   [6] *TMS* VII.iv.37 (p. 342).

importance of articulating "principles" of "natural jurisprudence," even characterizing it in the 1790 edition of the *Moral Sentiments* as "of all the sciences by far the most important, but hitherto, perhaps, the least cultivated."[7] Of course, he regularly evaded this science – for example, concluding in the passage just cited that "it belongs not to our present subject to enter into any detail";[8] or most famously in the final paragraph of the 1759 edition of the *Moral Sentiments* where he reserved engagement with "the laws of all nations" for "another discourse," which of course never came.[9] I am inclined to agree with Cremaschi, Fleischacker and Griswold that Smith's proposed foundational system was incompletable, *at least in the terms of his general approach to morality*.[10] But this incompletability, this "aporia," also confirms the very point I have been driving at here: that justice for Smith works along very different channels than the processes that governed ordinary morality; and that it yields a minimal sort of universal jurisprudence. Perhaps its simplicity required no elaborate articulation, essential though it was to the "defence" of humanity.[11] Smith was not unaware of the aporia, but I'm not sure he was terribly troubled by it. Like Shklar, it seems he proceeded with a simple truth.

It is interesting from this perspective that Smith frequently voiced serious concerns about the positive *content* of international law in the eighteenth century, about the "principles upon which those rules either are, or ought to be founded"[12] – quite independent of the problems of implementation. Smith's substantive concerns here about articulating affirmative principles, about what they "ought" to be, move him decisively beyond *realism* I believe, and toward a position that was more assertive, and potentially more optimistic from a cosmopolitan perspective. In this sense I have characterized Smith as a *troubled realist*. To explore this, one might begin in the *Lectures on Jurisprudence*. At first blush, Smith is remarkably optimistic about the progress of international law by the middle of the eighteenth century, reflecting the optimism of the Enlightenment itself. Rehearsing the same progressive impulses that propelled his well-known stadial account of history elsewhere in the *Lectures*, in which mankind moved forward through time, according to its mode of subsistence, from the savage simplicity of the "Age of Hunters" to the polite humanity of "The Age of Commerce,"[13] Smith here constructed a comparative typology of

---

[7] *TMS* VI.ii.intro.2 (p. 218).   [8] *TMS* VI.ii.intro.2 (p. 218).   [9] *TMS* VII.iv.37 (p. 342).
[10] Cremaschi, "Adam Smith," pp. 100–101; Fleischacker, *Wealth of Nations*, ch. 8; Griswold, *Virtues of Enlightenment*, p. 258; Griswold, "On the Incompleteness of Adam Smith's System," pp. 181–186.
[11] The "defence of humanity" idea comes from *TMS* II.ii.1.4 (p. 79). See also II.ii.3.4 (p. 86).
[12] *TMS* VI.ii.intro.2 (p. 218).   [13] *LJ* (A) i.27–35 (pp. 14–16); and *LJ* (B) 149–150 (pp. 459–460).

"the laws of nations" in which he contrasted "ancient" and "modern" laws along the classic Enlightenment binaries of barbarian/civilized, crude/refined, hostile/gentle, passionate/mannered.[14] He observed that the moderns had introduced great improvements over ancient and "barbarian" life with such innovative practices as: the humane treatment of prisoners of war (who "are now as well treated as other people"[15]); showing leniency and "humanity" when an enemy capitulates (which tends to make modern nations capitulate more readily);[16] allowing a captive nation, as it "changes masters," to retain its possessions, its religion and its laws;[17] sparing the life of a defeated monarch (which served to augment the institutional authority of monarchy everywhere);[18] the introduction of fire-arms (which made modern armies "less irritated with one another" and less likely to "slaughter" since they are at a "greater distance" and not "mixed with one another");[19] the practice of exchanging resident ambassadors,[20] and so on. Clearly Smith was encouraged by such "humane" innovations over "barbarian" rape, pillage and plunder.

But when he stepped down from the lectern and the Enlightenment binaries that were useful for teaching students about stadial drifts in jurisprudence, he was not always so sanguine. Observe his description of the state of international law in the 1790 revision to the *Moral Sentiments*. Not only were "laws of nations" nearly impossible to implement (for the *realist* reasons I explored in Chapter 6), but furthermore:

the laws *themselves* are, the greater part of them, laid down with very little regard to the plainest and most obvious rules of justice.[21]

One such poignant violation for Smith was the widespread convention that the victor in war reaps the spoils. In the course of discussing the barbarity of this practice, Smith revealed exactly how he conceived the relation of negative justice to international law:

That the innocent, though they may have some connexion or dependency upon the guilty (which, perhaps, they themselves cannot help) should not, upon that account, suffer or be punished for the guilty, is one of the plainest and most obvious rules of justice. In the most unjust war, however, it is commonly the sovereign or

---

[14] And yet, I am convinced by Jennifer Pitts that Smith should not be reduced to that species of European "cultural and moral superiority" that justified the civilizing mission of imperial conquest. Pitts' account of Smith's "nontriumphalist account of history" and his "respectful posture toward non-European societies he regarded as being in earlier stages of development" is a contribution to our perception of Smith. *Turn to Empire* (pp. 25–58).

[15] *LJ* (B) 346 (p. 548).   [16] *LJ* (B) 346–347 (pp. 548–549).   [17] *LJ* (B) 350 (p. 550).

[18] *LJ* (B) 349–350 (pp. 549–550).   [19] *LJ* (B) 350 (p. 550).

[20] *LJ* (B) 354–358 (pp. 551–554).   [21] *TMS* III.3.42 (p. 155).

the rulers only who are guilty. The subjects are almost always perfectly innocent. Whenever it suits the conveniency of a public enemy, however, the goods of the peaceable citizens are seized both at land and at sea; their lands are laid waste, their houses are burnt, and they themselves, if they presume to make any resistance, are murdered or led into captivity; and all this in the most perfect conformity to what are called the laws of nations.[22]

The point is that Smith was focusing here on principles of international law, in terms that draw on Grotius and that prefigure just war theory today. Smith was gesturing toward an affirmative, universal idea of justice conceived negatively as the avoidance of human suffering, as the condemnation of cruelty toward innocents. Though he never completed his jurisprudence, or elaborated this in further examples, clearly he aspired to a system of justice that might serve as a basis for political judgment in international affairs, independent of national interests and cultural norms, which are always partial, self-serving, and easily corruptible by zealots, both political and commercial.

CULTURAL PLURALISM

Part V is a short and relatively understudied chapter in the *Moral Sentiments*.[23] There Smith considered the "Influence of Custom and Fashion upon the Sentiments of Moral Approbation and Disapprobation."[24] He began as follows:

There are other principles besides those already enumerated, which have a considerable influence upon the moral sentiments of mankind, and are the chief causes of the many irregular and discordant opinions which prevail in different ages and nations concerning what is blamable or praise-worthy. These principles are custom and fashion.[25]

In this introductory statement Smith affirmed what he already had richly demonstrated in moral psychological terms throughout the *Moral Sentiments*: that our sentiments are largely a product of social discipline. In Part V Smith elaborated this basic idea, primarily to demonstrate the phenomenon of cultural diversity, and also, through that, to affirm the essential corruptibility of ordinary moral life. Indeed, he asserted that "custom" sometimes sanctions practices "which shock the plainest principles of right and wrong."[26] Before moving forward, a few preliminaries about using the language of culture to describe what Smith was doing in the Part V of *Moral Sentiments*. In this book I often refer to Smith's theory of "moral culture." Here now I similarly refer to

---

[22] *TMS* III.3.42 (p. 155).   [23] A recent exception is Pitts, *Turn to Empire*, ch. 2.
[24] *TMS* V (pp. 194–211).   [25] *TMS* V.1.1 (p. 194).   [26] *TMS* V.2.14 (p. 209).

Smith's views on "cultural pluralism." Of course Smith himself never used the term "culture" to describe what he was doing, so there is clearly some anachronism here. In Part V, he tended to refer to "nations" and "societies" and their "general style of conduct or behavior"; but since this resonates with what we call "culture" today, I use the concept as a shorthand that captures well enough what Smith was doing, but also signifies Smith's relevance to contemporary discussion. One key difference is that I occasionally extend the concept of "culture" to refer to things that Smith might have characterized as practices, or "particular usages." In Part V, we will see, Smith differentiated culture (understood as the "general style of conduct or behavior" of a nation) from cultural practices (what he referred to as "particular usages") in order to argue that cultures are far less corruptible than practices are. He had specific reasons for believing this, which I will explore later. But for the moment, I think the binary creates an artificial conceptual landscape that is far too rigid to accommodate practices or events that *rest on* perverting the "general style of conduct or behavior" of a people. Nazism of course is the classic example. Twentieth-century social psychologists understood that we cannot possibly make sense of the widespread acquiescence of the German population to Nazi "practices" without appreciating the extent that German culture was driven to embrace them through techniques of fear, propaganda, ideology, desensitization and so forth. To carve up group reality as Smith did in Part V into general tendencies and practices, in which the first is stable and the second is not, is highly problematic in this sense. And thus my analysis of Smith's thought here will occasionally use the language of "culture" to characterize things that might have looked to Smith like perverse practices.

Part VI was divided in two. First Smith considered the "dominion" of custom and fashion over our aesthetic sensibilities.[27] His discussion of human "beauty" conveys his general purpose in Part V: to assert the wide variability of tastes, beliefs and values across cultures. He reads here like Montaigne in "Of Cannibals" as he described exotic ideas of beauty in Guinea, China and North America, not for purposes of asserting the superiority of European ideas, but quite explicitly the opposite: to demonstrate variety, and to ride astonished Europeans for their own practice of corsetting. Montaigne had observed that "each man calls barbarism whatever is not his own practice."[28] I cite the following passage at length for its rich Montaigneian resonances:

---

[27] *TMS* V.1 (pp. 194–200).
[28] Michel de Montaigne, "Of Cannibals," in *The Complete Essays of Montaigne*, trans. Donald M. Frame (Stanford, CA: Stanford University Press, 1965), pp. 150–159, at p. 152.

What different ideas are formed in different nations concerning the beauty of the human shape and countenance? A fair complexion is a shocking deformity upon the coast of Guinea. Thick lips and a flat nose are a beauty. In some nations long ears that hang down upon the shoulders are the objects of universal admiration. In China if a lady's foot is so large as to be fit to walk upon, she is regarded as a monster of ugliness. Some of the savage nations in North-America tie four boards round the heads of their children, and thus squeeze them, while the bones are tender and grisly, into a form that is almost perfectly square. Europeans are astonished at the absurdity of this practice, to which some missionaries have imputed the singular stupidity of those nations among whom it prevails. But when they condemn those savages, they do not reflect that the ladies in Europe had, til within these very few years, been endeavoring, for near a century past, to squeeze the beautiful roundness of their natural shape into a square form of the same kind. And that, notwithstanding the many distortions and diseases which this practice was known to occasion, custom had rendered it agreeable among some of the most civilized nations which, perhaps, the world ever beheld.[29]

This technique of asserting cultural variety to illustrate the hypocrisies of modern European assertions of superiority over "savages" is evident once again when Smith turned from aesthetics to his second subject in Part V: the influence of custom and fashion on *moral sentiment*.[30] Here he contrasted the severity of the savage whose life of hardship makes him entirely insensible to the weak and effeminate passions that drive civilized and polite people, who live under general conditions of security and happiness.[31] Clearly Smith held a stadial view of history; he believed deeply in human progress and valued the humanity and delicacy of civilized life. But in these passages, again like Montaigne, he also conveyed a certain reverence and awe for the "magnanimity and self-command" of the savage which are "almost beyond the conception of Europeans."[32]

There is not a negro from the coast of Africa who does not, in this respect, possess a degree of magnanimity which the soul of his sordid master is too often scarce incapable of conceiving.[33]

We shouldn't get too distracted by Smith's language of "barbarians" and "savages," for Smith used these terms in a "descriptive" sense rather than in the "evaluative" sense that was so common among his contemporaries.[34] Indeed, though he articulated his arguments in Part V in language that might repel a twenty-first-century reader, it is noteworthy that Smith in

---

[29] *TMS* V.1.8 (p. 199).   [30] *TMS* V.2 (pp. 200–211).   [31] *TMS* V.2.8–11 (pp. 204–209).
[32] *TMS* V.2.9 (p. 205). Compare with Montaigne on the warfare of "barbarians" in "Of Cannibals," p. 156.
[33] *TMS* V.2.9 (p. 206).   [34] See Pitts, *Turn to Empire*, p. 264, n. 2.

these passages sought to reveal the many hypocrisies of European civility, revealing a strain of openness and self-reflexivity that has been largely unrecognized and unappreciated in eighteenth-century European thought generally, and in the abuse of Smith's thought over the past two centuries. Smith is an important eighteenth-century European theorist of cultural diversity who keenly understood the particularity of European beliefs and practices.

He concluded his discussion of cultural diversity with an important distinction between culture and practices – between the "general style of character and behaviour" of a given society with its "particular usages."[35] The reason for this is that sometimes societies that are perfectly polite and civilized in their general tendencies engage in activities, entertain certain practices, that are fundamentally horrific – that "shock the plainest principles of right and wrong."[36]

All these effects of custom and fashion, however, upon the moral sentiments of mankind, are inconsiderable, in comparison of those which they give occasion to in some other cases; and it is not concerning the general style of character and behaviour, that those principles produce the greatest *perversion* of judgment, but concerning the propriety or impropriety of particular usages.[37]

Smith's primary example here was a particular European perversion: the practice of infanticide in all the states of ancient Greece, "even among the polite and civilized Athenians."[38] Smith characterized the exposure of infants as a "dreadful violation of humanity" – "can there be greater barbarity … than to hurt an infant?" Even Plato and Aristotle were "led away by the established custom":

Uninterrupted custom had by this time so thoroughly authorized the practice, that not only the loose maxims of the world tolerated this barbarous prerogative, but even the doctrine of philosophers, which ought to have been more just and accurate, was led away by the established custom, and upon this, as upon many other occasions, instead of censuring, supported the horrible abuse by far-fetched considerations of public utility.[39]

Smith's reflections here on the barbarity of this culturally sanctioned practice foreshadow assumptions that are axiomatic for anthropologists today, particularly the extent that one's context will condition one's view of the world, including one's understanding of harm. The examples from which we could draw to illustrate this are infinite – the normalization of

---

[35] *TMS* V.2.12 (p. 209). [36] *TMS* V.2.14 (p. 209). [37] *TMS* V.2.12 (p. 209), emphasis added.
[38] *TMS* V.2.15 (p. 210). [39] *TMS* V.2.1 (pp. 209–210).

violent death experienced by children saturated in cultures of violence; the modern sterilization of violence in Foucault's history of punishment; Arendt's banality of evil; Milgram's capitulation to authority; Zimbardo's "power of the situation." Without acknowledging the power of culture to distort natural human inhibitions and sanction horrific practices, how can we make any sense of the following speech delivered by Heinrich Himmler to an audience of senior SS officers in 1943:

> I ... want to speak to you ... of a really grave chapter. Amongst ourselves ... it shall be said quite openly, but all the same we will never speak about it in public ... I am referring ... to the extermination of the Jewish people ... Most of you men know what it is like to see 100 corpses side by side, or 500, or 1,000. To have stood fast through this and ... to have stayed decent – that has made us hard. This is an unwritten and never-to-be-written page of glory in our history ... All in all ... we can say that we have carried out this most difficult of tasks in a spirit of love for our people. And we have suffered no harm to our inner being, our soul, our character.[40]

Raw material abounds in terrifying quantities over the last century – from "decent SS" to "freedom fighters" blowing themselves apart on packed city busses, from "ethnic cleansers" to "good folks" using war and torture to "smoke out evil." One thing here is certain: in the twenty-first century, we cannot accept claims about the universalizability of harm without asking how the birthplace of Goethe and Mozart could have erected a death machinery that efficiently exterminated millions of innocents, among them one-and-a-half million children. The cold, depersonalized bureaucratic functioning of this machinery needs explanation, but also the infinite narratives of sheer cruelty that have been reported in such unbearable detail in Daniel Goldhagen's *Hitler's Willing Executioners* and Iris Chang's *The Rape of Nanking*. In a key that resonates powerfully with so many recent memories of radical evil, Smith concluded his discussion of Greek infanticide as follows:

> When custom can give sanction to so dreadful a violation of humanity, we may well imagine that there is scarce any particular practice so gross which it cannot authorize. Such a thing, we hear men every day saying, is commonly done, and they seem to think that this is a sufficient apology for what, in itself, is the most unjust and unreasonable conduct.[41]

---

[40] Himmler, speech to senior SS officers, Poznań, October 4, 1943; cited in Lucy S. Davidovich, *A Holocaust Reader* (New York: Behrman House, 1976), pp. 344–345. See Friedländer's interpretation in *Kitsch and Death*, pp. 102–105.

[41] *TMS* V.2.15 (p. 210).

Smith even seemed to understand the effect of this phenomenon on soldiers who are "under the necessity of submitting" to difficult orders. To relieve cognitive dissonance and preserve psychic integrity, they tend to silence the voice of conscience, and cultivate a language in which their actions are justified and their moral universe is reconciled. Ultimately they become "hardened against all sense of either justice or humanity":

For his own ease, he is too apt to learn to make light of the misfortunes which he is so often under the necessity of occasioning; and the situations which call forth the noblest exertions of self-command, by imposing the necessity of violating some-times the property, and sometimes the life of our neighbor, always tend to diminish, and too often to extinguish altogether, that sacred regard to both, which is the foundation of justice and humanity.[42]

Smith richly understood the pathologies of social conformism, how easily individuals can be swept along in the current, in the "general contagion."[43] He recognized the extent that culture orders our sentiments. Of course this was a central feature of his account of ordinary morality throughout the *Moral Sentiments*, and something that he tended to value for its stabilizing effects on modern society, as I have argued. Nevertheless he also understood that our conformism was responsible for both good and bad consequences:

Those who have been educated in what is really good company, not in what is commonly called such, who have been accustomed to see nothing in the persons whom they esteemed and lived with, but justice, modesty, humanity, and good order; are more shocked with whatever seems to be inconsistent with the rules which those virtues prescribe. Those, on the contrary, who have had the misfortune to be brought up amidst violence, licentiousness, falsehood, and injustice; lose, though not all sense of the impropriety of such conduct, yet all sense of its dreadful enormity, or of the vengeance and punishment due to it. They have been fami-liarized with it from their infancy, custom has rendered it habitual to them, and they are very apt to regard it as, what is called, the way of the world.[44]

This Janus-faced view of culture was confirmed elsewhere in the *Moral Sentiments* as well:

This natural disposition to accommodate and to assimilate, as much as we can, our own sentiments, principles and feelings, to those which we see fixed and rooted in the persons whom we are obliged to live and converse a great deal with, is the cause of the contagious effects of both good and bad company.[45]

---

[42] *TMS* III.3.37 (p. 153).   [43] *TMS* III.3.43 (p. 155).
[44] *TMS* V.2.2 (pp. 200–201).   [45] *TMS* VI.ii.1.17 (p. 224).

Indeed, culture was "contagious" for Smith and highly deterministic, for better or for worse. The key point, however, is that Smith was never sanguine or apologetic about it (at least when talking about European corruption, as we will see). One cannot hide behind it. Smith never allowed culture to trump justice; he never allowed diversity to trump "the strongest and most vigorous passions of human nature."[46] As such he was always perfectly contemptuous of those who inflict cruelty on innocents:

> the characters and conduct of a Nero, or a Claudius, are what no custom will ever reconcile us to, what no fashion will ever render agreeable; but the one will always be the object of dread and hatred; the other of scorn and derision ... [T]he sentiments of moral approbation and disapprobation, are founded on the strongest and most vigorous passions of human nature; and though they may be somewhat warpt, cannot be entirely perverted.[47]

In this vein Smith categorically condemned what he called the "violation of humanity"[48] wherever he came upon it: African slavery in which "Fortune never exerted more *cruelly* her empire over mankind"[49] and the "savage injustice" committed by Europeans against aboriginals in America.[50] It is interesting to note in this context, however, again following Montaigne, that Smith regularly condemned the "barbarity" of European practices like corsetting, infanticide, slavery and imperial conquest without *ever* extending this same sort of condemnation to the practices of non-European cultures. In Part V, he described in sometimes gruesome detail such activities as Chinese foot-binding, and the Amerindian practice of torturing and slowly roasting captive prisoners, not to condemn their inhumanity, but rather to shame Europeans for their hypocrisy! I will return to this important wrinkle in Smith's thought below, for it would seem to bear importantly on Smith's thoughts about the universality of justice.

CULTURE AND HARM

In recent work, Amartya Sen seizes on Smith's condemnation of culturally sanctioned practices in Part V and elsewhere, and argues that Smith's *Moral Sentiments* offers important resources for "scrutinizing ... the impact of entrenched tradition and custom" – that is, it is useful for responding "objectively" to "practices as different as the stoning of adulterous women

---

[46] *TMS* V.i.1 (p. 200). [47] *TMS* V.2.1 (p. 200).

[48] This arises during his discussion of Greek infanticide at *TMS* V.2.15 (p. 210).

[49] *TMS* V.2.9 (p. 206), emphasis added.

[50] *WN* IV.i.32 (p. 448); *WN* IV.vii.c.80 (p. 626). Again, Pitts' interpretation in *A Turn to Empire*, ch. 2, is essential here.

in Afghanistan, selective abortion of female fetuses in China, Korea, and parts of India, and the use of capital punishment (with or without opportunity for celebratory public jubilation) in the United States."[51] I am not certain whether Smith would have agreed with Sen that his system enables the "forceful scrutiny of local values," the "adequately objective scrutiny of social conventions and parochial sentiments"[52] – although if he did agree, it would not be because his sympathy mechanism produced "open impartiality," as Sen argues, but because of the instinctive revulsion toward human suffering that Smith connected with justice. These are two very different processes, as we've seen.

Surely the idea of *intervening* to save distant victims from injustice would have struck Smith as absurd. But the problem of agreeing with Sen goes deeper than this.[53] I believe we are left with a relatively clear idea of what harm meant for Smith in a European context, but with a very hazy sense of whether he believed that this European understanding of harm can be universalized. Given Smith's absolute commitment to individual liberty, it may strike a reader as surprising that he condemned only European barbarities, but used his violent, graphic examples of Chinese foot-binding and Amerindian torture, among others, only to demonstrate cultural diversity and the hypocrisies of European civility. One might have expected Smith to be shocked by such practices; but he was not, particularly in the Amerindian case where, like Montaigne, his fascination latched on to savage virtues. I believe Smith deliberately hedged in these cases, and that his reason was established very clearly in his mind. As Part V came to a close, Smith asserted something profound, and too rarely noticed.[54] He said that "nations" develop the manners and general tendencies that are best suited to them, and that this phenomenon of cultural expediency should necessarily diminish our sense of their perversion: "Hardiness is the character most suitable to the circumstances of a savage; sensibility to those of one who lives in a very civilized society."[55] Thus, he concluded, "we cannot complain that the sentiments of men are very grossly perverted." A culture becomes what it must be. Of course, practices can sometimes go awry, and "shock the plainest principles of right and wrong." But Smith was surprisingly sanguine about this. If somehow a culture's perverse practices should begin to infect "the general style and character of conduct" – in other words, if a culture

---

[51] Sen, "Impartiality," p. 459.   [52] *Ibid.*, pp. 458–459.
[53] My thanks to Amartya Sen, who later clarified to me that he was concerned less with being faithful to Smith's theory, and more to what might be made of it for other purposes. My challenge to Sen's interpretation of Smith here should be considered in this light. And yet, I think Smith himself provides us with independent and compelling reasons to question these other purposes, regardless of their intellectual lineage. In other words, my engagement here with Sen is not merely an historical or textual one.
[54] Pitts, *Turn to Empire*, ch. 2, is an important exception.   [55] *TMS* V.2.13 (p. 209).

itself becomes perverse to the core – it will simply perish. Here we see Smith's cosmopolitan providence from Section VI.ii of the *Moral Sentiments* at work, protecting the general well-being of mankind: wholly perverse cultures will necessarily self-destruct:

> There is an obvious reason why custom should never pervert our sentiment with regard to the general style and character of our conduct and behaviour, in the same degree as with regard to the propriety or unlawfulness of particular usages. There never can be any such custom. No society could subsist a moment, in which the usual strain of men's conduct and behaviour was of a piece with the horrible practice I have just now mentioned [infanticide].[56]

Clearly wholly perverted cultures frequently persist beyond a moment, and from a cosmopolitan perspective Smith seems a bit cavalier about human suffering in the interim. In this passage, Smith made a far-reaching claim that should not be overlooked or dismissed for its brevity, for it seems to exempt the Amerindian from the absolute demands of justice as Smith conceived it, and ultimately thus from the "laws of nations." If Amerindian practices are internally justified as necessary to the very existence of Amerindian culture for Smith, the grounds for external critique would seem to be largely nullified or side-lined. This leaves wide open the question of whether justice for Smith had transcultural teeth, or whether, in his mind, it was intended only for peoples who had achieved a certain degree of civilization, only for those whose violations could be conceived as hypo-critical to the civilized values that governed the rest of their lives.

SMITH AND UNIVERSAL HUMAN RIGHTS

Inevitably, the question must be put to us: does harm signify something consistent and intelligible across contexts – or is harm itself a cultural artifact and necessarily particular to the person/group who inflicts or experiences it?[57] As this book comes to a close, I would like to reflect on what Knud Haakonssen describes as the "critical potential" of Smith's jurisprudence – that it is "somehow outside the grip of social change"[58] – and to highlight the significance of this sort of critique for current discus-sions about human rights in political, moral and legal theory. It should be noted that in recent years Haakonssen has pulled back somewhat from the zeal of his universalist position, emphasizing less the "critical" potential of Smith's jurisprudence, and more its contingent and "historical" nature,

---

[56] *TMS* V.2.16 (p. 211).   [57] A major theme in Fleischacker's interpretation in *Wealth of Nations*, ch. 8.
[58] Haakonssen, *Science of a Legislator*, p. 147.

which would seem to make critical jurisprudence a substantially immanent activity.[59] Perhaps it is a reflection of the multicultural mode in which we all now live, think and write that Haakonssen no longer asserts such things as: "some situations involving injury are so basic to human life that the spectator's verdicts will always be recognizably similar."[60] Instead, he now writes: "what counts as injury is not a universal matter, it varies dramatically from one type of society to another," and "you would have to know what society you are talking about if your specification of rights and duties were to be of any use."[61]

In his recent discussion of Smith's view of justice, Samuel Fleischacker rejects Haakonssen's earlier, more universalist claims about Smith's critical jurisprudence and offers a set of arguments that in many ways align with Haakonssen's later gravitation toward historical-cultural variation.[62] While it has been clear throughout this book that I am deeply persuaded by Fleischacker's general insistence on the historical quality of Smith's moral theory and the criteria it produces, I resist taking this "all the way down" into Smith's views of justice, so to speak – at least as Smith conceptualized his own unfinished project. Although I agree with many of Fleischacker's insightful textual and philosophical refutations of the coherence and plausibility of Smith's articulation of negative justice, I tend nevertheless, as a faithful historian of Smith's thought, to align with the impulses behind Haakonssen's earlier argument. Smith's jurisprudential gestures in the *Moral Sentiments* assumed a very specific place in his thought that can only be appreciated when situated in the larger context of his concerns about moral judgment. I believe Smith's theory of negative justice was a very deliberate attempt to address a gnawing preoccupation with bias and stabilizing the standards by which we judge – a problem that becomes particularly acute in the society of nations, where people and practices are distant and unfamiliar.

Whether or not we ultimately agree that negative justice does the universalizing work that Smith suggested it can (though he never actually completed his project to prove it!) – whether we think that Smith's turn from ordinary morality to negative justice in the *Moral Sentiments* adequately confronts cultural bias; indeed, whether or not we ultimately believe that harm is intelligible across contexts and that our aversion to it sustains a cosmopolitan

---

[59] See Knud Haakonssen, "Introduction" to *The Cambridge Companion to Adam Smith*, ed. Knud Haakonssen (Cambridge: Cambridge University Press, 2006), pp. 1–21, at pp. 5–6.
[60] Haakonssen, *Science of a Legislator*, p. 148.   [61] See "Introduction," pp. 5–6.
[62] Fleischacker, *Wealth of Nations*, ch. 8.

ethics – we must recognize the extent that engaging Smith's thought becomes productive for twenty-first-century moral and political theory, particularly in discussions about human rights. For generating such questions, struggling with them, and attempting to provide creative solutions, Smith is remarkably relevant to current thinking about moral and political judgment in a deeply pluralistic world. Human rights discourse has always struggled with precisely the same issues – from the articulation of universal rights in such eighteenth-century documents as the "Declaration of Independence" of 1776 and the "Declaration of the Rights of Man" of 1789, to the creation of the United Nations and its more expansive articulation of universal rights in the "Universal Declaration of Human Rights" in 1948 – which declared, in terms that resonate with Smith's thought as much as with Locke's, that "the recognition of inherent dignity and of the equal and inalienable rights of all members of the human family is the foundation of freedom, justice and peace in the world," and that "disregard and contempt for human rights have resulted in barbarous acts which have outraged the conscience of man-kind"[63] – to very current discussions in international law and ethics about our ability to articulate, measure and assess the minimal conditions of a flourishing human life.[64] The fundamental problem in human rights discourse has always been the extent that universal claims are possible in light of the vast plurality of cultural norms and practices, and the inevitable resistance among some to concur.

Smith is highly relevant and helpful here not only because he articulated the problem of plural moral goods in a sophisticated, psychologically textured, distinctively Scottish way; but because his jurisprudence points to ways we might navigate beyond the problem so richly conceived. When Smith cultivated a theory of negative justice to ground universal criteria for moral judgment, and to serve as a bulwark of "defence" for the protection of innocents,[65] he was deliberately seeking to navigate a course between the inherent particularity of moral culture and the contentious certitude of positive conceptions of the good. In Griswold's words, he was "attempting

---

[63] *Universal Declaration of Human Rights*, United Nations General Assembly Resolution 217A (III) of 10 December 1948. Smith was not inclined to use the language of rights, and did so only occasionally, but note the sanctity of such protection for Smith: "by the wisdom of Nature, the happiness of every innocent man is … rendered holy. Consecrated, and hedged round against the approach of every other man; not to be wantonly trod upon, not even to be, in any respect, ignorantly and involuntarily violated, without requiring some expiation, some atonement in proportion to the greatness of such undesigned violation." *TMS* II.iii.3.4 (p. 107).

[64] See the work of Martha Nussbaum and Amartya Sen in *The Quality of Life* (Oxford: Clarendon Press, 1993).

[65] *TMS* II.ii.1.4 (p. 79).

to carve out logical space for reason-giving that is neither free from historicity nor reducible to it."[66] His attempt to ground this universal perspective in a *summum malum* derived from an instinctive human revulsion broadly confirmed through human experience, rather than a casuistic *summum bonum* which is necessarily partial and contentious, resonates profoundly with attempts today to develop a minimal, or thin, conception of shared moral goods. Note for example Sen's gesture toward minimalism in the closing paragraphs of his essay on Smith's "open" view of impartiality. He writes: "a common resolve to fight for the abolition of famines, or genocide, or terrorism, or slavery, or untouchability, or illiteracy, or epidemics, and so on" does not require "agreed complete orderings or universally accepted full partitionings of the just from the unjust."[67] Addressing just how Smith fits into this very lively contemporary debate about plural moral goods, and whether he ultimately makes progress on the project of minimalism with his idea of negative justice, is a big agenda for another project. In this book I sought to provide a fresh interpretation of Smith's thought that opens itself to such questions; but applications are beyond my scope. If I have succeeded in demonstrating Smith's salience for international human rights by situating his thoughts about physical distance, affective "connexion" and historical familiarity within a larger problematic of moral epistemology and judgment, I believe I have accomplished much.

In the end, however, I will say that I am inclined to agree with Knud Haakonssen that the "socially formed" nature of Smith's moral philosophy need not mean "that there are no universally constant features of humanity."[68] I fully recognize the problems with claiming that negative justice has "universal" significance, and that asserting this may ultimately require grafting an additional thought (or two) onto Smith's sociological project. As Fleischacker notes, anyone who wants to proceed from Smith in a universalist mode must:

face the possibility that we might need to come to the realm of harm with a demand for precise rules already in hand: that we might need to *carve out* some precise set of harms to protect people against, out of all the possible harms they might undergo.[69]

As a political and moral theorist, and a human being, and not only an historian of Smith's thought, I am not uncomfortable passing Smith's universal gesture through a critical sift, preserving insights I find compelling,

---

[66] Griswold, "Incompleteness," p. 185.   [67] Sen, "Impartiality," pp. 468–469.
[68] Knud Haakonssen, *Natural Law and Moral Philosophy*, p. 131.
[69] Fleischacker, *Wealth of Nations*, p. 167.

letting pass those I don't, and moving constructively beyond him, "carving out" as I go.

Committed as I am to peace and cross-cultural understanding in an unstable and dangerous world, I am not inclined to surrender to the particularism of Smith's moral psychology. Smith's description of ordinary morality illuminates the perils of aiming too high and expecting too much – which is why I have found his project so important. But the world is also too dangerous for a *laissez-faire* attitude toward the horrific things regimes and moral cultures too often do in the name of self-determination, often in service of "higher" purposes though very often in pursuit of base and revolting ones. Relativism is a luxury of the safe and privileged, whose lives tend to be ordered and protected by moral goods woven deeply and often imperceptibly into the fabric of their reality. This is not the place to develop this (one needs only to read the morning paper), but merely to say that I, like Smith, am a *troubled* particularist.

Bibliography

A. PRIMARY SOURCES

à Kempis, Thomas. *The Imitation of Christ*, trans. Leo Sherley-Price. London: Penguin, 1952.

Aristotle. *Nicomachean Ethics*, trans. M. Ostwald. Indianapolis, IN: Bobbs-Merrill, 1962.

   The Politics and The Constitution of Athens, ed. Stephen Everson. Cambridge: Cambridge University Press, 1996.

Burke, Edmund. "Philosophical Inquiry into the Origin of Our Ideas of the Sublime and Beautiful." In *The Works of the Right Honorable Edmund Burke*, 12 vols. Boston: Little Brown, 1881, vol. II.

   "Reflections on the Revolution in France." In *The Writings and Speeches of Edmund Burke*. Oxford: Clarendon Press, 1981–2000, vol. VIII.

Butler, Joseph. "Fifteen Sermons Preached at the Rolls Chapel, vol. I." In *The Works of Bishop Butler*, ed. J. H. Bernard. 1726, 2 vols. London: Macmillan, 1900.

Cicero. *De Finibus Bonorum et Malorum*, trans. H. Rackham. Cambridge, MA: Harvard University Press.

   De Officiis, ed. M. Winterbottom, trans. M. T. Griffin and E. M. Atkins. Oxford: Oxford University Press, 1994.

   On Duties. Cambridge: Cambridge University Pres, 1991.

Descartes, René. *Discourse on the Method of Properly Conducting One's Reason and of Seeking the Truth in the Sciences*, trans. F. E. Sutcliffe. London: Penguin, 1968.

Emerson, Ralph Waldo. "Circles." In *Emerson: Essays*. Cambridge, MA: Harvard University Press, 2005.

Herder, Johann. "Yet Another Philosophy of History for the Education of Humanity." In *Herder on Social and Political Culture*, ed. and trans. F. M. Barnard. Cambridge, 1969.

Hobbes, Thomas. *On the Citizen (De Cive)*, ed. Richard Tuck and Michael Silverthorne. Cambridge: Cambridge University Press, 1998.

   Leviathan, ed. Richard Tuck. Cambridge: Cambridge University Press, 1991.

Hume, David. *An Enquiry Concerning the Principles of Morals*, ed. J. B. Schneewind. Indianapolis, IN: Hackett, 1983.

   A Treatise of Human Nature. London: Penguin Books, 1993.

Political Essays, ed. Knud Haakonssen. Cambridge: Cambridge University Press, 1994.

Hutcheson, Francis. "Reflections on the Common Systems of Morality" and "Inaugural Lecture on the Social Nature of Man." In *Francis Hutcheson, Two texts on human nature*, ed. T. Mautner. Cambridge: Cambridge University Press, 1993.

"Reflections upon Laughter and Remarks upon the 'Fable of the Bees.'" In *Collected Works of Francis Hutcheson*, 7 vols. Hildesheim: G. Olds, 1971. Vol. 7: *Opera Minora*, pp. 144–156.

Kant, Immanuel. "An Answer to the Question: What Is Enlightenment?," trans. H. B. Nisbet. In *Political Writings*, ed. Hans Reiss. Cambridge: Cambridge University Press, 1970, pp. 54–60.

Critique of Pure Reason, trans. Norman Kemp Smith. New York: St. Martin's Press, 1929.

"The Metaphysics of Morals, Part II: Metaphysical First Principles of the Doctrine of Virtue." In *Practical Philosophy*, trans. and ed. Mary J. Gregor. Cambridge: Cambridge University Press, 1996, pp. 509–603.

Leslie, T. E. Cliffe. "The Political Economy of Adam Smith," *Fortnightly Review*, November 1, 1870, p. 12.

Locke, John. *Two Treatises of Government*, ed. Peter Laslett. Cambridge: Cambridge University Press, 1960–1992, pp. 265–428.

Mandeville, Bernard de. *The Fable of the Bees, or Private Vices, Publick Benefits*, ed. F. B. Kaye. 2 vols. Oxford: Oxford University Press, 1924; reprint ed. Indianapolis, IN: Liberty Press, 1988.

Marcus Aurelius, *Meditations*, ed. and trans. C. R. Haines. Cambridge, MA: Harvard University Press, 1916.

The Meditations, trans. G. M. A. Grube. Indianapolis, IN: Hackett, 1983.

Marx, Karl. "Preface" to *Capital: A Critique of Political Economy*. In *Marx and Engels: Basic Writings on Politics and Philosophy*, ed. Lewis S. Feuer. New York: Anchor, 1959, pp. 133–146.

Millar, John. *An Historical View of the English Government* (1803). 4 vols. London, 1812.

Montaigne, Michel de. *The Complete Essays of Montaigne*, trans. Donald M. Frame. Stanford, CA: Stanford University Press, 1965.

Nicole, Pierre. "De la charité et de l'amour-propre." In *Oeuvres philosophiques et morales de Nicole, comprenant un choix de ses essais*, ed. Charles Jourdain. Paris: L. Hachette, 1845, trans. Elborg Forster, "Of Charity and Self-Love." In *Moral Philosophy from Montaigne to Kant: An Anthology*. 2 vols., ed. J. B. Schneewind. Cambridge: Cambridge University Press, 1990, vol. I, pp. 370–387.

Pascal, Blaise. *Penseés*, trans. W. F. Trotter. New York: E. P. Dutton, 1958.

Plato. *Republic*, trans. G. M. A Grube, ed. C. D. C. Reeve. Indianapolis, IN: Hackett, 1992.

Phaedo, ed. C. J. Rowe. Cambridge: Cambridge University Press, 1993.

Pufendorf, Samuel. *De iure naturae et gentium libri octo*, ed. J. S. Brown, trans. C. H. and W. A. Oldfather. Oxford, 1934.

Rousseau, Jean-Jacques. *The Basic Political Writings*, trans. Donald A. Cress. Indianapolis, IN: Hackett, 1987, pp. 23–109.

Considérations sur le gouvernement de Pologne et sur sa réformation projettée. In *Jean-Jacques Rousseau: Œuvres complètes*. 4 vols., ed. Bernard Gagnebin and Marcel Raymond. Paris: Gallimard, Bibliothèque de la Pléiade, 1959–1966, vol. III, pp. 951–1041.

Du Contrat Social; ou, principes de droit politique, Œuvres complètes. In *Jean-Jacques Rousseau: Œuvres complètes*. 4 vols., ed. Bernard Gagnebin and Marcel Raymond. Paris: Gallimard, Bibliothèque de la Pléiade, 1959–1966, vol. III, pp. 347–470.

Discours sur les sciences et les arts. In *Jean-Jacques Rousseau: Œuvres complètes*. 4 vols., ed. Bernard Gagnebin and Marcel Raymond. Paris: Gallimard, Bibliothèque de la Pléiade, 1959–1966, vol. III, pp. 1–30.

Discours sur l'origine et les fondements de l'inégalité parmi les hommes. In *Jean-Jacques Rousseau: Œuvres complètes*. 4 vols., ed. Bernard Gagnebin and Marcel Raymond. Paris: Gallimard, Bibliothèque de la Pléiade, 1959–1966, vol. III, pp. 109–223.

Fragments politiques. In *Jean-Jacques Rousseau: Œuvres complètes*. 4 vols., ed. Bernard Gagnebin and Marcel Raymond. Paris: Gallimard, Bibliothèque de la Pléiade, 1959–1966, vol. III, pp. 469–560.

Lettre à M. D'Alembert sur son Article Genève, ed. Michel Launay. Paris: Garnier-Flammarion, 1967.

Projet de constitution pour la Corse. In *Jean-Jacques Rousseau: Œuvres complètes*. 4 vols., ed. Bernard Gagnebin and Marcel Raymond. Paris: Gallimard, Bibliothèque de la Pléiade, 1959–1966, vol. III, pp. 899–950.

Seneca, "De Beneficiis." In *Moral Essays*, vol. III, ed. and trans. John Basore. Cambridge, MA, 1928.

Epistulae Morales, ed. L. D. Reynolds. Oxford, 1965, trans. Robin Campbell, *Letters from a Stoic*. New York, 1969.

Shaftesbury, Anthony Ashley Cooper, the third Earl of. "Soliloquy or Advice to an Author." In *Characteristics of Men, Manner, Opinions, Times, etc.* 2 vols., ed. John M. Robertson. Gloucester, MA, 1963, 1:121. Reprint *Moral Philosophy from Montaigne to Kant: An Anthology*. 2 vols., ed. J. B. Schneewind. Cambridge: Cambridge University Press, 1990, vol. I, pp. 486–488.

Smith, Adam. *The Correspondence of Adam Smith*, ed. Ernest Campbell Mossner and Ian Simpson Ross, as vol. VI of *The Glasgow Edition of the Works and Correspondence of Adam Smith*. Oxford: Oxford University Press 1977; reprint Indianapolis, IN: Liberty Press, 1987.

Essays on Philosophical Subjects, ed. W. L. D. Wightman, as vol. III of *The Glasgow Edition of the Works and Correspondence of Adam Smith*. Oxford: Oxford University Press 1977; reprint Indianapolis, IN: Liberty Press, 1982.

An Inquiry into the Nature and Causes of the Wealth of Nations (1776), ed. R. H. Campbell and A. S. Skinner, as vol. II of *The Glasgow Edition of the Works and Correspondence of Adam Smith*. Oxford: Oxford University Press 1977; reprint Indianapolis, IN: Liberty Press, 1981.

Lectures on Jurisprudence (1762–1766), ed. R. L. Meek, D. D. Raphael and P. G. Stein, as vol. V of *The Glasgow Edition of the Works and Correspondence of Adam Smith.* Oxford: Oxford University Press 1977; reprint Indianapolis, IN: Liberty Press, 1982.

The Theory of Moral Sentiments (1759), ed. D. D. Raphael and A. L. Macfie, as vol. I of *The Glasgow Edition of the Works and Correspondence of Adam Smith.* Oxford: Oxford University Press 1977; reprint Indianapolis, IN: Liberty Press, 1982.

B. SECONDARY MATERIALS

Abdel-Nour, Farid. "An International Ethics of Evil?" *International Relations*, vol. 18, no. 4 (2004), pp. 425–439.

Abrams, M. H. *Natural Supernaturalism: Tradition and Revolution in Romantic Literature.* New York: W. W. Norton and Company, 1971.

Anderson, Amanda. *The Powers of Distance: Cosmopolitanism and the Cultivation of Detachment.* Princeton, NJ: Princeton University Press, 2001.

Andrew, Edward G. "Anarchic Conscience and Enlightenment Reason." In *Philosophical Designs for a Socio-Cultural Transformation*, ed. Tutsuju Yamamoto. Ecole des Hautes Etudes en Sciences Culturelles and Rowman & Littlefield, 1998, pp. 77–85.

Conscience and Its Critics: Protestant Conscience, Enlightenment Reason, and Modern Subjectivity. Toronto: University of Toronto Press, 2001.

Annas, Julia. *The Morality of Happiness.* New York: Oxford University Press, 1993.

Archibugi, Daniele, and David Held, eds. *Cosmopolitan Democracy: An Agenda for a New World Order.* Cambridge: Polity, 1995.

eds. *Debating Cosmopolitics.* London: Verso, 2003.

Arendt, Hannah. *Between Past and Future: Eight Exercises in Political Thought.* New York: Viking Press, 1960; reprint New York: Penguin, 1977.

Auerbach, Erich. *Mimesis: The Representation of Reality in Western Literature*, trans. and ed. Willard R. Trask. Princeton, NJ: Princeton University Press, 1968.

Baker, Keith Michael. *Condorcet: From Natural Philosophy to Social Mathematics.* Chicago: University of Chicago Press, 1975.

Ball, Terence, James Farr and Russell L. Hanson, eds. *Political Innovation and Conceptual Change.* Cambridge: Cambridge University Press, 1989.

Barber, Benjamin R. *Jihad vs. McWorld: How Globalism and Tribalism Are Reshaping the World.* New York: Ballantine Books, 1995.

Barry, Brian. "International Society from a Cosmopolitan Perspective." In *International Society: Diverse Ethical Perspectives*, ed. David R. Mapel and Terry Nardin. Princeton, NJ: Princeton University Press, 1998, pp. 144–163.

Becker, Gary S. *The Economic Approach to Human Behavior.* Chicago: University of Chicago Press, 1976.

Beiser, Frederick C. *The Sovereignty of Reason: The Defense of Rationality in the Early English Enlightenment.* Princeton, NJ: Princeton University Press, 1996.

Beitz, Charles. *Political Theory and International Relations.* Princeton, NJ: Princeton University Press, 1979.

Benhabib, Seyla. *Another Cosmopolitanism.* Oxford: Oxford University Press, 2006.

Bénichou, Paul. *Man and Ethics: Studies in French Classicism* (Paris: Editions Gallimard, 1948), trans. and ed. Elizabeth Hughes. New York: Anchor, 1971.

Bergson, Henri. *The Two Sources of Morality and Religion,* trans. Ashley Audra, Cloudesley Brereton, W. Horsfall Carter. New York: Doubleday, 1956.

Berlin, Isaiah. *Five Essays on Liberty,* ed. Henry Hardy. Oxford: Oxford University Press, 2002.

Vico and Herder. London, 1980.

Berry, Christopher. *Hume, Hegel and Human Nature.* The Hague: Martinus Nijhoff, 1982.

The Idea of Luxury: A Conceptual and Historical Investigation. Cambridge: Cambridge University Press, 1994.

Social Theory of the Scottish Enlightenment. Edinburgh: Edinburgh University Press, 1997.

"Sociality and Socialisation." In *The Cambridge Companion to the Scottish Enlightenment,* ed. Alexander Broadie. Cambridge: Cambridge University Press, 2003, pp. 243–257.

Bettelheim, Bruno. "Remarks on the Psychological Appeal of Totalitarianism." *American Journal of Economics and Sociology,* vol. 12, October (1952), pp. 89–96. Reprint Bruno Bettelheim, *Surviving and Other Essays.* New York: Alfred A. Knopf, 1979, pp. 317–332.

Bloch, Marc. *The Historian's Craft,* trans. Peter Putnam. New York: Vintage, 1953.

Blom, Hans W., and Laurens C. Winkel, eds. *Grotius and the Stoa.* Assen: Van Gorcum, 2004.

Boltanski, Luc. *Distant Suffering: Morality, Media and Politics.* Cambridge: Cambridge University Press, 1999.

Bonar, James, ed. *A Catalogue of the Library of Adam Smith, Author of the "Moral Sentiments" and "The Wealth of Nations."* New York: Augustus M. Kelley Publishers, 1966.

Breckenridge, Carol A., Sheldon Pollock, Homi K. Bhabha and Dipesh Chakrabarty. "Cosmopolitanism." *Public Culture,* vol. 12, no. 3 (2000).

Brown, Vivienne. *Adam Smith's Discourse: Canonicity, Commerce and Conscience.* London, 1994.

"Dialogism, the Gaze and the Emergence of Economic Discourse." *New Literary History,* vol. 28, no. 4 (1997), pp. 697–709.

Brubaker, Lauren. "'A Particular Turn or Habit of the Imagination': Adam Smith on Love, Friendship and Philosophy." In *Love and Friendship: Rethinking Politics and Affection in Modern Times,* ed. Eduardo Velasquez. Lanham, MD: Lexington Books, 2003, pp. 229–262.

"Does the 'Wisdom of Nature' Need Help?" In *New Voices on Adam Smith,* eds. Leonidas Montes and Eric Schliesser. London: Routledge, 2006, pp. 168–192.

Buber, Martin, "The Question to the Single One." In *Between Man and Man*, trans. Ronald Gregor Smith. Glasgow: Collins, 1979, pp. 60–108.
Tales of the Hasidim. New York: Schocken, 1957.
Burtt, Shelley. *Virtue Transformed: Political Argument in England, 1688–1740*. Cambridge: Cambridge University Press, 1992.
Butler, Judith. "'Conscience Doth Make Subjects of Us All.'" *Yale French Studies*, no. 88 (1995), pp. 6–26.
Campbell, David, and Michael J. Shapiro, eds. *Moral Spaces: Rethinking Ethics and World Politics*. Minneapolis, MN: University of Minnesota Press, 1999.
Campbell, T. D. *Adam Smith's Science of Morals*. London: Allen & Unwin, 1971.
Caputo, John. *Against Ethics: Contributions to a Poetics of Obligation with Constant Reference to Deconstruction*. Bloomington, IN: Indiana University Press, 1993.
Cassirer, Ernst. *The Philosophy of the Enlightenment*, trans. Fritz C. A. Koelln and James P. Pettegrove. Princeton, NJ: Princeton University Press, 1951.
Castiglione, Dario. "Mandeville Moralized." *Annali della Fondazione Luigi Einaudi*, vol. 17 (1983), pp. 239–290.
"Considering Things Minutely: Reflections on Mandeville and the Eighteenth-Century Science of Man." *History of Political Thought*, vol. 7 (1986), pp. 463–488.
"Excess, Frugality and the Spirit of Capitalism: Readings of Mandeville on Commercial Society." In *Culture in History: Production, Consumption and Values in Historical Perspective*, ed. Joseph Melling and Jonathan Barry. Exeter: University of Exeter Press, 1992, pp. 155–179.
Cavell, Stanley. *Must We Mean What We Say?* Cambridge: Cambridge University Press, 1969–1976.
Chatterjee, Margaret. "The Oceanic Circle." In *Gandhi's Diagnostic Approach Rethought: Exploring a Perspective on His Life and Work*. New Delhi: Promilla and Co. and Bibliophile South Asia, 2007, pp. 148–174.
Cheah, Pheng, and Bruce Robbins, eds. *Cosmopolitics: Thinking and Feeling Beyond the Nation*. Minneapolis, MN: University of Minnesota Press, 1998.
Chong, Kim-chong, Sor-hoon Tan and C. L. Ten, eds. *The Moral Circle and the Self: Chinese and Western Approaches*. Peru, IL: Open Court, 1993.
Clark, Henry C. "Conversation and Moderate Virtue in Adam Smith's 'Theory of Moral Sentiments.'" *Review of Politics*, vol. 54, no. 2 (1992), pp. 185–210.
Clarke, P. H. "Adam Smith and the Stoics: The Influence of Marcus Aurelius." University of the West of England, Faculty of Economics and Social Science, Working Papers in Economics No. 18, April 1996.
"Adam Smith, Stoicism and Religion in the 18th Century." *History of the Human Sciences*, vol. 13, no. 4 (2000), pp. 49–72.
"Unity in the Influences on Adam Smith." *History of Economics Review*, vol. 26 (2002), pp. 10–25.
Cohen, Joshua, ed. *For Love of Country: Debating the Limits of Patriotism*. Boston: Beacon, 1996.
Coles, Romand. *Rethinking Generosity: Critical Theory and the Politics of Caritas*. Ithaca, NY: Cornell University Press, 1997.

Colletti, Lucio. "Mandeville, Rousseau and Smith." In *From Rousseau to Lenin: Studies in Ideology and Society*, trans. John Merrington and Judith White. New York: Monthly Review Press, 1972, pp. 195–216.

Collingwood, R. G. *The Idea of History*. Oxford: Oxford University Press, 1946–1980.

Connolly, William E. "Suffering, Justice, and the Politics of Becoming." In *Moral Spaces: Rethinking Ethics and World Politics*. Minneapolis, MN: University of Minnesota Press, 1999.

Why I Am Not a Secularist. Minneapolis, MN: University of Minnesota Press, 1999.

"Eccentric Flows and Cosmopolitan Culture." In William E. Connolly, *Neuropolitics: Thinking, Culture, Speed*. Minneapolis, MN: University of Minnesota Press, 2002, pp. 177–201.

Cooper, John M. "Eudaimonism, Nature, and 'Moral Duty' in Stoicism." In *Aristotle, Kant, and the Stoics: Rethinking Happiness and Duty*, ed. Stephen Engstrom and Jennifer Whiting. Cambridge: Cambridge University Press, 1996, pp. 261–284.

Cremaschi, Sergio V. "Adam Smith: Skeptical Newtonianism, Disenchanted Republicanism, and the Birth of Social Science." In *Knowledge and Politics: Case Studies in the Relationship between Epistemology and Political Philosophy*, ed. Marcelo Dascal and Ora Gruengard. Boulder, CO: Westview Press, 1989, pp. 83–110.

Cropsey, Joseph. *Polity and Economy: An Interpretation of the Principles of Adam Smith*. The Hague: Martinus Nijhoff, 1957.

"Adam Smith." In *History of Political Philosophy*, ed. Leo Strauss and Joseph Cropsey. Chicago: University of Chicago Press, 1963, pp. 607–630.

Darwall, Stephen. *Impartial Reason*. Ithaca, NY: Cornell University Press, 1983.

The British Moralists and the Internal "Ought": 1640–1740. Cambridge: Cambridge University Press, 1995.

"Empathy, Sympathy, Care." *Philosophical Studies*, vol. 89 (1998), pp. 261–282.

"Sympathetic Liberalism: Recent Work on Adam Smith." *Philosophy and Public Affairs*, vol. 28, no. 2 (1999), pp. 139–164.

"Equal Dignity in Adam Smith." *Adam Smith Review*, vol. 1 (2004), pp. 129–134.

Davidovich, Lucy S. *A Holocaust Reader*. New York: Behrman House, 1976.

de Waal, Alex. "The Humanitarian Juggernaut." *London Review of Books*, June 22, 1995.

Den Uyl, Douglas, and Charles L. Griswold. "Adam Smith on Friendship and Love." *Review of Metaphysics*, vol. 49, March, pp. 609–637.

Dennett, Daniel C. "Why You Can't Make a Computer That Feels Pain." In *Brainstorms: Philosophical Essays on Mind and Psychology*. Hassocks: Harvester, 1979, pp. 190–229.

Derathé, Robert. *Rousseau et la science politique de son temps*. Paris: Presses Universitaire de France, 1950.

des Jardins, Gregory. "Terms of *De Officiis* in Hume and Kant." *Journal of the History of Ideas*, vol. 28 (1967), pp. 237–242.

Dickey, Laurence W. "Historicizing the 'Adam Smith Problem': Conceptual, Historiographical, and Textual Issues." *Journal of Modern History*, vol. 58, September (1986), pp. 579–609.

"Pride, Hypocrisy and Civility in Mandeville's Social and Historical Theory." *Critical Review*, Summer 1990, pp. 387–431.

"Appendices I–IV." In Adam Smith, *An Enquiry into the Nature and Causes of the Wealth of Nations*, ed. Laurence W. Dickey. Indianapolis, IN: Hackett, 1993, pp. 213–263.

"*Doux-Commerce* and Humanitarian Values: Free Trade, Sociability and Universal Benevolence in Eighteenth-Century Thinking." In *Grotius and the Stoa*, ed. Hans W. Blom and Laurence C. Winkel. Assen: Van Gorcum, 2004, pp. 271–318.

Dufour, Alfred. "Pufendorf." In *The Cambridge History of Political Thought, 1450–1700*, ed. J. H. Burns and Mark Goldie. Cambridge: Cambridge University Press, 1991, pp. 561–588.

Dumont, Louis. *From Mandeville to Marx: The Genesis and Triumph of Economic Ideology*. Chicago: University of Chicago Press, 1977.

Dunn, John. "Democracy Unretrieved, or the Political Theory of Professor Macpherson." *British Journal of Political Science*, vol. 4, no. 4 (1974).

"From Applied Theology to Social Analysis: The Break between John Locke and the Scottish Enlightenment." In John Dunn, *Rethinking Modern Political Theory, Essays 1979–83*. Cambridge: Cambridge University Press, 1985, pp. 55–67.

Dupuy, Jean-Pierre. "Invidious Sympathy in the *Theory of Moral Sentiments*," *Adam Smith Review*, vol. 2 (2006), pp. 98–123.

Dwyer, John. "Theory and Discourse: The 6th Edition of The Theory of Moral Sentiments." In *Virtuous Discourse: Sensibility and Community in Late Eighteenth-Century Scotland*. Edinburgh: John Donald Publishers, 1987, pp. 168–185.

Einstein, Albert. Letter of 1950. Cited in the *New York Times*, March 29, 1972.

Elster, Jon, ed. *The Multiple Self*. Cambridge: Cambridge University Press, 1986.

Engberg-Pedersen, Troels. "Discovering the Good: *Oikeiōsis* and *Kathēkonta* in Stoic Ethics." In *The Norms of Nature: Studies in Hellenistic Ethics*, ed. Malcolm Schofield and Gisela Striker. Cambridge: Cambridge University Press, 1986; and Paris: Editions de la Maison des Sciences de l'Homme, 1986, pp. 145–183.

The Stoic Theory of Oikeiōsis. Aarhus: Aarhus University Press, 1990.

Evensky, Jerry. *Adam Smith's Moral Philosophy*. Cambridge: Cambridge University Press, 2005.

Feinberg, Joel. "Supererogation and Rules." In *Doing and Deserving: Essays in the Theory of Responsibility*. Princeton, NJ: Princeton University Press, 1970, pp. 3–24.

Fitzgibbons, Athol. *Adam Smith's System of Liberty, Wealth and Virtue: The Moral and Political Foundations of the Wealth of Nations*. Oxford: Oxford University Press, 1995.

Fleischacker, Samuel. "Philosophy in Moral Practice: Kant and Adam Smith." *Kant-Studien*, vol. 82 (1991), pp. 249–269.

Integrity and Moral Relativism. Leiden: Brill, 1992.

The Ethics of Culture. Ithaca, NY: Cornell University Press, 1994.

A Third Concept of Liberty: Judgement and Freedom in Kant and Adam Smith. Princeton, NJ: Princeton University Press, 1999.

On Adam Smith's Wealth of Nations. Princeton, NJ: Princeton University Press, 2004.

"Smith und der Kulturrelativismus." In *Adam Smith als Moralphilosoph*, ed. Christel Fricke and Hans-Peter Schütt. Berlin: De Gruyter, 2005 (trans. as "Smith and Cultural Relativism").

Foley, Vernard. *The Social Physics of Adam Smith*. West Lafayette, IN: Purdue University Press, 1976.

Forbes, Duncan. "Natural Law and the Scottish Enlightenment." In *The Origins and Nature of the Scottish Enlightenment*, ed. R. H. Campbell and A. S. Skinner. Edinburgh: John Donald Publishing Ltd, 1982, pp. 186–204.

Force, Pierre. *Self-Interest before Adam Smith: A Genealogy of Economic Science*. Cambridge: Cambridge University Press, 2003.

Forman-Barzilai, Fonna. Book review of Charles Griswold, *Adam Smith and the Virtues of Enlightenment*. *Political Theory*, vol. 28, no. 1 (2000), pp. 122–130.

"Whose Justice? Which Impartiality?: Reflections on Griswold's Smith." *Perspectives on Political Science*, vol. 30, no. 3 (2001), pp. 146–150.

"Adam Smith as Globalization Theorist." *Critical Review*, vol. 14, no. 4 (2002), pp. 391–419.

"The Emergence of Contextualism in Rousseau's Political Thought: The Case of Parisian Theatre in the Lettre à d'Alembert." *History of Political Thought*, vol. 24, no 3 (2003), pp. 435–463.

"And Thus Spoke the Spectator: Adam Smith for Humanitarians: On Luc Boltanski, *Distant Suffering: Morality, Media and Politics (Cambridge 1999)*," *Adam Smith Review*, vol. 1, Fall (2004), pp. 167–174.

"Sympathy in Space(s): Adam Smith on Proximity." *Political Theory*, vol. 33, no. 2 (2005), pp. 189–217.

"Smith on 'Connexion', Culture and Judgment." In *New Voices on Adam Smith*, ed. Leonidas Montes and Eric Schliesser. London: Routledge, 2006, pp. 89–114.

Book review of Jennifer Pitts, *A Turn to Empire: The Rise of Imperial Liberalism in Britain and France*. Princeton, NJ: Princeton University Press, 2005. In *Ethics and International Affairs*, vol. 21, no. 2 (2007), pp. 265–267.

"Adam Smith." In *Sage Encyclopedia of Political Theory*, ed. Mark Bevir. Thousand Oaks, CA: Sage Publications, forthcoming.

Foucault, Michel. *Discipline and Punish: The Birth of the Prison*, trans. Alan Sheridan. New York: Vintage Books, 1977.

Freud, Sigmund. *Civilization and Its Discontents*, trans. and ed. James Strachey. New York: W. W. Norton, 1961.

Friedländer, Saul. *Reflections of Nazism: An Essay on Kitsch and Death.* New York: Harper & Row, 1984.

Friedman, Milton. *Essays in Positive Economics.* Chicago: University of Chicago Press, 1953.

Fries, Thomas. "Dialog und Soliloquium." In *Dialog der Aufklärung, Shaftesbury, Rousseau, Solger.* Tübingen: Francke Verlag, 1993, pp. 49–97.

Galston, William A. "Cosmopolitan Altruism." In *Altruism,* ed. Ellen Frankel Paul, Fred D. Miller, Jr., and Jeffrey Paul. Cambridge: Cambridge University Press, 1993, pp. 118–134.

Gascoigne, John. *Cambridge in the Age of the Enlightenment: Science, Religion, and Politics from the Restoration to the French Revolution.* Cambridge: Cambridge University Press, 1988.

Geertz, Clifford. "The Uses of Diversity," *Michigan Quarterly Review,* vol. 25 (1986), pp. 105–123.

Giddens, Anthony. *Runaway World.* New York: Routledge, 2000.

Goldsmith, M. M. *Private Vices, Public Benefits: Bernard Mandeville's Social and Political Thought.* Cambridge: Cambridge University Press, 1985.

Gordon, Daniel. *Citizens Without Sovereignty: Equality and Sociability in French Thought, 1670–1789.* Princeton, NJ: Princeton University Press, 1994.

Gray, John. *Enlightenment's Wake: Politics and Culture at the Close of the Modern Age.* London: Routledge, 1995.

    Isaiah Berlin. Princeton, NJ: Princeton University Press, 1996.

Green, Lewis F. *Chronicle into History: An Essay on the Interpretation of History in Florentine Fourteenth-Century Chronicles.* Cambridge: Cambridge University Press, 1972.

Griswold, Charles L., Jr. "Rhetoric and Ethics: Adam Smith on Theorizing about the Moral Sentiments." *Philosophy and Rhetoric,* vol. 24, no. 3 (1991), pp. 213–237.

    Adam Smith and the Virtues of Enlightenment. Cambridge: Cambridge University Press, 1999.

    "Reply to My Critics." *Perspectives on Political Science,* vol. 30, no 3 (2001), pp. 163–167.

    "Imagination: Morals, Science, and Arts." In *The Cambridge Companion to Adam Smith,* ed. Knud Haakonssen. Cambridge: Cambridge University Press, 2006, pp. 22–56.

    "On the Incompleteness of Adam Smith's System." *Adam Smith Review,* vol. 2 (2006), pp. 181–186.

    Forgiveness: A Philosophical Exploration. Cambridge: Cambridge University Press, 2007.

Gunn, J. A. W. *Politics and the Public Interest in the Seventeenth Century.* London: Routledge & Kegan Paul, 1969.

Haakonssen, Knud. *The Science of a Legislator: The Natural Jurisprudence of David Hume and Adam Smith.* Cambridge: Cambridge University Press, 1981.

    ed. *Traditions of Liberalism: Essays on John Locke, Adam Smith and John Stuart Mill.* Sydney: Center for Independent Studies, 1988.

"Natural Law and Moral Realism: The Scottish Synthesis." In *Studies in the Philosophy of the Scottish Enlightenment*, ed. M. A. Stewart. Oxford: Clarendon Press, 1990, pp. 61–85.

ed. *Enlightenment and Religion: Rational Dissent in Eighteenth-Century Britain*. Cambridge: Cambridge University Press, 1996.

Natural Law and Moral Philosophy: From Grotius to the Scottish Enlightenment. Cambridge: Cambridge University Press, 1996.

ed. "Introduction." In Adam Smith, *Theory of Moral Sentiments*. Cambridge: Cambridge University Press, 2002, pp. vii–xxiv.

ed. *The Cambridge Companion to Adam Smith*. Cambridge: Cambridge University Press, 2006.

Haakonssen, Knud, and Donald Winch. "The Legacy of Adam Smith." In *The Cambridge Companion to Adam Smith*, ed. Knud Haakonssen. Cambridge: Cambridge University Press, 2006, pp. 366–394.

Hampshire, Stuart. *Morality and Conflict*. Cambridge, MA, 1983.

Hanley, Ryan. "Adam Smith, Aristotle and Virtue Ethics." In *New Voices on Adam Smith*, ed. Leonidas Montes and Eric Schliesser. London: Routledge, 2006, pp. 17–39.

"Commerce and Corruption: Rousseau's Diagnosis, Adam Smith's Cure." *European Journal of Political Theory*, vol. 7, no. 2 (2008), pp. 137–158.

Harkin, Maureen. "Adam Smith's Missing History: Primitives, Progress and Problems of Genre." *English Literary History*, vol. 72 (2005), pp. 429–451.

Hayek, Friedrich A. von. *Individualism and the Economic Order*. Chicago: University of Chicago Press, 1948.

Heath, Eugene. "The Commerce of Sympathy: Adam Smith on the Emergence of Morals." *Journal of the History of Philosophy*, vol. 33, no. 3 (1995), pp. 447–466.

Heilbronner, Robert L. "The Wonderful World of Adam Smith." In *The Worldly Philosophers: The Lives, Times and Ideas of the Great Economic Thinkers*. New York: Simon & Schuster, 1953, pp. 40–72.

Heise, Paul A. "Stoicism in Adam Smith's Model of Human Behavior: The Philosophical Foundations of Self-Betterment and the Invisible Hand." *Oekonomie und Gesellschaft: Adam Smith's Beitrag zur Gesellschaftswissenshaft*, vol. 9 (1991), pp. 64–78.

"Stoicism in the EPS: The Foundations of Adam Smith's Moral Philosophy." *Perspectives in the History of Economic Thought*, vol. 11 (1995), pp. 17–30.

Held, David. *Democracy and the Global Order: From the Modern State to Cosmopolitan Governance*. Stanford, CA: Stanford University Press, 1995.

Held, David, and Tony McGrew, eds. *Governing Globalization*. Cambridge: Polity, 2002.

Heyd, David. *Supererogation: Its Status in Ethical Theory*. Cambridge: Cambridge University Press, 1982.

Hill, Lisa. "The Hidden Theology of Adam Smith." *European Journal of the History of Economic Thought*, vol. 8, no. 1 (2001), pp. 1–29.

"Adam Smith and the Theme of Corruption." *Review of Politics*, vol. 68 (2006), pp. 636–662.

Hill, Lisa, and Peter McCarthy. "On Friendship and Necessitudo in Adam Smith." *History of the Human Sciences*, vol. 17, no. 4 (2004), pp. 1–16.

Hirschman, Albert O. *The Passions and the Interests: Political Arguments for Capitalism before Its Triumph.* Princeton, NJ: Princeton University Press, 1977.

"Rival Views of Market Society." *Journal of Economic Literature*, vol. 20, December (1982). Reprint *Rival Views of Market Society and Other Recent Essays.* Cambridge: Cambridge University Press, 1992, pp. 105–141.

Hollinger, David. "How Wide Is the Circle of the 'We'?," *American Historical Review*, vol. 98, no. 2 (1993), pp. 317–337.

"Not Universalists, Not Pluralists: The New Cosmopolitans Find Their Own Way." In *Conceiving Cosmopolitanism: Theory, Context, and Practice*, ed. Steven Vertovec and Robin Cohen. Oxford: Oxford University Press, 2002, pp. 227–239.

Hollis, Martin. *The Cunning of Reason.* Cambridge: Cambridge University Press, 1987.

Holmes, Stephen. "The Secret History of Self-Interest." In *Beyond Self-Interest*, ed. Jane J. Mansbridge. Chicago: University of Chicago Press, 1990, pp. 267–286.

Honig, Bonnie. "Another Cosmopolitanism?" In *Another Cosmopolitanism*, ed. Seyla Benhabib. Oxford: Oxford University Press, 2006, pp. 102–127.

Hont, Istvan. "'The Rich-Country – Poor-Country' Debate in Scottish Classical Political Economy." In *Wealth and Virtue: The Shaping of Political Economy in the Scottish Enlightenment*, ed. Istvan Hont and Michael Ignatieff. Cambridge: Cambridge University Press, 1985, pp. 271–315.

"The Language of Sociability and Commerce: Samue Pufendorf and the Theoretical Foundations of the 'Four-Stages Theory.'" In *The Languages of Political Theory in Early-Modern Europe*, ed. Anthony Pagden. Cambridge: Cambridge University Press, 1987, pp. 253–276.

"Free Trade and the Economic Limits to National Politics: Neo-Machiavellian Political Economy Reconsidered." In *The Economic Limits to Modern Politics*, ed. John Dunn. Cambridge: Cambridge University Press, 1990, pp. 41–120.

"The Permanent Crisis of a Divided Mankind: 'Contemporary Crisis of the Nation State' in Historical Perspective." In *Contemporary Crisis of the Nation State?*, ed. John Dunn. Oxford: Blackwell, 1995, pp. 166–231.

Jealousy of Trade: International Competition and the Nation-State in Historical Perspective. Cambridge, MA: Harvard University Press, 2005.

Hont, Istvan, and Michael Ignatieff, eds. *Wealth and Virtue: The Shaping of Political Economy in the Scottish Enlightenment.* Cambridge: Cambridge University Press, 1985.

Hope, Vincent. "Smith's Demigod." In *Philosophers of the Scottish Enlightenment*, ed. Vincent Hope. Edinburgh: Edinburgh University Press, 1984, pp. 157–167.

Virtue by Consensus: The Moral Philosophy of Hutcheson, Hume and Adam Smith. Oxford: Clarendon Press, 1989.

Horne, Thomas. "Envy and Commercial Society: Mandeville and Smith on 'Private Vices, Public Benefits.'" *Political Theory*, vol. 9, no. 4 (1981), pp. 551–569.

Hundert, E. J. *The Enlightenment's Fable: Bernard Mandeville and the Discovery of Society*. Cambridge: Cambridge University Press, 1994.

Hurka, Thomas. *Perfectionism*. Oxford: Oxford University Press, 1993.

Hutchinson, Terence. *Before Adam Smith: The Emergence of Political Economy, 1662–1776*. Oxford: Basil Blackwell, 1988.

Ignatieff, Michael. "Smith, Rousseau and the Republic of Needs." In *Scotland and Europe, 1200–1850*, ed. T. C. Smout. Edinburgh: John Donald Publishers, 1986, pp. 187–206.

The Needs of Strangers. London: Chatto & Windus, 1984; reprint London: Hogarth Press, 1990.

Blood and Belonging: Journeys into the New Nationalism. New York: Noonday, 1993.

Inwood, Brad. "Hierocles: Theory and Argument in the Second Century AD." *Oxford Studies in Ancient Philosophy*. Oxford: Oxford University Press, 1984, vol. 2, pp. 151–183.

Jardins, Gregory des. "Terms of *De Officiis* in Hume and Kant." *Journal of the History of Ideas*, vol. 28 (1967).

Jones, Charles. *Global Justice: Defending Cosmopolitanism*. Oxford: Oxford University Press, 1999.

Jones, Deiniol. "The Origins of the Global City: Ethics and Morality in Contemporary Cosmopolitanism." *British Journal of Politics and International Relations*, vol. 5, no. 1 (2003), pp. 50–73.

Justman, Stuart. *The Autonomous Male of Adam Smith*. Norman, OK: University of Oklahoma Press, 1996.

Kalyvas, Andreas, and Ira Katznelson, "The Rhetoric of the Market: Adam Smith on Recognition, Speech and Exchange." *Review of Politics*, vol. 63, no. 3 (2001), pp. 549–579.

Kennedy, Gavin. *Adam Smith's Lost Legacy*. Basingstoke and New York: Palgrave Macmillan, 2005.

Keohane, Nannerl O. *Philosophy and the State in France: The Renaissance to the Enlightenment*. Princeton, NJ: Princeton University Press, 1980.

Kidd, I. G. "Stoic Intermediates and the End for Man." In *Problems in Stoicism*, ed. A. A. Long. London: Athlone Press, 1971, pp. 150–172.

Kingston, Rebecca. "The Political Relevance of the Emotions from Descartes to Smith." In *Bringing the Passions Back In: The Emotions in Political Philosophy*, ed. Rebecca Kingston and Leonard Ferry. Vancouver, BC: University of British Columbia Press, 2008, pp. 108–125.

Kleer, Richard. "Final Causes in Adam Smith's *Theory of Moral Sentiments*." *Journal of the History of Philosophy*, vol. 33, no. 2 (1995), pp. 275–300.

"The Role of Teleology in Adam Smith's *Wealth of Nations*," *History of Economics Review*, vol. 31 (2000), pp. 14–29.

Klein, Lawrence E. *Shaftesbury and the Culture of Politeness: Moral Discourse and Cultural Politics in Early Eighteenth-Century England*. Cambridge: Cambridge University Press, 1994.

Kleinig, John. "Butler in a Cool Hour." *Journal of the History of Ideas*, vol. 7 (1969), pp. 399–411.

Koselleck, Reinhart. *Futures Past: On the Semantics of Historical Time*. Frankfurt: Suhrkamp Verlag, 1979; trans. and ed. Keith Tribe. Cambridge, MA: MIT Press, 1985.

Krieger, Leonard. *The Politics of Discretion: Pufendorf and the Acceptance of Natural Law*. Chicago: University of Chicago Press, 1965.

Kuiper, Edith. "The Construction of Masculine Identity in Adam Smith's Theory of Moral Sentiments." In *Towards a Feminist Philosophy of Economics*, ed. Drucilla K. Barker and Edith Kuiper. London: Routledge, 2003, pp. 145–160.

"Adam Smith and His Feminist Contemporaries." In *New Voices on Adam Smith*, ed. Leonidas Montes, and Eric Schliesser. London: Routledge, 2006, pp. 3–60.

Kwok-Bun, Chan. "Both Sides, Now: Culture Contact, Hybridization and Cosmopolitanism." In *Conceiving Cosmopolitanism: Theory, Context, and Practice*, ed. Steven Vertovec and Robin Cohen. Oxford: Oxford University Press, 2002, pp. 191–208.

LaCapra, Dominick. "Rethinking Intellectual History and Reading Texts." In *Modern European Intellectual History: Reappraisals & New Perspectives*, ed. Dominick LaCapra and Steven L. Kaplan. Ithaca, NY: Cornell University Press, 1982, pp. 47–85.

Lamb, Robert Boyden. "Adam Smith's System: Sympathy Not Self-Interest." *Journal of the History of Ideas*, vol. 35 (1974), pp. 671–682.

Larmore, Charles E. *Patterns of Moral Complexity*. Cambridge: Cambridge University Press, 1987.

The Morals of Modernity. Cambridge: Cambridge University Press, 1996.

Lear, Jonathan. "Transcendental Anthropology." In *Subject, Thought, and Context*, ed. Philip Pettit and John McDowell. Oxford: Clarendon Press, 1986, pp. 267–298.

Lecky, W. E. H. *History of European Morals from Augustus to Charlemagne*. New York: George Braziller, 1955, vols. I and II.

Leslie, T. E. Cliffe. "The Political Economy of Adam Smith," *Fortnightly Review*, November 1, 180.

Levi, Anthony. *French Moralists: The Theory of the Passions, 1585–1659*. Oxford: Oxford University Press, 1964.

Levy, David M., and Sandra J. Peart . "Adam Smith and His Sources: The Evil of Independence." *Adam Smith Review*, vol. 4 (2008), pp. 57–87.

Lomonaco, Jeffrey. "Adam Smith's 'Letter to the Authors of the *Edinburgh Review.*'" *Journal of the History of Ideas*, vol. 64, no. 4 (2002), pp. 659–676.

Long, A. A. *Hellenistic Philosophy: Stoics, Epicureans, Sceptics. 2nd edn*. Berkeley, CA: University of California Press, 1986.

Long, A. A., and D. N. Sedley, eds. *The Hellenistic Philosophers, 2 vols*. Cambridge: Cambridge University Press, 1987.

Lovejoy, Arthur O. "The Supposed Primitivism of Rousseau's 'Discourse on Inequality.'" *Modern Philology*, vol. 21 (1923).

Reflections on Human Nature. Baltimore, MD: Johns Hopkins University Press, 1961.

Löwith, Karl. *Meaning in History*. Chicago: University of Chicago Press, 1949.

Lukes, Steven. "On Trade-offs between Values." European University Institute Working Papers in Political and Social Sciences, No. 92–94 (1992).

Macfie, A. L. *The Individual in Society*. London: Allen & Unwin, 1967.

Macpherson, C. B. *The Political Theory of Possessive Individualism*. Oxford: Oxford University Press, 1962.

Book review of D. Winch, Adam Smith's Politics. *In History of Political Economy*, vol. 11 (1979), pp. 450–454.

Madsen, Richard, and Tracy B. Strong. *The Many and the One: Religious and Secular Perspectives on Ethical Pluralism in the Modern World*. Princeton, NJ: Princeton University Press, 2003.

Mapel, David R., and Terry Nardin, eds. *International Society: Diverse Ethical Perspectives*. Princeton, NJ: Princeton University Press, 1998.

Markell, Patchen. *Bound by Recognition*. Princeton, NJ: Princeton University Press, 2003.

Marshall, David. "Adam Smith and the Theatricality of Moral Sentiments." *Critical Inquiry*, vol. 10, June (1984), pp. 592–613.

"Adam Smith and the Theatricality of Moral Sentiments." In David Marshall, *The Figure of Theatre: Shaftesbury, Defoe, Adam Smith, and George Eliot*. New York: Columbia University Press, 1986.

Marshall, T. H. *Citizenship and Social Class*. Cambridge: Cambridge University Press, 1950; reprint London: Pluto, 1992.

McDonough, Kenneth. "Cultural Recognition, Cosmopolitanism and Multicultural Education." *In Philosophy of Education 1997*, ed. L. Stone. Urbana, IL: Philosophy of Education Society, 1998.

McDonough, Kevin, and Walter Feinberg, eds. *Citizenship and Education in Liberal-Democratic Societies: Teaching for Cosmopolitan Values, and Collective Identities*. Oxford: Oxford University Press, 1993.

McKenna, Stephen J. *Adam Smith: The Rhetoric of Propriety*. Albany: State University of New York Press, 2006.

McLean, Iain. *Adam Smith: Radical and Egalitarian: An Interpretation for the 21st Century*. Edinburgh: Edinburgh University Press, 2006.

McNamara, Peter. *Political Economy and Statesmanship: Smith, Hamilton, and the Foundation of the Commercial Republic*. Dekalb: University of Illinois Press, 1998.

Medema, Steven G. "Adam Smith and the Chicago School." *In The Elgar Companion to Adam Smith*, ed. Jeffrey Young. Cheltenham: Edward Elgar, forthcoming 2009.

Mehta, Pratap Banhu. "Self-Interest and Other Interests." In *The Cambridge Companion to Adam Smith*, ed. Knud Haakonssen. Cambridge: Cambridge University Press, 2006, pp. 246–269.

Mehta, Uday Singh. *Liberalism and Empire: A Study in Nineteenth-Century British Liberal Thought*. Chicago: University of Chicago Press, 1999.

Miller, David. "The Resurgence of Political Theory." *Political Studies*, vol. 38 (1990), pp. 421–437.

Miller, David, and Michael Walzer, eds. *Pluralism, Justice, and Equality*. Oxford: Oxford University Press, 1995.

Minowitz, Peter. *Profits, Priests, and Princes: Adam Smith's Emancipation of Economics from Politics and Religion*. Stanford, CA: Stanford University Press, 1993.

Mitchell, Harvey. "The Mysterious Veil of Self-Delusion in Adam Smith's *Theory of Moral Sentiments*." *Eighteenth-Century Studies*, vol. 20 (1987), pp. 405–421.

Montes, Leonidas. *Adam Smith in Context: A Critical Reassessment of Some Central Components of His Thought*. Basingstoke: Palgrave Macmillan, 2004.

"Adam Smith as an Eclectic Stoic." *Adam Smith Review*, vol. 4 (2008), forthcoming.

Montes, Leonidas, and Eric Schliesser, eds. *New Voices on Adam Smith*. London: Routledge, 2006.

Moon, J. Donald. *Constructing Community: Moral Pluralism and Tragic Conflicts*. Princeton, NJ: Princeton University Press, 1993.

Morrow, Glenn R. *The Ethical and Economic Theories of Adam Smith*. New York, 1923; reprint New York: Augustus M. Kelley, 1973.

"The Significance of the Doctrine of Sympathy in Hume and Adam Smith." *Philosophical Review*, vol. 32, no. 1 (1923), pp. 60–78.

Muller, Jerry Z. *Adam Smith in His Time, and Ours: Designing the Decent Society*. New York: Free Press, 1993; Reprint Princeton, NJ: Princeton University Press, 1995.

Muthu, Sankar. *Enlightenment Against Empire*. Princeton, NJ: Princeton University Press, 2003.

"Adam Smith's Critique of International Trading Companies: Theorizing 'Globalization' in the Age of Enlightenment." *Political Theory*, vol. 36, no. 2 (2008), pp. 185–212.

Myers, Milton L. "Adam Smith as Critic of Ideas." *Journal of the History of Ideas*, vol. 32, no. 2 (1975), pp. 281–296.

The Soul of Modern Economic Man: Ideas of Self-Interest, from Thomas Hobbes to Adam Smith. Chicago: University of Chicago Press, 1983.

Mayerfield, Jamie. *Suffering and Moral Responsibility*. New York: Oxford University Press, 1999.

Nagel, Thomas. *The View from Nowhere*. Oxford: Oxford University Press, 1986.

Neili, Russell. "Spheres of Intimacy and the Adam Smith Problem." *Journal of the History of Ideas*, vol. 47, no. 4 (1986), pp. 611–624.

North, Helen. *Sophrosyne: Self-Knowledge and Self-Restraint in Greek Literature*. Ithaca, NY: Cornell University Press, 1966.

Nussbaum, Martha C. *The Fragility of Goodness*. Cambridge: Cambridge University Press, 1986.

The Therapy of Desire: Theory and Practice in Hellenistic Ethics. Princeton, NJ: Princeton University Press, 1994.

"Kant and Stoic Cosmopolitanism." *Journal of Political Philosophy* (1995).

Poetic Justice: The Literary Imagination and Public Life. Boston: Beacon, 1995.

"Compassion: The Basic Social Emotion." *Social Philosophy and Policy*, vol. 13 (1996), pp. 27–58.

ed. *For Love of Country: Debating the Limits of Patriotism*. Boston: Beacon, 1996.

Cultivating Humanity: A Classical Defense of Reform in Liberal Education. Cambridge, MA: Harvard University Press, 1997.

"'Mutilated and Deformed': Adam Smith on the Material Basis of Human Dignity." In Martha Nussbaum, *The Cosmopolitan Tradition*. Cambridge, MA: Harvard University Press, forthcoming.

Nussbaum, Martha C., and Amartya Sen, eds. *The Quality of Life*. Oxford: Clarendon Press, 1993.

Nussbaum, Martha C., *et al*. "Patriotism and Cosmopolitanism." *Boston Review*, October/November 1994.

Nygren, Anders. *Eros and Agape*. London: SPCK, 1954.

Otteson, James R. "Adam Smith on the Emergence of Morals: A Reply to Eugene Heath." *British Journal for the History of Philosophy*, vol. 8, no. 3 (2000), pp. 545–551.

Adam Smith's Marketplace of Life. Cambridge: Cambridge University Press, 2002.

"Shaftesbury's Evolutionary Morality and Its Influence on Adam Smith." *Adam Smith Review*, vol. 4 (2008), forthcoming.

Pagden, Anthony. *Lords of All the World: Ideologies of Empire in Spain, Britain, and France, c.1500–c.1800*. New Haven, CT, 1995.

Page, James. *Peace Education: Exploring Ethical and Philosophical Foundations*. New York: Information Age Publishing, 2008.

Penelhum, Terence. *Butler*. London: Routledge & Kegan Paul, 1985.

Peters, John Durham. "Publicity and Pain: Self-Abstraction in Adam Smith's *Theory of Moral Sentiments*," *Public Culture*, vol. 7 (1995), pp. 657–684.

Pettit, Philip. "A Sensible Perspectivism." In *Pluralism: The Philosophy and Politics of Diversity*, ed. Baghramian, Maria, and Attracta Ingram. London: Routledge, 2000, pp. 60–82.

Phillipson, Nicholas. "Adam Smith as Civic Moralist." In *Wealth and Virtue: The Shaping of Political Economy in the Scottish Enlightenment*, ed. Istvan Hont, and Michael Ignatieff. Cambridge: Cambridge University Press, 1985, pp. 179–202.

"Politics and Politeness in the Reigns of Anne and the Early Hanoverians." In *The Varieties of British Political Thought, 1500–1800*, ed. J. G. A. Pocock with Gordon J. Schochet and Lois G. Schwoerer. Cambridge: Cambridge University Press, 1993, pp. 211–245.

Pitts, Jennifer. *A Turn to Empire: The Rise of Imperial Liberalism in Britain and France*. Princeton, NJ: Princeton University Press, 2005.

Pocock, J. G. A. *The Machiavellian Moment: Florentine Political Thought and the Atlantic Republican Tradition*. Princeton, NJ: Princeton University Press, 1975.

The Political Works of James Harrington. Cambridge: Cambridge University Press, 1977.

"Authority and Property: The Question of Liberal Origins." In *After the Reformation: Essays in Honor of J. H. Hexter*, ed. Barbara C. Malament. Philadelphia: University of Pennsylvania Press, 1980, pp. 331–354.

Virtue, Commerce, and History: Essays on Political Thought and History, Chiefly in the Eighteenth Century. Cambridge: Cambridge University Press, 1985.

"Cambridge Paradigms and Scotch Philosophers: A Study of the Relations between the Civic Humanist and Civil Jurisprudential Interpretation of Eighteenth-Century Social Thought." In *Wealth and Virtue: The Shaping of Political Economy in the Scottish Enlightenment*, ed. Istvan Hont and Michael Ignatieff. Cambridge: Cambridge University Press, 1985, pp. 235–252.

"Time Institutions and Action: An Essay on Traditions and Their Understanding." In J. G. A. Pocock, *Politics, Language and Time: Essays on Political Thought and History*. Chicago: University of Chicago Press, 1989, pp. 233–272.

"Political Thought in the English-Speaking Atlantic, 1760–1790, Part 2: Empire, Revolution and the End of Early Modernity." In *The Varieties of British Political Thought, 1500–1800*, ed. J. G. A. Pocock with Gordon J. Schochet and Lois G. Schwoerer. Cambridge: Cambridge University Press, 1993, pp. 283–317.

Portman, John. *When Bad Things Happen to Other People*. New York: Routledge, 2000.

Radner, John B. "The Art of Sympathy in Eighteenth-Century British Moral Thought." *Studies in Eighteenth-Century Culture*, vol. 9 (1980), pp. 189–210.

Raphael, D. D. *The Moral Sense*. Oxford: Oxford University Press, 1947.

"Bishop Butler's View of Conscience." *Philosophy*, vol. 24 (1949), pp. 219–238.

ed. *British Moralists 1650–1800*, 2 vols. Oxford: Clarendon Press, 1969; reprint Indianapolis, IN: Hackett, 1991.

"Hume and Adam Smith on Justice and Utility." In *Proceedings of the Aristotelian Society*. London: Methuen & Co., 1972/73. New Series, vol. 73, pp. 87–103.

"The Impartial Spectator." In *Essays on Adam Smith*, ed. Andrew S. Skinner and Thomas Wilson. Oxford: Clarendon Press, 1975, pp. 83–99.

Moral Philosophy. Oxford: Oxford University Press, 1981.

Adam Smith. Oxford: Oxford University Press, 1985.

"Adam Smith 1790: The Man Recalled, the Philosopher Revived." In *Adam Smith Reviewed*, ed. Peter Jones and Andrew Skinner. Edinburgh: Edinburgh University Press, 1992, pp. 93–118.

The Impartial Spectator: Adam Smith's Moral Philosophy. New York: Oxford University Press, 2007.

Rasmussen, Dennis. "Rousseau's 'Philosophical Chemistry' and the Foundations of Adam Smith's Thought." *History of Political Thought*, vol. 27, no. 4 (2006), pp. 620–641.

The Problems and Promise of Commercial Society: Adam Smith's Response to Rousseau. University Park, PA: Pennsylvania State University Press, 2008.

"Whose Impartiality? Which Self-Interest?: Adam Smith on Utility, Happiness and Cultural Relativism." *Adam Smith Review*, vol. 4 (2008), pp. 247–261.

Rawls, John. *A Theory of Justice*. Cambridge, MA: Belknap Press, 1971.

Raynor, David. "Hume's Abstract of Adam Smith's *Theory of Moral Sentiments*." *Journal of the History of Philosophy*, vol. 22 (1984), pp. 52–79.

Raz, Joseph. *The Morality of Freedom*. Oxford: Oxford University Press, 1988.

Ritter, Alan, and Julia Conaway Bondanella, eds. *Rousseau's Political Writings*. New York: W. W. Norton, 1988.

Robbins, Bruce. Feeling Global: *Internationalism in Distress*. New York: New York University Press, 1999.

Robertson, John. *The Scottish Enlightenment and the Militia Issue*. Edinburgh: John Donald Publishers, 1985.

"The Scottish Enlightenment at the Limits of the Civic Tradition." In *Wealth and Virtue: The Shaping of Political Economy in the Scottish Enlightenment*, ed. Istvan Hont and Michael Ignatieff. Cambridge: Cambridge University Press, 1985, pp. 137–179.

ed. A Union for Empire: *Political Thought and the Union of 1707*. Cambridge: Cambridge University Press, 1995.

Robin, Corey. Fear: *The History of a Political Idea*. New York: Oxford University Press, 2004.

Rorty, Amélie Oskenberg. "Butler on Benevolence and Conscience." *Philosophy*, vol. 53 (1978), pp. 171–184.

"Akrasia and Pleasure." In *Essays on Aristotle's Ethics*, ed. Amélie O. Rorty. Berkeley, CA: University of California Press, 1980, pp. 267–284.

Rorty, Richard. *Contingency, Irony and Solidarity*. Cambridge: Cambridge University Press, 1989.

"Justice as a Larger Loyalty." In *Cosmopolitics: Thinking and Feeling beyond the Nation*, ed. Pheng Cheah and Bruce Robbins. Minneapolis, MN: University of Minnesota Press, 1998, pp. 45–58.

Ross, Ian Simpson. *The Life of Adam Smith*. Oxford: Clarendon Press, 1995.

"'Great Works upon the Anvil' in 1785: Adam Smith's Projected Corpus of Philosophy." *Adam Smith Review*, vol. 1 (2004), pp. 40–59.

Rothkrug, Lionel. *Opposition to Louis XIV: The Political and Social Origin of the French Enlightenment*. Princeton, NJ: Princeton University Press, 1965.

Rothschild, Emma. "Adam Smith and Conservative Economics." *Economic History Review*, vol. 45 (1992), pp. 74–96.

Economic Sentiments: Adam Smith, Condorcet, and the Enlightenment. Cambridge, MA: Harvard University Press, 2001.

"Dignity or Meanness." *Adam Smith Review*, vol. I (2004), pp. 150–164.

Saint-Amand, Pierre. *The Laws of Hostility: Politics, Violence, and the Enlightenment*, trans. Jennifer Curtiss Gage. Paris, 1992; Minneapolis, MN: University of Minnesota Press, 1996.

Sakamoto, Tatsuya, and Hideo Tanaka, eds. *The Rise of Political Economy in the Scottish Enlightenment*. London: Routledge, 2003.

Sandbach, F. H. *The Stoics*. Indianapolis, IN: Hackett, 1975, 1994.

Sandel, Michael. *Liberalism and the Limits of Justice*. Cambridge: Cambridge University Press, 1982.

"The Procedural Republic and the Unencumbered Self." *Political Theory*, vol. 12, no. 1 (1984), pp. 81–96.

Sartre, Jean-Paul. *Being and Nothingness*, trans. Hazel E. Barnes. New York: Philosophical Library, 1956.

Schlereth, Thomas J. *The Cosmopolitan Ideal in Enlightenment Thought*. Notre Dame, IN: University of Notre Dame Press, 1977.

Schliesser, Eric. "The Obituary of a Vain Philosopher: Adam Smith's Reflections on Hume's Life." *Hume Studies*, vol. 29, no. 2 (2003), pp. 327–362.

"Adam Smith's Benevolent and Self-Interested Conception of Philosophy." In *New Voices on Adam Smith*, ed. Leonidas Montes, and Eric Schliesser. London: Routledge, 2006, pp. 328–357.

"Articulating Practices as Reasons: Adam Smith on the Social Conditions of Possibility of Property." *Adam Smith Review*, vol. 2 (2006), pp. 69–97.

Schliesser, Eric, and Spencer Pack. "Adam Smith's 'Humean' Criticism of Hume's Account of the Origin of Justice." *Journal of the History of Philosophy*, vol. 44, no. 1 (2006), pp. 47–63.

Schneewind, J. B. "The Divine Corporation and the History of Ethics." In *Philosophy in History: Essays on the Historiography of Philosophy*, ed. Richard Rorty, J. B. Schneewind and Quentin Skinner. Cambridge: Cambridge University Press, 1984, pp. 173–191.

The Invention of Autonomy: A History of Modern Moral Philosophy. Cambridge: Cambridge University Press, 1998.

Schofield, Malcolm. *The Stoic Idea of the City*. Chicago: University of Chicago Press, 1991–1999.

Schumacher, Millard. "Rights, Duties, and Supererogation." PhD thesis, Queen's University, Ontario, 1970.

Schumpeter, Joseph. *History of Economic Analysis*. London: G. Allen and Unwin, 1954.

Sekora, John. *Luxury: The Concept in Western Thought, Eden to Smollett*. Baltimore, MD: Johns Hopkins Press, 1977.

Sen, Amartya. *On Ethics and Economics*. Oxford: Basil Blackwell, 1987.

"Open and Closed Impartiality." *Journal of Philosophy*, vol. 99, no. 9 (2002), pp. 445–469.

Shapiro, Michael. *Reading "Adam Smith": Desire, History and Value*. Newbury Park, CA: Sage Publications, 1993.

"The Ethics of Encounter: Unreading, Unmapping the Imperium." In *Moral Spaces: Rethinking Ethics and World Politics*, ed. David Campbell, and Michael J. Shapiro. Minneapolis, MN: University of Minnesota Press, 1999, pp. 57–91.

Shaver, Robert. "Virtues, Utility, and Rules." In *The Cambridge Companion to Adam Smith*, ed. Knud Haakonssen. Cambridge: Cambridge University Press, 2006, pp. 189–213.

Sher, Richard B. *Church and University in the Scottish Enlightenment: The Moderate Literati of Edinburgh*. Princeton, NJ: Princeton University Press, 1995.

Shklar, Judith N. "Facing up to Intellectual Pluralism." In *Political Theory and Social Change*, ed. David Spitz. New York: Atherton Press, 1967, pp. 275–295.

Men and Citizens: A Study of Rousseau's Social Theory. Cambridge: Cambridge University Press, 1969.

Freedom and Independence: A Study of the Political Ideas of Hegel's Phenomenology of Mind. Cambridge, MA: Harvard University Press, 1976.

Ordinary Vices. Cambridge, MA: Belknap Press, 1984.

"Liberalism of Fear." In *Liberalism and the Moral Life*, ed. Nancy Rosenblum. Cambridge, MA, 1989, pp. 21–39; reprint *Political Thought and Political Thinkers*, ed. Stanley Hoffman. Chicago: University of Chicago Press, 1998, pp. 3–20.

"Giving Injustice Its Due." *Yale Law Journal*, vol. 98, April (1989).

Faces of Injustice. New Haven, CT: Yale University Press, 1990.

"Obligation, Loyalty and Exile." In *Political Thought and Political Thinkers*, ed. Stanley Hoffman. Chicago: University of Chicago Press, 1998, pp. 38–55.

"The Bonds of Exile." In *Political Thought and Political Thinkers*, ed. Stanley Hoffman. Chicago: University of Chicago Press, 1998, pp. 56–72.

Silver, Allan. "Friendship in Commercial Society: Eighteenth-Century Social Theory and Modern Sociology." *American Journal of Sociology*, vol. 30 (1990), pp. 274–297.

"'Two Different Sorts of Commerce' – Friendship and Strangership in Civil Society." In *Public and Private in Thought and Practice: Perspectives on a Grand Dichotomy*, ed. Jeff Weintraub and Krishan Kumar. Chicago: University of Chicago Press, 1997, pp. 43–74.

Singer, Peter. *The Expanding Circle: Ethics and Sociobiology*. New York: Farrar, Straus & Giroux, 1981.

Skinner, Andrew S. *A System of Social Science: Papers Relating to Adam Smith*. Oxford: Clarendon Press, 1979.

Skinner, Quentin. "Hobbes' *Leviathan*." *Historical Journal*, vol. 7 (1964), pp. 321–133.

"Meaning and Understanding in the History of Ideas." *History and Theory*, vol. 8 (1969), pp. 3–53.

The Foundations of Modern Political Thought. Cambridge: Cambridge University, Press, 1978, vols. I and II.

"The Idea of Negative Liberty: Philosophical and Historical Perspectives." In *Philosophy in History: Essays on the Historiography of Philosophy*, ed. Richard Rorty, J. B. Schneewind and Quentin Skinner. Cambridge: Cambridge University Press, 1984, pp. 193–221.

"The Paradoxes of Political Liberty." *The Tanner Lectures on Human Values*. Salt Lake City, UT: University of Utah Press, 1986, vol. VII, pp. 227–250.

"A Reply to My Critics." In *Meaning and Context: Quentin Skinner and His Critics*, ed. James Tully. Princeton, NJ: Princeton University Press, 1988.

"Rhetoric and the Constitution of Reality." *Proceedings of the British Academy*, vol. 76 (1990), pp. 1–63.

"The Republican Ideal of Political Liberty." In *Machiavelli and Republicanism*, ed. Gisela Bock, Quentin Skinner and Maurizio Viroli. Cambridge: Cambridge University Press, 1990, pp. 293–309.

Smith, Craig. *Adam Smith's Political Philosophy*. London: Routledge, 2006.

Smith, David. "How Far Should We Care? On the Spatial Scope of Beneficence." *Progress in Human Geography*, vol. 22, no. 1 (1998), pp. 15–38.

Smith, Vernon L. "The Two Faces of Adam Smith." *Southern Economic Journal*, vol. 65, no. 1 (1998), pp. 1–19.

Solomon, Robert C. *A Passion for Justice: Emotions and the Origins of the Social Contract*. Lanham, MD: Rowman & Littlefield, 1995.

Starobinski, Jean. *Blessings in Disguise; or, The Morality of Evil*, trans. Arthur Goldhammer. Cambridge, MA: Harvard University Press, 1989, 1993.

Stewart, Dugald. *Biographical Memoirs of Adam Smith, of William Robertson, and of Thomas Reid*. Edinburgh: George Ramsay and Company, 1811.

Stewart, M. A. "The Stoic Legacy in the Early Scottish Enlightenment." In *Atoms, Pneuma, and Tranquility: Epicurean and Stoic Themes in European Thought*, ed. Margaret J. Osler. Cambridge: Cambridge University Press, 1991, pp. 273–296.

Stewart-Robertson, J. C. "Cicero among the Shadows: Scottish Prelections of Virtue and Duty." *Rivista critica storia della filosofia*, vol. I (1983), pp. 25–49.

Stigler, George. "Smith's Travels on the Ship of State." *History of Political Economy*, vol. 3 (1971), pp. 265–277.

Stocker, Michael. *Plural and Conflicting Values*. Oxford: Oxford University Press, 1992.

Stout, Jeffrey. *Ethics after Babel: The Languages of Morals and Their Discontents*. Boston: Beacon, 1988.

Striker, Gisela. *Essays on Hellenistic Epistemology and Ethics*. Cambridge: Cambridge University Press, 1996.

Taylor, Charles. "The Diversity of Goods." In *Philosophy and the Human Sciences: Philosophical Papers II*, ed. Charles Taylor. Cambridge: Cambridge University Press, 1985, pp. 230–247.

Sources of the Self: The Making of Modern Identity. Cambridge, MA: Harvard University Press, 1989.

Teichgraeber, Richard. "Rethinking *Das Adam Smith Problem*." *Journal of British Studies*, vol. 20, no. 2 (1981), pp. 106–123.

"Free Trade" and Moral Philosophy: Rethinking the Sources of Adam Smith's Wealth of Nations. Durham, 1986.

"History, Political Theory and Interpretations of Adam Smith." *Political Theory*, vol. 23, February (1995), pp. 147–195.

Tribe, Keith. "Adam Smith: Critical Theorist?" *Journal of Economic Literature*, vol. 37 (1999), pp. 609–632.

"The German Reception of Adam Smith." *A Critical Bibliography of Adam Smith*, ed. Keith Tribe. London: Pickering and Chatto, 2002, pp. 120–152.

Tuck, Richard. *Natural Right Theories: Their Origin and Development*. Cambridge: Cambridge University Press, 1979.

"The Contribution of History." In *A Companion to Contemporary Political Philosophy*, ed. Robert E. Goodin and Philip Petit. Oxford: Blackwell, 1983, pp. 72–89.

The Rights of War and Peace: Political Thought and the International Order from Grotius to Kant. Oxford: Oxford University Press, 1999.

Tugendhat, Ernst. "Universalistically Approved Intersubjective Attitudes: Adam Smith," trans. Bernard Schreibl. *Adam Smith Review*, vol. 1 (2004), pp. 88–104.

Tully, James. "Governing Conduct." In *Conscience and Casuistry in Early Modern Europe,* ed. Edmund Leites. Cambridge: Cambridge University Press, 1988, pp. 12–71.

"Introduction." In *Samuel Pufendorf, On the Duty of Man and Citizen*, ed. James Tully. Cambridge: Cambridge University Press, 1991, pp. xxi–xxix.

An Approach to Political Philosophy: Locke in Contexts. Cambridge: Cambridge University Press, 1993.

ed. *Philosophy in an Age of Pluralism: The Philosophy of Charles Taylor in Question*. Cambridge: Cambridge University Press, 1994.

Strange Multiplicity: Constitutionalism in an Age of Diversity. Cambridge: Cambridge University Press, 1995.

Public Philosophy in a New Key, 2 vols. Cambridge: Cambridge University Press, 2009.

Urmson, J. O. "Saints and Heroes." In *Essays in Moral Philosophy*, ed. A. I. Melden. Seattle: University of Washington Press, 1958, pp. 198–216.

Valihora, Karen. "The Judgement of Judgement: Adam Smith's *Theory of Moral Sentiments.*" *British Journal of Aesthetics*, vol. 41 (2000), pp. 138–159.

Van Kley, Dale. "Pierre Nicole, Jansenism and the Morality of Enlightened Self-Interest." In *Anticipations of the Enlightenment in England, France, and Germany*, ed. Alan C. Kors and Paul Korshin. Philadelphia: University of Pennsylvania Press, 1987, pp. 69–85.

Veblen, Thorstein. *The Theory of the Leisure Class: Introduction by Robert Lekachman*. London: Penguin, 1967.

Vertovec, Steven, and Robin Cohen, eds. *Conceiving Cosmopolitanism: Theory, Context, and Practice*. Oxford: Oxford University Press, 2002.

Veyne, Paul. *Bread and Circuses: Historical Sociology and Political Pluralism*. Paris, 1976; trans. and ed. Brian Pearce, London: Penguin, 1990.

Viner, Jacob. "Power versus Plenty as Objectives of Foreign Policy in the Seventeenth and Eighteenth Centuries." *World Politics*, vol. I, October (1948), pp. 1–29.

The Role of Providence in the Social Order: An Essay in Intellectual History. Princeton, NJ: Princeton University Press, 1972.

Religious Thought and Economic Society. Durham, NC: Duke University Press, 1978.

Essays on the Intellectual History of Economics, ed. Douglas A. Irwin. Princeton, NJ: Princeton University Press, 1991.

Vivenza, Gloria. *Adam Smith and the Classics: The Classical Heritage in Adam Smith's Thought*. Oxford: Oxford University Press, 2002.

"Reading Adam Smith in the Light of the Classics." *Adam Smith Review*, vol. 1 (2004), pp. 107–124.

Voegelin, Eric. "Helvétius and the Heritage of Pascal." In *From Enlightenment to Revolution*, ed. John H. Hollowell. Durham, NC: Duke University Press, 1975, pp. 53–73.

von Holthoon, F. L. "Adam Smith and David Hume: With Sympathy." *Utilitas*, vol. 5, no. 1 (1993), pp. 36–48.

von Villiez, Carola. "Double Standard – Naturally! Smith and Rawls: A Comparison of Methods." In *New Voices on Adam Smith*, ed. Leonidas Montes and Eric Schliesser. London: Routledge, 2006, pp. 115–139.

Waldron, Jeremy. "What Is Cosmopolitan?" *Journal of Political Philosophy*, vol. 8, no. 2 (2000), pp. 227–243.

Waller, James. *Becoming Evil: How Ordinary People Commit Genocide and Mass Killing*. 2nd edn, New York: Oxford University Press, 2007.

Waltz, Kenneth. *Man, the State and War*. New York: Columbia University Press, 1959.

Walzer, Michael. *Spheres of Justice: A Defense of Pluralism and Equality*. New York: Basic Books, 1983.

"Nation and Universe." *Tanner Lectures 1989*. The Tanner Lectures on Human Values, xi, pp. 509–556, ed. G. B. Petersen. Salt Lake City, UT: University of Utah Press, 1990.

Thick and Thin: Moral Argument at Home and Abroad. Notre Dame, IN: University of Notre Dame Press, 1994.

Waszek, Norbert. "Two Concepts of Morality: A Distinction of Adam Smith's Ethics and Its Stoic Origin." *Journal of the History of Ideas*, October (1984), pp. 591–604.

Man's Social Nature: A Topic of the Scottish Enlightenment in Its Historical Setting. Frankfurt am Main: Peter Lang, 1986.

Watson, Matthew. "Trade Justice and Individual Consumption Choices: Adam Smith's Spectator Theory and the Moral Constitution of the Fair Trade Consumer." *European Journal of International Relations*, vol. 13, no. 2 (2007), pp. 263–288.

Weinstein, Jack Russell. "Sympathy, Difference, and Education: Social Unity in the Work of Adam Smith." *Economics and Philosophy*, vol. 22, no. 1 (2006), pp. 1–33.

Werhane, Patricia. *Adam Smith and His Legacy for Modern Capitalism*. New York: Oxford University Press, 1991.

Whelan, Frederick G. "Legal Positivism and International Society." In *International Society: Diverse Ethical Perspectives*, ed. David R. Mapel and Terry Nardin. Princeton, NJ: Princeton University Press, 1998, pp. 36–53.

White, Stephen K. *Political Theory and Postmodernism*. Cambridge: Cambridge University Press, 1991.

Williams, Bernard. *Moral Luck: Philosophical Papers, 1973–1980*. Cambridge: Cambridge University Press, 1981.

Ethics and the Limits of Philosophy. Cambridge, MA: Harvard University Press, 1985.

Winch, Donald. *Adam Smith's Politics: An Essay in Historiographic Revision.* Cambridge: Cambridge University Press, 1978.

"Adam Smith's 'Enduring Particular Result': A Political and Cosmopolitan Perspective." In *Wealth and Virtue*, ed. Istvan Hont and Michael Ignatieff. Cambridge: Cambridge University Press, 1985, pp. 253–269.

"Adam Smith and the Liberal Tradition." In *Traditions of Liberalism: Essays on John Locke, Adam Smith and John Stuart Mill*, ed. Knud Haakonssen. Sydney: Center for Independent Studies, 1988, pp. 82–104.

"Adam Smith: Scottish Moral Philosopher as Political Economist." *Historical Journal*, vol. 35, no. 1 (1992), pp. 91–113.

Riches and Poverty: An Intellectual History of Political Economy in Britain, 1750–1834. Cambridge: Cambridge University Press, 1996.

Wokler, Robert. "Rousseau's Pufendorf: Natural Law and the Foundations of Commercial Society." *History of Political Thought*, vol. 15, no. 3 (1994), pp. 373–402.

Wolf, Susan. "Moral Saints." *Journal of Philosophy*, vol. 79, no. 8 (1982), pp. 419–439.

Wolin, Sheldon. *Politics and Vision: Continuity and Innovation in Western Political Thought.* Boston: Little Brown, 1960.

Xenos, Nicholas. "Classical Political Economy: The Apolitical Discourse of Civil Society." *Humanities in Society*, vol. 3 (1980), pp. 229–242.

Yack, Bernard. *The Problems of a Political Animal: Community, Justice, and Conflict in Aristotelian Political Thought.* Berkeley, CA: University of California Press, 1993.

ed. *Liberalism without Illusions: Essays on Liberal Theory and the Political Vision of Judith N. Shklar.* Chicago: University of Chicago Press, 1996.

Index

IDEAS IN CONTEXT

Edited by Quentin Skinner and James Tully